MORE PRAISE FOR
HERE IS WHERE

"*Here Is Where* is remarkable for the painstaking research on display and its yield of rescued-from-obscurity stories. **Many of the true incidents Andrew Carroll has uncovered aren't just surprising but powerful. Others are simply laugh-out-loud funny, but all are described with considerable skill.** America has always had among its citizenry a number of individuals whose legacy is immense but unappreciated, and Carroll has truly done them justice."

—Steven Pressfield, bestselling author of *Gates of Fire,*
Tides of War, and *Killing Rommel*

"Both a fascinating excavation of underappreciated events and agents and a compelling analysis of what binds us together, *Here Is Where* makes for **rich and vivid reading. It seems to me that Andrew Carroll has become the Charles Kuralt of American history.**"

—Les Standiford, bestselling author of *Desperate Sons* and
Last Train to Paradise

"**In *Here Is Where,* one of our best historian-sleuths, Andrew Carroll, has given us a fresh and irresistible approach to experiencing history.** Until someone invents a time machine, it's the next best thing to being there—and he's such a vivid, engaging writer that it's probably more fun."

—James Donovan, author of *A Terrible Glory* and *The Blood of Heroes*

"Writing with a historian's insight and the skill of a master storyteller, Andrew Carroll reminds us to look for the fascinating bits of history that lie just behind the curtains of our modern surroundings. *Here Is Where* is a captivating, thoroughly enjoyable journey across the country with a friend who knows all the cool places to stop and have a look.**"

—Gregory A. Freeman, author of *The Last Mission of the*
Wham Bam Boys and *The Forgotten 500*

HERE IS WHERE

HERE IS WHERE

Discovering America's Great
Forgotten History

ANDREW CARROLL

CROWN ARCHETYPE
· NEW YORK ·

Library of Congress Cataloging-in-Publication Data is available upon request.

ISBN 978-0-307-46397-5
eISBN 978-0-307-46399-9

Printed in the United States of America

Book design by Maria Elias
Jacket design by Jessie Sayward Bright
Jacket photograph: David Bassett/Getty Images

1   3   5   7   9   10   8   6   4   2

First Edition

The mind is not a vessel to be filled,
but a fire to be kindled.

—*From "On Listening to Lectures" by Plutarch*

To Andrew Delbanco, John Elko, Robert Herman,
David Kastan, Victoria Silver, Arnold Rampersad,
Neal Tonken, and Ellis Turner—
the teachers and professors in my life who lit the fire.

CONTENTS

HERE IS WHERE

INTRODUCTION

THE EXCHANGE PLACE

No, Cassius, for the eye sees not itself
But by reflection, by some other things.

—*Brutus, in Shakespeare's* Julius Caesar

HERE IS WHERE it all began: the Exchange Place PATH station in Jersey City, New Jersey, just across the Hudson River from Manhattan. This is the spot that sparked my almost compulsive desire to seek out unmarked history sites throughout the country. It's been fifteen years since I first read about what happened here a century and a half ago, and while in New York visiting family I thought I'd subway over from Manhattan and finally see the place for myself.

During the Civil War, the New Jersey Railroad Company ran trains through here, and one night in 1863 or '64 (the exact date isn't known) a young man fell between the loading platform and a Washington, D.C.–bound train. Just as the steam-powered locomotive began to lurch forward, potentially crushing the man to death under its massive wheels, a bystander rushed over and pulled him to safety. The man in peril was Robert Todd Lincoln, the president's eldest son. His quick-thinking rescuer was the prominent Shakespearean actor Edwin Booth, brother of John Wilkes Booth. Robert and Edwin had never met, and there's no indication that they ever saw or communicated with each other again. Nor does it seem that the story made its way to President Lincoln himself. He and Mary had already buried two other sons: three-year-old Eddie, who succumbed to tuberculosis in 1850, and eleven-year-old Willie, who died in the White House on February 20, 1862, from typhoid fever. The couple was still grief-stricken from Willie's death, and a third loss might have proved emotionally incapacitating. Mary had all but physically barred Robert Todd from fighting in the war and, after he enlisted, made certain he landed a desk job on General Ulysses S. Grant's staff.

I don't remember exactly where I first heard about the Exchange Place story, but I do recall thinking, initially, that it must have been apocryphal. Perhaps the two men had bumped into each other on the train platform and exchanged a few cordial words, and then over the years this brief encounter blossomed into the sensationally ironic tale of how a Booth had saved the life of a Lincoln not long before Edwin's younger brother assassinated Robert's father. Or maybe Robert had indeed fallen onto some railroad tracks and Edwin was at the station but only as a witness while another man swiftly came to Robert's aid. The possibility that their lives had intersected in the dramatic manner I'd read about seemed far-fetched.

Except that the story turned out to be true. Robert Todd Lincoln himself described the episode in a February 1909 letter to Richard Watson Gilder, editor of *The Century Magazine*. "The incident occurred while a group of passengers were late at night purchasing their sleeping car places from the conductor who stood on the station platform at the entrance of the car," Lincoln explained.

The platform was about the height of the car floor, and there was of course a narrow space between the platform and the car body. There was some crowding, and I happened to be pressed by it against the car body while waiting my turn. In this situation the train began to move, and by the motion I was twisted off my feet, and had dropped somewhat, with feet downward, into the open space, and was personally helpless, when my coat collar was vigorously seized and I was quickly pulled up and out to a secure footing on the platform. Upon turning to thank my rescuer I saw it was Edwin Booth, whose face was of course well known to me, and I expressed my gratitude to him, and in doing so, called him by name.

What especially intrigued me when I first read this was the possibility that, if the station were still active, each day thousands of commuters, tourists, and other travelers would wait for their trains near the very spot where this extraordinary encounter had occurred—and would probably be unaware of it. I started to wonder what other great unmarked sites are all around us that we pass by or walk over every day.

Stories began to accumulate. Whenever a newspaper, magazine, book, radio program, documentary, lecture, or cocktail conversation alluded to a relatively unknown incident, I jotted it down and slipped the note into a manila file titled "Forgotten History." That slim folder grew fatter and has since multiplied into twenty-four bulging cabinets full of articles, clippings, and hastily scrawled reminders of places to research. I've also discovered that while I'm digging about for smaller nuggets, my eye often catches the glint of something bigger and more striking. This happened when I delved into the Lincoln/Booth story.

Obviously I'd heard of John Wilkes Booth, but I knew nothing about his brother. Did he harbor the same pro-Confederacy views? Was he complicit in the assassination? Or was their relationship antagonistic?

No on all counts. Edwin was close to his younger brother, and apparently there was tension only if they discussed politics. The last time the two had met, John Wilkes stormed out of the room after Edwin told him he'd voted for Lincoln.

When Edwin saw the April 15, 1865, newspaper article naming his brother as the president's assassin, he immediately wrote to a colleague that he felt as if he "had been struck on the head with a hammer." The manager of the playhouse where Edwin was performing notified him by messenger that, in light of his relationship to the killer, "out of respect for the anguish which will fill the public mind as soon as the appalling fact shall be fully revealed, I have concluded to close the Boston Theatre until further notice." Edwin agreed and confided privately to his very close friend Adam Badeau: "The news of the morning has made me wretched indeed, not only because I received the unhappy tidings of the suspicion of a brother's crime, but because a good man, and a most justly honored and patriotic ruler, has fallen by the hand of an assassin."

In his next letter to Badeau, Edwin, his anger clearly growing, referred to John as an outright "villain."

One of the final meetings between Edwin and John—and this was the larger gem that sparkled into view as I poked around the Exchange Place story—occurred in New York City on November 25, 1864, known back then as Evacuation Day. (The anniversary commemorates both the departure of British troops from the colonies in 1783 and the last shot of the war; as His Majesty's ships sailed out of New York Harbor past jeering mobs on Staten Island, a British gunner petulantly fired a cannonball toward the crowd. He missed.) On this same night, Confederate officers led by Lieutenant Colonel Robert M. Martin scattered throughout lower Manhattan glass bottles containing a highly flammable phosphorous liquid known as "Greek fire." Their mission was to burn the city to the ground in what would be the first major domestic terrorist strike on New York.

Martin and his seven coconspirators had all checked in to hotels under assumed names. At a prearranged time they would pour the incendiary chemicals on the floors and beds of their suites and disperse once the fires became uncontrollable. The flames would then ignite a firestorm through the densely packed wooden homes and buildings of Manhattan and kill scores of innocent men, women, and children.

This was just one of many schemes to inflict widespread suffering on Northern civilians, and the plots were often sanctioned at the highest levels of the Confederate government. Texas state senator Williamson Simpson Oldham explained to President Jefferson Davis in explicit detail one particular plan to "devastate the country of the enemy, and fill his people with terror." In mid-October 1864 an American doctor and acquaintance of Oldham's named Luke Blackburn sailed to Bermuda to care for patients in the final throes of yellow fever. Blackburn's intentions, however, were far from charitable; the forty-five-year-old Kentuckian was secretly collecting soiled bedsheets and garments to ship back to the States in sealed trunks. He hoped the linens and clothing could then be used to unleash an outbreak of the fatal disease throughout the North. He especially wanted to get a "gift" of fancy—and contaminated—dress shirts into the hands of Abraham Lincoln. (The war would be over by the time Blackburn could start his pandemic, and it wouldn't have worked anyway. Yellow fever is spread by mosquitoes.)

For die-hard Rebs such as Lieutenant John Headley, Robert Martin's second-in-command, extreme measures against the North were entirely justified. "Ten days before this attempt of Confederates to burn New York City," Headley wrote in his journal, "General Sherman had burned the city of Atlanta, Georgia, and the Northern papers and people of the war party were in great glee over the miseries of the Southern people."

The Confederate attack on Manhattan was started by Headley himself, in Suite 204 of the Astor House hotel, when he lit his room's carpet and bedsheets on fire and then set out into the night. At the North River Wharf, Headley lobbed bottles of Greek fire at wooden vessels and hay barges. While passing Phineas T. Barnum's American Museum, he was delighted to see smoke pouring out of the building and terrified patrons leaping from windows. Headley bumped into fellow conspirator Robert Cobb Kennedy and learned that Kennedy had impulsively tossed a bottle into a museum stairwell because he figured it would be "fun to start a scare." With bells clamoring in every direction, Headley and Kennedy rushed like giddy pranksters to the rendezvous house in the Bowery, laughing and backslapping the whole way.

Just north of them, John T. Ashbrook was setting fire to Lafarge House at 671 Broadway. Right next door was the Winter Garden Theatre, where a production of Shakespeare's *Julius Caesar* was under way. Edwin and John Wilkes Booth, along with their older brother, Junius, were the featured performers. Smoke from the Lafarge seeped into the theater, and Edwin, according to a *New York Times* article the next day, calmed the frightened crowd as alarms began ringing.

Order was quickly restored at the Winter Garden and throughout Manhattan. No one died, and the fires failed to ignite a citywide conflagration. There was, however, significant property damage, and some New Yorkers were injured scrambling for their lives, but that was the extent of the crisis. Fear and hysteria turned to outrage as the Confederate plot was revealed in morning newspapers, and a massive hunt for the perpetrators was launched. All of them were able to evade capture except Robert Cobb Kennedy, who was tried and, on March 25, 1865, hanged at Fort Lafayette in New York Harbor.

The November 25, 1864, performance of *Julius Caesar* represented the first and last time the three Booth brothers shared a stage. Edwin starred as the assassin Brutus; Junius played Cassius, who instigated the plot against Caesar; and John was Mark Antony, whose funeral oration deftly stirred the vacillating Roman crowd against Caesar's killers. In the play's penultimate lines, however, it is also Antony who concedes that at least Brutus's motivations were honorable: "All the conspirators save only he / Did that they did in envy of great Caesar." Antony says of Brutus:

He only in a general honest thought
And common good to all made one of them.
His life was gentle and the elements
So mixed in him that nature might stand up
And say to all the world "This was a man."

The production was a one-night-only benefit to raise funds for a statue of William Shakespeare in Central Park. The life-sized monument was erected in May 1872 and stands there to this day.

Before heading over to see the Exchange Place for the first time, I decide to pay Will a visit. I have a general idea where his memorial is supposed to be, but foolishly I've neglected to bring a map.

"Excuse me," I ask a middle-aged couple (the man is wearing a Yankees cap, so I assume they're locals), "do you all know where the Shakespeare statue is? It's around here somewhere."

Contrary to stereotype, I've always found New Yorkers to be very helpful with directions. They stop and she says, "That sounds *vaguely* familiar," then looks at him.

He shakes his head. "I didn't know there was one."

I get a similar response from almost everyone else I ask (a few, to be expected, are tourists), and several positively know where it is and send me in the absolutely wrong direction. After forty-five disorienting minutes, an obliging soul finally points me to Literary Walk, and sure enough, there's Shakespeare. A sign a few feet away chronicles the history of the memorial and acknowledges Edwin Booth's fund-raising efforts. Brother John isn't mentioned.

After snapping a few pictures I take the bus to lower Manhattan in search of sites related to the November 25, 1864, attack. There's now a Best Buy electronics store where the Winter Garden Theatre used to be. All the other buildings have been replaced by more formidable structures or paved over completely. By midafternoon I've found most of the addresses where the Confederate agents had struck. A majority of them, it's hard not to notice, are only a block or two away from where the Twin Towers once stood.

From lower Manhattan I head to the Exchange Place, the first stop outside of New York City on the PATH train route. After I climb the stairs out of the underground station, I see train tracks several hundred feet away. And a waiting platform. I trot over, and all the signs read EXCHANGE PLACE.

I circle the small, above-ground station to shoot pictures and search for any sort of historic plaque or marker. Nothing. I set my camera bag on the ground and suddenly stand bolt upright. I take a step back and realize that I'm on top of a giant cast-iron map of the New Jersey and Manhattan waterfronts. I must have walked over it a dozen times since I've been here.

Looking closer, I find little boxes of text by their respective points of interest: "Communipaw Massacre 1643—Dutch settlers massacred 80 Indians as they slept"; "July 30, 1916—Ammunition trains and barges exploded at Black Tom Wharf. The shock wave was felt as far away as Philadelphia. Many believed it to be the work of saboteurs"; "1954—*On the Waterfront* filmed with Marlon Brando." I search for the Exchange Place itself on the map, and the only little box near it says, "You are here." There's nothing about Booth and Lincoln.

Over the next twenty minutes or so, not a single soul looks at the map. I start photographing the folks on the platform, all of whom seem (as I was) oblivious to the bounty of historical information directly beneath them. It's possible that they're regular commuters well familiar with the map and its inch-long boxes, but I doubt this is true of all of them.

"I hope you don't mind my asking," a woman says to me, "but I was just wondering what you were doing." Far from minding, I'm happy to tell her that we're standing right on top of a great cartographic treasure trove of historic places, and no one appears to notice. "So I was photographing them not noticing," I say.

She looks down and reacts exactly as I did, instantly stepping back as if the ground had vanished and then reappeared before her eyes. "I've been commuting from here for almost a month, and I've never seen this before."

I point out a few favorite spots and then repeat the Booth/Lincoln story.

"Right where we're standing?" she asks.

"I'm not sure if it's here *exactly,* but somewhere around this place."

"That's amazing," she says. I tell her I think so, too.

By this time I have to race to Penn Station to catch a train for Washington, D.C. As I'm dashing off I glance back and see the woman conversing amiably with two other people as all three look intently at the map under their feet.

My epiphany comes minutes after Amtrak Northeast Regional 137 rolls out of Manhattan: I will search for unmarked sites across America that have been forgotten over time. One trip, all regions of the country. And not only in major metropolitan areas but in small towns and communities from coast to coast. Historic sites aren't just clustered in Beacon Hill, Greenwich Village, Hyde Park, Fisherman's Wharf, and other big-city neighborhoods. They are everywhere.

Since I've recently lost both the one stable job I've ever held and a pretty wonderful girlfriend (no hard feelings), the timing is perfect. My calendar, to say the least, is clear. And if I don't do this now, I doubt the opportunity will ever arise again.

Back in Washington I pull from my bookshelf a road atlas purchased years ago that has sadly gone unused, and I flip through the pages. My mind begins racing as I contemplate the sheer logistics of such an undertaking, of researching and pinpointing so many little-known sites, finding historians and experts to guide me along the way, and coordinating (even though I'll probably drive much of the trip) countless airline, train, and bus schedules. Weather will be a factor, too; flight delays and cancellations are all but assured during summer hurricane season in the South and winters in the North and Midwest.

There are those who can toss some underwear and extra pairs of socks into a backpack, leap out the front door, and cast their fortunes to the wind. I'm not that kind of traveler. I'm all for spontaneity and serendipitous discoveries, but with limited funds and time, I'll have to maintain a tight schedule and know exactly where I'm going from the start. There'll be no margin for error. Ultimately I estimate that it will require five to six months to plan the trip and then at least as long to visit every site on my itinerary.

This is madness, I begin to think, a whim-driven folly better suited for the young and not a man nearing his forties.

All the more reason to go. It's decided.

From the outset I need to establish my terms. Words like *forgotten* and *overlooked* are, admittedly, subjective; what might be unfamiliar to one person is another's area of expertise. Many of the stories I've collected in those twenty-four filing cabinets were referenced in obscure magazines and journals or cited in footnotes and parenthetical asides from out-of-print books. They haven't permeated the popular culture and, at best, only hazily ring a bell to some people. It's not the most scientific criterion, but part of the reason for visiting the sites—along with confirming that they're not marked—is to ascertain how well they're known to those who live nearby. I want even the locals to be surprised.

Every spot must also be nationally significant and represent a larger narrative in American history. Ideally, I plan to cover the full sweep of our nation's past, from the first Native Americans, Spanish explorers, and Pilgrims who set foot on this land to the pioneers, patriots, inventors, soldiers, artists, and activists who transformed it. Not every story can or will be epic in scope, but the impact of each protagonist should reverberate beyond any one state or region.

Priority one is to plot out where I'm going and what I hope to find, and by that I don't mean just the actual sites. This journey must be more than a grand sightseeing adventure. Along with searching for the physical places, I want to explore why any of this matters. Ever since a fire gutted our family's home in Washington, D.C., destroying hundreds of personal letters, photos, and other irreplaceable memorabilia, I've become more conscientious about preserving history. But beyond mere sentimentality, what difference does it honestly make if historic sites are torn down, boarded up, bulldozed, or simply neglected?

And why have so many of them been forgotten in the first place?

PART I

WHERE TO BEGIN

Starting Points

NIIHAU

The whole object of travel is not to set foot on foreign land; it is at last to set foot on one's own country as a foreign land.

—G. K. Chesterton

LOCATED ABOUT TWENTY-TWO hundred miles from the continental United States and nicknamed "the Forbidden Island," Niihau is the westernmost inhabited isle on the Hawaiian chain. The seal-shaped speck of land is also the world's largest privately owned island, stretching approximately nineteen miles long and six miles across at its widest point. In 1864 a clan of Scottish ranchers, the Sinclairs, purchased Niihau for $10,000 in gold from King Kamehameha V, and their descendants—the Robinsons—still own it to this day. (The king also offered the Sinclair family Waikiki, but they passed.)

No tourists are allowed on Niihau except those who are personally invited by the Robinson family or who fly in from neighboring Kauai ("the Garden Isle") on Niihau Helicopters Inc., a Robinson-operated

business that offers four-hour tours and daylong safaris. Other companies run sightseeing and snorkeling boat trips that skirt the coast
from a mile out. But I need to go ashore; the story I'm pursuing involves a small plane that made an emergency landing near the main
village more than seventy years ago, and the ensuing manhunt for the
pilot sparked a panic on America's mainland that had major social and
political repercussions. Getting to the island is no easy feat, and its re-
moteness, I suspect, accounts for why "the Niihau incident" isn't better
known.

Hawaii was slotted for the end of my travels, when I planned to be
in the neighborhood anyway (that is, around Washington State), but
while piecing together my itinerary, I called Niihau Helicopters and
immediately hit a snag.

A very pleasant woman named Shandra told me that the pilot
couldn't shuttle just one passenger out to the island, so I'd have to
join an already scheduled party of three or more. Shandra could find
only one day on their calendar when they had a group short by a single
person, and I confirmed on the spot. Liftoff would be in three months,
which cut my preparation time for the entire journey in half.

There was another problem.

If a storm blew in or the other passengers canceled at the last minute, the flight to Niihau would be postponed indefinitely. I wouldn't be
charged, but I'd have gone all the way to Hawaii for nothing. My only
option was to make a reservation and hope for the best.

Over the next three months, I frantically began coordinating the
remainder of my itinerary. The original plan, and certainly the most
logical and economical strategy, was to zigzag across the country in one
clean, continuous line, either from side to side or top to bottom. But, as
with Niihau, I had to schedule my visits according to what worked best
for the various guides and historians who'd be touring me around in
their respective towns. My final route looked as if it had been mapped
out more by Jackson Pollock than by Rand McNally.

Every few weeks I called Shandra to make sure the other parties hadn't pulled out, and every time she assured me that they were still committed.

On my way to Kauai, I hopscotched the Hawaiian Islands, hitting Maui first to check out Charles Lindbergh's grave near a small abandoned church in Kipahulu. There's room for two but he's buried alone; his wife, Anne, instructed that her ashes be scattered in Maine, thousands of miles away. The legendary pilot's nearest neighbors are a row of gibbon apes named Kippy, Keiki, Lani, and George—the beloved pets of Lindbergh's close friend Sam Pryor.

Later that afternoon I flew to Oahu and photographed a statue of Abraham Lincoln outside the Ewa Elementary School. A memorial to Lincoln here seems odd, considering that Hawaii wasn't a state in Lincoln's day and was officially neutral in the Civil War. As it turns out, a handful of Hawaiians volunteered to fight for the Union, and Lincoln, as president, endeared himself to the territory by writing a heartfelt letter of condolence to King Kamehameha V in February 1864 after his younger brother, King Kamehameha IV, passed away.

From Oahu, it was on to Kauai.

With twenty-four hours to go, I phoned Shandra one last time. "Sorry to keep bugging you," I said, well aware that I must have been testing her patience. Hawaii's relaxed, aloha spirit hadn't yet permeated my East Coast, type A disposition. "I'm a bit of a control freak," I explained apologetically.

"As long as you're the one who said it," Shandra replied, laughing, and then confirmed that, yes, everything was looking good. "Just be here no later than eight thirty A.M."

I told her I was setting not one but two alarms and arranging for a wake-up call.

"Somehow that doesn't surprise me," she said.

With alarms and phones ringing at 7:00 A.M., I'm up.

So is the sun, which is a welcome sight, although a slow-rolling avalanche of dark clouds is encroaching on the horizon.

At the office for Niihau Helicopters I wait nervously in the parking lot.

One car pulls up, then a second. I finally meet my fellow passengers—
a couple in their fifties from New Jersey and a former Marine from San
Diego, who's with his wife and their young daughter. They're an affable
group, but frankly I'm just thrilled they all showed up.

During a brief orientation, we're told that we'll be flying on an Agusta
A-109 (its predecessor, also owned by the Robinsons, was used in the
opening scene of *Jurassic Park*); once we're on the island we may pick
up shells as souvenirs; the black rocks along the beach are very slick, so
be careful; sandwiches will be served for lunch; and we'll have several
hours to rove around, snorkel, take pictures, and so on. We learn a little
about the island's history, but there's no mention of the Niihau incident.

From the heliport it's a fifteen-minute ride out to the island, and
once Niihau comes into view, our pilot, Dana Rosendal, who flew
Cobras and Hueys in the Army, dips and swoops the copter above
points of interest and offers additional tidbits of information. The
number fluctuates, but approximately 130 people live there now, Dana
tells us. An eco-Luddite's dream, Niihau has few cell phones, televi-
sions, or personal computers, and what minimal power the villagers do
require is wind- and solar-generated. They drink and wash with fresh
rainwater. None of the roads are paved, and most islanders rely on
bikes and horses for transportation. It's also the only island where Hawaiian is the primary language. There is one modern structure, a U.S.
Navy installation far from the central village, that conducts missile defense operations. (Three weeks before I arrived in Kauai, North Korea
threatened to shoot a Taepodong-2 ballistic missile "toward" Hawaii to
test its range. I almost called Shandra to see if this might scuttle our
flight but, in a rare instance of self-restraint, decided against it.)

We pass high over three villagers, and they wave at us. "Everyone
here is real friendly," Dana says. Niihau doesn't even have a jail.

The copter sets down on a dirt landing pad near a tin-covered shed,
and immediately we all go our separate ways. With no commercial
buildup (not even restaurants or supermarkets; everything is boated or
flown in), there's a timeless quality to the landscape, which makes it
easier to envision what happened here some seven decades ago.

I hike inland a bit and try to imagine what Hawila Kaleohano, a twenty-nine-year-old villager who had stepped outside of his home to see why his horse was neighing loudly and acting spooked, must have thought when, from out of nowhere, a small plane came in low and fast and slammed into the rough soil, kicking up clouds of dirt until finally skidding to a stop in front of his house.

The pilot, who appeared to be Japanese, had sustained minor injuries and was barely conscious. Kaleohano pulled him from the smoking wreckage and then searched through the cockpit, hoping to find some form of identification. Kaleohano discovered a pistol and a stash of documents. He learned that the pilot's name was Shigenori Nishikaichi, and he was twenty-one years old.

More villagers rushed to the scene. They only spoke Hawaiian, so someone sent for Ishimatsu Shintani, an older man who had been born in Japan and could speak the language fluently. By the time Shintani arrived, the pilot was alert, and the two had a brief conversation—and then Shintani left without explanation.

Perplexed, the villagers located the Robinsons' caretaker and assistant beekeeper Yoshio Harada, a thirty-eight-year-old Hawaiian-born man who, like his wife, Irene, was of Japanese ancestry. Nishikaichi, the pilot, confided to Harada that the Imperial Navy had just bombed Pearl Harbor and the United States and Japan were now at war. Harada shared none of this with the villagers.

Although the islanders were without electricity and phone lines, they were aware that diplomatic relations between the two countries had been strained. None of them knew, however, that the U.S. naval base on the main island of Oahu was under attack and that Nishikaichi had flown in the invasion's second wave. After his plane was struck by enemy fire, Nishikaichi was forced to crash-land on Niihau.

That afternoon the villagers threw a party for the young pilot. They roasted a pig and sat around the fire playing guitar and singing. With everyone at ease, Nishikaichi asked Hawila Kaleohano for his papers back. Kaleohano politely refused.

Hours later, from a crackling, battery-powered radio, the villagers heard about Pearl Harbor and realized that Nishikaichi was an enemy combatant. They decided to detain him until the island's owner, Aylmer Robinson, arrived the next morning from his main residence in Kauai. He could then take Nishikaichi back to the proper authorities.

Monday came but no Aylmer.

Yoshio and Irene Harada offered to house Nishikaichi, and the villagers agreed—so long as he remained under close watch.

Tuesday, Wednesday, and Thursday passed with still no sign of Aylmer, who'd never been absent this long. The villagers climbed to the top of the highest point on Niihau and, after waving kerosene lanterns in the direction of Kauai, lit a massive bonfire. They didn't know that the Navy had imposed an emergency ban on all travel in the area, and Aylmer—who is believed to have seen the flickering lights and suspected that they signaled trouble—could only watch helplessly. Nishikaichi used the delay to his advantage, gaining the trust of the Haradas.

On Friday, December 12, Shintani attempted to bribe Kaleohano for the airman's papers. Despite the significant amount of cash offered (about $200), Kaleohano, convinced that they must contain sensitive military information, said no.

By some accounts, later that afternoon Irene Harada began playing a record on the couple's hand-cranked phonograph. The music was not for entertainment but to muffle the sounds of what was about to happen next. Her husband and Nishikaichi snuck up behind the lone villager guarding their home and wrestled him to the ground. They locked him in a warehouse and gathered up a shotgun and pistol before setting out to retrieve Nishikaichi's papers and additional weapons.

From his outhouse, Kaleohano spied Harada and Nishikaichi approaching his home. Knowing that eventually they'd find him unless he made a break for it, when the two men momentarily looked in the opposite direction, Kaleohano dashed toward the village. Harada pivoted, aimed his shotgun at Kaleohano, and fired but just missed him. Kaleohano shouted at the top of his lungs for everyone to run, that Harada had helped the Japanese pilot escape and they were both armed. The villagers, at first incredulous that their friend and neighbor had turned on them, scattered.

Harada and Nishikaichi rushed to Nishikaichi's plane to use the radio. It didn't work. They torched the plane and, out of spite, returned to Kaleohano's home and burned it to the ground.

By this time Kaleohano was off the island, paddling a small decrepit whaling boat to Kauai with five other villagers.

Back on Niihau, Harada and Nishikaichi continued searching for Kaleohano. The sun was rising—it was the morning of December 13, almost a full week since the assault on Pearl Harbor—and the two men, exhausted and desperate, captured a cowhand named Ben Kanahele and his wife, Ella, and threatened to shoot the couple if they didn't reveal where Kaleohano was hiding. Ben knew that Kaleohano had left the island but played dumb and assured Harada that they'd locate him together.

After fifteen excruciating hours rowing to Kauai, Kaleohano and the other villagers tracked down Aylmer Robinson. They updated him on the situation, and Robinson along with twelve armed soldiers from the 299th Infantry's M Company rushed to Niihau.

Meanwhile, still held at gunpoint, Ben Kanahele silently vowed that if the opportunity arose, he would disarm Nishikaichi. That chance came around 1:00 P.M. on December 13, when Nishikaichi lowered his guard while passing the shotgun to Harada.

Kanahele pounced.

Nishikaichi reached for the pistol stashed in his boot and shot Ben three times at close range, piercing his ribs, groin, and hip. Ben stayed on his feet and with a surge of adrenaline lunged toward Nishikaichi, lifted him off the ground, and then slammed him into a stone wall. Before the stunned pilot could recover, Ella cracked his skull with a rock and Ben sliced his throat open with a hunting knife.

When they turned around, Harada was facing them with the shotgun in hand. After a few tense moments, he aimed the barrel at himself and pulled the trigger. The shell blew a hole through his abdomen, and he slowly bled to death.

Robinson and the soldiers arrived the next day and hurried Kana-hele to Kauai for medical treatment. (Niihau did not then, nor does it now, have a hospital.) Kanahele survived and was later awarded the Purple Heart.

After a few hours spent wandering around Niihau, I return to the shed for lunch. Everyone else is already snacking away on chips and sand-wiches, chatting, and picking through small, colorful piles of gathered seashells. (I collected some myself, including a scoopful of sand, and the grains are like nothing I've ever seen; each one is as large as a poppy seed.) A light mist turns into rain. We expect it to pass quickly, but it explodes into a ferocious storm, pounding our little metal hut for almost an hour. "Any chance we'll get stuck on the island?" someone asks Dana.

"It won't last much longer," he says.

I'm so elated to be here that I don't care how long we're delayed. Fif-teen minutes later, shafts of sunlight appear, and Dana tells us we'll be heading back soon. I commiserate with my fellow explorers about how nerve-racking it was traveling to Niihau and worrying the whole time that the trip might be canceled at any moment.

"We were thinking the same thing," the former Marine from San Diego says, "and we were only coming in from California. This place really is in the middle of nowhere."

Guadalcanal is often cited as the Americans' first amphibious land-ing and ground campaign of World War II, but technically speaking, the twelve men of Company M, 299th Infantry who embarked from Kauai on December 13 executed the first U.S.-led ship-to-shore offen-sive of the war. The real significance of the Niihau incident, however, isn't just what occurred on the island but its repercussions. By Decem-ber 16 the Niihau incident was front-page news in papers across the country, and the brief but violent episode was described in graphic, sensationalistic accounts: HAWAIIAN WOMAN BRAINS JAP PILOT, one headline blared. What most terrified Americans were the actions of

Shintani and the Haradas, whose sudden betrayal of their neighbors further enflamed public sentiment against Japanese Americans.

That fear received a federal stamp of approval on January 26, 1942, when Congress released the findings of its Pearl Harbor investigation, formally known as the Roberts Commission Report. A substantial portion of the proceedings was dedicated to the Niihau incident. "It is worthy of note that neither SHINTANI nor HARADA had previously exhibited un-American tendencies," the report stated. It then concluded that there was a "strong possibility" that "Americans of Japanese descent, who previously have shown no anti-American tendencies and are apparently loyal to the United States, may give valuable aid to Japanese invaders in cases where the tide of battle is in favor of Japan."

"Since the publication of the Roberts Commission Report," California governor Culbert Olson declared on January 27, "[the people of my state] feel that they are living in the midst of a lot of enemies. They don't trust the Japanese, none of them." Buried in the report, and unmentioned by Olson and like-minded politicians, was the fact that the U.S. soldier who led the raid on Niihau to hunt down Nishikaichi was a Japanese American lieutenant named Jack Mizuha. Mizuha went on to serve heroically in the famed 442nd Regimental Combat Team, one of the most highly decorated units in American military history.

On February 19, 1942, President Franklin D. Roosevelt signed Executive Order 9066, which led to the internment of 120,000 men, women, and children of Japanese descent, many of them American-born citizens. The Niihau incident was not solely responsible for the order, but it galvanized the public and fortified Roosevelt's decision to uproot thousands of families from their homes for the duration of the war.

Exactly thirty-four years after Executive Order 9066 was issued, the federal government began making amends to those who were forced into the camps. "We now know what we should have known then—not only was that evacuation wrong, but Japanese-Americans were and are loyal Americans," President Gerald Ford stated in Proclamation 4417. On August 10, 1988, President Ronald Reagan signed the Civil Liberties Act into law, officially expressing regret for the government's actions and appropriating $1.2 billion in monetary reparations ($20,000 each for all surviving detainees) to be disbursed over ten years. Presidents Bush and Clinton included a signed letter of apology with the payments sent during their respective administrations.

While Niihau's far-flung location is one of the primary reasons the Niihau incident hasn't garnered more attention, its association with a dark moment in American history is responsible as well. And this notion—of shameful events intentionally being relegated to the most distant regions of the nation's collective memory—would take me back to the East Coast, 5,500 miles away.

ONA JUDGE'S HOME
AND GRAVE

In your patriotic address to us of the last year we regret that you tell us that the oil is almost extinguished in the lamp and that old age has rendered it impossible for you to attend. Altho we are again pushed by our fellow citizens to give you an invitation to come and join in the festivities of the day—The toast Sir which you sent us in 1809 will continue to vibrate with unceasing pleasure in our ears— Live free or die, death is not the greatest of evils.

—From a July 25, 1810, letter by the Battle of Bennington Committee to the New Hampshire–born Revolutionary War hero John Stark, whose toast "Live free or die" became New Hampshire's official motto 135 years later

UNLIKE THE THOUSANDS of slaves who would escape from plantations and manor houses in the years and decades after her, Ona "Oney" Judge did not flee across moonlit fields chased by dogs or wade through dark, waist-high swamps teeming with water moccasins and alligators. No, Judge simply walked out of her master's Philadelphia mansion on High Street as he and his family ate supper. She had even packed a suitcase. But by stepping through the white-columned doorway and into the bustling city, America's capital at the time, Judge became one of the earliest and boldest pioneers of the Underground Railroad.

In the May 24, 1796, *Pennsylvania Gazette,* a notice announced Judge's disappearance. "Absconded," it declared,

> . . . a light mulatto girl, much freckled, with very black eyes and bushy black hair. She is of middle stature, slender, about 20 years of age and delicately formed.
>
> She has many changes of good clothes, of all sorts, but they are not sufficiently recollected to be described—As there was no suspicion of her going off, nor no provocation to do so, it is not easy to conjecture whither she has gone, or fully, what her design is. . . .
>
> Ten dollars will be paid to any person who will bring her home, if taken in the city, or on board any vessel in the harbour;—and a reasonable additional sum if apprehended at, and brought from a greater distance, and in proportion to the distance.

The exact day that Judge left Philadelphia aboard a northern-bound sloop named *Nancy* and landed in Portsmouth, New Hampshire, isn't known. She had no family or friends there but assimilated quickly into the town's free black community. Judge herself, however, was in no way free; because of the 1793 Fugitive Slave Act, she lived in constant fear that at any moment she could be snatched up by slave hunters. Within two months of her escape, that threat became all the more imminent.

"Oney!" a voice called out as Judge was walking in Portsmouth's Market Square. She turned and there was Bets Langdon, the teenage daughter of Senator John Langdon, an old family friend of Judge's master. Her identity was revealed.

"Why, Oney," Bets asked, knowing that slaves rarely traveled alone, "where in the world did you come from?"

"Run away, missis." Judge saw no point in lying.

"Run away! And from such an excellent place! Why what could induce you? You had a room to yourself, and only light, nice work to do, and every indulgence—"

"Yes—I know—but I wanted to be free, missis."

Judge knew that word of her whereabouts would quickly get back to Philadelphia, and she could only brace herself for the consequences.

"Are you allergic to poison ivy?" Vicky Avery asks me as we tramp through a wooded area between the intersection of Dearborn Road and Martin Brook in Greenland, a small town that borders Portsmouth. I look down and notice clusters of a three-leafed plant brushing against my bare ankles.

"I had a pretty bad case as a kid," I reply with some concern. "Doesn't everyone get a rash if they touch it?"

"Only certain people. Well, I guess you'll know later," Vicky says, moving briskly ahead of me.

A local historian who's lectured and written extensively about Judge and other slaves in the region, Vicky is also a busy mom raising three young girls (she drives her fourteen-year-old daughter four hours, every weekday, to dance with a ballet company in Maine). And yet she's gone out of her way to educate me about Ona Judge and is interrupting a packed schedule to show me spots relevant to Judge's life in Portsmouth and Greenland.

As we're walking, I explain to Vicky that, in all of my preparations for this cross-country trip, few stories have intrigued me more than fugitive-slave accounts. To set out alone, as thousands did, often carrying with them nothing at all, knowing they would be hunted, entrusting their lives to strangers along the way, and recognizing that if caught they risked a savage beating, if not death, represents a courage beyond all measure.

Those who fled did not just fly impulsively into the night. They plotted and planned, some devising clever schemes to evade their pursuers. In 1848 an elderly gentleman named William Johnson, his head wrapped in a bandage and his right arm in a sling, boarded a train in Georgia with a male slave to seek medical treatment in the North. In fact, they were both slaves; William Johnson was a frail, light-skinned woman named Ellen Craft, and her manservant was her real-life husband. They made their way to Pennsylvania and then Great Britain, which had abolished slavery in 1833. After the Civil War they returned to the States and founded a school for young African American children in Georgia, not far from their master's old plantation.

On March 29, 1849, Henry "Box" Brown famously shipped himself in a wooden crate from Richmond to Philadelphia, barely surviving the twenty-two-hour ordeal.

John Fairfield, a white man born into a slaveholding family, became a staunch abolitionist renowned for his creative tactics. He once dressed as an undertaker and conspired with more than two dozen slaves, all posing as mourners carrying a corpse (who was very much alive), to embark on a "funeral march" to freedom.

And in the early-morning hours of May 13, 1862, a twenty-three-year-old South Carolina slave named Robert Smalls boarded a Confederate gunship, *Planter,* docked outside the Charleston quarters of General Roswell Ripley while the general and his crew slept onshore. Smalls had served as the ship's deckhand and was able to fool the Confederate sentinels along the coast by blowing the correct whistle signals at every station. After sighting the USS *Speed,* which almost fired on him, Smalls raised a white flag and proudly "surrendered" the *Planter* to the Union vessel. Smalls was hailed as a national hero, earned the rank of captain in the U.S. Navy, and was elected to Congress after the war.

Although Judge's flight from Philadelphia wasn't as harrowing or elaborate as other escapes, by remaining in New Hampshire she was publicly defying the most powerful and admired man in the country. Her master had won the War of Independence, helped craft the Constitution, and, among many other legislative acts, signed the fugitive slave law into effect inside the very house from which she had run away.

Ona Judge's master was the president of the United States, George Washington.

As a dower slave, Judge legally belonged to Washington's wife, Martha, but the president was for all intents and purposes her owner as well, and he was adamant that she be returned to him. The situation, though, had to be handled delicately.

"Enclosed is the name, and description of the Girl I mentioned to you last night," President Washington wrote to Secretary of the Treasury Oliver Wolcott on September 1, 1796. "She has been the particular attendant on Mrs. Washington since she was ten years old; and was handy and useful to her being perfect Mistress of her needle."

Having heard through the political grapevine that Ona was in Portsmouth, Washington asked Wolcott to enlist the aid of New Hampshire's collector of customs, Joseph Whipple, whose brother William had signed the Declaration of Independence.

"What will be the best method to [retrieve her], is difficult for me to say," Washington continued in his confidential letter to Wolcott:

> To seize, and put her on board a Vessel bound immediately to this place, or to Alexandria which I should like better, seems at first view, to be the safest and leas[t] expensive [option]. . . .
>
> I am sorry to give you, or anyone else trouble on such a trifling occasion, but the ingratitude of the girl, who was brought up and treated more like a child than a Servant (and Mrs. Washington's desire to recover her) ought not to escape with impunity if it can be avoided.

Joseph Whipple was eager to please the president and, under the pretext of offering Judge employment, convinced her to meet with him. After talking with the young woman at length, however, he became genuinely moved by her desire to be free. She remarked that she'd never been mistreated by the Washingtons but was opposed, not unreasonably, to being enslaved for the rest of her life. In fact, Judge surprised Whipple by offering to return to President Washington if he would promise to manumit her upon his death. Whipple was relieved to have struck a compromise and communicated Judge's proposal to the president.

The commander-in-chief was not in the habit of negotiating with slaves and upbraided Whipple for even considering her offer. "I regret that the attempt you made to restore the Girl should have been attended with so little Success," Washington replied frostily. "To enter into such a compromise with _her_, as she suggested to _you_, is totally inadmissible."

Making matters worse for Washington was that by December 1796, Judge was engaged to Jack Staines, a sailor of mixed race who had fought in the Revolution. Any hope of delivering Judge back to Virginia against her will and without "exciting a mob or a riot—or creating uneasy sensations in the minds of well disposed Citizens," as Whipple humbly (very, _very_ humbly) wrote to Washington on December 22, was complicated by this new state of affairs. To prove his fealty to the president, Whipple persuaded the Portsmouth town clerk to deny Judge and Staines their marriage license.

The couple simply applied for one in a nearby town, Greenland, where it was granted, and they wed in January 1797. Judge gave birth to their first child, a baby girl, that summer.

By then Washington was a former president, having retired to his beloved Mount Vernon, and Judge believed that at long last she could achieve some peace of mind.

She could not. In the fall of 1799, almost three and a half years after abandoning Philadelphia, Judge received a visitor traveling through Portsmouth on business. He was Martha Washington's nephew, Burwell Bassett. Judge's husband was out to sea, leaving her unprotected and alone with their daughter. (Because Judge was a fugitive slave, the child was born a slave, too.) At first Bassett tried flattery and persuasion, entreating Judge to move to Mount Vernon with the Washingtons. She held firm: No.

Bassett left but disclosed to his Portsmouth host later that night his intention to abduct "[Judge] and her infant child by force" if necessary. Aghast, Bassett's host secretly relayed a message to Judge that she was in grave danger. Judge went into hiding, and Martha's nephew returned to Virginia empty-handed. Judge's guardian angel was Senator John Langdon, whose teenage daughter had bumped into Judge three years earlier and inadvertently blown her cover.

George Washington passed away just months after Bassett's visit, and with his death all attempts to cajole or capture Ona Judge finally ended.

Judge died a widow in 1848, alone and impoverished. Before passing away, she was asked by an abolitionist newspaper reporter if she ever regretted relinquishing the relative comfort of the Washingtons' presidential mansion for the hardships she'd later face. "No," Judge said. "I am free and have, I trust, been made a child of God by the means."

Vicky and I step over a trickling creek and approach two squat rock walls shaped like an *L,* the last remnants of the property boundary in Greenland where Judge and Jack Staines made their home. About a hundred feet away is her grave marker, now just a nub of gray stone poking through a thin carpet of red pine needles on the forest floor. There's a sense of privacy and serenity to this spot that befits a woman who wasn't seeking acclaim or recognition but only to live her life, marry, and worship as she chose.

"I'm really torn about all of this," I confide to Vicky as we walk back to her car. "I've always considered Washington a heroic soul—"

"I think he was heroic, too!" she interjects.

"—and I'm not out to bash his reputation." This was a man renowned for valor under fire, emerging from a single battle in the French and Indian War with two horses shot out from under him and four bullet holes through his coat. As a general during the Revolution, he was no less audacious, repeatedly putting himself in harm's way and suffering through many of the same deprivations as his soldiers. Through word and action he rallied an inexperienced, despondent army teetering on the brink of collapse, and prevented a mutiny after the Revolution when those same troops were treated shoddily by Congress. And although ambitious, he was not ruthlessly so. He could easily have held on to and expanded his power as president, but, among other noble acts, he decided against running for a third term to set an example to his successors.

"I knew—I think we all know—he owned slaves," I continue, still trying to untangle my knotted thoughts on the matter. "But that was in the abstract. Seeing where Judge lived and died, and learning about her story has made his role as a slave owner all the more real."

Washington himself was conflicted. As aggressive as his efforts to retain Judge were, Martha was closer to the young slave and, by all accounts, led the charge to have her returned. On the larger issue of slavery, Washington deserves credit at least for evolving. He was born into a slaveholding family and personally inherited ten slaves at the age of eleven. Never an impassioned advocate for the institution, he later believed it should be ended entirely. A year before he died he changed his will so that all of his personal slaves would be freed. "I never mean," Washington wrote to a friend in 1786, "to possess another slave by purchase; it being among my first wishes to see some plan adopted, by which slavery in this Country may be abolished by slow, sure and imperceptible degrees."

Vicky has to pick up her daughter, and after we say good-bye, I head to downtown Portsmouth by myself to find where the *Nancy* would have docked more than two hundred years ago.

There's no record of Judge's first thoughts upon landing here, and I can't even imagine the mix of terror and exhilaration she must have felt setting foot in New Hampshire for the first time, neither enslaved nor entirely free.

"What I don't understand," I asked Vicky before she left, "is why there isn't a memorial or even a small plaque honoring Ona Judge anywhere in New Hampshire, when she's *the very personification* of the state's motto and its love of independence. Is it simple racism or sexism?"

"I don't think that's it entirely," Vicky said. "The town of Milford recently erected a full-sized statue to Harriet Wilson, who wrote *Our Nig,* the first novel by an African American woman. But what makes Ona different is that she was a slave and, therefore, a reminder that New Hampshire was a slave state for quite a long time—until 1857, actually. There are some aspects of our history, I think, we'd just rather ignore."

I figured this might be the case months ago while preparing my full itinerary. When I first started phoning around Portsmouth to inquire about George Washington's slave, I received the same reply in so many words as when I called other cities about unpleasant periods from their past. I heard it when I asked the Cincinnati Zoo about the exhibition of live Native Americans there in 1887; the Owensboro, Kentucky, chamber of commerce about America's last public execution next to the old courthouse on August 14, 1936 (the circuslike atmosphere at the hanging mortified the nation); and the Sonoma Developmental Center in Northern California about the forced sterilizations conducted there on thousands of men and women labeled "subhuman" in the 1920s through 1950s. "That's just not something," I was told time and time again, "we really want to remember."

MOUND CITY

"Ma, I've enlisted," he had said to her diffidently. There was a short silence. "The Lord's will be done, Henry," she had finally replied, and had then continued to milk the brindle cow.

When he had stood in the doorway with his soldier's clothes on his back, and with the light of excitement and expectancy in his eyes almost defeating the glow of regret for the home bonds, he had seen two tears leaving their trails on his mother's scarred cheeks.

Still, she had disappointed him by saying nothing whatever about returning with his shield or on it.

—*From* The Red Badge of Courage (1895) *by Stephen Crane*

PICKING ONE NAME at random from among the more than two thousand Civil War soldiers sailing north on the Mississippi aboard the doomed *Sultana* in late April 1865, local historian Jerry Potter begins telling me about Samuel Jenkins. Jerry and I are trudging down a thick, muddy trail that cuts through a panoramic expanse of farmland in Mound City, Arkansas, where Jerry believes the charred, scattered remains of the *Sultana* lie buried.

A teenager from North Carolina, Samuel Jenkins had yearned to emulate his two older brothers and fight in the Civil War. For which side didn't much seem to matter; when the Confederacy rejected him for being too young, Jenkins volunteered for the Union Army's Third Tennessee Cavalry, and the undermanned regiment gladly accepted him. (Although Tennessee had seceded, pro-Union communities in the state's eastern half mustered up troops to serve with federal divisions.) Jenkins was captured in September 1864 at the battle of Sulphur Creek Trestle and shipped off to the Castle Morgan prison in Cahaba, Alabama, where he remained until the South surrendered. On April 24, 1865, he boarded the *Sultana* in Vicksburg, Mississippi, along with hundreds of other troops who'd endured both the hellfire of battle and the torments of a Confederate POW camp. Most would not survive the boat ride home.

"I've gotten to know Jenkins's daughter, Glenda Green," Jerry says.

"His daughter?" I ask, astonished that anyone alive today had a parent living 150 years ago.

"Jenkins was in his early seventies when Glenda was born—these were *men* back then," Jerry adds with a wry smile, "and she told me a story about sitting with him by the fireplace when he was eighty or so. Out of nowhere he says to her, 'It's been well over sixty years now, and not a day's gone by that I don't hear those boys screaming in the water.'" We stop for a moment.

"Now, think of that," Jerry says, turning to face me. "He lived with that memory every day for his entire life. Every—single—day."

We've only walked about half a mile, but with the humidity we're both drenched. Jerry points out coyote and raccoon tracks as we continue slogging through the sticky mud, or "gumbo," as the locals call it. I look down at my boots, and with layers of mud caked around them they're clownishly large. Each step feels heavier than the last.

"There sure are a lot of butterflies," I mention as blue, white, black, and orange wings flit around us.

Jerry nods. "It's really quite beautiful out here." We pause again as he pulls out a map. "The river used to be here, right where we're standing. It's shifted over the years."

Acres of dense green soybean fields surround us.

"So this is where they all died?" I ask, trying to re-create the scene from almost a century and a half ago.

"Not all. Many of the bodies drifted downstream, a few as far as Vicksburg, and some were pulled out of trees. What little remained of the *Sultana* ended up here, too," he says, directing my attention to a massive ridge a hundred or so feet away.

Launched on January 3, 1863, the *Sultana* was a gleaming, state-of-the-art steamer originally built to haul cotton and other merchandise for trade up and down the Mississippi and Ohio Rivers. But during the Civil War it transported an even more lucrative cargo: Union soldiers. The *Sultana*'s captain, J. Cass Mason, contracted with the federal government to move troops, earning up to $10 a man.

When the *Sultana* left New Orleans on April 21, 1865, for St. Louis, the seventeen-hundred-ton boat was carrying about ninety passengers and crew, a mere quarter of its legal limit. Just south of Mississippi, Captain Mason was alerted that one of the boilers was leaking. During a stop in Vicksburg he assessed the damage and determined that it needed to be replaced entirely, a three-day task. Mason was anxious to keep heading upriver and ordered his engineers to weld a patch over the defective seam. They could install a new boiler in St. Louis.

By the time they shoved off from Vicksburg, an additional two thousand people, most of them Union troops released from Cahaba and Andersonville, another POW camp, had boarded the 260-foot-long boat along with several hundred head of cattle, horses, and Army mules. While the *Sultana* docked in Helena, Arkansas, on April 26, a photographer noticed the massive steamer bulging with soldiers and began setting up his tripod to capture the image. Word quickly spread on board, and as men rushed sternside to be included in the picture, the boat nearly capsized.

Later that night, at about eleven o'clock, the *Sultana* departed from Memphis with an additional 300 passengers and then made a brief stop in Hopefield, Arkansas, to load up 1,000 bushels of coal. A boat meant to carry only 376 people was now crammed with 2,400.

Most of the passengers settled down to rest, but for many sleep was elusive. Huddled on the decks under thin and tattered blankets, some men shivered uncontrollably in the cold, drizzling rain, while those delirious with joy at the prospect of freedom danced and sang in the dark. "We were all talking of home and friends and the many good things we would eat," an Indiana lieutenant named William Dixon recalled. "We had no thought but that we would be at home in a few days feasting with our loved ones once more."

Around midnight, Nathan Wintringer informed his second engineer, Samuel Clemens (no relation to Mark Twain), that the boilers were running smoothly.

At 2:00 A.M., almost exactly, they exploded.

Those closest to the eighteen-foot boilers were instantly scalded to death or blown mangled and lifeless into the Mississippi. "The wildest confusion followed," one soldier recollected. "Some sprang into the river at once, others were killed, and I could hear the groans of the dying above the roar of the flames."

Within minutes the entire boat was consumed by fire, leaving those who couldn't swim with a grotesque choice—burn or drown. "Women and little children in their night clothes, brave men who have stood undaunted on many a battle field," recalled survivor J. Walter Elliott, "suddenly [saw] the impending death by fire, and wringing their hands, tossing their arms wildly in the air, with cries most heartrending, they rush[ed] pell-mell over the guard and into the dark, cold waters of the river."

"Some were swearing a 'blue streak,'" another survivor later wrote about the final moments of soldiers who jumped to their death. "Some would curse Abe Lincoln, Jeff Davis, General Grant—any and everybody prominently connected with the war. Some were crying like children. . . . Some prayed very loud, and most passionately; others were getting off very formal and graceful prayers, all in dead earnest."

Men thrashed in the water, fighting one another over floating debris—wooden doors, bales of hay, mule carcasses, barrels, anything—to cling to. Those who couldn't swim frantically grasped onto and dragged down those who could. And many, after surviving the blast, the fire, the suffocating smoke, the violent clashes in the icy river, eventually succumbed to hypothermia, their bodies already weakened by war and imprisonment.

Confirming exactly how many died is impossible. The government's official tally was 1,547 fatalities, which is about 30 more than were lost on the *Titanic*. But the consensus among contemporary historians is that 1,800 perished, making it America's worst maritime disaster. Out of the 760 passengers who made it ashore, approximately 300 later died of burn wounds or from their prolonged immersion in the freezing Mississippi.

"None of this had to be," Jerry says as we stand looking over the now serene farmland, a place he's visited countless times. "It was all so unnecessary." He relates the events of April 27, 1865, with genuine emotion, clearly affected by what happened here. "What really gets me are the mothers who were waiting for their boys to return, after everything they had been through, after all those years. And they were so close."

"What did Samuel Jenkins do after making it home?"

"Because of what he had seen that night he dedicated his life to medicine. He became a doctor."

I ask Jerry how a tragedy such as this can be so overlooked, especially considering that more people died on the *Sultana* than on the *Titanic,* which inspired hundreds of books, numerous documentaries, and one of the highest-grossing movies ever made. And the *Sultana* didn't just fade from view over time; it was forgotten almost immediately. "Only a few days ago 1,500 lives were sacrificed to fire and water, almost within sight of the city," a Memphis journalist lamented. "Yet, even now, the disaster is scarcely mentioned—some new excitement has taken its place."

"Apathy was part of it," Jerry says. "Four years of battle after battle—sometimes with tens of thousands killed and wounded in just days—had cauterized the nation, emotionally, to the carnage of war. It was just too much to bear."

But the main reason the story vanished so quickly was timing. "Lincoln had been assassinated just two weeks before," Jerry reminds me. While grieving for the slain president, the country was also riveted by the manhunt for John Wilkes Booth, who was finally cornered and shot dead on April 26. Terrible though it was, the *Sultana* got eclipsed by other events.

Many national tragedies have been similarly overshadowed. Three years before the *Sultana* blew up, an explosion at the Allegheny Arsenal in Pittsburgh killed 78 workers, mostly women. It was the worst loss of civilian life during the Civil War but was nevertheless relegated to a historical footnote because it occurred on September 17, 1862, which was also the date of Antietam, the war's bloodiest one-day battle. On October 8, 1871, a firestorm swept through rural Peshtigo, Wisconsin, incinerating upward of 2,500 men, women, and children. Peshtigo almost certainly would be better remembered had Chicago not suffered its "Great Fire," which left 200 to 300 people dead, that very same day. And more recently, when American Airlines Flight 587 plummeted from the sky into the Belle Harbor neighborhood of Queens, New York, killing all 260 on board and 5 on the ground, it was our country's second-deadliest airline disaster. But because it happened on November 12, 2001, when the nation was petrified by anthrax-laced mail and a possible second wave of strikes following the September 11 attacks, there was almost relief that the crash was due to pilot error and not sabotage.

Jerry and I cross over the Arkansas/Tennessee border and drive into the Memphis National Cemetery, where ten thousand American servicemen are buried. Although born and raised in the South, Jerry has become very protective of the *Sultana*'s Union soldiers—or "his boys," as he refers to them—and wants to check the grave of an Ohio officer named John Ely. "Originally they had him being from Illinois, and I asked them to change it." Jerry finds the new marker and confirms it's been corrected.

"Good," he says.

We then walk over to a section that, Jerry tells me, emphasizes the final, heartbreaking indignity of the *Sultana's* aftermath. In row after row we see white markers with only UNKNOWN U.S. SOLDIER engraved in the marble. There are more unidentified U.S. troops buried here, I learn, than anywhere else except Arlington National Cemetery.

"It didn't have to be this way," Jerry says again. This time, however, he isn't referring to the disaster but the anonymous headstones. Soon after the corpses of several hundred Union troops killed on the *Sultana* were recovered, they were identified and laid to rest in Elmwood Cemetery, just south of Memphis. When government officials disinterred the soldiers from Elmwood in 1867 to rebury them with honors here, they wrote their names on the wooden coffins before loading them onto railcars. All of these young men who had died so pointlessly would, at the very least, have a permanent grave site with their name on it, a place where their family members could come and find their lost son or husband or brother, mourn for them, and pay tribute to their sacrifice. The dead would be remembered as individual heroes of the war and not just anonymous victims of a catastrophic accident.

But it was not to be; as the trains rolled through Tennessee to carry the bodies to this cemetery, a thunderstorm erupted. The men's names, which had been written on the coffins in chalk, got washed away by the rain.

RICHARD "TWO GUN"
HART'S HOUSE

I am not shy about admitting that I am an incorrigible Peeping Tom. I have never passed an unshaded window without looking in, have never closed my ears to a conversation that was none of my business. I can justify or even dignify this by protesting that in my trade I must know about people, but I suspect that I am simply curious.

—From Travels with Charley (1962) by John Steinbeck

BEFORE EMBARKING ON my trip, I established three unbreakable rules. First, no trespassing. Tempted as I am to join the growing band of thrill seekers flashlighting their way through abandoned asylums, prisons, sanatoriums, hospitals, and similar institutions, these subversive expeditions are usually illegal and can damage the physical structures themselves. (Plus, I hate spiders.) Rule number two is a corollary of the first: Respect the privacy of those who live in historic homes. This means keeping addresses confidential unless the current occupants agree to disclose them and making no surprise visits.

In a few cases, alas, I strike sites off my itinerary because the home owners haven't answered my letters asking for their consent. One especially disappointing loss has been César Chávez's birthplace in Arizona, a forty-acre ranch that was essentially stolen by a greedy neighbor in cahoots with the Chávez family's own lawyer. César was eleven when his parents were robbed of the land, and according to his autobiography, seeing them get swindled incited his lifelong passion for social justice. Also off-limits for now is the house in Connecticut where Ely Parker lived. A full-blooded Seneca Indian, Parker served as General Ulysses S. Grant's personal aide during the Civil War and handwrote the surrender papers signed by General Robert E. Lee at Appomattox.

Fortunately, most of the people I've contacted have agreed to let me visit, starting with Kelly King, who now resides in the Homer, Nebraska, house once owned by Richard "Two Gun" Hart. A famous Prohibition agent during the 1920s, Hart was renowned for hunting down and capturing bootleggers and busting up stills nationwide. He was also harboring a family secret that made his chosen career all the more remarkable.

On my way to Homer, I'm planning to meet with Richard Hart's eighty-three-year-old son, Harry, to learn more about his father's eventful life. And while zipping down the highway en route to Lincoln, where Harry lives, I have my own troubling encounter with the law.

"Do you have any idea how fast you were going?" a patrolman asks after pulling me over.

There's really no correct response to this, but I proceed nevertheless to give one of the dumbest answers possible: "I'm driving all over the country, and every once in a while I just kind of zone out behind the wheel and don't know what I'm doing."

Barely containing his anger, the officer warns me that I was a mere few miles per hour shy of reckless driving, a jailable offense. He hands over the ticket and sternly advises me to set my cruise control to the speed limit and leave it there. I swear to him I will.

Ten minutes later, as the shock of my near arrest wears off, I hastily pencil three words on my ticket, the only scrap of paper I have on hand: "Cruise control inventor?"

Delayed by the stop and having crept along at what feels like a painstakingly slow pace (that is, the posted speed limit), I arrive late at Harry's. Despite my tardiness, he gives me a warm welcome and invites me into his apartment.

As Harry pours me a glass of water in the kitchen, I glance at the awards and photographs lining his walls. One plaque, surrounded by letters of recognition, is inscribed to Harry from the Homer Fire Department and honors his almost six decades of service. Harry walks in and sees me looking at a picture of a beautiful woman.

"That was my wife, Joyce," Harry says. "We were married forty-nine years."

By the dining room table, Harry has two trunks of memorabilia that, together, contain a physical timeline of his father's peripatetic life as a runaway, a World War I soldier, and, eventually, one of the nation's most celebrated G-men. Harry begins pulling out leather holsters, half a dozen Indian Police and Special Agent badges, and fan mail. In lieu of an actual address, one letter mailed to his father simply has a drawing of two guns and the word *HART* in all caps on the envelope. The post office knew exactly where to send it.

"Where does the nickname come from?" I ask Harry, expecting a rousing story about his dad blasting his way through a circle of outlaws.

"He usually carried two guns with him, and he could shoot with both hands."

"Well," I say, nodding, "that would explain it."

There are also stacks of large black binders inside the trunks, each one crammed with pictures and newspaper articles. From a random culling of clips I jot down several headlines: TWO-GUN HART SNARES QUINTET, R. J. HART RECEIVES THREATENING LETTERS—BELIEVES AUTHORS ARE BOOTLEGGERS, and TWO-GUN HART MAKES RAIDS HERE [IN SOUTH DAKOTA]; LIVES UP TO REPUTATION.

One biographer who apparently nursed a vendetta against Richard

Hart claimed, among other accusations, that Hart never served in the Army. The numerous pictures that Harry shows me of his father standing in formation with other troops while being reviewed by senior officers all look pretty authentic.

Flipping through the binders, I come across a photo of Harry himself in his late teens or early twenties. Boyishly handsome, half grinning with a hint of a rebellious smirk and his hair slicked back, he's standing next to a tubby, bald man in his late forties. "That's Al Capone!" I blurt out. "Holy smokes. What was he like in person?"

Harry shrugs. "He seemed like a guy."

From his response, I'm uncertain if Harry wasn't able to form much of an impression or doesn't remember him well.

Fat-cheeked and smiling, Capone is wearing a plain white dress shirt tucked into khaki pants. He looks like a nebbishy middle-aged man and not the murdering Chicago boss whose lavish lifestyle was paid for by running illegal booze, robbery, shakedowns, and prostitution. Harry doesn't appear eager to elaborate, so I don't press it.

I do, however, ask him why he thinks men like his father—the "good guys"—are often overshadowed by the Al Capones, John Dillingers, and Bugsy Siegels of the world.

"Bad guys are more interesting," Harry replies.

I'd be disingenuous to suggest that I don't find them alluring as well. Indeed, what initially drew me to Harry's father was the fact that his real name was Vincenzo Capone. Richard "Two Gun" Hart was Al Capone's older brother.

Born outside of Naples, Italy, in 1892, Vincenzo immigrated with his parents to Brooklyn about a year later. Around the age of sixteen, he fled New York's cramped tenements for the spacious Midwest and earned his keep laboring on ranches and working as a circus roustabout. He admired silent-film star William Hart, a quiet but fearless law-and-order type, and changed his own name to Richard James Hart. After World War I, he rode a freight train west and hopped off in Homer, where he worked a series of odd jobs. Richard yearned to be more than a bit player in life, and he stepped into the spotlight as a real-life action hero when he rescued a young woman named Kathleen Winch during a flash flood. Like a true leading man he even got the girl; Richard and Kathleen fell in love and married.

With his newfound fame he became town marshal, and by the early 1920s he was chasing moonshiners as a federal agent. Starting in 1926, the Bureau of Indian Affairs assigned him to several Native American reservations (including in Cheyenne, South Dakota, Harry Hart's place of birth), and as a bodyguard to President Calvin Coolidge. When Prohibition ended in 1933, Richard became a justice of the peace. He had scant communication with his six younger brothers, each of whom had become entangled in nefarious activities, and met Al only a few times. By the late 1930s, Al was a powerless ex-con, his criminal empire gone and his mind ravaged by syphilis. He died of a heart attack in 1947, and Richard suffered a cardiac arrest himself five years later, dying at the age of sixty.

Before I leave, Harry gives me a short, self-published biography of his father that he's written as well as specific directions to the family's old house in Homer. I thank him profusely for his time and head to my hotel.

WELCOME TO HOMER—LITTLE BUT LIVELY, a tall red-and-white sign proclaims as I pull off Route 77 after driving up from Lincoln the next morning. I cross over a short bridge that leads directly onto Homer's main avenue, John Street. With American flags hanging from every lamppost, the tiny, immaculate town looks like something out of a Norman Rockwell painting.

From John Street I take a right on Third and, after a few blocks, park in front of a light-blue two-story house on the corner of Spring Street. The lawn is large and bright green. There's a birdbath in the front yard nestled within a cluster of white, pink, and purple flowers. Another small garden presses up against the garage. Kelly King, the house's current owner, has maintained the property wonderfully.

Before coming here, I asked Kelly how she learned that Richard Hart used to live in the house.

"First the realtor mentioned it," Kelly told me. "And then I met Harry, and he gave me more of the details."

"What was your reaction?"

"I thought it was very interesting."

"Did you find anything exciting when you moved in, like trapdoors or hidden contraband?" I asked, instantly realizing that the question made me sound like a kid raised on too many Hardy Boys mysteries.

Kelly laughed and said, "Well, we did look through the basement and the crawlspace in the attic real carefully, but there was nothing there."

I now photograph the house from different angles, and while I'm shooting it from the side, an older woman drives by, stops, and asks me if I'm friends with Kelly King.

"Not personally," I say. "She's at work now, but she gave me permission to take pictures, and last night I met with Harry Hart in Lincoln, who used to live here and was telling me all about his father, Richard. I just wanted to come and see the house for myself."

"He was a very nice man," the woman says. I'm about to ask her if she means Richard or Harry, but she rolls up her window and waves good-bye.

A private house can't be designated a national landmark without the owner's approval, and while I more than understand why some individuals aren't enthusiastic about gawkers congregating on their front lawn and snapping photos of where they live, it's frustrating to consider how many intriguing places will remain indefinitely unknown. There's more than just idle curiosity at stake; these "regular" homes are reminders that history doesn't dwell solely in the estates and manor halls of the privileged. It can also be found in suburban split-levels, on family farms, and within public housing projects that people pass by every day—or actually live in, often without even knowing it.

Fortunately, for every site like Ely Parker's house or César Chávez's ranch that remains hidden, new possibilities constantly reveal themselves. As I'm leaving Nebraska, I get a call from a woman named Marjorie Teetor Meyer, who's responding to the message I had recently left asking about her father, an influential inventor, and their family home in Hagerstown, Indiana. Marjorie kindly gives me the address, and although I doubt I'll have a chance to stop by during my upcoming trip to Indiana, I can save it for another visit.

Marjorie's father, Ralph Teetor, was a brilliant mechanical engineer who built a full-sized car at the age of twelve and, after graduating from the prestigious University of Pennsylvania in 1912, developed a revolutionary procedure for balancing turbine rotors in warships. Teetor received numerous patents throughout his life, mostly related to cars, and he served as president of the Society of Automotive Engineers. And he did all of this despite being blind since childhood; at the age of five, Teetor was jimmying open a locked drawer with a penknife when the blade slipped and pierced his eyeball. Both retinas became infected and Teetor lost all vision.

Although extremely independent and familiar with every component of an automobile, Teetor obviously couldn't get behind the wheel of a car and drive himself. While riding around one day with his attorney, Harry Lindsey, he became annoyed by Lindsey's lurching, gas-and-brake driving habits. Later, in the basement workshop of his Hagerstown home, Teetor began tinkering with accelerator and brake pedals, throttles, control cables, and manifold vacuum power sources to design a regulating system for cars that maintained their speed with just the touch of a button. He christened it the Speedostat. Automakers loved the invention, and Cadillac was among the first to offer it commercially, in its 1959 models, with one slight change. The company called it "Cruise Control."

FORT MEADE

A belief in supernormal perception, and especially in the clairvoyant vision, is apparent in the history, however meager it may be, of every ancient nation.

Hebrew history is full of instances of it. A striking example is recorded as occurring during the long war between Syria and Israel. The King of Syria had good reasons for suspecting that in some manner the King of Israel was made acquainted with all his intended military operations, since he was always prepared to thwart them at every point. Accordingly he called together his chiefs and demanded to know who it was among them who thus favored the King of Israel, to which one of the chiefs replied: "It is none of thy servants, O King: but Elisha, a prophet that is in Israel, telleth the King of Israel the words thou speakest in thy chamber."

—From Telepathy and the Subliminal Self (1897) by Dr. Rufus Osgood Mason, the U.S. Navy assistant surgeon during the Civil War and an early proponent of using psychic powers for military ends

MY THIRD SELF-IMPOSED rule while planning the itinerary was: No weird stuff.

I'll plead agnostic about the existence of haunted mansions, alien abductions, demonic possessions, and other extraterrestrial or supernatural manifestations, but regardless of how entrenched these tales might be in a community's local lore, they're not verifiable or consequential and therefore wouldn't be relevant to my trip.

Much to my own astonishment, I had to break rule number three while doing last-minute research on Niihau and Pearl Harbor, which led me to a bizarre but historically significant site at Fort Meade, Maryland, along with other top-secret places I hadn't otherwise considered.

The route to Fort Meade, figuratively speaking, was a winding one but strangely enlightening. Before arriving in Hawaii, I read about a UFO sighting over Los Angeles in February 1942 that startled a nation still jittery from the attack on Pearl Harbor. I would have dismissed this incident out of hand if it weren't for the fact that, whether or not an actual flying saucer appeared over L.A., seven people were killed or seriously injured due to the late-night scare. ANTI-AIRCRAFT GUNS BLAST AT L.A. MYSTERY INVADER the Associated Press exclaimed the morning of February 25, 1942. Under a banner headline, ARMY SAYS ALARM REAL, the *Los Angeles Times* breathlessly reported: "Powerful searchlights from countless stations stabbed the sky with brilliant probing fingers while anti-aircraft batteries dotted the heavens with beautiful, if sinister, orange bursts of shrapnel."

Those gorgeous shell bursts sent jagged chunks of metal plummeting back to earth, critically wounding civilians scurrying to safety as air-raid sirens wailed and all electricity was cut off, plunging the city into darkness. Five people also died, two from heart attacks and three in traffic accidents caused by panicked motorists. "The spectacular anti-aircraft barrage came after the 4th Interceptor Command ordered the blackout when strange craft were reported over the coast line," the *Los Angeles Times* also noted.

Initially, the military couldn't explain with certainty what had set off "the Battle of Los Angeles," and forty-two years passed before an official report blamed weather balloons for being the most likely cause.

For understandable reasons, government agencies tend not to go on the record about UFO sightings, but those who believe that aliens have visited planet Earth frequently roll out two "official" documents to buttress their case. The first dates back to the seventeenth century. "In this year one James Everell, a sober, discreet man, and two others, saw a great light in the night at Muddy River," Massachusetts Bay Colony governor John Winthrop wrote in his journal in 1639. "When it stood still, it flamed up, and was about three yards square; when it ran, it was contracted into the figure of a swine: it ran as swift as an arrow towards Charlton, and so up and down about two or three hours. . . . Divers[e] other credible persons saw the same light, after, about the same place."

Some 330 years later, Jimmy Carter spotted a UFO minutes before attending a Lions Club meeting in Leary, Georgia. The Jimmy Carter Library was surprisingly helpful when I called to verify the October 1969 story, and staff members even sent me a photocopy of the questionnaire that Carter, by that time Georgia's governor, dutifully filled out from the International UFO Bureau. "Seemed to moved [*sic*] toward us, stop, move partially away, return, then depart," Carter handwrote on the form. He described the object as "bluish at first— then reddish—Luminous—not solid." In the spirit of bipartisanship, I contacted the Ronald Reagan Presidential Library to confirm that Reagan also claimed to have once seen a UFO. The staff there, alas, did not respond.

Intriguing as Carter's account was, the sighting didn't cause much of a stir at the time or impact his presidential campaign, although questions about it have dogged him over the years. "I never knew of any instance where it was proven that any sort of vehicle had come from outer space to our country and either lived here or left," he stated in a September 1995 speech at Emory University, apparently trying to shake off rumors that as commander-in-chief he'd been shown evidence of recovered alien aircraft.

At this same presentation, however, the Q&A period took a peculiar turn when Carter began talking about a "special" Soviet military plane that went down in Zaire during his presidency. After U.S. satellites scanned the area and found nothing, the CIA conferred with a clairvoyant who, Carter told the Emory students, "went into a trance and gave some latitude and longitude figures. We focused our satellite cameras on that point, and the plane was there."

Hello? Here was a former president of the United States openly discussing government-sponsored paranormal operations. Now, *this* had potential.

Sure enough, intelligence agencies had been utilizing psychic espionage for years. "There are legitimate laboratory projects that may eventually unlock the mysteries of the human mind," Pulitzer Prize–winning columnist Jack Anderson reported in the *Washington Post* on April 23, 1984. "One of the most promising is the testing of 'remote viewing'—the claimed ability of some psychics to describe scenes thousands of miles away."

Anderson went on to describe a remote-viewing operation, code-named Project Grill Flame, that was producing "astonishing results." In one test, a psychic was given latitudinal and longitudinal coordinates and, based solely on those numbers, stated that the site was a Soviet nuclear-testing area, a fact that U.S. satellites verified. Grill Flame and its variously named offshoots, including Sun Streak, Center Lane, and Star Gate (also Stargate), focused not only on espionage but also on predicting terrorist attacks and locating hostages, POWs, and kidnapped government officials.

In a follow-up piece on remote viewing, Jack Anderson claimed that former CIA director Stansfield Turner and General William Odom, the Army's intelligence chief, were concerned that the Soviets might surpass the United States in psychic research. "Inside the Pentagon, [Odom] has raised the question of whether the Soviets could use psychics to penetrate our secret vaults," Anderson stated in a sober tone. "This has led to talk in the backrooms about raising a 'psychic shield' to block this sort of remote viewing." Anderson recognized how crack-

potty this all seemed but still defended it: "At the risk of being ridiculed over a 'voodoo gap,' advocates like Rep. Charlie Rose (D-N.C.),
support continued research into the more promising areas of this mysterious field. After all, the atomic bomb was once thought to be a hare-
brained idea."

And Grill Flame was an idea with consequences. Whether the program led to actionable intelligence (and there's debate about this) or
was really just a major disinformation campaign to spook the Soviets, it
consumed tens of millions of federal tax dollars and thousands of manpower hours that critics argue could have been used more productively.

By the mid-1990s remote-viewing operations were shut down and
declassified. After reading through hundreds of pages of documents
and autobiographical material by former "viewers," I learned that Fort
Meade was where Grill Flame was hatched. Buildings 2650 and 2651,
to be exact. I contacted Meade's public affairs office several times to
ask where the buildings were and if I could come by to photograph
them. The staff members were always courteous but never gave me a
definitive reply. Running short on time, I decided to drive there and,
without doing anything illegal or unethical, explore the base myself.

Located twenty-five miles northeast of Washington, D.C., Fort George
G. Meade is named after the U.S. general who was wounded five times
during the Civil War and unexpectedly given command of Union
forces at Gettysburg right before the battle. Meade prevailed, and
the victory was a turning point in the war. (His post-Gettysburg record was spottier. Lincoln rebuked him for not aggressively pursuing
and destroying Lee's army, and Meade's luster dimmed as Ulysses S.
Grant's star began to rise.) Access to Fort Meade is generally restricted,
but the public is allowed inside under certain circumstances.

A guard at the main gate asks me why I'm here.

"I'm going to the museum," I say. This is true. I'm curious to see if
they have any exhibits about remote viewing. The guard notices my
camera in the front seat.

"No pictures, okay?"

"It's for the museum," I say. This is mostly true.

Photography isn't exactly encouraged on any military base, but there's particular reason for sensitivity here: Fort Meade is home to the NSA—the National Security Agency or, as Washington insiders joke, "No Such Agency" because its cryptological operations are so secretive. I place the camera inside my backpack, and after the guard completes a security check of my car, he tells me where to go. I follow his directions to the letter, and as much as I'd hoped to catch a glimpse of Buildings 2650 and 2651 along the way, there's no sign of them.

Inside the museum, I start with the Meade Room, which features a plaster bust, portrait, and photographs of the general, along with numerous pictures of his beloved but battered horse Old Baldy. During the First Battle of Bull Run an artillery fragment bloodied Old Baldy's nose; at Antietam his neck was gashed; a bullet ripped into his stomach at Gettysburg; and at Petersburg he got punched in the ribs by another shell, prompting Meade to retire him for the duration of the war. Old Baldy made his last ceremonial appearance as the "riderless horse" at Meade's own funeral, and he outlived his owner by ten years. Euthanized and buried, Old Baldy was later disinterred and decapitated so a taxidermist could mount his head for public display.

There's nothing in the museum about remote viewing anywhere. Machine guns, howitzers, and captured enemy uniforms, including a German *Pickelhaube* helmet with the little spiky thing on top, fill the glass cases, and the exhibit culminates with the prized "big toys," as one docent calls them, in the last room—three full-sized tanks, the Mark VIII Liberty, the M3-A1, and a Renault FT-17. With such impressive weaponry on display, I suppose a bunch of guys sitting behind a desk squeezing their brows to envision Soviet sub bases overseas wouldn't fit in.

Bob Johnson, the museum's director, has agreed to meet with me, and he's familiar with the remote-viewing program.

"Do you know where Buildings 2560 and 2561 are?" I ask.

"I'm pretty sure they've been torn down," he says. "They were over near Kimbrough, the hospital. Those are all empty fields now." I have a map of the base, and he indicates where he thinks they would have been.

Even broaching the subject makes me feel a little silly, and I emphasize to Bob that my overall trip is a serious enterprise. But researching Fort Meade's psychic warriors did open up a whole category of historic sites that are unmarked for reasons of national security. Many a hair-raising moment has occurred in these tourist-unfriendly places—be they military bases, radar installations, nuclear-missile silos, or "undisclosed locations" where senior government officials are secreted away in public emergencies—and the relevant stories are barricaded behind steel-reinforced walls and razor-topped electric fences guarded by armed sentries. Stopping by to photograph them isn't a question of bad manners, like visiting a private home uninvited. It's grounds for arrest.

But as with private homes, for every great story that remains hidden for now, new ones crop up over time. Before leaving Fort Meade, I show Bob a memoir I've brought along by a former World War II soldier who did basic training here and then joined the 603rd Camouflage Battalion. Their main assignment, something of a ghost story in itself, was classified for decades. "The 603rd was one of four noncombat units that were part of a phantom division called the Twenty-third Headquarters Special Troops," the seventy-eight-year-old veteran, William Ralph Blass, reminisced.

> Our identity was kept secret for the simple reason that we were posing as other Allied troops in order to fool the enemy. . . . [We were] pretending to be Patton's armor, the Fifteenth Tank Battalion. Except, that instead of Shermans, we had rubber ones that we inflated at night and left in his same tank tracks. We even had ways of faking tank fire and noise, which the men in the sonic unit blasted all night long at the Germans. So when Von Ramcke looked the next morning through the haze and battle smoke with his field glasses, he thought he was seeing Patton's forces. In a matter of hours he would have known it was a ruse,

but by then, Patton had attacked somewhere else, and we and our portable dummy tanks had vanished.

Hundreds of artists, many with theater and design backgrounds, served in the so-called Ghost Army painting inflatable rubber "tanks" to make them look real, constructing fake ammunition dumps and troop cantonments to dupe German air reconnaissance, and coloring and arranging camouflage netting to appear as if rows of warplanes and assorted military equipment lay hidden underneath, all to convince the Wehrmacht that Allied forces were more formidable than their actual numbers. This turned out to be handy training for Bill Blass, who after the war built a fashion empire worth half a billion dollars. Among his most cherished possessions were the notebooks he sketched in while at Fort Meade.

Bob photocopies the pages in my copy of Blass's memoir about Fort Meade, and we discuss the remote-viewing buildings one more time. "Just don't take any pictures," he advises.

I promise him I won't.

After driving around the post for a few minutes, I locate the spot and pull off on a side road. As I'm surveying the empty fields, a pickup truck parks right behind me.

"You lost?" a helpful voice calls out.

I look over and see a guy in his early forties, sporting a crew cut. I'm almost certain he's military, although he's not wearing a uniform, just a light-brown polo shirt and jeans.

"Well . . . ," I begin, not sure who he is and how much I should say, "I'm trying to figure out where some buildings were."

"What buildings?"

"They were numbered 2560 and 2561."

"Can I see that?" he asks, pointing at the map sticking out of my front pocket.

"Uh, yeah."

"I think they were demolished a while ago," he says, tracing a small circle with his index finger over the same area Bob had indicated.

"It's okay if they're no longer there. I'm just curious where they used to be. . . ."

Now he's a bit wary. "Why's that?"

I downplay it. "Oh, it's just for this little project I'm working on."

That sounds suspiciously evasive, so I elaborate. "It's about a top-secret program the CIA was doing using psychics."

Much better.

He looks at me like I'm a nutcase. "Sorry I can't help you there. Do you know how to find your way back to the main exit?" he asks. "It can be confusing."

"Not really."

He turns toward the street and says, "Drive out here, make a left onto Llewellyn Avenue, take your first left onto Ernie Pyle Road, go right on Mapes Road, and then you'll turn right to 175."

"Left, left, right, right. Got it. And I'll pass by the barracks, right?"

"I don't believe so."

I had forgotten to ask Bob where they were. "I need to find those, too. Bill Blass trained here during World War II."

"The fashion guy?"

"That's the one."

He hands back the map and shakes his head. "Lotta funny stories about this place."

"Any that come to mind?" I ask, smiling.

He thinks for a moment, gives me a long, hard look, and says, "Almost forgot. They're doing construction on Llewellyn, so you might have to jog around that a bit."

That would be a no.

It's also a good indication, even I can intuit, that it's time to move on.

MARY DYER'S FARM

We suppose you [in Rhode Island] have understood that last year a company of Quakers arrived at Boston upon no other account than to disperse their pernicious opinions had they not been prevented by the prudent care of that Government.... We therefore make it our request that you as well as the Rest of the Colonies take such order herein that Your Neighbors may be freed from that Danger; That you Remove those Quakers that have been Received, and for the future prohibit their coming amongst you.

—From a September 12, 1657, letter by the Commissioners of the United Colonies to Rhode Island's governors, who ultimately refused the request on the grounds that laws enacted against the Quakers only encouraged them. "They delight to be persecuted," Rhode Island replied.

IN THE FAMILY of American states, Rhode Island and Providence Plantations (the state's official name) is the runt of the brood. Wyoming is the least populated, but Rhode Island is geographically the smallest. And like many diminutive siblings, what the Ocean State lacks in physical brawn it compensates for in bravado and scrappy determination. Rhode Island was first to declare independence from Great Britain and boasts having fired the earliest shots of the Revolution; on June 9, 1772, almost three years before Massachusetts minutemen clashed with redcoats at Lexington and Concord, Sons of Liberty patriots from Warwick, Rhode Island, shot up and torched a British schooner, HMS *Gaspée,* that had been harassing colonial mailboats. Newspapers across the colonies cheered the brazen strike, which exacerbated tensions with England, and Warwick residents celebrate the *Gaspée* affair every June by burning the ship in effigy.

This rebellious streak dates back to the late 1630s, when Roger Williams, with other like-minded souls banished from Massachusetts because of their faith, established the colony as a haven from persecution. Among those exiled was Mary Dyer, an early heroine in the battle for religious freedom. (The correct spelling of her last name is somewhat elusive; Dyre, Dyer, and Dyar all appear on contemporaneous documents.) Today, a statue honoring Dyer stands in Boston, where she died. But there is no tribute or memorial to her of any kind in Newport, where she lived.

Described by her peers as "comely"—the Puritans' uncomely word for "attractive"—Dyer was admitted to the Boston church in December 1635 at the age of twenty-four. She had emigrated from England a year before with her husband, William, but by the spring of 1638 she was cast out of Massachusetts. Her friendship with Anne Hutchinson, who was labeled a heretic for leading unauthorized Bible meetings, had already raised suspicions, and Governor John Winthrop became convinced that Dyer was wicked when he learned that she had prematurely given birth to a deformed, stillborn girl. To prove his case, Winthrop disinterred the tiny corpse that Dyer had secretly buried in grief and shame. "It was of ordinary bigness; it had a face, but no head," Winthrop wrote in his journal. "The navel and all the belly, with the distinction of the sex, were where the back should be; and . . . between the shoulders, it had two mouths, and in each of them a piece of red flesh sticking out; it had arms and legs as other children; but, instead of toes, it had on each foot three claws, like a young fowl."

For her "monster birth," Dyer was expelled. She and her husband joined Roger Williams, Anne Hutchinson, and other exiles from Massachusetts to found Rhode Island, the first government in the New World to establish freedom of worship as a fundamental human right.

In 1652 the Dyers traveled to England, where Mary came under the spiritual wing of George Fox and his newly formed Society of Friends, or Quakers. Mary converted and returned to New England in 1657. Her timing couldn't have been worse. Massachusetts's new governor, John Endicott (also spelled Endecott), was more intolerant than Winthrop and supported increasingly vituperative punishments against the Quakers, from extravagant fines and whippings to slicing off their ears and slitting their tongues. In October 1658, Massachusetts passed a law condemning them to death if they even entered the state.

Nine months later, Marmaduke Stephenson and William Robinson did just that, intentionally challenging the law. They were promptly tossed into prison. When Mary Dyer visited them, she, too, was jailed. William Dyer went ballistic, excoriating the magistrates by letter for mistreating his wife. "You have done more in persecution in one year than the worst bishops [back in England] did in seven," he raged. Although William Dyer no longer lived in Massachusetts, he still commanded respect and was able to secure Mary's release. Stephenson and Robinson were freed as well.

But precisely as the Rhode Island authorities had forewarned in their September 1657 letter to the United Colonies, the draconian laws only served as a magnet to the Quakers. Stephenson and Robinson marched right back into Massachusetts and were arrested, and Mary Dyer left Newport for Boston to offer moral support. Once again, she was incarcerated. All three received death sentences.

On October 27, 1659, Dyer, Stephenson, and Robinson were led to the gallows. Stephenson went first. "Be it known unto all this day that we suffer not as evil-doers, but for conscience sake," he said when the noose was draped over his head. After a final prayer was uttered by the local minister, Stephenson went off the platform. The rope snapped straight; his body tensed, shuddered, and then went limp.

Robinson followed.

Dyer was saved for last so she could watch the other two die. Her legs and arms were bound, and the noose was placed around her neck. Suddenly a voice cried out, "Stop! For she is reprieved." Unbeknownst to Dyer, Endicott had conceded to giving her one last chance, after first giving her a memorable scare. Dyer was untied, taken down from the gallows, and escorted out of Boston.

Far from being shaken by the experience, Dyer was furious that she'd been spared while her fellow Quakers had been killed. Seven months later, on May 31, 1660, Governor Endicott and Dyer were once more face-to-face.

"Are you the same Mary Dyer that was here before?" he asked, incredulous.

"I am the same Mary Dyer that was here at the last General Court," she said.

Endicott had lost all patience. "Tomorrow," he told her, "[you will] be hanged till you are dead."

"This is no more than what you said before," Dyer replied.

"But now it is to be executed."

The next morning she again calmly approached the gallows on Boston Common. The noose was tightened. A minister placed a handkerchief over her face so that the assembled crowd would not witness her final, involuntary contortions. A signal was given, and she dropped. Her neck broke the instant the rope went taut, and Mary Dyer was dead.

Dyer was not the last Quaker to be martyred; one year later, a man named William Leddra was hanged. Influenced by a prominent Quaker in England named Edward Burrough, King Charles II ordered that the executions stop.

A U.S. Naval Hospital stands where Dyer's farm used to be in Newport, just off Third Street. Outside the hospital's entrance, a security officer asks me the nature of my visit. I describe my search for unmarked sites and Mary Dyer's connection to the place. He smiles and from out of nowhere asks: "Okay, history guy. Where'd the name Jeep come from?" (I'm thrown at first but then realize that my latest rental car is a Jeep, so the question isn't totally irrelevant.)

His tone is playful, but for a moment I'm afraid that if I fail to answer correctly, he might actually turn me away, like the Sphinx blocking passage to Thebes. If memory serves, there are a couple of theories about the etymology of Jeep, but I'm so caught off-guard, I can't recall a single one of them.

"C'mon," he says, "it's short for 'general purpose,' or GP, which became *Jeep*. Also, I need to see your ID." I'm not sure that he's entirely accurate, but as I hand him my driver's license, I'm not about to argue.

He seems genuinely intrigued by Dyer's story, but he's confused by my intentions; if I know there are no plaques or signs about Dyer, "What's the point of coming here?" he asks. Cars are starting to line up behind me.

"I just have to see it firsthand," I say quickly.

"Happy hunting."

Over the past three and a half centuries the land around the hospital has changed, and no structures or foundations from the seventeenth century have survived. Anything, everything, related to Mary Dyer is gone.

"That's probably why there's no marker about her—there's nothing there," a staff member at the Newport Historical Society suggested when I called them months ago to verify where Dyer's property was. "Preservation funds are limited as it is, and priority is usually given to sites where there's *something* to point to."

A tangible link to the past certainly has its advantages. Ideally, we hope to see the original building or fort or house because these help us to summon the memory of those who worked or fought or lived there. An empty spot of land often isn't as evocative as the genuine article.

But even if "nothing" remains, there is value still in visiting the general area, I think. The stories, not the physical sites, are what's paramount, and they become more indelibly impressed in our minds when we travel to where they occurred. The journey alone inspires thought-ful contemplation, and inevitably we chat with others about our en-deavor along the way, as I did with the security guard and also with a woman on the train to Providence, who saw me reading Dyer's biogra-phy and was curious about "the Quaker Martyr from Rhode Island."

At the destination itself all of our senses are engaged. Dyer's old homestead presses up against what is now Coasters Harbor. Strolling around this picturesque neighborhood, hearing the light lapping of the waves and taking in the briny air, I have a better idea of her life here in Newport and how far she was from her first home in Boston. For us it's an easy ninety-minute drive to Massachusetts. In Dyer's time the journey took days, and she often went by foot. I can't imagine how punishing this must have been in both body and spirit, especially her final trip. With every step she knowingly moved closer to a horrific death—and yet kept walking. I doubt I ever would have focused on the depth of her courage had I not come here. Now I'll never forget it.

My contact at the Newport Historical Society touched on one other matter that can't be overstated when it comes to why historical sites often go unmarked: lack of funding. Obviously it costs money to get these signs and plaques made, to say nothing of the hefty expenses re-quired to erect a statue or refurbish an old property, and preservation and historical societies across the country are operating on shoestring budgets as it is. They also rely extensively on dedicated volunteers, and, having called on many of them already, I can attest that they are a con-sistently helpful and knowledgeable bunch.

At the forefront of the movement to protect America's past is the revered and privately funded National Trust for Historic Preservation, and each year the organization releases a list of the nation's most "en-dangered sites." It is a sobering catalog of extraordinary landmarks that have either been neglected or are at risk of being destroyed. The Trust recently included on its list the Human Resources Center in Yankton, South Dakota (formerly the South Dakota Hospital for the Insane), and the building is historically significant because its winged design and sun-drenched rooms were intended to create a soothing environment for patients. I immediately contacted the center about coming out for a visit before it was demolished, and the administrator said that there was no rush; in this case, a recent cut in the state budget had ironically saved the old hospital—for the time being. "The truth is," the administrator told me, "we don't have the money to tear it down."

From Newport I drive to Boston, where I check in to the Omni Parker House. Terrible as this is to confess, I've always avoided historic hotels. Aside from usually being out of my price range, they sometimes seemed to trade comfort for ambience. Descriptions like "old-fashioned elegance," "quaint," and "period architecture" were, I assumed, just code words for "no Wi-Fi," "cramped rooms," and "dodgy air-conditioning."

The Parker House has prompted me to reevaluate my bias. Billing itself as the longest continuously operated hotel in America, it turns out to be sensational, and I'm especially fascinated by the cast of characters who've served on its staff. In the 1980s a budding opera singer named Denyce Graves studying at the nearby New England Conservatory of Music worked the night shift as a telephone operator. She is now one of the world's foremost mezzo-sopranos. During the 1940s a young Malcolm Little bussed tables in the hotel's restaurant before converting to Islam and changing his name to Malcolm X. And nearly a century ago, a Vietnamese man in his early twenties named Nguyen That Thanh traveled throughout the United States and worked as a pastry chef here. He later returned to his homeland, assumed the name Ho Chi Minh, and became the Communist revolutionary who ruled North Vietnam from the mid-1940s until his death in 1969.

After a few days finalizing last-minute reservations and assembling what's turned into a phone-book-sized itinerary, I'm good to go. And with a clearer understanding of the reasons why so many historical sites remain unrecognized—they evoke shame, they're inaccessible, the original structure is gone, there's no funding to mark them, they've been overshadowed by other events, and so on—I'm ready to tackle the larger question of what makes them worth remembering at all.

PART II

THE WORLD BEFORE US

Coming to, Exploring, and
Conserving America

THE PAISLEY FIVE MILE
POINT CAVES

In a manner of speaking, the fact that humankind itself is unpredictable is the quintessential stumbling-block for archaeologists. We have to assume that the people whose dwelling-places, artefacts, lives even, we are dealing with were rational, integrated, sane and sensible human beings. Then we look around at our own contemporaries and wonder how this belief can possibly be sustained.

—From Ancient Ireland: Life Before the Celts (1998) by archaeologist Laurence Flanagan

THERE IS NO WELCOME TO PAISLEY sign gracing the outskirts of the 240-person town in southeast Oregon, just a long white banner strung over Main Street between two telephone poles that announces in big red and black letters:

Paisley Mosquito Festival
Last Full Weekend in July

Upon seeing this I'm torn between admiring their aplomb for celebrating a nuisance most communities would probably downplay, if not deny completely, and dreading what is evidently going to be twenty-four hours of nonstop slapping and scratching.

Presently I have more urgent matters to contend with. After leaving the Redmond airport, I accidentally clicked on the Mute button of my new GPS device, causing me to roll down Highway 97 about forty miles too far. By the time I noticed how uncharacteristically quiet the GPS had been and backtracked to the exit I missed, I'd wasted more than ninety minutes. Now I'm late to an early-evening meeting with my host, Dr. Dennis Jenkins, and to top it off I've misplaced his cell phone number. Without him I can't get out to Five Mile Point Caves tomorrow morning, and touring that excavation site is the whole reason I've flown across the country and driven for the past four and a half hours.

While checking in to the Sage Rooms, I ask owner Michelle Huey if they have Wi-Fi. (Dr. Jenkins's contact information is in an old e-mail.)

"We don't have any way to connect to the Internet," she tells me, "and there's no wireless in town."

"Is there anyplace with computers that are already hooked up?"

"Only the public library, and they're closed."

Everything about this trip has me anxious. Like Niihau, Paisley is a one-shot deal. This week Dr. Jenkins and his team pack up for the year, so tomorrow is my only chance to tag along. My apprehension goes beyond any logistical concerns, however. Originally I thought it would be "fun" to include an archaeological dig on my itinerary and watch the past be unearthed, literally, before my eyes. When I read in an obscure science monthly about what had been found at the Paisley Caves, a discovery so momentous I still believe it deserves paparazzi-like attention, I contacted Dr. Jenkins, and he approved my visit. That was months ago.

Awed as I was by the site's significance, now that I'm actually focused on the larger story, I have no clue how to humanize the protagonists, who are—give or take a few centuries—14,500 years old.

Immersing myself in Prehistoric Archaeology 101 has only confused me more, since so much of the subject matter appears disputable and uncertain. There are obviously no letters, journals, documents, film clips, photographs, or sketches of any kind to offer reliable insight into what Pleistocene people thought or felt or looked like. What *is* put forth seems wildly speculative. Clay-molded "interpretations" of Stone Age faces are reconstructed using a single tooth or strand of hair, and entire metropolises are imagined based on nothing more than the discovery of two beads and a femur. And whenever a theory finally does gain wide acceptance in the scientific community, some groundbreaking new find sends it toppling. It becomes difficult, especially for a newcomer, to maintain firm footing on such shifting, unstable terrain.

For six decades the prevailing wisdom held that about 13,500 years ago, *Homo sapiens* trekked across an exposed land bridge from Siberia into what is now Alaska and then fanned out across the continent. Distinctive fluted spear points and other manmade objects dug up in 1926 at what turned out to be a bison-killing ground in Folsom, New Mexico, followed by similar items found in nearby Clovis, represented the first hard proof of these Paleo-Indian pioneers. (Still contested is who most deserves credit for the discoveries. An African American cowboy named George McJunkin tried bringing attention to the Folsom site in 1908, but no one listened. And in 1929, three years before Edgar Billings Howard excavated Clovis, a local teenager named Ridgely Whiteman mailed the Smithsonian Institution a "warhead" point he'd found in the area while hunting for artifacts and insisted there were more. He too was ignored.) "Clovis" became the defining adjective for anything related to the earliest people in either North or South America.

That is, until the late 1990s. After two decades of research, Universidad Austral de Chile professors Mario Pino and Tom Dillehay convinced a blue-ribbon panel of archaeologists in 1997 that a Monte Verde, Chile, settlement predated Clovis by one thousand years. Cordage, stone tools, and the remains of edible plants, potatoes, nuts, berries, and even seaweed were uncovered, along with evidence of hearths and tents made of animal hides.

At about the same time, the Meadowcroft Rockshelter near Pittsburgh was earning recognition as another pre-Clovis settlement, dating back to 14,000 B.C. Suddenly, pre-Clovis sites started popping up everywhere. Cactus Hill in Virginia, Lovewell in Kansas, La Sena in Nebraska, and South Carolina's Topper dig, among others, all claimed to beat Clovis by upward of two, five, six, and possibly twenty *thousand* years, respectively. None of these places, however, have yielded human DNA. This isn't absolutely necessary to date a site, but uncontaminated human DNA adds a degree of certainty that tools and weapons made of stone (which can't be radiocarbon-dated), charred wood (which could be from a manmade hearth—or a natural forest fire), and other detritus and artifacts do not.

Then, in 2003, a University of Oregon archaeologist radiocarbon-dated the first pre-Clovis human DNA in North America. That archaeologist was Dr. Dennis Jenkins.

Who, praise the heavens, I've finally located at the university's temporary dormitory a block off Main Street. "Join us," he says, inviting me inside, where he's reviewing with his students today's haul from Paisley Caves. Dressed in jeans and a blue button-down shirt, Dr. Jenkins has the distinguished silver-haired mien of a tenured professor, but his ruddy complexion hints of a life spent in the great outdoors and he exudes a youthful vigor and warmth. Two students are splayed out on the living room sofa, exhausted, while others are either preparing dinner or tapping away on their computers. One young woman, rifling through the refrigerator, opens a container and wrinkles her nose. "Eww, is this cole slaw? It looks *really* old. I think there's something growing on it."

"Catalog it," a tired voice from the sofa calls out.

Plastic sandwich bags are clustered everywhere, each one neatly labeled and filled with what appear to be little bones, dirt, and dark clumps I can't identify but am assuming will be analyzed later. Discreetly, I take a closer peek to determine if they look anything like the discovery that put Paisley Caves on the archaeological map: human coprolite.

Yes, when everything is said and done, it is 14,500-year-old poo that has brought me here and, more important, furthered our understanding of when the first primitive souls walked, hunted, ate, slept, and defecated in what is now the United States of America.

After Dr. Jenkins finishes speaking with his students, I apologize for being late and recount my series of technological mishaps. He waves it off and we step outside, where the scent of mosquito-killing DEET saturates the evening air.

We chat casually for a minute on the front stoop and then get to the matter at hand. "Your discovery," I say, "makes Paisley a kind of prehistoric Jamestown or Plymouth where the *truly* first Americans set foot, and yet I doubt many people outside of the archaeological world have heard of it."

While slicing small chunks of watermelon with his pocketknife, Dr. Jenkins gently corrects me. Another University of Oregon professor, named Luther Cressman, he says, was actually the first to excavate Paisley Caves back in 1938. (I'd heard that, too, but Dr. Jenkins is being modest; he—Dr. Jenkins—found the coprolites.)

Dr. Jenkins also cautions me on being fanciful (his word) about portraying the caves as some sort of way station for America's earliest explorers. It's possible, he explains, that the Paleo-Indians actually lived here and weren't just passing through. Plus, we don't know if they were indeed "truly first" on the continent or even in this area. He believes it's only a matter of time before another archaeologist unearths older DNA.

"But even if someone else digs up an earlier specimen," I ask, "Paisley Caves will forever be where the first pre-Clovis human DNA was found in North America, right?"

"I suppose that's true," he says.

"What I'm also trying to understand is what relevance these sites and stories have to us now. On the flight over, I read an article about a 35,000-year-old flute made from the bone of a vulture's wing recently found in caves near Ulm, Germany. There's something poignant about this image of early humans sitting around a fire playing instruments to entertain each other. Is there anything similar you've found at Paisley, anything that 'humanizes' these people?"

"That sounds a bit fanciful to me. We have no idea how those flutes were used. They could have been for signaling. We have to stick with facts and be very careful about extrapolating certain theories based on our own feelings."

"Is there *anything* we can know for certain about the people who lived here?" I ask.

"Quite a lot," he says, and then proceeds to lay out a convincing summary of their dietary and living habits based on their feces. From threads found in their stool, we assume they could sew. From salt deposits, moss spores, and various chemical signatures, we can track their movements according to which rivers they drank from and what plants they ate—and even when they consumed them, based on their seasonal availability. (Dr. Jenkins segues a moment to emphasize how the winters here used to be −10 to −20 degrees Fahrenheit.) We know they used digging sticks to harvest a root vegetable known as Indian carrots.

"Have you ever tried them?" I ask.

Dr. Jenkins nods, grimacing. "They taste like turpentine."

He goes on to say that we can also determine what parasites were in their system, and as DNA technology gets more advanced, we'll be able to determine what illnesses they had.

"I hadn't thought about the health problems they had to suffer through. I can't imagine living in a world without Novocain," I say, half kidding.

Dr. Jenkins responds seriously: "I've seen abscessed teeth, entire mandibles rotted away—not here, but from other sites. Think of living with that kind of pain every day. These were *tough* individuals, and I have enormous respect for them. We've grown a little soft in comparison."

"Along with disease and harsh weather, what else—"

"And starvation periods."

"And those, right. Along with all that, what other threats did they face? I'm guessing there were any number of deadly animals they had to look out for."

"Rattlesnakes, scorpions, black widows, and also your more warm and fuzzy predators, all of them extinct now, like American lions, cheetahs, short-faced bears, saber-toothed tigers—though it's possible they weren't around here then—and the dire wolf."

"Those sound bad."

"They were."

The more we talk, the more questions I want to ask, but I know Dr. Jenkins has to get back to his students, and I clearly have homework to do.

"See you tomorrow, seven A.M. Six thirty if you want breakfast," he says.

"Sounds like a long day."

"It'll go quicker than you think."

That evening I pore through a stack of academic journals and articles I've brought detailing Native American history. Dr. Jenkins is among those who believe that contemporary tribes are direct descendants of Paleo-Indians, but there is, of course, raucous debate about this as well. On July 18, 1996, two spectators at a hydroplane race on the Columbia River in Kennewick, Washington, stumbled upon a nine-thousand-year-old skull, which scientists said appeared to be a "caucasoid" of European ancestry. (A gray-putty reconstruction of his face bears an uncanny resemblance to British actor Sir Patrick Stewart.) After the full skeleton was retrieved, local tribes demanded the remains so they could be buried immediately. Archaeologists insisted on examining them longer, and a series of lawsuits followed. As of now, "Kennewick Man" resides under lock and key at the Burke Museum in Washington, his fate still undetermined. Dr. Jenkins's coprolite DNA corroborates an unbroken link between Paleo-Indians and Native Americans, but it's also possible that there have been multiple migration routes.

At the crack of dawn, I'm back at the dorms. Dr. Jenkins and his team pile into two white vans, and we drive a quarter of a mile along Route

31 and then turn right onto a bumpy dirt road that cuts through an open valley blanketed by sage and rabbit brush. Dusty lime-green sandbags mark a trail up to the caves, and within minutes the crew is bustling away. My goal is to stay out of everyone's path and, for the love of God, try not to destroy a major scientific breakthrough by accidentally stepping into fifteen-thousand-year-old poo.

Part construction project, part military operation, the site is surprisingly tidy considering how many tons of dirt have been processed. Everyone moves with purpose, and spirits seem high. Over at Cave 2, Scott, a graduate student from Washington State University, is helping his classmate Jen into a full-body Tyvek suit (to prevent the contamination of ancient coprolites with modern DNA). Jen carefully inches her way down a large plank into the cave's deeper well, while Marci, another student, stands a few feet higher up loading large plastic buckets with freshly mined soil.

The system moves with assembly-line efficiency. Buckets are carried out of the caves, their contents dumped onto three-by-two-foot screens with wooden handles on each side. Before shaking the sifter for a good twenty or thirty seconds, whoever's manning the contraption yells out, "Dirt!"—the archaeological equivalent of "Fire in the hole!"—and everyone in the immediate vicinity shields his or her eyes from the ensuing dust cloud. Finer particles fall through the mesh wire, while the larger, more promising objects on top are picked out with forceps and placed in plastic bags.

I see a small bone and get excited.

"It's probably animal," I'm told. The Paisley Caves are a veritable charnel house of fish, bird, horse, coyote, and even camel bones.

Moments later, someone yells out the magic words: "I've got poo!!"

Dr. Jenkins walks over, takes a look. "Bag it."

The student nods and plops it into a sterile specimen cup.

No matter how serious about the work a person might be (and every academic journal I've read lauds Dr. Jenkins for his professionalism and rigorous standards), one does not spend six physically arduous weeks digging through layers of prehistoric bat, deer, coyote, and rat feces in search of their human equivalent without engaging in some scatological humor. After overhearing a student discussing a "groaner," I tentatively ask if they've nicknamed the different types of excrement.

"Of course," I'm told.

Thus begins my brief education in coprolite slang. "You have your princess poo, which is very small and dainty," one student says, "while the groaner is bigger, and the Hershey's Kiss has a little pinched point on top."

"Don't forget the groaner maximus," another adds.

I'm not going to name names, but apparently one very esteemed archaeologist on the premises has his own favorites. "Oh, his are the *worst*," a student says. "Ask him what a Klingon is."

No, I don't think I will.

For a few minutes I duck into Cave 5 and rest, wiped out by the afternoon heat and impressed by how hard these students and volunteers labor under such enervating conditions. The cave feels noticeably cooler and offers a sensational view of the surrounding valley. Whoever these folks were, they had impeccable real estate sense.

Dr. Jenkins walks by.

"Quick question?" I ask.

"Sure."

"Do you think the Paleo-Indians who lived here would have appreciated all of this?" I say, gesturing at the magnificent scene spread out before us.

"Keep in mind it would have looked much different fourteen thousand five hundred years ago. A lot of what's below us might have been water." I'm expecting to hear the word *fanciful* as well. Instead he surprises me. "But yes, actually, I think they would have."

Dr. Jenkins was absolutely right about the day passing swiftly. Before I know it we're hiking down the trail and returning to town. After washing up, everyone gathers for a late-afternoon cookout at a small park by the dormitory.

"Yesterday I talked with Dr. Jenkins about the significance of the work you're doing here," I say to the students while they grill up hamburgers and chicken. "What do you all think we can learn, if anything, from the primitive folks who once lived in these caves?"

Mike, an Iraq War veteran in his late twenties, mildly reprimands me. "First of all, I wouldn't use the word *primitive*. These were sophisticated people. They created an atlatl, a very complicated hunting device, and sandals out of sagebrush bark. They carved heat-tempered spear points, and they—"

"Wait," I interrupt. "Explain that last thing, about the spear points."

"They heated rocks to a certain temperature so they'd flake a specific way."

"That's incredible."

"Everything they had, they made with their own hands," Jen says. "We're overly dependent on technology to do things for us. I'm not suggesting technology is bad, just that we can hardly exist without it, and this dulls our ability to function when it breaks down. Personally I admire how resourceful and self-reliant they were."

After thanking Dr. Jenkins and his students for their hospitality, I get back into my car and drive under the Paisley Mosquito Festival banner one last time. Since my flight into Salt Lake City isn't until tomorrow morning, there is, in contrast to my frantic dash down here, no need to rush. Long stretches of the two-lane highway to Redmond are walled in by ponderosa pines, and upon spotting a break in the trees, I pull off to look out over a valley aglow with orange sunlight. Whether the men and women who roamed this region 14,500 years ago would have gazed at this land with equal joy—or, possibly, cursed it as one more obstacle to overcome—is impossible to know. But the notion that their very survival, in the face of infinite hardships and dangers, is proof of a resilience and ingenuity that we can draw strength and inspiration from today, doesn't seem the least bit fanciful at all.

THE REMAINS OF
PROMETHEUS

> . . . Let [Zeus] wreathe
> Curls of scorching flame around me;
> Let him fret the air with thunder,
> And the savage-blustering winds!
> Let the deep abysmal tempest
> Wrench the firm roots of the Earth! . . .
> Let the harsh-winged hurricane sweep me
> In its whirls, and fling me down
> To black Tartarus: there to lie
> Bound in the iron folds of Fate.
> I will bear, but cannot die.

—From Prometheus Bound by Aeschylus
(translated in 1906 by John Stuart Blackie)

IT'S NOT UNTIL I hit the Utah/Nevada border that I begin to appreciate just how old Prometheus was when his life ended abruptly twenty miles west of here. While eating ice cream inside the Border

Inn Restaurant & Motel, which cleverly straddles the two states to offer Utah's cheaper gas prices on one half of the property and booze and slot machines on the other (I'm on the Nevada side), I skim through Gordon Kerr's *Time Line: History of the World*. Prometheus himself isn't mentioned, but the chronology puts his 4,900-year life span into context.

Prometheus was born about 2900 B.C., some two hundred years before the Egyptians began constructing the Great Pyramids. He was a wee sprout when Sargon of Akkad, the world's first emperor, rose to power around 2300 B.C. near what is present-day Iraq, and he was just entering adulthood when the Trojan War began in 1190 B.C. (As lopsided juxtapositions go, Kerr's two-sentence entry for 961 B.C. is a delight: "[Israel's King] David dies and is succeeded by his son, Solomon. The Olmec invent the tortilla.") By the time Prometheus was well into middle age, Solon had introduced democracy to Athens, the Buddha had found enlightenment, Brutus had stabbed Caesar, and Christ had been crucified. Prometheus was getting on in years but still strong and vigorous when Spanish explorers first set foot in America during the early 1500s. Then, on August 6, 1964, five men led by a thirty-year-old University of North Carolina graduate student named Donald R. Currey found Prometheus on the north slope of Wheeler Peak along Nevada's Snake Range and literally chopped him to pieces. Despite having endured for five millennia in conditions that are fatally inhospitable to most living creatures, the ancient bristlecone pine tree was no match for half a dozen men armed with chainsaws.

A quote about trees by the naturalist John Muir, patron saint of America's environmental movement, first set me on the trail to Prometheus. "Though fast rooted they travel about as far as we do," Muir wrote. "They go wandering forth in all directions with every wind, going and coming like ourselves." This shook me from my human-centric selection process and made me investigate trees connected to American history. Most, it turned out, were remembered for being in proximity to something like a treaty signing, duel, battle, or execution.

Then I read about Prometheus, who wasn't a mere bystander. Prometheus *was* history, in both life and death. When his rings were finally counted, the full horror of Currey's actions became apparent. He and his team had not just destroyed a 4,900-year-old tree (some estimates have put the number closer to 5,100), they had killed *the oldest living thing* in the United States and, quite possibly, the world.

They even had government approval to do so. Under a National Science Foundation fellowship, Currey was studying the Little Ice Age, which began around 1250 and lasted four to five centuries, and he'd hoped that by examining tree rings he could better analyze regional climate changes. He convinced a U.S. Forest Service district ranger named Donald Cox that while "WPN-114," Currey's more clinical name for Prometheus, was in his scientific opinion "super old" and larger than other bristlecone pines in the stand, he wasn't different enough to warrant special protection. (Although there are indeed male and female trees, bristlecone pines are monoecious, so I'm technically incorrect in referring to Prometheus as a "he" or "him." Considering his impressive longevity, however, I don't have the heart to call him just an "it," and his mythological namesake happens to be male.) "No one would have walked more than a hundred yards to see it," Cox purportedly said later, defending his and Currey's decision to have WPN-114 "sectioned."

There is, to be accurate, an honest debate about the designation "oldest living thing." A quaking-aspen grove nicknamed "Pando" (Latin for "I spread") in Utah's Fishlake National Forest is considered to be the oldest *clonal* organism in America; the individual trees live only to the age of 120 or so, but they share a root system that supposedly has been expanding for 80,000 years. It's also possible that deep within some foreign cave, there's a plucky little million-year-old microbe that has escaped notice all these years. But for all intents and purposes, when it comes to the oldest single living organism in the United States, Prometheus was the champ. (Methuselah, a 4,800-year-old bristlecone pine named after the oldest person in the Bible, is now, by default, believed to be the current title holder. Located in California's Inyo National Forest and sheltered under a kind of arboreal witness protection plan, the tree's exact location is kept a secret.)

After unearthing the Prometheus story, I phoned the National Park Service's Washington, D.C., headquarters to inquire about his precise whereabouts.

"We had nothing to do with that," a staff member told me right off the bat. "The Forest Service approved the request to cut it down, not us."

"But Prometheus—well, the stump or whatever," I said, "is now in Great Basin National Park, and I need the Park Service's permission to go out there and find it."

"Contact the folks at Great Basin."

"Do you know if there's a sign or plaque by the stump already?"

"Not to my knowledge, and I doubt that's something anyone is eager to bring attention to, but the folks there can tell you." Before hanging up he added: "Good luck."

I called over to Great Basin and was transferred to the park's chief of interpretation, Betsy Duncan-Clark, who couldn't have been nicer and was soon sharing with me great stories about her home state of Alaska. But she also said it was unlikely that anyone at Great Basin could help me. Finding Prometheus would require a full day of mostly off-trail hiking, the site wasn't easily accessible, and the staff couldn't escort every visitor wanting a personal tour.

"I totally understand," I said, "but what if I tagged along with a ranger who had to hike out there anyway for some other reason?"

"That might be an option, but then you'd have to go on the exact day we tell you, weather permitting, and abide by other conditions. So no promises." Betsy recommended I consider using GPS coordinates to find it on my own.

"I'm fine with that, but I have a horrible sense of direction—I once drove from Toledo to Detroit and ended up in Canada—and I guarantee you I'll get lost. Then you'll have a search-and-rescue mission on your hands, which will be much more time-consuming in the end."

My passive-aggressive logic apparently paid off. Several days later, Betsy gave me a fixed date and time to meet with Ranger Bryan Petrtyl at the Great Basin Visitor Center. "I'll be right on time," I assured her.

From the Border Inn to Great Basin is only about a thirty-minute drive, and, after meeting in the visitor center, Bryan and I waste no time before we're plotting our day. Bryan is soft-spoken and friendly and clearly seems to know what he's doing, and I feel I'm in capable hands.

Water bottles filled, trail mix packed, suntan lotion applied, and boots tied, we hit the trail. I'm not sure if I'm light-headed because we're almost two miles above sea level or giddy with excitement because everything is going according to plan, but for some reason the hike transforms me into a chatty, inquisitive six-year-old. "Bryan, what's that tree over there?" (It's a spruce, he says.) "When did you become a ranger?" (Six years ago.) "How old are you now?" (Twenty-seven.) "What got you interested in the great outdoors?" (Hunting fossils as a boy back home.) "Where are you from?" (Ohio.) "When do you think we'll find Prometheus?" (About three more hours.) I suspect he's secretly hoping I'll run out of questions or, ideally, enough oxygen to walk and talk at the same time.

Up ahead I notice a sign and ask Bryan what it says before stopping to read it for myself. "This tool is called an 'increment borer,'" states the text, accompanied by an image of the T-shaped device.

> It is used by scientists to obtain a "core sample" from a limb or the trunk of a tree. The core is a cross section of a portion of the tree's annual growth rings. Use of the increment borer makes it unnecessary to cut down a tree in order to measure and count its rings. The borer does not endanger the life of a tree.

Why Donald Currey didn't use an increment borer is one of the more contentious aspects of the Prometheus story. Currey claimed that he started to, but after several attempts it cracked and there wasn't enough time left in the season to get a replacement.

Bryan and I break from the trail and the terrain becomes considerably more precarious. In order to reach Prometheus we have to hike up a steep incline of glacier-piled quartzite rocks and boulders that feel unstable in spots.

"What're the chances that some of these could give way?" I ask.

"It's possible," Bryan replies, stepping nimbly from stone to stone. "But if anything bad happens," he deadpans, "they might name a trail after you."

I stop for a minute to take a slug of water. "You ever use one of those GPS things when you hike?"

"I prefer maps," Bryan says. "That way you can see the whole area around where you're going and places you might have missed otherwise." He then expounds on the benefits of exploring without either. "There's nothing like suddenly coming upon a special canyon or waterfall, and it's like when two people meet for the first time. The probability of these two things happening simultaneously is so slim, it makes the experience even more meaningful."

We resume our march up the talus, and after passing by limber pines and Engelmann spruces, we're encountering more and more bristlecone pines. Bryan points one out to emphasize a particular survival technique. "When a root or branch gets infected, like on this section here, the tree stops sending nutrients to the dying part to ensure that the rest will remain healthy. They can also shut down photosynthesis to conserve energy."

Bryan also tells me that the trees have migrated to higher altitudes, where the thin air makes forest fires less likely.

From an aesthetic standpoint, bristlecone pines are wonderfully expressive, almost humanlike in their proportions and poses. The trees grow out instead of up, making them more stout than towering. (At 17 feet in height, Prometheus would have looked like a bonsai next to the 379-foot Hyperion, the world's tallest tree, located in Northern California's Redwood National Forest.) We pass by one I name the Opera Singer because she's facing the open valley with arms outstretched, back slightly arched, and, through a large mouth-shaped hole, seems to be belting a prolonged aria to her adoring audience below. Another, the Soldier, is ramrod straight with a branch angled out and then in toward its crown like a bent elbow, crisply saluting. Most of the trees, however, are twisted and contorted, as if writhing in pain. Had Edvard Munch designed a tree, the bristlecone pine would be it.

As I'm mentally strolling about in my own happy little world assigning names and personalities to this odd cast of characters, Bryan stops and without much fanfare (I'm guessing he's not a fanfare kind of guy) says, "This is it."

This is what? I think, glancing over a scattered pile of large gray rocks. I lean closer and realize that mixed among them are chunks of curved gray wood. Then I see the base of the tree jutting about a foot and a half out of the ground, cut unevenly across the top. Prometheus.

I had expected the stump, but not these large portions of the actual tree strewn about. He must have been enormous, I think, reassembling the pieces in my mind. Currey reported the circumference to be 252 inches, or exactly 21 feet.

I tell Bryan I need about a half hour to make notes and take a few pictures of the site. He says that's fine and goes off to conduct whatever duties he's officially here to perform.

Before coming to Nevada, I had considered Prometheus's fate—in that he had been cut down by those who, ostensibly, should have been protecting him—as comically ironic. But looking over his withered remains, I'm struck by how profoundly sad a loss this is. A tree that had tenaciously survived for approximately five thousand years, through droughts and blizzards and windstorms and avalanches, was knocked down, just like that, in an afternoon.

Currey later expressed regret for what he had done, and before he passed away in 2005 at the age of seventy he was an impassioned voice for both the creation of Great Basin National Park and a law that would protect bristlecone pines on federal property, legislation that Congress eventually enacted.

Currey's defenders believe that, ultimately, he made an honest mistake and that human inquiry often relies on poking holes in the natural world to study what's inside. "Archaeologists," the old saying goes, "burn the pages of history as they read them," and the same can be said of many other researchers. Some scientific data were gleaned from Prometheus's rings, aiding climatologists in measuring temperature fluctuations and weather patterns over thousands of years, as well as archaeologists who utilize tree rings to verify radiocarbon-tested data. Like the Greek titan of myth who was condemned to endless suffering for stealing fire (representing knowledge) from his fellow gods and sharing it with man, WPN-114 also sacrificed for the sake of humanity.

Currey's detractors, and there are many, argue that he acted recklessly and with a touch of hubris. He was a geographer, after all, not a dendrologist. And while useful information was indeed acquired by sectioning Prometheus, it should be weighed against what else might have been learned over time if the tree had been spared. Any hope of following Prometheus's life span to its natural conclusion ended irrevocably on August 6, 1964.

There's another long-term factor that comes to mind as I amble about the wide sunlit area where Prometheus once grew. It relates to something Bryan told me soon after we met, when he was extolling Great Basin National Park's scientific value as an "eighty-thousand-acre living laboratory where ecological, biological, and genetic diversity can be studied." There is also, he said, the park's human story, from the Fremont Indians and sheepherders who once lived and hunted in this area to the day hikers and overnight campers who now visit this peaceful, pristine environment for mental and spiritual renewal. They—all of us—need time to reflect and think and imagine, undistracted by gadgets, deadlines, and incessant chatter. Great Basin offers that sense of solace and respite.

Bryan is particularly heartened by the number of families he sees come here and reconnect with one another, communicating in whole sentences—as opposed to abbreviated texts—and bonding over a shared discovery, whether it's an intricate rock formation, a hidden bird's nest, or stands of bristlecone pine trees that first sprang to life about the same time Homer was composing *The Iliad*. When these are destroyed, whether through vandalism or carelessness, future visitors are denied memories and experiences that have nourished the souls of so many others. The impact of these irreparable losses cannot be quantified.

Bryan has returned and is eating quietly about thirty feet away from me. I'm not hungry but decide I'll need energy for our descent and begin nibbling on some granola and a green apple. After I finish, Bryan stands up and adjusts his backpack, a silent signal that it's time to leave. I check around to make sure I haven't dropped anything and then pocket my notebook. My mind was a whirlwind of questions coming up here, but now I'm just lost in the scenery.

Bryan looks over to see if I'm ready, and I nod.

We head down, neither of us saying a word.

MOUND KEY ISLAND

JUAN PONCE DE LEÓN, believing the reports of the Indians of Cuba and San Domingo to be true, made an expedition into Florida to discover the river Jordan. This he did either because he wished to acquire renown, or, perhaps, because he hoped to become young again by bathing in its waters. While I was a prisoner in those parts, I bathed in a great many rivers, but I never found the right one. It seems incredible that JUAN PONCE DE LEÓN should have gone to Florida to look for such a river.

—*From* Memoir of Hernando D'Escalante Fontaneda (1575)

THE ISLAND, FROM half a mile away, seems to be floating above the ocean.

"That's because of the red mangroves," Bobby Romero explains to me as we approach Mound Key in Estero Bay, Florida. "Inland you have the black, white, and buttonwood trees. The red ones, which thrive in saline, are mostly on the edges, and their roots grow straight down from the branches, right into the water." Clustered together they create a dark, shadowy ring around the island, giving the illusion that it's hovering several feet in the air.

Fifty-six years old and semiretired, Bobby charters tours of Estero Bay and is motoring me out to Mound Key on his catamaran *Beachcomber*. After we nestle the boat in a tiny lagoon called North Landing, I lower myself into a kayak and paddle around the island's edge to take pictures. Up close the mangrove roots appear ominous, a dense tangle of fingerlike undergrowth waiting to grab anything that ventures too near. I head out into the deeper water.

The island, Bobby also told me earlier, is growing. "It's much larger now than it was during Fontaneda's time," he says, referring to Hernando D'Escalante Fontaneda, whose story is my reason for coming here. For seventeen years the young Spaniard was held captive by the Calusa Indians in La Florida, as the territory was then known, and Mound Key is the one verifiable place he lived before gaining his freedom.

This was in 1556, more than fifty years before Captain Christopher Newport brought the first Virginia Company settlers to a swampy outpost called Jamestown and almost sixty-five years before the Pilgrims rowed ashore at Cape Cod. Fontaneda, whose writings about the New World influenced European royalty and future explorers, gold seekers, and colonists, is significant in his own right. But he's also representative of an entire era—starting from the time Christopher Columbus reached the Bahamas in 1492 to the arrival of English entrepreneurs and Pilgrims more than a century later—that is something of a historical blind spot in our nation's rearview mirror.

A few brief highlights from this period: In early April 1513, Juan Ponce de León waded onto a Florida beach, making him the first nonnative individual to set foot on what would eventually be the United States of America. Beginning in 1524, Giovanni da Verrazano made three trips to North America, sailing up and down the Atlantic coast until he was eaten by Carib Indians in 1528. That's also the year Pánfilo de Narváez organized the first—and, to this day, most catastrophic— overland expedition across the continent. It started near Tampa Bay with more than four hundred men and ended in present-day Arizona with four, including the Spanish nobelman Álvar Núñez Cabeza de Vaca and a Muslim slave named Estevanico—but not Narváez, who perished along the way. A decade later, fellow Spaniard Hernando de Soto led a six-hundred-man army from Florida to the Mississippi River, thinking he would do better. He would not. By 1542 half of his troops were dead, as was de Soto, and the rest had given up. And in 1565 the Spanish Navy's Admiral Pedro Menéndez de Avilés founded St. Augustine, the oldest permanent European settlement in the States.

When Hernando D'Escalante Fontaneda landed in Florida in 1523, he had no intention of exploring or schlepping around the New World. Born in 1536 (possibly '37; the records are iffy) to wealthy Spanish parents living in Peru, the thirteen-year-old Fontaneda was sailing to Spain with his older brother when their ship sank near the Florida Keys. Fontaneda was "rescued" by the Calusa Indians, who stole whatever treasure could be salvaged from the ship and murdered most of the other passengers. Killing and robbing the near-drowned survivors wasn't very hospitable, but the Calusas were motivated by more than greed; previous light-skinned visitors were known to carry a nasty array of incurable infections and did not, themselves, always play nice. Fontaneda's life was spared because he danced and sang for the Calusas' chief, Carlos, who considered him a harmless amusement. Carlos ruled from Mound Key, and from there Fontaneda was granted release and allowed to return home after seventeen years in captivity.

The water around the island is choppier than I'd anticipated, and my kayak is rocking unsteadily. I'm a fair distance from shore at this point and having trouble putting out of my mind what one of the local park rangers told me when I called to ask if there were sharks in Estero Bay: "Yes," he said. There might have been more to that response— something about the odds of an attack being about a billion to one— but I don't remember anything after the "Yes" part.

When a speedboat's wake almost tips me over, I snap one more picture of the island and paddle back to North Landing. Bobby and I hoist the kayak onto his boat, and after gathering together my camera gear, food, and water, I set out on foot for the other side of the island.

Ten minutes later, I'm there.

Mound Key is about a thousand yards across at its waist, and a trail of crushed seashells leads from North Landing to an even smaller beachhead on the south side. The path is meant to discourage visitors from veering off into the wooded areas where archaeological digs are ongoing, and it's mostly straight except for a slight wiggle near Mound 1, where Carlos is believed to have released Fontaneda. Interpretive signs about the Calusas, which are the only historical markers on the trail, make no mention of Fontaneda. Instead they focus on the inventive assortment of tools and mechanisms the Calusas devised for cooking and hunting—bow drills to start fires, spears with replaceable stone points, snares, traps, and atlatls—along with sophisticated awning-covered canoes.

Before finding Mound Key, I'd sought out where Fontaneda had shipwrecked in the Keys, which would have added some variety to my landlocked itinerary. Florida has an exceptional historical marker program, and they've even mounted plaques on the ocean floor next to sunken steamers, World War II cruisers, and Spanish treasure ships from the early 1700s. Fontaneda's ship has yet to be recovered, and the Florida treasure hunters I contacted said there was little financial incentive to locate the vessel because the Calusas had stripped it clean.

Five years after returning to Spain, Fontaneda published an account of his New World experiences. *Travels with Charley* it is not. Although written in the first person, the narrative is dry and impersonal. There's only one perfunctory sentence about the shipwreck that claimed Fontaneda's brother and so dramatically altered his own fate, and he spills considerably more ink on Ponce de León's supposed search for the fountain of youth, a story that, although Fontaneda made famous, he himself didn't believe. But whatever Fontaneda lacked in literary style he made up for in expertise. No other European had spent more time in the New World, and his observations were widely disseminated and carefully scrutinized. Author and conservationist Marjory Stoneman Douglas, herself a notable figure for her work saving the Everglades, notes that Fontaneda penned "the first book about Florida, or, indeed, about the whole mainland of North America."

And Fontaneda does flash an intriguing light on the land's flora and fauna. He writes of giant eels as thick as "a man's thigh," tortoises "the size of a large shield . . . with as much flesh as a cow," and the ubiquitous *Guaiacum officinale* tree, "which physicians know is useful for many purposes." Possibly he's being coy; the tree's gum was used primarily for treating syphilis, which was ravaging Europe in the sixteenth century. What Fontaneda did *not* find, much to his extreme displeasure, was gold or silver. By my count, he harps on this half a dozen times.

Fontaneda also goes on at length about the Native Americans, describing their diet, customs, weapons, and clothing—or lack of it. "These Indians," he remarks of one tribe, "go almost naked, wearing only a sort of apron. The dress of the men consists of braided palm-leaves, and that of the women of moss." He goes on to portray them as being "a tall race of men and women graceful and well-featured."

It is by far his most charitable comment. Unlike Cabeza de Vaca, who had good relations with and espoused fair treatment of the natives, Fontaneda refers to various tribes as "rascals and beggars" and others as "barbarous" and perceives the whole lot of them as "treacherous." He warns that the natives are skillful warriors and would not be easy to subjugate. "They are very adroit at drawing the bow," he says, "and I am convinced they can never be made submissive and become Christians."

He concludes: "They should all be taken, men and women, after terms of peace have been offered them, placed on ships, and scattered throughout the various islands, and even on the Spanish main, where they might be sold as his Majesty sells his vessels to the grandees [noblemen] in Spain." Fontaneda was by no means the sole voice calling for such measures (Columbus proposed something similar about two minutes after making landfall), but he was certainly one of the most authoritative.

From the 1600s through the early 1800s, tens of thousands of Native Americans were enslaved, but men, women, and children imported from Africa were ultimately preferred over the indigenous population. Torn from their homes and tribes and thrust into unfamiliar territory after a debilitating mid-Atlantic crossing, they were easier to dominate. The natives, as Fontaneda noted, were well armed, knew the terrain, and could band together. They were also being decimated by European diseases. There were simply too few of them left to satisfy the avarice of slaveholding merchants and plantation owners.

As I walk back to North Landing and reflect on the legacy of men such as Fontaneda, my first thought is how unfortunate it was that the Calusas ever let him go. But that, I realize, might be too harsh a judgment. Fontaneda didn't ask to be a castaway at age thirteen and held captive until he was thirty. The real pity, I suppose, is that he ended up here in the first place.

After Bobby drops me off at a marina in Fort Myers Beach, I drive over to the ranger station in Estero that manages Mound Key. (No one is posted on the island itself.) I need to pick up some literature related not to Fontaneda but to my next site, in Indiana. Mound Key is a perfect example of how stories, somewhat haphazardly, lead to other stories.

While planning my itinerary months ago, I needed to confirm with the rangers in Estero that Mound Key was accessible, and when I phoned, a male voice on the other end said: "Hello, and thanks for calling the Koreshan State Historic Site."

"Sorry, I was looking for Mound Key," I said, assuming I'd called the wrong number. Mike Heare, the Park Service specialist who answered, informed me that they covered the island, too. I asked who or what a Koreshan was, and he explained that they were a cult that tried to establish a utopian colony here more than a hundred years ago. Their founder, Dr. Cyrus Reed Teed, had changed his name to Koresh and founded a religion that promoted reincarnation, communal living, celibacy, and the belief that the universe is contained *within* the earth, which is actually a concave sphere.

"Koresh like David Koresh from Waco?"

"Not related." (The Waco guy did share one thing with Teed. He, too, felt that *Koresh*—referenced in Isaiah 44 as God's shepherd—had a stronger, more messianic ring to it than his given name, which was Vernon Wayne Howell.)

"That's pretty crazy," I said, dismissing the story as a kind of fringe footnote.

Mike set me straight. "Communities like this sprouted all around the United States, and they've been a major part of American history."

They have indeed, I learned after plunging into the topic. They also represented a natural continuation from the early explorers and pilgrims who had once perceived this country as a Garden of Eden or New Jerusalem. By as early as the 1840s, many citizens were bemoaning that the American experiment had failed, and they went off to build new societies untainted by the sins and vices they believed were contaminating mainstream society. These utopian communities attracted the lunatic crowd, no doubt, but they also appealed to many sensible and distinguished individuals, including the eminent publisher and one-time presidential candidate Horace Greeley, who famously advised, "Go west, young man."

So, after thanking Mike Heare for his help, I'm going west to Grand Prairie, Indiana, in search of Greeley's promised land.

THE GRAND PRAIRIE
HARMONICAL ASSOCIATION

The last time I slept or ate with a floor under me (our wagon-box and mother earth excepted) was at Junction-City, nearly four weeks ago. The "Denver House," which is the Astor House of the gold region, has walls of logs, a floor of earth, with windows and roof of rather flimsy cotton-sheeting. . . . Still, a few days of such luxury surfeited me, mainly because the main or drinking-room was also occupied by several blacklegs as a gambling-hall, and their incessant clamor . . . persisted in at all hours up to midnight, became at length a nuisance, from which I craved deliverance at any price. Then the visitors of that drinking and gambling-room had a careless way, when drunk, of firing revolvers, sometimes at each other, at other times quite miscellaneously, which struck me as inconvenient for a quiet guest with only a leg and a half, hence in poor condition for dodging bullets. So I left.

—From An Overland Journey from New York to San Francisco (1859)
by Horace Greeley

INDIANA NATIVE JOHN Babson Lane Soule, not Horace Greeley, was actually the first journalist to exhort his readers to "go west," but few Americans promoted the new frontier as emphatically as Greeley, even if he found the raucous, brawling territories a tad coarse for his own tastes.

Born to impoverished New Hampshire farmers in 1811, Greeley dropped out of school at the age of fourteen to apprentice with a printer, founded a weekly newspaper at the age of twenty-three, and was a dominant publishing force by his thirties, espousing everything from vegetarianism and temperance to the abolition of slavery. Greeley aspired to hold elected office, but a three-month stint in Congress filling a vacated seat and a disastrous presidential campaign represented the extent of his political career.

After writing sympathetically about the "filth, squalor, rags, dissipation, want, and misery" of New York's destitute in 1840, Greeley was contacted by Albert Brisbane, an American educated by philosopher François Marie Charles Fourier in France. Fourier was an early champion of women's rights (according to some scholars he coined the word *féminisme*) and pushed for utopian communities, or "Phalanxes," that fostered cooperation over individualism. Upon Fourier's death in 1837, Brisbane took up the cause and found a kindred spirit in Greeley, who began publicizing utopian concepts in his influential *New York Tribune* and organizing Phalanxes wherever there was interest. He embraced Fourier's idealistic belief that, as Greeley paraphrased him, "the true Eden lies before, not behind us."

One of these Fourier- and Greeley-inspired Edens, the Grand Prairie Harmonical Association, was established in Warren County, Indiana, named after the Revolutionary War hero Dr. Joseph Warren. And he deserves a mention. An outspoken voice for American independence, the thirty-four-year-old Warren fought as a private on Bunker Hill despite having been appointed a major general; his official promotion was several days away, and he preferred serving with the common soldiers. After he was killed by a shot to the head, British soldiers rolled his lifeless body into a ditch and stabbed it repeatedly with their bayonets.

Warren's brother John and their friend Paul Revere later identified Warren's decomposed corpse by a false tooth.

My guide for this particular sojourn into western Indiana is Terri Wargo, president of the Warren County Historical Society. Before I arrived, Terri sent me several articles about Grand Prairie and went out of her way to visit the site to make sure we could locate it. "There's nothing really there," she warned me.

"It's okay," I said. "That's true for a lot of the places I'm visiting."

After staying overnight just across the border in Danville, Illinois, I meet with Terri at West Lebanon's public library, where she's worked for more than two decades.

"How long have you been with the historical society?" I ask.

"About ten years. I never thought I'd be running it, though. I guess I went to one too many meetings and was elected president," she says, laughing.

We drive north on State Road 63, which becomes U.S. 41, and then go west on Route 26 for a few miles. As we near a slight rise in the two-lane highway, Terri pulls onto the shoulder.

"Here we are," she says.

Well, Terri was dead-on; there's not much around except an everywhere-you-look vista of lush green bean fields and tiny white farmhouses dotting the landscape.

Nineteenth-century maps and records confirm that this ridge is where the main building, the Community House, would have sat, overlooking the 350 acres purchased by the Association in 1851.

"This shouldn't take long," I say as I photograph the surrounding terrain from the middle of the road. Terri watches the highway to make sure I'm not flattened by a truck zooming over the incline.

Greeley never lived in or even visited Grand Prairie, but he outlined its intellectual foundation. Using language similar to that of other Fourier Phalanx charters, the Association's manifesto declared that its intent was to educate members in "the three following departments, viz., educational, agricultural, and mechanical . . . for the culture of both mind and body." There was a "college" to teach applied trades such as carpentry and blacksmithing along with more academic pursuits, and all money was held collectively by the board of trustees, of which Greeley was one. Few other specifics are known about the Association except its mission "to forward the elevation, peace and unity of the human family."

It lasted just over a year.

The only first-person narrative I could find from a surviving member was dictated by a ninety-year-old man named Philander Child. He faulted a poor harvest, summer drought, and lack of employment for the Association's demise and not any philosophical deficiencies in the overall plan. He conceded, however, that he remembered mostly the positive side of the experience because it was at Grand Prairie that he met his future wife, Eve.

In his 1868 autobiography, *Recollections of a Busy Life,* Horace Greeley skips over Grand Prairie and profiles three other ventures instead (all of which, like most Fourier Phalanxes, have historical markers). Brook Farm in West Roxbury, Massachusetts, was launched in 1840 and counted the famed author Nathaniel Hawthorne as a founding member. Sylvania in Pike County, Pennsylvania, covered a whopping 2,300 acres and folded in 1845 after two years. And the longest-lasting was the North American Phalanx, a 673-acre property in Monmouth County, New Jersey, which started in 1843 and held up for seven years. (A real estate company selling posh mansions in Monmouth recently tried to capitalize on the area's utopian history, luring prospective buyers with the promise that, although "a group of idealists" were unable to build "the particular future they dreamed of, . . . their spirit continues to influence the Monmouth County luxury homes and the region's colorful lifestyle of today." The fact that most of these nineteenth-century idealists disdained flamboyant displays of wealth is, I guess, beside the point.)

Greeley had made Fourier's Phalanxes a trendy utopian brand name, but they weren't the only product on the ideological market. A capitalist version was set up fifteen miles outside of Chicago in the

1880s by railroad magnate George Pullman. His aim was to build an attractively designed community for his workers—with public parks, fountains, and manicured gardens—but where unions were banned and, in his words, "strikes and other troubles that periodically convulse the world of labor would need not be feared." It endured for almost two decades; the recession of the 1890s sparked what Pullman most dreaded, a workers' strike, and his dream died just before he did in 1897.

Although utopian communities tended to follow a socialist economic model, many were founded on religious principles. (Some blended the two, using Acts 2:44–45 as their justification: "And all that believed were together, and had all things common; / And sold their possessions and goods, and parted them to all men, as every man had need.") Among the most enduring faith-based utopias were those built by the Shakers, who at their peak in the mid-1800s had approximately six thousand members in more than twenty communes nationwide. Maine's Sabbathday Lake Shaker Village is still up and running after 220 years. With only about two or three members left, however, its future is grim. Shaker numbers have dwindled over the past two centuries mostly due to their strict no-sex policy. Ever. Even between married couples. The Shakers could expand only through the recruitment of new members, and celibacy was a hard sell.

Such was not the case with the Oneida Community, founded in 1848 by John Humphrey Noyes fifteen miles east of Syracuse, New York. Oneida was a carnal free-for-all compared with the Shakers' communes or, for that matter, even your average swingers' resort. Noyes, a former Yale Divinity School student, and his followers practiced "complex marriage," which *prohibited* couples from being monogamous. Instead, everyone was essentially married to everyone and encouraged to have multiple sex partners. Oneida grew to several hundred people in just two years.

Noyes's "Heaven on Earth" began to unravel in the mid-1870s due to various factors, including a backlash among younger members who actually grew tired of the forced promiscuity and wanted to settle down with a single person. Noyes fled America after learning he'd been accused of statutory rape, and in 1881 the Oneida Community disbanded. Its reputation wasn't exactly enhanced when, later that year, a former member named Charles Guiteau assassinated President James Garfield. (As chance would have it, Secretary of War Robert Todd Lincoln was standing near the president when he was hit. Lincoln was also at the Pan-American Exposition when President William McKinley was shot, and while he declined an invitation to Ford's Theatre the night of April 14, 1865, Robert was at his father's bedside before he died. No other American has been in such relatively close proximity to three presidential assassinations.) Even before Charles Guiteau killed Garfield, his fellow Noyesians had written Guiteau off as a bit creepy, nicknaming him Charles Git-out.

Calculating exactly how many utopias, or "intentional communities" as academics now refer to them, have been attempted is challenging because the definition is subjective. One person's bright, happy collective is another's oppressive, maniac-led cult. The stuffy but reliable *Oxford English Dictionary* adheres to the word *utopia*'s original meaning—conceived by Thomas More—as a perfect place that can never truly exist, while the *OED*'s more optimistic American cousin, *Merriam-Webster,* allows for it potentially to be real. But what can be said with certainty is that, from the Puritans' shining city on a hill to "just leave me alone, man" hippie enclaves, no other nation on earth has attracted and hosted more of these colonies, ecovillages, and communes than the United States.

Horace Greeley himself conceded defeat on their long-term prospects in this country or anywhere else. They might be "excellently calculated for use on some other planet," he concluded in his *Recollections,* "but not on this one."

In 1869 the *New York Tribune*'s agricultural editor, Nathan Meeker, helped establish a "temperance colony" about fifty miles north of Denver that eventually became Greeley, Colorado, named in honor of his abstemious boss. Greeley, the place, was intended to be not a Fourier Phalanx but a clean, family-friendly town where faith, education, culture, and hard work were celebrated and alcohol was illegal. (The ban lasted a whole century.)

In an odd historical postscript, Greeley has sporadically been in the media spotlight for the past decade because of an Egyptian student named Sayyid Qtub, who lived there more than sixty years ago and attended classes at what is now the University of Northern Colorado. Qtub came to the United States in 1948 and passed through New York City first before his six-month stay in Greeley.

New York's frenzied, menacing streets, with their noisy gin joints, brothels, and seedy drug dens, had traumatized the shy and soft-spoken Qtub, and Greeley should have seemed, in comparison, like heaven on earth. Classical concerts, free public lectures, sock hops, and potluck suppers were the town's main entertainment, and religious services were always fully attended. But again, one man's Shangri-la is another's Hades, and Qtub saw only decadence in Greeley. "Dancing naked legs filled the hall, arms draped around the waists," he later wrote of one church-sponsored event. When he went on to fume that "the atmosphere was full of love," he did not mean the chaste and innocent kind. Qtub was especially revolted by the latest musical craze. "Jazz is the American music," he seethed, "created by Negroes to satisfy their primitive instincts, their love of noise and their appetite for sexual arousal."

After returning to Egypt, he traveled throughout the Middle East lecturing and writing extensively about the West's spiritual wickedness, as evidenced in little Greeley, Colorado. Qtub isn't exactly a household name in the United States, but the movement of like-minded souls he inspired, "the Base," is universally recognized. The original Arabic translation is probably more familiar to most of us: al-Qaeda.

PIKES PEAK'S SUMMIT

We were now nearly fourteen thousand feet above the sea level. But we could not spend long in contemplating the grandeur of the scene for it was exceedingly cold, and leaving our names on a large rock, we commenced letters to some of our friends, using a broad flat rock for a writing desk. When we were ready to return I read aloud the lines from Emerson.

> "A ruddy drop of manly blood,
> The surging sea outweighs;
> The world uncertain comes and goes,
> The looser rooted stays."

. . . We pursued our journey in all possible haste, anxious to find a good camp for the night before dark. At last when I thought I could not go a rod further, we found a capital place, a real bear's den it seemed, though large enough for half a dozen. And here we are, enclosed on every side, by huge boulders, with two or three large spruce trees stretching their protective arms over our heads.

Yours truly,
J. A. Archibald

J. A. ARCHIBALD wrote these words in early August 1858 after climbing the Colorado mountain named after Zebulon Montgomery Pike Jr., the twenty-eight-year-old Army officer who began mapping out the southern regions of the Louisiana Purchase in 1805 while Meriwether Lewis and William Clark, somewhat more famously, charted the north. Pike attempted to scale the 14,115-foot mountain in late November 1806, but after several days without food and blanketed up to his waist in snow, the starving and frostbitten explorer gave up. "No human being," Pike concluded, "could have ascended its pinical [sic]." Pike is believed to have been the first non–Native American to make the attempt, and he never tried again. J. A. Archibald would go on to accomplish what Pike himself could not, earning a spot among our nation's most notable mountaineers.

Archibald's parents, John and Jane, undoubtedly contributed to their child's bold, adventurous spirit. In 1854 the family was living in Massachusetts when the Kansas-Nebraska Act passed, granting settlers in these relatively wild, unruly territories the right to decide whether or not slavery should be allowed there. Mr. and Mrs. Archibald saw an opportunity to promote their abolitionist beliefs, so they packed up their eight children and headed for Kansas. Soon after arriving, they offered their new home as both a meeting place for fellow Free Staters and a safe house, or "station," on the Underground Railroad. There is no record of violence against the Archibalds, but their actions could have easily gotten them killed; pro-slavery thugs from Missouri poured into what became known as "Bleeding Kansas" to murder and terrorize anyone aligned with the Free State cause. From these brutal clashes emerged the abolitionists' fiercest advocate—some would say madman—a New York–born cattle raiser and tanner named John Brown.

In the early summer of 1857, twenty-year-old J. A. Archibald set out with a younger brother, Albert, to join gold hunters from Lawrence, Kansas. "I was much pleased to learn on my arrival, that the company contained a lady [Mrs. Robert Middleton]," Archibald noted in a long letter detailing the journey. Middleton was one of the few fellow travelers Archibald wrote about, but a lasting friendship wasn't in the cards; Middleton was put off by Archibald's progressive views, even if they benefited Middleton herself. "I soon found that there could be no congeniality between us," Archibald wrote. "She proved to be a woman unable to appreciate freedom or reform . . . and confined herself the long days to feminine impotence in the hot covered wagon."

Alternately riding in these ox-drawn wagons and walking in thin leather moccasins across the kiln-hot plains, Archibald and the Lawrence party trekked more than five hundred miles from Kansas to Colorado. Whether or not they found gold (and they didn't) mattered little to Archibald, whose aim was to rove "across the prairie sea."

Traveling for the sake of traveling I understand, having already covered thousands of miles by car, boat, helicopter, kayak, train, plane, bus, and hiking boots. The beauty of this country is simply breathtaking. Even the gas stations and chain restaurants I'm passing on I-25, as I drive south from Denver to Manitou Springs, can't diminish the magnificent sight before me of a dark-blue mountain range backlit by the rays of a vanishing sun. But what these early pioneers endured seems beyond comprehension. Aside from the physical exhaustion, thirst, and hunger they experienced, they had to maintain constant, hyperalert preparedness for everything from rattlesnakes underfoot to thieving bandits around every trail bend, while also staving off long periods of mind-numbing boredom.

Although there is one passage dedicated to the "disgusting inactivity, and monotony" of their expedition, Archibald's letters and journal are free of grievances or grumblings. Mostly they contain descriptions of the land's infinite splendor and surreal, dreamlike images—"The Indians have the custom of suspending their dead in trees, where the dry air of this elevated plain speedily shrivels them up"—as well as the small unfolding dramas of the natural world: "The buffalo cow as well as the bull is naturally a very timid animal, save when wounded or driven to bay. I learned that the mother of the captured calf made a heroic stand, and presented a beautiful illustration of maternal feeling over fear. . . . She died in his defence."

In Archibald's time, the only way to ascend Pikes Peak was by foot. Now going up "America's most visited mountain" can also be accomplished by bike, car, or cog railway. I'm choosing the latter because I, blessedly, share none of Archibald's craving for self-punishing exploration. Adventure, yes; misery, no. I justify my laziness by reasoning that I'm on a tight schedule and don't have several days to spare trudging up and down a fourteen-thousand-foot mountain. I'm also curious to see what our tour guide will say about Archibald's momentous climb to the top.

"She's not a tour guide," a staff member at the Manitou & Pikes Peak Railway corrects me. "She's a *conductor,* and her name is Erin." Attractive and (I'm guessing) in her mid- to late twenties, Erin teaches high school history most of the year and works here in the summer. She is personable, funny, and very smart, and she keeps all 180 of us engaged and entertained for the entire ninety-minute trip. We first learn some basics about the Cog Railway itself. After enduring a painfully bumpy two-day burro ride up Pikes Peak, inventor and businessman Zalmon Simmons (of Simmons BeautyRest mattress fame) resolved to finance a more comfortable mode of transportation. On June 30, 1891, the inaugural steam-powered train safely transported its first paying customers, a Denver church choir, up the 26-degree incline to the summit. Tickets back then were $5 apiece, or approximately $135 in today's dollars. (I paid $33.50.) Erin assures us that, since the maiden voyage well over a century ago, there hasn't been a single passenger fatality or serious injury. Our ninety-ton train, we also learn, is powered by a diesel/electric engine and chugs the 8.9 miles up the mountain no faster than 10.5 miles per hour.

Regional one-upmanship is inevitable in these types of talks, and Erin lands a few good-natured jabs. "How many of you are from Texas? I know you all think everything's bigger in Texas, but see those large rocks over there?" she asks, pointing to a sprawling pile of boulders on our right. "We Coloradoans call that gravel." She also puts Delaware in its place. "You can fit the entire state in Pike National Forest," she says.

Erin also directs our attention to the various trees along the way: blue spruces, Douglas firs, ponderosa pines, and quaking aspens, whose bark, we learn, can be rubbed on the skin to prevent sunburn. "It has a natural SPF of seven," she informs us. There are also some two-thousand-year-old bristlecone pines, mere babes in the woods, I think, compared with the dearly departed Prometheus.

By the time we reach 10,000 feet (we left at 6,320), the temperature has plunged substantially. Windbreakers and sweaters are being pulled out of backpacks and handbags, and Erin starts walking up and down the train making sure everyone is doing all right and answering questions. I ask her what types of dangers hikers would have encountered back in the 1850s.

"There were—and still are—black bears, mountain lions, and poisonous snakes, but the weather would have been the greatest threat," she says. "It can be warm and sunny one moment, then a blizzard can come in before you know it."

I'm about to ask her about J. A. Archibald, whom she hasn't mentioned, but a teenage girl gets Erin's attention, and I miss my chance.

While Archibald was motivated mostly by the thrill of discovery and not wealth when setting out with the Lawrence party from Kansas, there was one other goal, and it was fully realized at the top of Pikes Peak. "I have accomplished the task which I marked out for myself," Archibald wrote home on August 5, 1858,

> and now I feel amply repaid for all my toil and fatigue. Nearly everyone tried to discourage me from attempting it, but I believed I should succeed; and now, here I am, and I feel that I would not have missed this glorious sight for anything at all.
>
> In all probability I am the first woman who has ever stood upon the summit of this mountain and gazed upon this wondrous scene which my eyes now behold.
>
> How I sigh for the poet's power of description, so that I might give you some faint idea of the grandeur and beauty of the scene.

At a time when even other women—see "Middleton, Mrs. Robert," above—disparaged the suffragists, Julia Anna Archibald Holmes (she often dropped her married name in her letters and journals) became one more irrefutable example that women could achieve whatever men could.

To some degree, they had to be tougher. Female explorers were often ostracized and denigrated by their male peers (one of Archibald's fellow travelers fumed in a letter home about being stuck with "strong willed women and weak-minded men"), their clothing was traditionally less suitable for rugged travel than garments worn by men (the most scandalous and politically radical aspect of Archibald's journey was her dressing in pantlike "bloomers"), and they had to constantly guard against sexual assault and harassment. No accounts suggest that Archibald was subjected to either, but she modestly alluded to her appeal among the Native Americans. "One Indian wanted to trade [me for] two squaws," she wrote, while others "approaching the wagon made signs for me to jump behind them on their ponies." Archibald declined with a polite shake of the head. (I've only seen one picture of her, and in my opinion she looks like the movie star Julia Roberts.)

Memorials nationwide pay homage to Amelia Earhart, Harriet Tubman, and Sacagawea, Lewis and Clark's indispensable Shoshone guide, all of whom charted new trails at enormous risk. But Julia Archibald remains largely forgotten, along with dozens of other intrepid women. Amanda Berry Smith, a former slave, crisscrossed four continents in the late nineteenth century as a missionary and educator, and her autobiography contains some of the earliest writings by any American on customs and daily life in remote African villages. Inspired by her globe-trotting father, Hawaiian-born Annie Montague Alexander traveled almost nonstop gathering fossils and hunting live animals for scientific study. She donated her massive collection along with considerable funding to create the Museum of Paleontology and the Museum of Vertebrate Zoology, both in Berkeley, California. While Alexander was digging up bones and shooting wild animals (the Alaskan bear *Ursus alexandrae* is named after her), botanist Ynes Mexia was logging thousands of miles in Mexico and South America collecting 150,000 plant specimens. And in the spirit of Julia Archibald, a fifty-eight-year-old mountaineer named Annie Smith Peck was the first person of either gender to summit Peru's 22,205-foot Mount Huascarán. A year later, in 1909, she planted a VOTES FOR WOMEN banner atop Peru's Mount Coropuna.

In her August 5 letter from Pikes Peak's summit, Archibald lamented her inability to adequately convey the "beauty and grandeur" around her. Thirty-four years later, a Wellesley College professor followed in Archibald's footsteps on July 22, 1893, and articulated the sentiments that had so eluded her predecessor. "It was then and there [on Pikes Peak]," Katharine Lee Bates recalled, "as I was looking out over the sea-like expanse of fertile country spreading away so far under those ample skies, that the opening lines of the hymn floated into my mind." Bates immediately began jotting down verses. Unsatisfied, though, with her first draft, she tinkered with it for two years before publishing the poem. "O beautiful for halcyon skies," it began,

> For amber waves of grain,
> For purple mountains majesties
> Above the enameled plain!
> America! America!
> God shed his grace on thee
> Till souls wax fair as earth and air
> And music-hearted sea!

Bates revised it several times before finalizing the version of "America the Beautiful" we sing today. A giant, three-paneled memorial at the summit pays tribute to Bates, but there's no mention of Archibald anywhere.

When our train left this morning the temperature was in the high seventies. Here it's in the low fifties. My T-shirt provides little protection against the stinging wind, and in no time I'm shivering so hard that I can barely hold my camera steady. There's at least another five minutes to go before we're supposed to be back on the train ("If you're late, you'll be left behind," Erin cheerfully warned us), and I doubt I'll be able to return here anytime soon. So this is really my only chance to photograph this historic view and fully take in the moment.

My teeth start chattering uncontrollably. I think of Julia Archibald spending two whole freezing nights up here and try to convince myself to tough it out for the remaining few minutes.

Another blast of cold air whips across the observation deck. Instinctively my shoulders hunch, and I cross my arms tightly against my chest. That does it for me. With head and pride hung low, I bolt for the train.

MADISON GRANT'S

RESIDENCE

[We] feel deeply the loss of our beloved President, Madison Grant. . . . No more will his familiar figure be seen among us. Around our council fires we shall sadly miss his ready wit, his wise decisions, and the inspiration to spur us on to high endeavor. Yet, believing with the poet that they who dwell in our hearts never die, we shall, like the Norsemen of old, carry him with us to the halls of Valhalla. . . .

Let us carve on the tablets of memory the Saga of Madison Grant.

—*From Madison Grant's obituary, written by Frederick Russell Burnham for the Boone and Crockett Club, an elite group of hunters founded by Grant, Teddy Roosevelt, and other avid outdoorsmen*

NO MAJOR TRIBUTES were ever carved on "the tablets of memory" for Madison Grant commensurate with his lifelong dedication to saving America's wilderness. No bronze plaques mark the

homes in which Grant lived, and there are no mountains, valleys, gla-
ciers, parks, hospitals, trails, or highways named in his honor. (There
is a Madison Grant elk refuge somewhere in California's Prairie Creek
Redwoods State Park, paid for by his brother after Grant died in 1937,
but when I called the park, no one on staff had heard of it.) Nor is
the Madison-Grant High School in Fairmount, Indiana, related to the
man; Madison and Grant, a school administrator informed me, are
simply the town's two neighboring counties. Whatever public memorials to Grant do exist are so obscure as to be essentially invisible.

Grant's name first came to my attention while I was researching
the pantheon of nature lovers who led America's nascent conservation
and preservation movements. (Although the words are often used in-
terchangeably now, they weren't originally synonymous: *conservation*
meant the responsible management of wild habitats to ensure their
long-term sustainability for the benefit of humans, especially hunters
and fishermen, while *preservation* was about safeguarding these places
for their own sake. The modern environmental movement is more
closely associated with the latter.) And I was struck by how many of
them were city boys, and, specifically, native New Yorkers. Along with
Grant, the prestigious group included President Teddy Roosevelt; Wilderness Society founder Bob Marshall, who has a million-acre Montana preserve named for him; artist William Henry Jackson, whose
1871 photographs of Yellowstone galvanized congressional support for
the national parks and who has Jackson Point in the Grant Tetons and
Mount Jackson in Yellowstone named in his honor; and anthropologist
and naturalist George Bird Grinnell, who has a mountain and a glacier
in Montana dedicated to him. Grinnell founded the Audubon Society
in 1886 and was an early advocate of saving the American bison.

Pulling the bison back from the precipice of extinction is, in particular, one of the most extraordinary reversals in preservation history. An
iconic photograph from the 1880s shows a gigantic mound, about forty
feet tall and several hundred feet around, of what appear to be bright
white rocks. Its size can be roughly estimated by the two unidentified
gentlemen in dark suits posing next to and on top of it. What the men

are posing with, in fact, is a small mountain made entirely of the skulls of slaughtered bisons.

Tens of millions of these animals once populated North America, but by the early 1900s, a mere one thousand of them remained. Ranchers and railroad companies wiped them out in droves to prevent the massive beasts from trampling their property, and hunters shot and sold them for their meat, hides (to make robes), tongues (considered a delicacy), bones (to be ground up into fertilizer), and horns (for umbrella handles).

At the forefront of the bison-rescue effort was Madison Grant. Working with Grinnell, Teddy Roosevelt, and the New York Zoological Society director William Hornaday, Grant was instrumental in establishing the Wichita Mountains Wildlife Refuge, Montana's National Bison Range, South Dakota's Wind Cave National Game Preserve, and Nebraska's Fort Niobrara National Wildlife Refuge as safe havens for the animals. There are now approximately half a million bison in America.

Despite his role in raising critical funds, helping to organize the American Bison Society, and educating Congress and the public about the animal's urgent plight, Grant has been largely ignored. Partly this was his own fault. According to his acquaintances, Grant was a modest soul who gave few newspaper interviews and was quite content to let Grinnell, Roosevelt, and Hornaday garner the lion's share of attention.

A later battle for imperiled redwood trees, however, drew Grant front and center. "The impending destruction of these forests is the most serious question confronting California in the effort for the preservation of some portion of her vast inheritance," Grant warned in the June 1920 issue of *National Geographic.* He then expounded on the history of the redwoods and their irreplaceable environmental and aesthetic worth. "The cutting of a Sequoia for grape stakes or railroad ties," Grant argued,

> is like breaking up one's grandfather's clock for kindling to save the trouble of splitting logs at the woodpile or lighting one's

pipe with a Greek manuscript to save the trouble of reaching for the matches.

After the fall of the Roman Empire the priceless works of classic art were "needed" for lime, and statues by Phidias and Praxiteles were slaked down for this purpose; but the men who did it are today rightly regarded as "vandals and barbarians."

At the end of the seventeen-page spread, Grant emphasized the "sentimental considerations" for ensuring the redwoods' survival. "No one who has seen these groves," he stated confidently, "can fail to love them."

Sentimentality itself must have momentarily gotten the better of Grant because he knew this wasn't true. Plenty of logging executives had visited these same woods and seen only a cash crop. Gold lured the first wave of prospectors to California in the 1850s, but the "Redwoods Rush" that followed was equally (if not more) profitable. Within three decades, hundreds of sawmills had popped up in the region to cut and grind giant redwoods into lumber that was prized for both its beauty and its durability. From cradle to casket, the booming American population was dependent on redwood-based products, furniture, buildings, and homes. In the early 1900s, 95 percent of the original forests were leveled, and the timber barons themselves were predicting that, to meet demand, the rest would be gone within sixty years.

Aghast at such a notion, Grant co-founded the Save the Redwoods League in 1918 with the paleontologists John C. Merriam and Henry Fairfield Osborn and proposed that the federal government use eminent domain to protect the trees, which all grew on private property. Grant, however, experienced staunch resistance to this suggestion, even among the League's own board of directors.

Then he had a brainstorm: Grant would appeal to his wealthy friends and colleagues to purchase from the landowners parcels of forests, or "memorial groves" as Grant called them, that would be maintained by the Save the Redwoods League in perpetuity. John C. Phillips, a Grant acquaintance who also served on the League's board, agreed to buy a thirty-five-acre grove as a tribute to his brother-in-law Colonel Raynal C. Bolling, the first high-ranking officer killed in World War I. "Colonel Bolling and his comrades dedicated their lives to their country," Grant remarked in a moving speech at the August 6, 1921, ceremony. "Let us dedicate ourselves to the task of keeping and preserving in its natural beauty a country which is worth fighting for." There are now almost one thousand of these memorial groves representing more than one million acres of redwood forests.

The corner of Seventy-seventh Street and Fifth Avenue in Manhattan hardly looks like an epicenter for America's early environmental movement, but it was from his home at 960 Fifth Avenue, as well as his office at the New York Zoological Society (which he cofounded and which is now the Bronx Zoo), that Madison Grant worked day and night to save endangered lands and species.

Had he wished, he could have lived a life of pampered self-indulgence. Born about a half mile from here into enormous wealth and privilege, Grant was educated by private tutors and traveled the world before attending Yale University, from where he was graduated with honors, and Columbia Law School.

"What's going on, my friend?" a burly doorman asks me after I've paced back and forth in front of the stately Upper East Side residence a few times to verify the address and find the best angle from which to photograph the building. I realize my wandering to and fro probably makes it seem like I'm casing the joint.

"I'm traveling the country looking for unmarked historical sites," I explain, "and this is one of them."

"Just don't shoot any of the people coming in or out," he says.

I assure him I will not.

Grant died here on May 30, 1937. Despite suffering from acute arthritis, up until the end of his life he was planning a trip to attend a conservation seminar in Berlin and exerting considerable energy helping newly created international organizations rescue species around the world at risk of dying out. His participation was critical in protecting, among many other animals, Sudanese white rhinos, koalas, African elephants, South African mountain zebras, and tortoises from the Galápagos Islands.

Unmarried, Grant had no children to promote his legacy, and while alive he was more comfortable advancing the issues he held dear, rather than himself. Though mostly forgotten now, he did not die in complete obscurity. "MADISON GRANT, 71, ZOOLOGIST IS DEAD—SAVED REDWOOD TREES," a long, glowing *New York Times* obituary announced. "Mr. Grant was born at the corner of Madison Avenue and Thirty-third Street on Nov. 19, 1865," the obituary continued. "Finding it unnecessary to earn a living, Mr. Grant turned a childhood interest in wild life into practical use. He first took up field zoology and then explored the scientific field of the higher forms of wild life [. . . and] is credited with the discovery of a number of North American mammals."

The obituary also listed many of Grant's numerous accomplishments, including an assortment of publications he either contributed to or authored.

Before flying off to visit Grant's redwoods in Humboldt, California, and then a residential facility in Sonoma Valley for people with developmental disabilities, I purchase a now out-of-print book by Grant to better comprehend his perspective on humanity and the natural world. It's a dense and academic work, not exactly light airplane reading, but it does help me understand why, despite Grant's Herculean efforts to preserve lands and wildlife that still bring a sense of wonder to millions, there's been no real push to build statues or memorials hailing him as a great and honorable man.

And why, as I would see in California, there shouldn't be.

PART III

THIS LAND IS
MY LAND

The Dark Side of Expansion
and Growth

THE SONOMA
DEVELOPMENTAL CENTER

There exists today a widespread and fatuous belief in the power of environment, as well as of education and opportunity to alter heredity, which arises from the dogma of the brotherhood of man.... Such beliefs have done much damage in the past and if allowed to go uncontradicted, may do even more serious damage in the future. Thus the view that the Negro slave was an unfortunate cousin of the white man, deeply tanned by the tropic sun and denied the blessings of Christianity and civilization, played no small part with the sentimentalists of the Civil War period and it has taken us fifty years to learn that speaking English, wearing good clothes and going to school and to church does not transform a Negro into a white man.... Americans will have a similar experience with the Polish Jew, whose dwarf stature, peculiar mentality and ruthless concentration on self-interest are being engrafted upon the stock of the nation.

—From The Passing of the Great Race (1916) by Madison Grant

EMBEDDED IN A rock next to the 364-foot-tall Founders Tree in California's Humboldt Redwoods State Park, a bronze plaque reads:

Dedicated to the Founders of the
Save-the-Redwoods League
Madison Grant • John C. Merriam • Henry Fairfield Osborn
by the California State Park Commission
September 13, 1931

None of the other tourists here seem to notice it. They are more inclined, as I was upon arriving, to crane their necks skyward. No photograph can capture the tree's booster-rocket height, and every person I see walk around its forty-foot circumference looks struck with a childlike sense of awe.

In 1991 one visitor did catch sight of Grant's name, however, and angrily shot off a letter to the California Department of Parks and Recreation: "Honoring Madison Grant with a plaque on public property is as historically bizarre as erecting a monument to Adolf Hitler for his part in founding the Volkswagen Company. Please have it removed."

Invoking Hitler can be unnecessarily provocative in some debates, but here the connection is apt. After reading the 1925 German translation of *The Passing of the Great Race,* the future führer sent Madison Grant a flattering letter, praising the book as his new "bible." And not without reason, for what Madison Grant most wanted to preserve, more than any giant sequoia or wild bison, was the white race. This was his main calling and his life's passion, regardless of how distasteful it might have seemed to others. "Race feeling may be called prejudice by those whose careers are cramped by it," Grant wrote bluntly in his book, "but it is a natural antipathy which serves to maintain the purity of type." Whites were endangered, Grant went on to argue, because

whether we like to admit it or not, the result of the mixture
of two races, in the long run, gives us a race reverting to the
more ancient, generalized and lower type. The cross between

a white man and an Indian is an Indian; the cross between a white man and a Negro is a Negro; the cross between a white man and a Hindu is a Hindu; and the cross between any of the three European races and a Jew is a Jew. . . .

This is a matter of every-day observation and the working of this law of nature is not influenced or affected by democratic institutions or by religious beliefs. Nature cares not for the individual nor how he may be modified by environment. She is concerned only with the perpetuation of the species or type and heredity alone is the medium through which she acts.

Hermann Göring, Hitler's deputy and designated successor, also admired Grant (the 1937 Berlin trip Grant was preparing for right before he died came at Göring's invitation), and the Third Reich's most influential eugenicists, Wilhelm Frick, Fritz Lenz, and Eugen Fischer, all counted Grant as both a colleague and good friend. He kept them apprised of new research in the United States and helped articulate the movement's "intellectual" foundation in Germany.

Especially appealing to them was Grant's endorsement of negative, as opposed to positive, eugenics. "Man has the choice of two methods of race improvement," Grant summarized in his book. "He can breed from the best or he can eliminate the worst by segregation or sterilization." The latter option better ensured long-term success, Grant believed. But much to his consternation, meddling human traits like "altruism [and] philanthropy" were preventing society from fully eradicating "the undesirable underclasses." He went on to say:

Mistaken regard for what are believed to be divine laws and a sentimental belief in the sanctity of human life tend to prevent both the elimination of defective infants and the sterilization of such adults as are themselves no value to the community. The laws of nature require the obliteration of the unfit and human life is valuable only when it is of use to the community or the race.

Monstrous as this sounds today, thanks to enthusiastic and outspoken proponents such as Madison Grant, eugenics was already being practiced in the United States. The Germans modeled their early sterilization efforts on what they saw occurring here.

Fifty miles north of San Francisco and nestled within the grape-scented valleys of wine country is the Sonoma Developmental Center, my destination after Humboldt Redwoods State Park. Conceived in the late 1800s, the Center was originally the California Home for the Care and Training of Feeble-Minded Children, and it expanded numerous times before settling into its present one-thousand-acre location.

"Sonoma Developmental Center," its literature states, "is the oldest facility in California established specifically for serving the needs of individuals with developmental disabilities. The facility opened its doors to 148 residents on November 24, 1891, culminating a ten-year project on the part of two prominent Northern California women who had children with developmental disabilities." By all accounts it was a model of humane care.

At first.

The literature goes on to note: "Many changes over the last 110 years include attitudes, philosophies, values, and beliefs in regard to the treatment of developmentally disabled people." This is a more pleasant way of saying: *For a while, some really terrible things went on here.* What happened, to be blunt, was the forced sterilization of thousands of men, women, and children deemed "unfit" or "subnormal"—an assessment made based on frighteningly arbitrary standards.

"You know we don't do that now, right?" a Sonoma receptionist said to me, clearly taken aback when I called to explain my request for a visit.

"Oh, absolutely," I replied. "And I'm not trying to make Sonoma look bad. This was all a long, long time ago. But I just want to see where the sterilizations took place."

"Let me connect you with Karen Litzenberg in our public information office."

I meant what I said; I'm honestly not picking on Sonoma or suggesting it should advertise the more chilling aspects of its past, but it is a significant historic site. California wasn't the first state to enact laws encouraging forced sterilizations (that would be Indiana, in 1907, followed by the majority of American states), but once the legislative green light blinked go in 1909, the state quickly made up for lost time and eventually surpassed all others. Out of sixty thousand involuntary sterilizations nationwide, one-third to a half of them were performed in California. And Sonoma bears the sad distinction of having carried out more than any other similar facility.

With its neoclassical buildings and well-manicured grounds, Sonoma looks more like an Ivy League campus than a government-run institution. "We want our residents to feel like it's a home," Karen Litzenberg says to me soon after we meet in the main administration building. "There's an equestrian ring with an indoor arena, a pool that's heated year-round, a softball field, a campground, and there are regular movie nights and dances, and also a coffee klatch."

Sonoma's mission now is to offer day-to-day living skills, vocational training, health education, and other guidance to developmentally disabled adults so they can live independently. "The population varies," Karen tells me as we pass newly renovated housing, "but about six hundred fifty people live here today." (I assure Karen that for reasons of privacy I won't photograph or write about any of the residents. I will say, and this is highly subjective and anecdotal, that all of the staff members Karen introduces me to are genial and forthcoming, and the overall atmosphere seems quite friendly.)

I need to find one of the hospitals where the sterilizations occurred, and Karen and I drive around the facility trying to match the current scenery with old photos she's dug up. A caption on one says that the original hospital, built in 1906, is where the carpenter shop sits now. "No, this is the *new* carpenter shop," a worker tells us. "I'm not sure where the old one was that replaced the hospital. That's before my time." Eventually we decide to focus on the Chamberlain Building, which was built in 1927. Long and beige with a red-tiled roof, the elegant three-story building is now home to clerical offices and laboratories.

Determining *exactly* how many sterilizations took place here is difficult because records have been lost and destroyed, and countless operations went unreported. Sonoma's superintendent Dr. F. O. Butler is believed to have conducted at least one thousand of the surgeries himself.

There is no indication that Madison Grant ever set foot here, but years before writing *The Passing of the Great Race* he helped lay the philosophical groundwork on which America's eugenics movement was constructed. (Grant also lobbied aggressively for racial segregation and anti-miscegenation laws.) Regrettably, he had no end of institutional allies. *Los Angeles Times* publisher Harry Chandler used his paper as a megaphone to promote eugenics, and universities such as Yale, Stanford, and Harvard bestowed their academic credibility to the cause. The Carnegie Institution funded a Long Island laboratory in 1904 that began keeping tabs on the physical traits of half a million American citizens (the information was often gathered voluntarily at state fairs, where "Fitter Family Contests" took place), and two decades later the Rockefeller Foundation helped establish the Berlin-based Kaiser Wilhelm Institute for Anthropology, Human Heredity and Eugenics. Grant's buddy Eugen Fischer served as its director until 1933.

Back in the States, people with mental retardation were among the first to go under the knife. Men received vasectomies and women salpingectomies (meaning, the removal of the fallopian tubes). California law gave doctors wide discretion in deciding who was eligible, and the labels "idiot," "imbecile," and "moron" were actual medical categories determined by intelligence tests. Idiots were a mental age of one to two, imbeciles three to seven, and morons eight to twelve.

Alcoholics, epileptics, schizophrenics, manic depressives, and others suffering from mental illnesses were also thrown into the "unfit" category. Blacks and Mexican Americans were disproportionately targeted, along with women of any ethnicity rumored to be promiscuous. "Something like 25 percent of the girls who have been sterilized were sent here solely, or primarily, for that purpose," wrote California's leading eugenicist, Paul Popenoe (a close friend of Grant's and, curiously, the "inventor" of marriage counseling), after inspecting Sonoma in 1926.

One year later, in *Buck v. Bell*, critics finally gained an audience before the U.S. Supreme Court and were confident that the justices would recognize the barbarity of forced sterilizations and their dangerous ethical implications. Carrie Buck was a twenty-one-year-old woman diagnosed as "feeble-minded," like her mother, and "immoral" for bearing an illegitimate child. Buck had actually been raped, and her foster family institutionalized her to protect their own good name. James Bell, the doctor petitioning to sterilize Buck, insisted that her child, a baby girl named Vivian, would also be mentally deficient. The Court passed down an overwhelming 8–1 ruling. Against Buck.

Chief Justice Oliver Wendell Holmes penned the majority opinion, which included these immortal words:

> It is better for all the world, if instead of waiting to execute degenerate offspring for crime, or to let them starve for their imbecility, society can prevent those who are manifestly unfit from continuing their kind. . . . Three generations of imbeciles are enough.

After the decision, the pace of forced sterilizations accelerated exponentially. Along with operating on Carrie Buck, Dr. Bell also sterilized her daughter, Vivian, for good measure. And yet, before she died at the age of eight from measles, Vivian turned out to be such a bright student that she had made her school's honor roll.

Charles Darwin's half cousin, the anthropologist and explorer Sir Francis Galton, conceived the word *eugenics*—"wellborn" or "of good stock"—in 1883. (A man of diverse interests, Galton also invented the dog whistle and introduced the idea of putting weather maps in newspapers.) Galton's aim was to apply the lessons of animal breeding to human beings, thereby promoting racial purity. His theories fit comfortably with early-twentieth-century American Progressivism, which had a borderline obsession with moral and physical cleanliness. Progressives, it's true, admirably supported suffrage, ended child labor, and enacted other necessary reforms, but it's also undeniable that many embraced eugenics as a potential cure-all for a host of social ills.

No one, however, rallied around the eugenics flag more fanatically than the Nazis, and after beginning with forced sterilizations, they concluded that operating on those deemed physically, psychologically, or morally defective was time-consuming and expensive. It was easier just to kill them.

One of the doctors most responsible for implementing this doctrinal shift in Nazi medical policies was Karl Brandt, Hitler's personal physician and the head of the Third Reich's euthanasia program. Buried among the thousands of documents from Brandt's trial at Nuremberg is this damning quote: "A strict selection by exterminating the insane or incapable—in other words, the scum of society—would solve the whole problem in one century, and would enable us to get rid of the undesirable elements who people our prisons, hospitals, and lunatic asylums." Although the passage articulated Brandt's opinion to the letter, he didn't write it. The excerpt, submitted by his lawyer as evidence that Brandt's views could not be judged abhorrent, came from Madison Grant's *The Passing of the Great Race*. Brandt was later hanged for war crimes.

"Do you want to see our petting zoo?" Karen asks me. My gut reaction is to say no. I have to catch a flight out of San Francisco at 7:00 P.M., and I want to avoid rush-hour traffic on Highway 101. I check my watch and decide a few minutes probably won't matter after all. It doesn't seem completely relevant to my visit, but I also don't want to appear rude. "Sure," I say.

As we drive up to the little farm, which has an indoor aquarium and an outdoor aviary, Karen familiarizes me with the animals. "We have llamas, ducks, rabbits, a guinea pig, sheeps, goats, and Pedro the bilingual parrot."

"Pedro the bilingual parrot?"

"He's an Amazonian parrot who knows words in both English and Spanish. Well, he speaks bird, too, so I guess he's trilingual."

We step into the barn, and Karen points out the buttons at wheelchair height along the stalls. "When you press one of these you get information about the animals. All of them have names. Deuce the pig is over there, and we also have two potbellied pigs, Breezy and Jethro. They've adopted a black rabbit named Louis, who prefers staying with them than the other rabbits."

"That's amazing."

"They're not the only ones like that. The llamas are very protective of the sheep, and Gretchen the turkey has been caring for some baby chickens that have taken to her as well. She's very maternal and likes to give them rides on her back."

We loop around to the parking lot, passing the outdoor pens along the way. I try to catch a glimpse of Louis snuggled under the watchful eye of his pig protectors, but he's apparently hidden himself somewhere.

"Well, I hope that was worth it."

"Oh, it was," I say, cheerfully thinking of how appalled Madison Grant, who based his vile and idiotic beliefs on the supposedly immutable laws of nature, would have been to find such an affectionate display among various creatures. It's a small example, no doubt, and I certainly knew before coming here that different species care for one another, especially the more vulnerable among them, and that nature—whether animal or human—isn't wholly cruel at heart. But every so often, it's nice to be reminded.

HAUN'S MILL

The victims of persecution had now turned persecutors on their own account, and persecutors of the most terrible description. . . .

At first this vague and terrible power was exercised only upon the recalcitrants who, having embraced the Mormon faith, wished afterwards to pervert or to abandon it. Soon, however, it took a wider range. The supply of adult women was running short, and polygamy without a female population on which to draw was a barren doctrine indeed. Strange rumours began to be bandied about—rumours of murdered immigrants and rifled camps in regions where Indians had never been seen. Fresh women appeared in the harems of the Elders—women who pined and wept, and bore upon their faces the traces of an unextinguishable horror.

—From A Study in Scarlet by Arthur Conan Doyle. The 1887 novel, in which Sherlock Holmes appears for the first time, is set partly in Utah and features a rogue band of violent Mormons. (During a visit to Salt Lake City in 1923, Doyle expressed regret for his depiction of Mormon culture.)

WHEN THE MASSACHUSETTS Bay Colony hanged Mary Dyer and three other Quakers on Boston Common, the executions—albeit indefensible—were not part of a larger campaign to actively hunt down and kill Quakers wherever they lived. Only once in American history have members of a particular faith been targeted for annihilation, specifically because of their religion, by a government directive. "The Mormons must be treated as enemies, and must be exterminated or driven from the state if necessary for the public peace—their outrages are beyond all description," Missouri governor Lilburn Boggs proclaimed on October 27, 1838.

Two days before Governor Boggs issued his decree, formally known as Executive Order 44, Missouri troops had skirmished with Mormon forces in Ray County, leaving three Mormons and one Missouri soldier dead. This was one Missouri soldier too many for Governor Boggs, and he declared open season on all Mormons. Taking his words to heart, the Livingston County Militia, led by Sheriff Thomas Jennings in nearby Caldwell County, descended on the Mormon settlement in northwestern Missouri that Jacob Haun had established three years earlier. Anti-Mormon sentiment had been building throughout the United States since 1830, when a twenty-four-year-old self-educated New Yorker named Joseph Smith Jr. published the Book of Mormon and laid the groundwork for what would become, officially, the Church of Jesus Christ of Latter-day Saints. (With more than fourteen million members today, Mormonism is now the largest American-born religion in the world. Early Mormons were especially hated and persecuted for engaging in "plural marriages," and the LDS Church banned polygamy among its followers in 1890.)

Since Haun's Mill wasn't in my trusty road atlas, I phoned the Caldwell County sheriff's office for information on how to find the place, and an officer kindly gave me detailed directions and also cautioned me that the dirt roads leading out to the remote spot can be impassable following a heavy rain and dicey even after a light one. Storm showers drenched the region two days ago, but fortunately, as I drive up

71 North for about thirty miles from St. Joseph and turn onto a series of increasingly narrow and rough roads, I'm encountering only a few shallow, muddy ditches along the way.

Finally I spy a thin vertical post that says HAUN'S MILL located just outside a large field. After parking, I walk through the thick unmowed grass and head toward a wooded area where many of the villagers had lived and which, according to more recent visitors, is supposedly haunted. It's hard to be spooked in broad daylight, but I do find myself flinching when I pass a small puddle and half a dozen tiny frogs jump up unexpectedly and plop back into the dark water.

Before coming here, I pored over numerous eyewitness testimonies, personal journals, affidavits, family histories, and other firsthand recollections describing what happened when Sheriff Jennings and his men invaded Haun's Mill. Although there are discrepancies in these accounts (some villagers claim that more than two hundred Missouri militia rode into Haun's Mill, while others put the number closer to three hundred), overall they are remarkably consistent.

What many survivors emphasized from the start was how pleasantly warm and serene October 30, 1838, had been—up until the crack of rifle shots and the rumble of galloping horses broke the tranquility. "While I was busily engaged getting supper, and two of the brethren, Mr. Rial Ames (my husband's brother) and Hyram Abbot, were sitting just outside the door, one cutting the other's hair," wrote Olive Ames in her journal (the last name is spelled Eames in other records), "they rose from the chair and remarked, 'I see some of the brethren coming from Far West,' when suddenly the party began firing. Then said Mr. Ames, 'It's the mob right on us.'" She continued:

> Men, women, and poor little children [began] running in every direction, not knowing what minute their lives would be taken. The mob continued firing, shooting at anyone they could see amidst the smoke. I rushed out of the house, crying, "Where are my children?" They gathered around me, then, with my babe,

but one month old, in my arms, I started to hide, not knowing where to go or what to do, so frightened was I, but anxious
to conceal my little ones somewhere. I soon found myself and
little ones hidden away down under the bluff in a little nook by
the creek. . . .

Isaac Laney crossed the creek above me. The mob saw him
and began firing. I saw him fall, then rise and climb the hill. He
escaped death, but carried a great many wounds.

"I made my escape by flight being shot four times through the body
and once across each arm," Laney recalled. One bullet struck his right
hip. "It hit the bone just above the joint[,] glanced out through the
skin and rolled down my drawer leg in to my boot." Bloody and almost
unconscious, he could hear the militia picking off defenseless villagers.
"I listened at them shooting the wounded which could not escape. I
was informed that one of these murderers followed old Father McBride
in his retreat and cut him down with an old scythe."

Thomas McBride was the local justice of the peace, and his death
is highlighted in almost every narrative. James McBride, in particular,
vividly recalled how his father was killed: "He had been shot with his
own gun, after having given it into the mobs possession. Was cut down
and badly disfigured with a corn cutter, and left lying in the creek. . . .
One of his ears was almost cut from his head—deep gashes were cut in
his shoulders; and some of his fingers cut till they would almost drop
from his hand."

Amanda Smith, a young mother who was only passing through
Haun's Mill with her family when they were caught up in the slaughter, elaborated in an affidavit how McBride's fingers came to be severed:
"His hands had been split down when he raised them in supplication
for mercy."

Smith lost her husband at Haun's Mill, and the fate of her children
is another story that, like McBride's, seared itself into the memories of
survivors. No one was more traumatized by what happened to them
than Smith herself, and in her affidavit she wrote:

[After the shooting began] I took my little girls (my boys I could not find) and started for the woods. The mob encircled us on all sides except towards the brook. I ran down the bank, across the mill pond on a plank, up the hill into the bushes. The bullets whistled around us all the way like hail, and cut down the bushes on all sides of us. One girl (Mary Steadwell) was wounded by my side and fell over a log; her clothes hung across the log, and they shot at them expecting that they were hitting her, and our people afterwards cut out of that log twenty bullets. . . .

I then came down to view the awful sight. Oh Horrible! What a sight! My husband and one son (Sardius), ten years old, lay lifeless on the ground, and another son (Alma) badly wounded, seven years old.

In a reminiscence for family members, Smith added:

Sardius and Alma had crawled under the bellows in the blacksmith's shop. . . . Alma's hip was shot away while thus hiding. Sardius was discovered after the massacre by the monsters who came in to despoil the bodies. In cold blood, one Glaze, of Carroll County, presented a rifle near the head of Sardius and literally blew off the upper part of it.

Out of approximately eighty Haun's Mill residents, eighteen men and boys were killed, and the number almost certainly would have been higher had the remaining villagers not fled deep into the woods. The militia simply ran out of people to shoot.

Most of the survivors moved to Illinois, followed by Joseph Smith, who'd been arrested by Missouri authorities but then "broke free" from custody while being transferred from one district court to another. Smith was purportedly allowed to escape in order to spare Missouri a prolonged and disruptive trial.

Fighting between Mormons and state militias throughout the West escalated into a kind of eye-for-an-eye vicious cycle, culminating in the

Utah War of 1857–58 and one of America's worst massacres, where the hunted became the hunters.

In early September 1857, an estimated 150 emigrants from Arkansas who were traveling by wagon train through Mountain Meadows in the Utah Territory found themselves pinned down for days by local Mormon militia originally disguised as Paiute Indians. In exchange for safe passage out of the valley, the Arkansans agreed to give up their weapons and leave the territory immediately, never to return. Considering that they hadn't wanted to stay in the first place, but only to rest for a few days en route to California, they readily consented.

On September 11, as the Arkansans were being escorted out of the valley by militia members, the commanding officers yelled to their men, "Do your duty!" Hearing the prearranged signal, the Mormons suddenly raised their rifles and began shooting the unarmed Arkansans where they stood, sparing only eighteen infants and children considered too young to be witnesses. (After leaving the parents' bodies to rot, the Mormons took the children home to raise as their own. When the Arkansans' remains were found two years later by U.S. Army investigators, most of the children were located and returned to relatives.) None of the Mormon militia members were punished except Colonel John Lee, who was excommunicated from the church, tried by an all-Mormon jury, and sentenced to death. Under Utah territorial law, Lee could choose whether he wanted to be hanged, beheaded, or shot, and he chose the last. Authorities brought him back to Mountain Meadows, where he was placed before a firing squad and executed.

According to my contact at the Caldwell County sheriff's office, a historical marker once stood at Haun's Mill describing in detail what had occurred here, but it was repeatedly defaced and then stolen. And that one was the replacement for another sign that had also been vandalized. "Ancestors of the militiamen still live around there," I was told. "It's not a proud moment in local history, and the signs kept getting torn down."

Which is a pity because remembering places like Haun's Mill and Mountain Meadows isn't about casting blame or embarrassing a single community. Rather, these tributes honor the dead and, more generally, serve as reminders of how violence begets violence and that otherwise decent and reasonable men (I'd like to give them the benefit of the doubt) can be stirred into a barbaric frenzy.

Memorializing "shameful" sites can also allow for other, more positive stories to be told. On September 11, 1999, a monument was erected at Mountain Meadows that includes this inscription:

Built by and maintained by
The Church of Jesus Christ of Latter-day Saints
out of respect for those who died and
were buried here and in the surrounding area
following the massacre of 1857.

On the day the memorial was dedicated, representatives from the Mormon Church met with descendants of the murdered Arkansans and demonstrated, through words of reconciliation and their very presence together, a powerful counterpoint to what had happened 142 years earlier.

Although no similar ceremony has taken place at Haun's Mill, some efforts have been made to atone for the atrocities committed there as well. "In this bicentennial year," Missouri's governor Christopher Bond proclaimed on June 25, 1976, "we reflect on our nation's heritage, [and] the exercise of religious freedom is without question one of the basic tenets of our free democratic republic." On behalf of his state, Bond expressed "deep regret for the injustice and undue suffering" inflicted on the Mormons. Bond's proclamation was among the first such apologies issued by a state, and numerous governors have since followed Missouri's lead on such evils as slavery, segregation, and forced sterilizations.

Bond also made certain to remedy a matter left unresolved for almost a century and a half. "I hereby rescind," he declared, "Executive Order Number 44."

UNION PACIFIC MINE #6

During all the summer and fall of 1976, China was an inferno. There was no eluding the microscopic projectiles that sought out the remotest hiding-places. The hundreds of millions of dead remained unburied and the germs multiplied themselves, and, toward the last, millions died daily of starvation. . . . Cannibalism, murder, and madness reigned. And so perished China.

Not until the following February, in the coldest weather, were the first expeditions made. . . . They found China devastated, a howling wilderness through which wandered bands of wild dogs and desperate bandits who had survived. All survivors were put to death wherever found. And then began the great task, the sanitation of China. Five years and hundreds of millions of treasure were consumed, and then the world moved in. . . . It was a vast and happy intermingling of nationalities that settled down in China in 1982 and the years that followed—a tremendous and successful experiment in cross-fertilization.

—From "The Unparalleled Invasion" (1910), a futuristic anti-Chinese story by Jack London about a American-led biological attack against China after it had tried to conquer the world through massive waves of emigration

BY THE TIME I drive into Rock Springs, Wyoming, at about 9:30 P.M., the only sit-down restaurant open is Bonsai, specializing in Japanese and Chinese cuisine. While waiting for my steamed chicken, I ask manager Sam Ha how many Chinese residents live in the area.

"There's me," he says, "my brother, one sister, my two daughters, five people from other families"—*This is going to take a while,* I say to myself—"and one, maybe two more."

"That's all? Only ten or twelve people out of what used to be almost twenty thousand?" Ethnic populations fluctuate in any community, but this is a steep plunge considering that Rock Springs once had its own bustling Chinatown.

He asks why I'm visiting.

"I'm researching the 1885 riot."

He nods, but I don't know if he's being polite or if he's truly familiar with the story of how at least two dozen Chinese immigrants were murdered here on that one day almost 140 years ago.

The next morning, when I see local historian Bob Nelson, I recap my conversation with Sam Ha, and Bob amends the count of how many Chinese residents live in Rock Springs, but only slightly. "I'd say the number's about fifteen or twenty, but it's definitely nowhere near its peak in 1885."

Bob and I have chatted on the phone a few times, and he's exactly as I imagined: early fifties and physically imposing with a voluble, outsized personality to match. Even though we've only just met, he embraces me like an old friend, and within minutes he's talking about his lap-band weight-reduction surgery—"I know, you don't have to say it, I'm still fat, but you should've seen me before"—and then pinballs wildly from one historical topic to the next, weaving in personal anecdotes and observations, all without taking a breath. I like him immensely.

An Illinois native, Bob moved to Wyoming in 1986 and currently runs the Rock Springs Historical Museum, now housed in a Romanesque-style sandstone building that originally served as city hall. Upon entering the museum, I'm drawn to a prominent display up front about a local meat cutter named Robert "Butch" Parker. Parker was falsely charged with stealing a drunken sheepherder's payday coins and, after being locked·up briefly, left the state in a huff, changed his last name as a tribute to an old friend, Mike Cassidy, and became a full-time outlaw.

"Is this where Butch Cassidy was jailed?" I ask Bob, while opening the heavy steel door of an old cell.

"No, Butch was held down the road. But a nineteen-year-old Dick Cheney spent the night here on a DWI charge," Bob says, referring to the former vice president.

Rock Springs grew from a remote coal-mining camp into the "home of fifty-six nationalities" when immigrants converged on the region during the 1860s and '70s. Looking around, I'm cheered by the black-and-white photos throughout the museum of nineteenth-century Austrian blacksmiths, kilted Scotsmen, and Bosnian jazz musicians side by side with aproned barkeeps from Slovenia and AME churchgoers, among many others, reflecting a diversity equaling that of most major cities.

Bob and I walk up to the museum's second floor. "Here's our main gallery," he says as we stand in front of a bright, stately room encircled by full-sized flags from around the world—a gift from Dick Cheney, Bob informs me.

"It's kind of inspiring," I say, "how Union Pacific created this tiny melting pot in the heart of America."

Bob quickly pops my happy little balloon with a pointed reality check: "U.P. brought in immigrants because they were cheaper and spoke different languages, which made it harder for them to unionize against the company."

"Oh."

We head back downstairs.

"There's not much on the '85 riot," I say, spying a single glass case with some pottery shards and broken rice-wine jugs below a *Harper's*

Weekly illustration depicting the violence. One Chinese man is drawn with his head flung back, arms outstretched, right at the moment he's been shot from behind.

"No," Bob admits, "this is all we have."

"It's a pretty significant event in American history."

"Look, more should be done to remember it," Bob says, "and I don't think people would be opposed to putting up a marker or memorial. Usually the push comes from within the community that was victimized, and we just didn't have that here. But we're working on it."

On our way to Mine #6, where the riot began, Bob wants to show me the site of the first settlement in Rock Springs. As we're about to drive onto a private lot posted with No Trespassing signs, I ask him to stop. "I can't go in there."

"Why not?"

"I have a strict no-trespassing rule."

"You are *such* a baby. Besides, I'm pretty sure I know the people who live here," he says unconvincingly.

Bob sees my hesitation and rolls his eyes. "Fine," he mutters, and we begin to back out. "*If,* however, one day you find that you need to go onto someone's property to research something—and *trespassing* usually implies criminal intent—carry a leash with you. If you're caught, just pretend you were out looking for your dog."

That's actually not a bad idea, I think, but no possible good could come from my saying so out loud, and I simply shake my head in mock disapproval.

Admiring the varied architecture as we drive through one neighborhood after another, I remark, "This really is an amazing town, all these different styles of homes and businesses." Bob agrees and points out Finnish, Spanish, Tyrolean, and Slovenian influences, along with places where the Italian newspaper, French bakery, Mexican chili parlor, German meat market (where Butch Cassidy worked), Jewish grocery, Greek candy shop, and Chinese pharmacy all once stood.

"When did the initial wave of Chinese immigrants arrive in Rock Springs?" I ask Bob.

"Around 1875, though some came earlier. Union Pacific brought the Chinese in after they worked on the railroads."

"Union Pacific owned the mines along with the railroads?"

"They owned everything," Bob says. "There used to be a U.P. billboard near here that said, 'We have what it takes—to take what you have.' This was for one of their hauling companies, but it might as well have been their corporate philosophy. They controlled the town."

Before the mid-1800s conjoined twins Eng and Chang Bunker were the first and only image most Americans had of Asian immigrants. Exhibited across the country by P. T. Barnum from 1830 to 1839 as "professional freaks," the famous brothers from Siam acquired enough wealth to purchase 110 acres of land in North Carolina, complete with slaves, and settle down with their wives. They raised twenty-one children between them; Eng fathered eleven, Chang ten. Fiercely pro-South, they each sent a son to fight for the Confederacy.

Then, beginning in 1848, thousands of Chinese men crossed the Pacific and poured into California after carpenter John Marshall serendipitously noticed some "bright, yet malleable" rocks while constructing a sawmill for his employer, John Sutter. (Ironically neither man profited from the gold rush triggered by Marshall's discovery.)

California governor John McDougall enthusiastically welcomed Chinese immigrants as the "most worthy of our newly-adopted citizens," and the *Pacific News* lauded them for "their industry, their quietness, cheerfulness and the cleanliness of their personalities." The *Daily Alta* predicted that "it may not be many years before the halls of Congress are graced by the presence of a long-queued Mandarin." (About 150 years, to be precise; in 1999, Oregon's First District elected David Wu, who sported a hip contemporary haircut and not the braided ponytail-like queue of his forefathers.)

Far from political podiums and newspaper editorial offices, however, resentments were already festering among white prospectors furious that they had to compete with "coolies," as the laborers were called. By 1850 tens of thousands of Chinese immigrants were not only panning for gold but tending orchards and vineyards, laying railroad tracks, working as domestic servants, and toiling in factories, jute mills, and canneries.

As their numbers surged, so did anti-Chinese hostility. Easy to identify by dress and appearance, the Chinese were despised for their willingness to perform menial jobs at low wages and were mistrusted because, instead of assimilating, they withdrew into Chinatowns—mostly to seek refuge from the very people harassing them. "As I write, news comes that in broad daylight in San Francisco, some boys have stoned an inoffensive Chinaman to death," a disgusted Mark Twain reported in *Roughing It,* "and that although a large crowd witnessed the shameful deed, no one interfered."

Other writers were less sympathetic. "The Chinese are uncivilized, unclean and filthy beyond all conception, lustful and sensual in their dispositions," *New York Tribune* publisher Horace Greeley editorialized in 1854. Legislators and judges began to codify this kind of bigotry that same year, when California's supreme court ruled that no Chinese person could testify against a white defendant because the Chinese were "a race of people whom nature has marked as inferior, and who are incapable of progress or intellectual development beyond a certain point." In 1870 the U.S. Congress passed the Naturalization Act, prohibiting the Chinese from gaining American citizenship.

Three years later the nation's economy plunged into what would turn out to be a six-year financial slump known as the Long Depression, casting millions from their jobs and exacerbating anti-immigrant prejudice. Pressured by the Knights of Labor, one of America's largest labor organizations, and other powerful unions, President Chester Arthur signed into law the Chinese Exclusion Act (which expanded restrictions put forth in the Page Act of 1875), in May 1882, representing the first time that the U.S. government officially barred a specific ethnic group from coming into this country.

Bob turns off Stage Coach Road where it intersects with Springs Drive and four-wheels it along the rocky edge of an eight-foot-deep gulch covered with reeds. He rolls down his window and points to a ridge. "Right about there is where the entrance for Mine Number Six used to be."

This would be the mine that British-born Isaiah Whitehouse walked into the morning of September 2, 1885, only to come face-to-face with two Chinese workers in his "room." Whitehouse ordered them to leave, but they insisted it was theirs. They were both right; mine superintendent Jim Evans had mistakenly assigned them the same spot.

Hearing shouts and cursing, white and Chinese miners stormed in, armed with hammers, drills, and anything else they were able to grab. By the time several foremen arrived minutes later, one Chinese worker had been struck through his skull with a pick and another had been beaten repeatedly in the head with a shovel. After the foremen broke up the fight and let the Chinese rush their wounded off to seek medical treatment, Evans implored the white miners to resume working. They refused. "Come on, boys," one exclaimed, adrenaline pumping, "we may as well finish it now, as long as we have commenced it; it has to be done anyway."

Within thirty minutes "an armed body of men . . . [came walking] down Front Street towards the hall of the Knights of Labor, shouting, while marching, 'White men fall in,'" one resident, Ralph Zwicky, later recalled during a congressional investigation into the incident. By 2:00 p.m. more than 150 men toting revolvers, shotguns, hatchets, and knives split up and headed into Chinatown. While passing the pump house for Mine #3, the first group spotted a trembling Lor Sun Kit and shot him in the back as he tried to run away. Leo Dye Bah tore off in the opposite direction—and straight into the second group, who gunned him down. Another man, Leo Kow Boot, also tried to escape but was struck by a bullet in the neck and bled to death.

"Soon the rioters came abreast of the outlying houses of Chinatown," Mr. Zwicky further testified. "What appeared at first to be the mad frolic of ignorant men was turning into an inhuman butchery of innocent beings. . . . Volley upon volley was fired after the fugitives. In a few minutes the hill east of town was literally blue with hunted Chinamen."

Chinese men and their families fled southeast to Burning Mountain and west toward Green River. Yee See Yen tried to escape across the railroad bridge but encountered an armed woman guarding the tracks. If he assumed a lady would be less likely to discharge her weapon, he guessed wrong. She shot him point-blank in the head.

Those who tried to hide in their own homes met the worst fate of all. "In the smoking cellar of one Chinese house the blackened bodies of three Chinamen were found," a September 3 newspaper reported. "Three others were in the cellar of another and four more bodies were found nearby. From the position of some of the bodies, it would seem as if they had begun to dig a hole in the cellar to hide themselves. But the fire overtook them when about halfway in the hole, burning their lower limbs to a crisp and leaving the upper trunk untouched."

By early evening, Chinatown was deserted. Most of the rioters, exhausted, went home for supper. Some returned afterward for a final looting and, once satisfied that all the valuables had been picked clean, torched whatever remained.

Huddled on windswept hillsides a mile or so away, hundreds of shivering Chinese men and women, many of them barefoot and underdressed, watched in disbelief as a red glow spread across the landscape where Chinatown once stood and then gradually flickered out, consumed by the darkness.

Twenty-five bodies were recovered, but the final number of fatalities is often cited as fifty because more than two dozen who fled into the night are believed to have died in hiding. One small family perished together; the baby and mother succumbed to dehydration and exposure, and the father, surrounded by wolves, shot himself. Whether it was twenty-five or more, the September 2, 1885, Rock Springs riot remains the single deadliest attack against any immigrant group in U.S. history.

After the riot, Wyoming Territory governor Francis Warren wired President Grover Cleveland for federal troops to quell future violence and allow the Chinese to return safely, but Cleveland, vacationing in the Adirondacks, didn't fully review the crisis until he came back to Washington almost a week later. Warren had meanwhile set out for Rock Springs himself and ordered train conductors to pick up and aid any Chinese stragglers they could find. Increasingly urgent cables from Warren finally convinced Cleveland to muster the necessary forces. Biting his political tongue, Warren thanked the president for his "prompt assistance." Approximately six hundred Chinese survivors returned to Rock Springs on September 9, protected by 250 rifle-wielding U.S. soldiers.

Sixteen men involved in the riot were charged with homicide, arson, and theft, but the trial was a farce. Jurors included men who led the mob; the local coroner, David Murray (another rioter), claimed the cause of death to be "unknown" for many who had clearly been gunned down or burned alive; the judge purportedly was himself a Knights of Labor member; no Chinese testimony was allowed; and defense witnesses lied through their teeth. The Reverend Timothy Thirloway was among the most egregious, declaring under oath that he watched the Chinese set their own homes on fire. *The Nation* magazine sarcastically commended Thirloway for his "moderation" in not blaming the Chinese for causing their own deaths, either by having murdered one another or engaged in a kind of mass spontaneous suicide.

All of the defendants were acquitted and released.

Far from inducing sympathy, the riot and subsequent acquittal only encouraged mobs in other regions. Nothing reached the level of bloodshed seen in Rock Springs, but Chinese immigrants were bashed, robbed, and hounded out of their neighborhoods, particularly in California and the Pacific Northwest.

President Cleveland tried to ignore the assaults, but Chinese ministers reminded him with composed, mafioso reasoning how regrettable it would be if they had to "withdraw [their] protection" from the thousands of Americans living in China, who'd then be forced to fend for themselves against vengeful hordes. Message received, President Cleveland issued a public condemnation of anti-Chinese violence and beseeched Congress to make financial amends to the "innocent and peaceful strangers whose maltreatment has brought discredit upon the country." Congress allotted almost $150,000 to the victims.

Standing over a narrow ravine close to where the mine used to be, I ask Bob if I can go into the gulch to take pictures.

"No problem. I can wait up here."

Leaning back to compensate for the steep, rocky incline, I carefully make my way down. Litter is everywhere. Candy wrappers. Crunched-up soda cans. A smashed television set and rusted air-conditioning unit. Tires. As I crouch down to photograph the mine entrance from a low angle, I take a small step back, hear a snap, and shoot forward, yelling, *What the hell is that?* I'm staring at a man-sized rib cage nestled in the reeds.

Bob comes over. "Probably an antelope," he says with a shrug, nonplussed.

"Scared the hell out of me," I say. "Have you seen all the trash down here?"

"People use this place as a dump."

Bob and I get back into his truck and drive over to Washington Elementary School, where Chinatown used to be. After the riot, the neighborhood was rebuilt under the watchful eye of federal troops who stayed for almost fifteen years, until they were called away to fight in the Spanish-American War. Gradually, most of the Chinese left Rock Springs, reflecting their downward population trend throughout the rest of America, too. When the 1892 Chinese Exclusion Act came up for renewal in 1902, Congress voted to make it "permanent." (An exemption was granted in 1917 to hundreds of Chinese living in Mexico who had aided General Jack Pershing during his hunt for Pancho Villa after he invaded Columbus, New Mexico.)

Time, however, plays havoc with the whole notion of enemies; after December 7, 1941, the Japanese, who had sided with us in World War I, were now reviled, and the once-hated Chinese became our close allies. Congress repealed the Chinese Exclusion Act for good in 1943.

. . .

As Bob drives me back to my car, I begin telling him about the other stories I'm covering on this part of the trip, such as the massacres at Haun's Mill and Mountain Meadows, the forced sterilizations at Sonoma, and Madison Grant's eugenics movement.

"Sounds uplifting," he says.

"Yeah, I'm kind of struggling with that," I confess. "But I actually think it's a sign of strength when a nation owns up to its past mistakes instead of hiding them. I also don't believe the darker incidents represent who we are fundamentally."

"I don't either. But you can't gloss over them," Bob says, sounding more serious than I've heard him before. "We get a lot of schoolkids coming through the museum, and I tell them that the problem is fear and intolerance. When people are afraid, they look for scapegoats, and often it's minorities or anyone considered 'different,' even if they're the least powerful part of a society."

"That does seem to be the pattern," I say.

"But we get better, and we learn."

"Did any good come out of the 1885 riot?" I ask.

"Around 1942 the federal government told Rock Springs it was planning on putting a Japanese internment camp here." Bob wasn't even alive when all this happened, but his answer conveys a sense of pride in his adopted town. "Our response was that we'd seen where this kind of discrimination can lead," he says, his mischievous grin returning. "We said no."

DOWAGIAC TRAIN STATION

Is not this crop of thieves and burglars, of shoulder-hitters and short-boys, of prostitutes and vagrants, of garroters and murderers, the very fruit to be expected from this seed so long being sown? What else was to be looked for? Society hurried on selfishly for its wealth, and left this vast class in its misery and temptation. Now these children arise, and wrest back with bloody and criminal hands what the world was too careless or too selfish to give. The worldliness of the rich, the indifference of all classes to the poor, will always be avenged. Society must act on the highest principles, or its punishment incessantly comes within itself. The neglect of the poor and tempted and criminal is fearfully repaid.

—From the Children's Aid Society's 1857 annual report, written by founder Charles Loring Brace

"AT THREE A.M. the children were taken off the train and slept here," Kay Gray tells me as we walk from the passenger platform into the quaint wood-paneled waiting room of the Dowagiac, Michigan, train depot. Although the original 1849 building was demolished in 1872, the current limestone-and-brown-brick station was erected over the same spot. "Later the next day, the children were brought to the local meetinghouse, where the Beckwith Theatre is now, for the selection process."

"Before I forget, how exactly do you pronounce the town's name?" I ask Kay, a grandmother and Dowagiac native who works at the local library.

"Doe-WA-jack," she enunciates.

"And this is where the very first orphan train arrived in 1854?"

"That's right. It all started here."

Even by today's standards, the numbers are whopping. Between 1854 and 1930, approximately two hundred thousand homeless children were loaded onto trains and hauled across the country in search of adults willing to take them in. This was not, however, an adoption service. Sponsors had to house the children only until they were a certain age, and their agreement to do so wasn't legally binding. Some adults were motivated by pity, but, for many, the children were seen as a labor force. Those physically able to work earned their room and board by performing farm and household chores, and it wasn't uncommon for them to be cast out after harvesting season was over. (And before child-labor laws were enacted in 1938, even five- and six-year-olds toiled long hours at dangerous jobs in mills, factories, and slaughterhouses.) Boys were preferred.

Several organizations conducted these "placing out" efforts, as they were called, but the largest and most influential agency was the New York Children's Aid Society (CAS), founded in 1853 by a twenty-seven-year-old Yale Divinity School graduate named Charles Loring Brace. Major eastern cities teemed with indigent children, and they were overwhelming orphanages, prisons, hospitals, and asylums. Brace spearheaded an "emigration plan" to ship the kids to mostly small rural towns in the Midwest, where fresh air and hard work, he believed, would enrich their bodies and souls. The first orphan train rolled into Dowagiac on October 1, 1854.

"Landed in Detroit at ten o'clock, Saturday night," CAS chaperone E. P. Smith wrote after the trip, "and reached [Dowagiac], a 'smart little town,' in S.W. Michigan, three o'clock Sunday morning." After spending the night at the station, the children, ages six to fifteen, were lined up at the meetinghouse and examined by potential sponsors, who could then bring their child home for the day before making a final decision. Out of forty-five children brought to Dowagiac from New York City, at least eight were unable to find anyone who wanted them. Dejected, they boarded another train and had to hope for better luck in the next town.

This routine—of shuffling kids from place to place until someone picked them—repeated itself across the country. Sponsors knew when to expect the newest batch of orphans primarily through newspaper notices and public flyers. The following advertisement, posted in Illinois, was fairly typical of these announcements:

ASYLUM CHILDREN!

A Company of Children, mostly Boys, from the New York
Juvenile Asylum, will arrive in

ROCKFORD, at the Hotel Holland,
THURSDAY MORNING, SEPT. 6, 1888,

And Remain Until Evening.
They are from 7 to 15 Years of age.

. . . Those who desire to take children on trial are requested
to meet them at the hotel at the times above specified.

Hotels, churches, opera houses, city halls, and other spacious venues hosted the initial meet and greet. Reception committees took responsibility for spreading the word and screening sponsors, but there were no real standards or criteria. An impromptu and whimsical nature ruled the whole affair. "The Darnells didn't know about it until a druggist told them," one observer recollected. "They went over and [a young boy] came up and hugged Mr. Darnell's legs. He said no at first, but came back and said he wanted the little fat boy."

Post-placement supervision was as lax as the matching process. Anecdotal evidence indicates that children were beaten and sexually abused, but determining exactly how many were victimized is impossible because CAS conducted no extensive long-term oversight or investigations. Left in a strange house hundreds of miles from home and often taunted by their peers, some children suffered from loneliness and emotional neglect. "They didn't want me to call them Mom and Dad," one young man lamented, recalling his unaffectionate guardians. Nor did they ever hug him or express any loving words to him. "Think what that does to you," he said.

Siblings were often separated, and CAS discouraged the children from communicating with blood relatives, recommending instead a clean break with the past. Many older kids quickly hightailed it out of their new homes, but whether they fled due to mistreatment or adolescent restlessness wasn't always clear. Undoubtedly some discovered that whatever romantic notions they had entertained (or been told) about pastoral life didn't prepare them for its arduous realities.

Despite a public perception that the children were orphans, a significant percentage had mothers and fathers who, although destitute, still loved them. Parents intent on finding their children encountered one obstacle after another. Agency records were shoddy and disorganized, and many children were filed under "whereabouts unknown" or had acquired new names from their present guardians. A mother hoping to reclaim her son who'd been placed far from his home in New York was brusquely told he had "no desire to return." But when the boy heard that his birth mother wanted to reunite with him, he was out the front door and Manhattan-bound.

Brace himself acknowledged that more follow-up was needed, and CAS made improvements over the years (and later revolutionized foster care in America). But logistically and financially it was impossible to check on every child. Visiting a single farm or prairie house could take days, and CAS was too short-staffed and underfunded to cover so much territory.

Catholics were among Brace's earliest and most vociferous opponents. Brace, a strict Protestant, had written crude statements about Catholicism in general, but what most angered various priests and bishops was CAS's habit of sending Catholic children to Protestant families. Levi Silliman Ives, founder of the Catholic Protectory, excoriated CAS in his organization's annual report:

> Concealment is first resorted to, a veil of secrecy is drawn over the proceedings, parental inquiries are baffled, the yearnings of the mother are stilled by tales of the wonderful advantages to her children, and promises of their speedy restoration to her arms. Yet all this while they are undergoing a secret process by which, it is hoped, that every trace of their early faith and filial attachment will be rooted out; and, finally, that their transportations to that indefinite region, "the far West," with changed names and lost parentage, will effectively destroy every association which might revive in their hearts a love for the religion of which they had been robbed.

Brace argued that, when possible, CAS tried to match Catholic children with Catholic adults, but there just weren't enough Catholic parents to meet the demand. Brace also had to contend with the prejudices of the times; like the majority of Americans, most sponsors were white and Protestant, and they wanted white, Protestant children. Ironically, a Catholic agency got into trouble when it tried to institute its own placing-out system and was accused of changing the surnames of Jewish children and sending them to live with Catholic families.

The harshest criticism leveled at Brace was that his efforts were comparable to the most heinous evil of the day—slavery. Along with the humiliating physical examinations the children had to endure publicly and the splitting apart of families, there were the often backbreaking working conditions. "If some Missionary Agent had taken that many little negroes from the plantations of Louisiana to Springfield or Jacksonville, and should have prepared to do the very thing with them that everybody knows will be done directly or indirectly with these poor children from New York," one newspaper editor raged, "our good abolitionist friends . . . would all have fainted at the horrid thought." Although Brace prohibited the practice, other placing-out programs inspired by CAS allowed children to become indentured servants, legally binding them to their sponsors for a set period.

Retracing the same route the children would have taken when they arrived in Dowagiac, Kay and I walk down West Railroad Street, hang a left at Commercial, and pass the district library where Kay works.

"What a cool little building," I say, looking at the Carnegie-funded library. It's an unusual mixture of modern and classical styles, and I've never seen anything like it. Kay isn't sure of the architectural design either but informs me that residents had a critical decision to make before construction began: Andrew Carnegie stipulated that the community had to contribute an annual appropriation for operating costs, and Dowagiac had only enough money to pay for either the library or a new hospital.

"And they chose the library," I say. "Wow, those are some hard-core book lovers."

"We did get a hospital eventually," Kay informs me.

Half a block away is the Beckwith Theatre. "The original building is gone," Kay says, "but the meetinghouse used to be here."

Spelled out on the Beckwith's marquee in black lettering is this week's show: *The Uninvited.*

No other stop on my itinerary, I tell Kay, resonates with me as personally as this one because I myself happen to be adopted. Not "plucked off the streets and shipped halfway across the country" adopted, but adopted nonetheless. Three days old at the time, I was placed by an agency into an unconditionally loving family, and I'd like to think that my experience, although wholly positive, has made me more sensitive to those whose experiences were not.

Which is why my immediate reaction to the orphan-train story was so negative. Abruptly uprooting children from the only community they've ever known, thrusting them into a series of degrading physical evaluations and potential rejections, and entrusting them to someone who's received less screening than your average bank-loan applicant seemed to me grossly irresponsible, if not criminal.

Kay reminds me to consider that "people had a different way of thinking back then," and that by all accounts Brace's motives were pure.

From everything I've read about Brace and CAS, this does seem to be true. Even his fiercest critics never accused him of corruption or selfishness. And in stark contrast to the eugenicist Madison Grant, Brace didn't believe that heredity determined one's worth as a human being. "The moral Brotherhood of man does not depend on community of descent, but on a common nature, a similar destiny, and a like relation to their common Father—God," Brace wrote in 1863, expressing a sentiment that Grant would probably have found emetic. Putting children into stable homes, Brace thought, would allow them to flourish. Every placement might have been a gamble, but Brace saw the alternative as guaranteed misery. Today it's hard to imagine thousands of children sleeping in doorways and picking through rotted trash heaps for anything edible, but this was reality in nineteenth-century American cities. Boys got drawn into criminal gangs, and young girls were forced into prostitution. There were orphanages and group homes, but many were cramped, unventilated breeding grounds of disease and abuse.

And while CAS administrators received blistering mail from grown orphan-train riders denouncing them for various transgressions, they also opened their share of appreciative letters. "I shall ever acknowledge with gratitude that the Children's Aid Society has been the instrument of my elevation," wrote a Yale University sophomore. "To be taken from the gutters of New York City and placed in a college is almost a miracle." Others sent in donations with their letters to repay the cost of their train ticket.

It's also only fair to note that foster care and adoption horror stories can be cherry-picked from today's headlines as well. Months before I left for Niihau, Hawaii, my hometown paper, the *Washington Post,* ran this grisly item: WOMAN IS CHARGED IN DEATHS OF 2 GIRLS: CHILDREN WERE FOUND IN ADOPTIVE MOTHER'S FREEZER LAST YEAR.

In 1895, Michigan became the first state to start clamping down on placing-out programs, followed by Illinois, Indiana, Kansas, Minnesota, Missouri, and Nebraska. But the children's welfare didn't seem to be the primary concern of legislators. "We cannot afford to have the state made a dumping ground for the dependent children of other states, especially New York," Kansas governor William Stanley declared, echoing the frustrations of elected officials throughout the west. Increasingly, small towns were coping with an influx of "big-city" crimes such as prostitution and murder as their populations swelled, and they had their own abandoned and needy boys and girls to care for.

Officially, placing out ended in 1929; most states had made the practice illegal and cities were offering better social services to poverty-stricken families so they wouldn't have to be separated. But a few orphans were still being put on trains as late as 1930.

The story of Alice Bullis, one of the very last riders, is emblematic of the program's contradictions. Bullis had been an orphan in New York for two years before she was transported to Kansas. "[We] were shipped like cattle," she recalled. "The adult agents who accompanied the children dressed them up and groomed them like livestock for a show. They taught them little poems and songs to present to their prospective owners." Bullis had to be removed from her first two homes because the men tried to molest her. "None of these people took me in because they wanted someone to love," she continued. "They just wanted me for work, and for whatever those old men wanted." Her luck changed when she fell in love with a high school classmate named Donald Ayler. They married when she turned twenty and eventually settled in Oklahoma City. "Everything happens for a reason," Alice Ayler said, looking back on her life. "I have been married to the same man for fifty-four years, proved that I had brains, and I have spent my life helping others. Some people are bitter about the trains, but not me. Even though there were some hard times, it probably saved my life."

PARIS-COPE SERVICE STATION

It is a heavy burden of responsibility for us to bear, since most of the victims of our bomb were only pawns. . . .

[But] there was never a way to solve the race problem which would be "fair for everybody" or which everyone concerned could be politely persuaded into accepting without any fuss or unpleasantness. . . . And the same has been true of the Jewish problem and the immigration problem and the overpopulation problem and the eugenics problem. . . .

And it is already clear that the controlled media . . . are deliberately emphasizing the suffering we have caused by interspersing gory closeups of the victims with tearful interviews with their relatives.

Interviewers are asking leading questions like, "What kind of inhuman beasts do you think could have done something like this to your daughter?" They have clearly made the decision to portray the bombing of the FBI building as the atrocity of the century.

And, indeed, it is an act of unprecedented magnitude.

—From The Turner Diaries (1978) by the white supremacist William Luther Pierce, who wrote under the pen name Andrew MacDonald

WHEN DONALD MURPHY, California's Department of Parks and Recreation director, read the complaint insisting that Madison Grant's name be stripped from the Founders Tree plaque in Humboldt Redwoods State Park, he didn't pass it off to an assistant or send back a perfunctory form letter. Instead, he personally composed a thoughtful, nuanced reply. "Is it 'historically bizarre' to commemorate Grant's undeniable efforts on behalf of conservation in light of his undeniable racism?" Murphy asked near the beginning of his lengthy response.

> Although he died in 1937 at age 72, Grant was a creature of the nineteenth century and as with many of his life contemporaries he held beliefs that most of us, hopefully, find both absurd and abhorrent today. Grant drew attention to his misguided deductions on race by setting them down on paper, but the sad truth is he probably did not think too differently than many others who've been "honored" for some historical role unrelated to the issue of race.

Murphy went on to explain why he took this so seriously:

> I don't ordinarily wear my ethnicity on my sleeve, so to speak, but in responding to your concerns I feel compelled to note that as an African American I think I have a personal perspective on the pain and suffering, the hurt and disappointment of racism....
>
> I say that only to let you know that I do not take lightly your request for removal of the plaque and that I can quite understand and appreciate the reasoning behind your request. I would hope you will understand too my decision to not have the plaque removed. Harmony among people comes from the true principles and attitudes of the present, not from purging the past.

I've been carrying Murphy's letter with me during this entire leg of my journey, which started in Northern California and ends here in Oklahoma City, and I've read it numerous times now. Whether or not the plaque should be removed is a tough call. Murphy is absolutely correct that Madison Grant wasn't alone in his views. President Teddy Roosevelt, birth control activist (and Planned Parenthood founder) Margaret Sanger, John Kellogg of breakfast-cereal fame, and Alexander Graham Bell, a lifelong advocate for deaf individuals who nevertheless believed they shouldn't marry lest they reproduce hearing-impaired offspring, were just a handful of illustrious Americans who endorsed some variation of selective breeding. But none of them, it's worth noting, collaborated with the Nazis or promoted eugenics as zealously as Grant. This might be a difference of degree rather than kind, but it's a difference nonetheless.

Ultimately, I side with Murphy on not removing the plaque. It's relatively small and unobtrusive and mostly states a historical fact—that Grant and two other men (also eugenics supporters) founded the Redwoods park—and doesn't exalt them as all-around super-great guys. In an ideal world there'd be a marker here that addresses the more appalling aspects of Grant's past. Although that, admittedly, might be a bit of a buzzkill in such an otherwise uplifting environment.

This whole issue also raises the question of what causes one generation of Americans to wrap its arms around noxious ideologies, while their descendants cast them off as repugnant. Social progress rarely moves forward with swift and deliberate speed but tends, it seems, to advance in fits and starts. Ideally, minds are changed when voices of conscience challenge the nation to live up to its fundamental principles. While it's true that eugenics enjoyed widespread approval in the early 1900s, its acceptance was by no means universal.

A small but growing community of prominent journalists, scientists, elected officials, academics, judges, lawyers, and other impassioned souls, along with the Catholic Church, all advocated the abolishment of forced sterilizations and other forms of negative eugenics. In the mid-1930s they found an unlikely ally in a poor, one-footed former chicken thief named Jack T. Skinner.

On July 31, 1934, the frail, five-foot-six-inch Skinner limped up to the Paris-Cope Service Station at 735 North Harvey in Oklahoma City and robbed the attendant of $17 at gunpoint. Caught and tried, Skinner was sentenced to ten years at McAlester Prison. While he was behind bars, Oklahoma passed a law compelling "habitual" criminals—anyone with three convictions or more—to be sterilized, and the state picked Skinner to undergo a mandatory vasectomy because he'd committed two other crimes. The first was a misdemeanor for stealing chickens (although not commendable, this wasn't exactly unheard-of during the Great Depression), and specifics about the second offense aren't known, but apparently it wasn't serious enough to warrant much prison time.

Skinner fought the punishment in court, paying his counseling fees with money pooled by fellow inmates. Pure selflessness was not, it's safe to assume, their prime motivation; they knew that if Skinner lost, they'd be next.

After the Oklahoma Supreme Court upheld the law, Skinner's attorney, Claud Briggs, doubted that the U.S. Supreme Court would even consider the case, let alone rule in Skinner's favor. Two new lawyers, Guy Andrews and H. I. Aston, joined the defense team and were more optimistic. Aston rushed to Washington and submitted an appeal on the very day of the Court's deadline, October 8, 1941. Although by this time Skinner had already been released from McAlester for good behavior, Oklahoma's assistant attorney general, Owen Watts, stated that, free or not, Skinner was still eligible for the chopping block, so to speak. On January 12, 1942, the Court agreed to hear *Skinner v. Oklahoma*.

Several legal principles were at issue, including cruel and unusual punishment, double jeopardy (that is, being penalized twice for the same crime), and the ex post facto nature of Oklahoma's law, in that it was passed after Skinner had been convicted for the third time. But the Court justices zeroed in on an argument first emphasized by the McAlester inmates themselves: Why should chicken thieves be sterilized and not embezzlers, who were exempt from the law?

When Justice Felix Frankfurter posed this exact question to Oklahoma's attorney general, Mac Williamson, during the May 6, 1942, oral arguments, Williamson replied, "There are elements of violence in stealing chickens."

"Not if done surreptitiously," interjected Chief Justice Harlan Stone, who fifteen years earlier had sided with the majority in *Buck v. Bell*, the infamous ruling that forced Carrie Buck and her young daughter to be sterilized. Williamson had no real answer to Stone's remark.

Skinner prevailed 9–0.

What most undermined Oklahoma's sterilization law, Justice William Douglas wrote in the Court's June 1, 1942, decision, was "its failure to meet the requirements of the equal protection clause of the Fourteenth Amendment," and he specifically delved into the chicken-stealing/embezzling comparison. On this the Court was in general agreement. But Douglas thought it necessary to add the following:

> We are dealing here with legislation which involves one of the most basic civil rights of man. Marriage and procreation are fundamental to the very existence and survival of the race. The power to sterilize, if exercised, may have subtle, far-reaching and devastating effects. In evil or reckless hands, it can cause races or types which are inimical to the dominant group to wither and disappear.

Across the Atlantic, those evil and reckless hands were already hard at work. In the summer of 1942, the Nazis had constructed fewer than one hundred concentration, labor, and extermination camps. Within two years, there were thousands of them.

Oklahoma v. Skinner did not officially reverse *Buck v. Bell*—which has yet to be overturned—or halt sterilizations in the United States, only "punitive" ones. But it represented the first major legal ruling against eugenics and lent enormous moral authority to its opponents. Along with the Court's warning on how such practices could lead to wholesale genocide (the irrefutable proof of which was revealed to the world after Soviet troops liberated Auschwitz on January 27, 1945), it also fortified the Fourteenth Amendment's "equal protection" clause and prompted certain legislation to be more "strictly scrutinized" to ensure that minority rights were being protected. As obvious as this sounds today, it was frighteningly less so generations ago.

Any number of locations could have served as a springboard to tell Skinner's story: his birthplace in Shawnee, Oklahoma; McAlester Prison; the county or state courthouses that first tried his case; or his grave in Tulare County, California, where he died at the age of seventy-seven, survived by six grandchildren and ten great-grandchildren. For me, the site of Skinner's botched holdup, which precipitated the constitutional legal fight, seemed a more offbeat and memorable choice and no less appropriate than the others. When I arrived at 735 North Harvey, where the Paris-Cope Service Station had been in 1934, it became all the more relevant.

Today, the site is a parking lot connected to a modern office building. Only three stories tall, the squat cement structure exudes a fortresslike impenetrability. The windows are thick and tinted green. Bulletproof. Brown metal poles topped with security cameras line the street. In front of the sleek all-glass entrance is a steel sign that reads GENERAL SERVICES ADMINISTRATION. But I know what this building is and why it's here. Whatever its official name might be now, it is, for all intents and purposes, the new Alfred P. Murrah Federal Building.

The old Murrah Building had, of course, stood across the street until the morning of April 19, 1995. At 9:02 A.M. a Ryder van packed with almost five thousand pounds of a diesel fuel and ammonium nitrate fertilizer mix exploded outside the nine-story building, killing 149 adults and 19 children. More than 320 buildings within a sixteen-block radius were damaged, and the blast could be heard in Stillwater, Oklahoma, some fifty-three miles away.

Coming two years after the 1993 World Trade Center bombing,

which was orchestrated and funded by Khalid Sheikh Mohammed (Osama bin Laden's partner in crime), the attack was initially blamed on Islamic extremists. But FBI agents traced the Ryder's identification number from a mangled axle back to a twenty-seven-year-old American named Timothy McVeigh, and the manhunt for McVeigh was on.

Incredibly, he was already in custody—for what began as a minor traffic violation. At around 10:30 A.M., a state trooper had pulled McVeigh over for driving without a rear license plate and ended up arresting him for possessing an unregistered gun. McVeigh was being booked when the Wanted bulletin came over the wires, and Oklahoma police, stunned that he was right in front of them, contacted the FBI.

During an inspection of McVeigh's car, detectives found, among a trove of incriminating evidence, photocopied pages from William Luther Pierce's *The Turner Diaries*. Published in 1978, the novel glorifies overthrowing the U.S. government and inciting a race war by, first, blowing up federal buildings. Pierce's description of an attack on the FBI's Washington headquarters is uncannily similar to what happened at the Murrah Building, where the FBI had regional offices. Just as Madison Grant's *The Passing of the Great Race* was a "bible" to Hitler, *The Turner Diaries* is practically a sacred text to neo-Nazis and has been linked to numerous killings. McVeigh, who sold the book at gun shows, cited it as an inspiration.

Whether or not Pierce ever read Grant isn't known, though I'd be surprised if he hadn't; *The Passing of the Great Race* is a classic among white supremacists. Regardless, the two men were kindred spirits who hated all the same people—blacks, Jews, immigrants, and most other minorities. Were he alive today, I'm sure Grant would be a dues-paying member of the National Alliance, the neo-Nazi organization Pierce founded in 1974.

While the impulse to excise men such as Pierce and Grant from our national autobiography with a hearty "Good riddance" is understandable, there's a risk in doing so. Sanitizing history prevents us from seeing the warning signs of another Haun's Mill, Mountain Meadows, or

Rock Springs. These incidents occurred so long ago they're almost un-real now, and the idea that similar massacres and riots could take place in our own time seems impossible. Such atrocities always do—right up until the moment they happen again.

The Oklahoma City National Memorial, directly across the street from the new Murrah Building, is a powerful reminder of this. Book-ending a one-hundred-yard-long shallow pool are two massive bronze walls, each about four stories tall, called the Gates of Time. Etched into one is 9:01 and the other 9:03. Between them, where the Murrah Building used to be, is a vast, empty space that forces the mind to re-flect on what happened at 9:02. I begin walking the length of the pool to look at both gates up close.

Most affecting, I think, are the memorial's 168 chairs, arranged by where the victims were sitting when the truck exploded. Nineteen of them, for the children, are smaller than the rest.

I absentmindedly step off the paved walkway and onto the grass, where the chairs are situated.

"Oh, sorry," I say to one of the park rangers, a guy in his twenties standing nearby. "Is it okay to walk on here?"

"You're fine."

While looking at the chairs more closely, I spot a discrepancy. "Why does that one have two names on it?" I ask the ranger.

The answer comes to me before he responds, but his reply is still a punch to the gut.

"There are three chairs like that," he tells me, "for the women who were pregnant. The second names are for the babies."

Unable to say anything, I just keep staring at the chairs.

"A lot of folks," he continues, "walk right past them without even noticing, but when they do, it's something I doubt they'll forget. It's the little things we almost miss that hit the hardest, you know?"

I do.

PART IV

LANDMARK CASES

Crimes and Lawsuits That
Changed the Nation

SLIP HILL GRADE SCHOOL

I'm in the Jehovah's Witness protection program. I have to go around knocking on people's doors and telling them I'm somebody else.

—*Steven Wright*

My Avon lady just became a Jehovah's Witness. That may not mean much to you, but it saves me one more trip to the door.

—*George Carlin*

What does Hannibal Lecter call a Jehovah's Witness? Free delivery!

—*Jay Leno*

UNLIKE JACK SKINNER, Marie Barnett was not a hard-core convicted felon looking to break the law for personal gain but an innocent soul caught up in a legal battle that also made its way to the U.S. Supreme Court. Actually, I didn't know all of this for certain before calling Marie at her home in West Virginia, but I figured it was a safe bet that she didn't have a criminal record when the Court took her case in 1943.

"How old were you at the time you got into trouble?" I asked Marie.

"I was nine."

"And you and your sister Gathie were in the fifth grade?"

"Fourth."

"Fourth grade, at Slip Hill Grade School?"

"That's correct."

On January 9, 1942, the West Virginia Board of Education, like many other public school boards across the United States, had made it mandatory for students to salute the American flag and recite the Pledge of Allegiance.

Marie and her sister refused.

"It wasn't that we weren't patriotic," Marie tells me. "Our faith teaches us to pledge allegiance only to God."

They, like other Jehovah's Witnesses, adhere to a literal reading of the Bible's commandment in Exodus 20:3–5 that states:

Thou shalt have no other gods before me.

Thou shalt not make unto thee any graven image, or any likeness of any thing that is in heaven above, or that is in the earth beneath, or that is in the water under the earth:

Thou shalt not bow down thyself to them, nor serve them.

"You and your sister weren't arrested, though, right?"

"No, but our father was—because we weren't in school, even though it was the principal who kept sending us home. He wasn't very nice about it."

Discrimination against Jehovah's Witnesses (who, before 1931, were called Bible Students) dates back to the late 1800s, when their founder, a charismatic Pittsburgh haberdasher named Charles Taze Russell, preached that Armageddon was imminent and that Christ had already returned to earth "invisibly" in 1874 but would be back for real about four decades later. Russell also claimed that, due to divinely inspired climate change, global temperatures would rise and the world would revert to a balmy, Genesis-like state. Russell's followers endured no end of insults, and this was before his successors encouraged door-to-door proselytizing, for which the Jehovah's Witnesses are perhaps best known and most ridiculed.

Beginning in the summer of 1940, mockery turned to bloodshed when physical assaults against Witnesses surged nationwide. Triggering the violence was the June 3, 1940, Supreme Court ruling against Walter Gobitas, a Jehovah's Witness from Minersville, Pennsylvania, who had told his children, Lillian and Billy, not to salute the flag or say the Pledge of Allegiance at school. They didn't, and they were expelled.

Both a district judge and a U.S. Court of Appeals sided with Gobitas, but the school board continued fighting until the cases landed before the nine justices of the Supreme Court. When they handed down their decision in *Minersville School District v. Gobitis* (a lower court misspelled Gobitas, and the error stuck), the final tally wasn't even close; 8–1 against Gobitas, with only Justice Harlan Stone dissenting. Justice Felix Frankfurter wrote the majority opinion. "National unity is the basis of national security," he argued.

> The ultimate foundation of a free society is the binding tie of cohesive sentiment. Such a sentiment is fostered by all those agencies of the mind and spirit which may serve to gather up the traditions of a people, transmit them from generation to generation, and thereby create that continuity of a treasured common life which constitutes a civilization. "We live by symbols." The flag is the symbol of our national unity, transcending

all internal differences, however large, within the framework of
the Constitution.

Almost overnight, Jehovah's Witnesses came under attack, vilified
by their assailants as un-American. "In June a mob of Legionnaires
dragged some of Jehovah's Witnesses from their automobiles as they
were sitting in the Court House Square at Jasper and beat them up,"
John Adams of Beaumont, Texas, recalled in a sworn affidavit. "When
some bystanders attempted to come to the rescue of these people," he
went on, "they likewise were beaten—two of them being a frail woman
and her daughter. When the woman and her daughter appealed to the
Sheriff and Deputy and Town Marshall of Jasper for protection, they
merely stood by and chuckled while the mob continued their 'dirty
work.'"

Hundreds of similar accounts were recorded throughout the country. Along with being punched, kicked, and shot at, Witnesses were
jailed without cause, fired from their jobs, and run out of their homes.
And this was all a year and a half before America declared war on Germany and Japan. Marie and Gathie Barnett declined to say the Pledge
barely a month after Pearl Harbor was bombed.

Thanks to Debra Basham and Midge Justice, who work for the State
of West Virginia and tracked down the 1942 records, I had Slip Hill
Grade School's original address at 2389 Hampshire Drive in Charles-
town. But street names have changed and the school was closed long
ago, so I needed to get specific directions from Marie.

"Is that far from where you live now?" I asked her during our first
conversation.

"Only a few miles away."

"Do you ever go back, like, for nostalgic reasons?"

"No," Marie replied without elaborating.

I invited her to come along with me, but Marie politely declined,
telling me she had to tend to her husband, who was recuperating from
an operation.

Marie's directions are clear enough, and I drive up to what I believe to be 2389 Hampshire. But apparently it's been so long since Marie has passed by here that even she didn't know Slip Hill has been razed, and there's nothing left but a gravel parking lot. I walk up to an AFL-CIO hall that sits close to where the school should be and ask a young woman inside if I have the right address.

"That's where the building used to be," she says, "before they tore it down. People thought it was an eyesore."

I'm tempted to remark that the empty space there now isn't exactly a thing of beauty, but I know it's not her fault that the school was leveled.

Marie couldn't recall in detail what happened the first day she and Gathie refused to say the Pledge, except that her teacher was quietly supportive but the principal would have none of it. For almost a month Marie and her sister walked a quarter of a mile to school each day, only to be turned away when they confirmed that, no, they hadn't changed their minds. "We were perfectly willing to stand there respectfully while the other students recited the Pledge, which we had done before," Marie said, "but the principal ordered us home every time."

Stare decisis, from the Latin *dictum stare decisis et quieta non movere* (meaning "to stand by and adhere to decisions and not disturb what is settled"), is Supreme Court gospel. Constantly overturning precedents is unwise, the reasoning goes, because it leads to judicial mayhem, and justices are especially averse to rehashing recently decided cases. But in light of the violent aftermath of *Gobitis,* the Court believed a second look was in order, and *West Virginia State Board of Education v. Barnette* was their opportunity for another chance at bat. (The extra *e* in Barnette was a mistake; as with the Gobitas family, the lower courts botched the name. I asked Marie if she thought the misspellings were an intentional slight. "No," she said. "I have relatives who write Barnett with an *e* at the end.")

Oral arguments were conducted on March 11, 1943, with Hayden Covington defending the Barnetts and two other families listed on the docket, McClure and Stull. Covington had served as lead counsel for several dozen major rulings involving Jehovah's Witnesses, many of which had broad implications that expanded freedom of speech, worship, and assembly rights to all Americans.

The *Barnette* decision came down three months later. Justices Stanley Reed and Owen Roberts saw no reason to overturn *Gobitis,* nor did they think it necessary to articulate why. Neither man contributed a written opinion.

Justices Hugo Black and William Douglas had also been in the majority for *Gobitis* but reversed themselves in *Barnette.* "Words uttered under coercion are proof of loyalty to nothing but self-interest," they wrote in a joint opinion. "Love of country must spring from willing hearts and free minds, inspired by a fair administration of wise laws enacted by the people's elected representatives within the bounds of express constitutional prohibitions."

Justice Robert Jackson, who had joined the Court only two years before, believed that *Gobitis* should be overturned, and he tackled Justice Frankfurter's "national unity is the basis of national security" argument head-on.

"National unity as an end which officials may foster by persuasion and example is not in question," Jackson wrote. "The problem is whether under our Constitution compulsion as here employed is a permissible means for its achievement." He then expounded on the slippery slope to which this coercion could lead:

> Nationalism is a relatively recent phenomenon but at other times and places the ends have been racial or territorial security, support of a dynasty or regime, and particular plans for saving souls. As first and moderate methods to attain unity have failed, those bent on its accomplishment must resort to an ever-increasing severity. . . .
>
> Ultimate futility of such attempts to compel coherence is the lesson of every such effort from the Roman drive to stamp out Christianity as a disturber of its pagan unity, the Inquisition, as a means to religious and dynastic unity, the Siberian

exiles as a means to Russian unity, down to the fast failing efforts of our present totalitarian enemies. Those who begin coer-
cive elimination of dissent soon find themselves exterminating
dissenters. Compulsory unification of opinion achieves only the
unanimity of the graveyard.

Notoriously combative, Frankfurter dug in his heels, defended
Gobitis, and responded with the longest and most impassioned of the
Barnette opinions. Perhaps stung by criticism after *Gobitis* that, as a
Jew, he should be more sympathetic to minority faiths, Frankfurter
began on a rare—for any justice—personal note:

> One who belongs to the most vilified and persecuted minority
> in history is not likely to be insensible to the freedoms guaran-
> teed by our Constitution. Were my purely personal attitude rele-
> vant, I should wholeheartedly associate myself with the general
> libertarian views in the Court's opinion, representing, as they
> do, the thought and action of a lifetime. But, as judges, we are
> neither Jew nor Gentile, neither Catholic nor agnostic. We owe
> equal attachment to the Constitution.

Frankfurter went on to stress his firm belief in judicial self-restraint,
that the Supreme Court should not behave like "a super-legislature"
subverting elected officials and the people's will. "Before a duly enacted
law can be judicially nullified," he wrote, "it must be forbidden by
some explicit restriction upon political authority in the Constitution."
Requiring students to affirm their allegiance to America did not, he
believed, run counter to any such restriction.

Ultimately Frankfurter's arguments lost out, and with newcomer
Wiley Rutledge joining the majority, *Gobitis* was overturned 6–3. By
sheer coincidence, the decision was announced on June 14—Flag Day.

. . .

After visiting Slip Hill, I phone Marie to ask her what happened when she heard the news.

"Where were you when you found out that you'd won the case?"

"Our lawyers called my dad, and he told us. We never went to the Supreme Court ourselves. I'm not sure at that age I even knew much about it. We hadn't gotten to that part of our schooling then."

"What's it like knowing you're part of a historic ruling like that?"

"I'm proud we stood up for our rights. I hope it paved the way for others, so they wouldn't have to go through what we did."

The two Barnett sisters went back to school, where they were top students. Marie eventually worked for an insurance company while also raising four children. She now has seven grandchildren and thirteen great-grandchildren.

"In retrospect would you do it all again?"

"Absolutely," she says.

I don't know if she'll take this as bad news or not, but I tell her the school isn't there anymore. "I did, however, find some small pieces of red bricks scattered about and picked up a few as keepsakes. I'd be happy to send you some, if you're interested." Since my earlier mention of the building didn't elicit positive memories, I expect Marie to say no.

"That would be nice. Thank you."

Of course, I'm the one indebted to Marie for sharing her memories, which shed light on a Supreme Court ruling I knew almost nothing about and, indirectly, introduced me to the surprising evolution of the Pledge of Allegiance itself.

The original 1892 version was first published in a wildly popular magazine called *The Youth's Companion,* and it made no mention of God; Francis Bellamy, the socialist minister who authored it, initially wrote: "I pledge allegiance to my Flag and the Republic for which it stands: one Nation indivisible, with Liberty and Justice for all." And while Bellamy was by all accounts a patriotic man, creating a "Pledge of Allegiance" was the brainstorm of *The Youth's Companion's* promotional wizard, James Upham.

Several weeks later, Bellamy added a "to" before "the Republic" because he thought it sounded better. In 1923 "my Flag" was altered to "the flag of the United States" and "of America" was tacked on a year later.

In 1942 a major change was made to the gesture that accompanied the Pledge. Traditionally, after students recited the words, they stretched their right arm straight out and at a raised angle, giving what was known as "the Bellamy salute." Small problem: This looked awfully Nazi-ish, so students were encouraged to place their hands over their heart instead.

"Under God" was included by an act of Congress in 1954. President Dwight D. Eisenhower enthusiastically signed the bill and proclaimed that the new addition would "strengthen those spiritual weapons which forever will be our country's most powerful resource, in peace or in war." Ike's words were a verbal volley aimed directly at the Soviet Union and "godless communists" everywhere.

Francis Bellamy had considered including "equality" along with "liberty and justice for all" in the original Pledge, but decided that in an era—the late nineteenth century—when segregation and other forms of racial discrimination were legal, the United States wasn't ready for something so radical.

Almost two generations later, during World War II, millions of minority troops were risking their lives overseas fighting for freedoms denied to them back home, prompting both black and white Americans to ask with growing impatience when their country *would* be ready to embrace equal rights. And some, like the woman whose spontaneous act of defiance against segregation would bring me to an old jailhouse in the South, were refusing to wait any longer.

SALUDA COUNTY JAIL

People always say that I didn't give up my seat because I was tired, but that isn't true. I was not tired physically, or no more tired than I usually was at the end of a working day. I was not old, although some people have an image of me as being old then. I was forty-two. No, the only tired I was, was tired of giving in.

—From My Story (1992) by Rosa Parks

AN AFRICAN AMERICAN woman riding on a bus is told to relinquish her seat for a white passenger. She says no. The driver warns her that if she doesn't move, she'll be arrested. The woman stays put, and the driver summons local police, who throw her in jail. Her case sparks a lawsuit that eventually helps bring an end to de jure discrimination on buses across the country and galvanizes early civil rights advocates. To the general public, however, she remains virtually unknown.

Her name was Irene Morgan, and on July 16, 1944, she boarded a Maryland-bound Greyhound Bus in Gloucester, Virginia. Twenty-seven years old, Morgan had suffered a miscarriage a few days earlier and scheduled an appointment with her family doctor back in Balti-more, where she had been raised. Morgan sat four rows from the rear in the "Colored" section and was minding her own business when the bus stopped just outside of Saluda, Virginia, to pick up a white couple. No empty seats were available, so the driver ordered Morgan onto her feet. Feeling ill and not wanting to stand the remainder of the trip, she wouldn't budge. "This is my seat," Morgan said. "Why should I?"

Upon entering Saluda, the driver pulled over and called the sheriff. An officer came onto the bus and issued Morgan a warrant, which she ripped up and tossed out the window. At that point a deputy grabbed her, causing Morgan to kick him, she later recounted, "in a very bad place." Then, she said: "He hobbled off, and another one came on. He was trying to put his hands on me to get me off. I was going to bite him, but he was dirty, so I clawed him instead. I ripped his shirt. We were both pulling at each other. He said he'd use his nightstick. I said, 'We'll whip each other.'"

Forcibly dragged out of the bus and onto the street, Morgan was locked up in Saluda's jail. All of this occurred eleven years before Rosa Parks famously refused to surrender her seat on a bus in Montgomery, Alabama.

"You're at the new county jail," a uniformed guard tells me after I briefly explain Morgan's story and the purpose of my visit. "You want the old jail."

"Is that a far drive from here?" I ask.

"This is Saluda; it's not even a far walk. Go left out of the park-ing lot, up the hill one block, and it's the building behind the old courthouse."

"So you're familiar with Irene Morgan and her arrest?"

"No, but back then the old jail is where she would've gone."

The square, two-story red-brick building is, I find, on the corner of

Bowden and Oakes Landing. According to a sign by the front door, it's now the Virginia Cooperative Extension for Middlesex County. Small and quaint, the structure itself suggests nothing of its former role.

After being incarcerated here, Morgan pled guilty to resisting arrest and paid a $100 fine. But on principle she would not pay the $10 for violating the state's segregation law.

Her attorney, Spottswood Robinson III, knew that Virginia wasn't about to overturn its race-based statutes and chose not to argue the case on moral grounds. Instead, he claimed that the law hindered interstate commerce because it placed an undue burden on bus companies by requiring them to constantly shift their passengers around depending on the region. Had Morgan's bus been in Washington, D.C., when the white passengers boarded, she wouldn't have been forced to move.

Unconvinced, the Middlesex Circuit Court ruled against Morgan, as did the Virginia Supreme Court.

With two new lawyers, William Hastie and Thurgood Marshall, now leading the fight, Morgan took her battle to the U.S. Supreme Court. Seven years earlier, President Franklin D. Roosevelt had appointed Hastie to the U.S. District Court for the Virgin Islands, making him the first African American federal judge. He served on the bench for two years and then became the dean of Howard University's School of Law, where he had been a professor. One of his students, in fact, was Thurgood Marshall. (President John F. Kennedy intended to make Hastie the first African American justice on the Supreme Court, but after Kennedy was assassinated, President Lyndon Johnson nominated Marshall instead.) Marshall was the NAACP's chief counsel, and in *Irene Morgan v. Commonwealth of Virginia*, he and Hastie built on Spottswood Robinson's original legal strategy, focusing less on the fundamental injustice of Virginia's discriminatory laws and more on the U.S. Constitution's commerce clause.

It worked. On June 3, 1946, the Court voted in favor of Morgan 6–1. (With Chief Justice Harlan Stone's recent death there were only eight justices, and Robert Jackson abstained because he was in Germany presiding over the Nuremberg trials.)

"The interferences to interstate commerce which arise from state regulation of racial association on interstate vehicles has long been recognized," Justice Stanley Reed wrote in the majority opinion.

> Such regulation hampers freedom of choice in selecting accommodations. The recent changes in transportation brought about by the coming of automobiles does not seem of great significance in the problem. People of all races travel today more extensively than in 1878, when this Court first passed upon state regulation of racial segregation in commerce.
>
> . . . It seems clear to us that seating arrangements for the different races in interstate motor travel require a single uniform rule to promote and protect national travel.

Justice Harold Burton, the lone dissenter, argued that if the Court imposed uniformity here, other segregation laws could be overturned as well. "On the precedent of this case," he wrote in his opinion, "the laws of the 10 states requiring racial separation apparently can be invalidated because of their sharp diversity from the laws in the rest of the Union."

Fortunately, he was correct; after Irene Morgan's case, a series of similar rulings followed that helped to systematically dismantle Jim Crow laws nationwide. In 1956 the Supreme Court upheld *Browder v. Gayle,* a case similar to *Morgan* that was sparked by the incarceration of Claudette Colvin, who, on March 2, 1955, wouldn't give up her seat on a city transit bus in Montgomery, Alabama. Colvin's act of civil disobedience preceded Rosa Parks's by nine months, and the local NAACP chapter was looking for just this type of incident, along with a sympathetic victim, to spark a bus boycott throughout Montgomery. A smart fifteen-year-old student on her way home from school, Colvin seemed perfect at first. And she might well have been lionized as a civil rights pioneer and achieved Rosa Parks's iconic status had it not turned out that the teenage girl was pregnant, and the father was a married man. Leaders within the African American community felt these revelations would undermine the greater cause, so they waited for another arrest. On December 1, 1955, police handcuffed the quiet, church-going seamstress Rosa Parks, and the historic boycott began two days later. It continued until December 1956, when *Browder v. Gayle* desegregated all Alabama city buses.

Stirred by Irene Morgan's courage and the outcome of her Supreme Court decision, sixteen young men (eight of them white, eight black) rode a bus together through Virginia and North Carolina in what they called a Journey of Reconciliation. This, in turn, inspired the Freedom Riders, a much larger group of whites and blacks who traveled on Greyhound and Trailways buses across the South during the summer of 1961. Their actions—along with nonviolent protests, sit-ins, and marches—shone a glaring spotlight on the racism that permeated much of the country and culminated in the sweeping Civil Rights Act of 1964.

While walking back to the parking lot near the new jail, I pass Saluda's sheriff's department and notice three officers leaning up against their squad cars, chatting casually. I jog over and, after giving them the thirty-second version of Irene Morgan's case, ask if her name sounds at all familiar.

They shake their heads, a collective nope.

"Kind of a Rosa Parks thing," one remarks.

"The stories are almost identical," I say. "But Morgan fought back and ended up kicking one of the deputies in the groin."

They all flinch.

"Ooh, not a good idea," one says, chuckling.

"Anyway, sorry for interrupting. I'm just trying to get a sense of how well known Irene Morgan is around here."

Morgan, who died in August 2007, would have been the first to acknowledge that, like Rosa Parks, she too had her predecessors. On

July 16, 1854, exactly ninety years to the day before Morgan landed in the Saluda jail, schoolteacher Elizabeth Jennings was roughed up on her way to church by a Manhattan carriage driver who wouldn't let her board his horse-drawn bus. Back then, African Americans were prohibited from riding in certain trolleys and buses entirely. Represented by twenty-four-year-old (and future U.S. president) Chester A. Arthur, Jennings forced the Third Avenue Railway Company to change its policy. "Colored persons if sober, well behaved and free from disease," Judge William Rockwell reasoned, "had the same rights as others and could neither be excluded by any rules of the Company, nor by force or violence." The case, however, had no bearing outside of New York.

And a mere ten days before Morgan's fateful stop in Saluda, twenty-five-year-old Lieutenant Jack Roosevelt "Jackie" Robinson was accosted by a driver for not moving from his seat on an Army bus—despite the recent integration of all military transportation. Robinson's furious reaction almost earned him a court-martial, but he was spared because he was already a star athlete (and this was three years before he broke professional baseball's color barrier in 1947). The fact that a world war was raging in July 1944 is another reason why Irene Morgan's run-in with the law didn't elicit the same attention as Rosa Parks's arrest did a decade later. The D-Day landings were barely a month old, and Americans were understandably preoccupied with frequent news updates about Allied troops thrashing their way across Europe. (And, not to belabor the point, Parks might have been regarded very differently if she had slammed her knee into a deputy sheriff's groin.)

After her husband passed away in 1948, Morgan left Virginia for Queens, New York, where she operated a child care business. At the age of sixty-eight she attended St. John's University to acquire her bachelor of arts degree, and five years later she earned a master's degree from Queens College. Morgan moved back to Virginia in 2002 and passed away at the age of ninety.

From her obituary and the few local newspaper articles written about Irene Morgan, what emerges is a portrait of a devout, humble individual who downplayed her actions and felt uncomfortable accepting accolades she believed were undeserved. When Howard University wanted to grant her an honorary doctorate for winning one of the first major national victories in the battle for civil rights, Morgan expressed enormous gratitude for the offer. But, having worked hard to receive her other degrees, she politely declined, explaining to university officials: "I didn't earn it."

JAMES JOHNSON'S LANDING SPOT (VIA THE DESERET CHEMICAL DEPOT)

WE HAVE A GRENADE, THE PIN HAS BEEN PULLED. WE HAVE PISTOLS, THEY'RE LOADED. WE HAVE C-4 PLASTIC EXPLOSIVES. IT'S A LONG WAY TO THE GROUND.

WE ARE TAKING THIS PLANE TO SAN FRANCISCO, NOT LOS ANGELES! SECURE PERMISSION TO LAND ON RUNWAY 19, AT EXACTLY 4:30 P.M. . . . WE WANT $500,000 IN CASH—DIFFERENT DENOMINATIONS. FOUR COMMANDER PARACHUTES WITH STOPWATCH AND WRIST ALTIMETER. . . . DON'T TELL THE PASSENGERS WHAT'S GOING ON.

—*From a hijacking note written on April 7, 1972, to the captain of United Flight 855 by a passenger listed as James Johnson*

DRIVING DOWN ROUTE 36 near Stockton, Utah, on my way to the Dugway Proving Ground, I notice a sign for the Deseret Chemical Depot and impulsively turn in to the unpaved entrance. At both Deseret and Dugway, the U.S. military conducted medical experiments on human subjects, and the testing at Dugway led to a lawsuit by one of the victims. I'd heard about the Deseret Chemical Depot while investigating Dugway and had assumed it was in the town of Deseret, some hundred miles south of here, so this is a pleasant and convenient surprise. Barely visible in the shallow valley about two miles below are rows of white rectangular buildings that, from here, look no bigger than grains of rice. I decide to linger at this overlook and shoot a few pictures of the old Army facility for my personal photo journal. Dugway is still active, but I remember reading that Deseret was closed years ago.

It was not.

After clicking off seven photographs of the main sign, I hear tires crunching on gravel and turn around just as a white sedan pulls up behind me. For a split second I think it might be a lost tourist in need of directions or another weekend history sleuth interested in obscure sites. Sun glare on the windshield prevents me from seeing a face, but through the side window I glimpse the driver's left arm. Desert cammies. Military police.

My heart starts pounding. I cap my camera and hesitantly walk over. The soldier is already on his cell phone reading off my license plate number.

"Hi," I say meekly after he hangs up. "I'm just taking some pictures of the sign. Is that okay?"

He rolls down his window and asks me why.

"I'm researching little-known history sites across America, and I just came across this abandoned Army post."

"It's not abandoned."

"I swear I didn't know that," I say. "I had read somewhere that it was closed." I show him the display screen of my digital camera. "Here are the photos I took so far, just seven of them, and I only shot the entrance, none of the buildings below. I can delete these right in front of you."

"I'm not sure you need to do that."

Relief. "Okay, well, I didn't mean to cause any trouble, and obviously I won't take any more pictures."

I am heading back to my car when he calls out, "Hey, I didn't say you could go. You gotta wait till my boss gets here."

Full-blown panic.

Several scenarios flash to mind. In the worst case, I'll be arrested. Or they might confiscate my camera, which would also be very bad because along with the depot there are pictures of other sites I haven't had time to back up on my computer. I can't surreptitiously switch the flash card with a blank one because the MP knows there are photos on here.

A white SUV comes up from the depot. And then two more, the first of which angles itself to block me in.

"What's up, buddy?" a soldier in his mid-thirties asks. Of the seven or eight other troops now on the scene, most stay in their vehicles, but two get out and keep an eye on me. I've never been good at determining enlisted ranks from uniforms, but I think the soldier questioning me is a staff sergeant. They all appear to be with the Utah National Guard.

I emphasize that I truly thought the base was inactive. "I mean, from up here. It *looks* deserted," I say. "I didn't see any signs saying no pictures, and this isn't even my destination. I'm headed to Dugway."

"What's in Dugway?"

"It's a military post—"

"I know that. Why do you need to go there? It's restricted."

For God's sake, don't mention illegal experiments on U.S. soldiers . . .

"Um, Dugway," I say cautiously, "is where the government—there was a lawsuit involving these tests done on—well, it's a really long story, but I pretty much just wanted to see if they have a museum or a post historian I could talk to."

I go on to explain my trip and that for this part of the journey I'm focusing on crimes and legal cases that have had national ramifications. "What happened at Dugway," I explain, "prompted a major court fight that—"

He cuts me off as another SUV rolls up. This, I find out, is "the boss."

"Wait here," the staff sergeant tells me.

He walks over and the two men start deliberating. The boss is clearly ticked. He keeps shaking his head, while the staff sergeant is shrugging this off as a false alarm. *He's an idiot, not a threat* is what I'm reading, and I'm perfectly fine with this line of reasoning.

Scowling, the boss gets back into his vehicle, and the staff sergeant walks toward me with his hand out. "Give me your camera."

Oh no.

"I'm not keeping it," he says. "Just show me how to delete the photos."

"Absolutely. Oh, man, I can't thank you enough."

"I hope we didn't mess up your Utah trip too much," the staff sergeant says, scrolling through my recent photographs one last time to make sure all the Deseret pictures are gone. He also advises me against going to Dugway because the boss has already alerted them to my intentions.

"I have a whole other Utah site near Provo I can pursue about a skyjacking that turned out to be pretty historic," I say. I almost add that the skyjacker himself was once part of the Utah National Guard but decide against it.

"All right," he says, handing me back my driver's license. "Take it easy."

"You, too, and thanks again."

Free to go, I drive off in the direction of Provo, about three hours away. My elation is tempered by the fact that I don't exactly know where I'm going, which is the reason I had nixed the skyjacking story in the first place. I have old photos of a relevant site in Springville, just south of Provo, but the area has changed drastically since the 1970s. When I called around before coming to Utah, no one I spoke with from this area—librarians, town officials, real estate agents—knew the specifics. Granted, the crime took place about forty years ago, but it's not often that someone carrying half a million dollars jumps out of a plane over one's town.

The incident began at 2:00 P.M. on April 7, 1972, when a man identified as James Johnson approached the United Airlines counter at Denver's Stapleton Airport and paid $59 for a one-way ticket on Flight 855 to Los Angeles. Holding his ticket daintily between the tips of his first finger and thumb so as not to leave any prints, Johnson boarded the Boeing 727 and sat in the last row, close to the aft stairwell.

Before takeoff, Johnson was in the bathroom altering his appearance with a wig and makeup when an announcement blared over the plane's loudspeakers, asking if any passenger had dropped a manila envelope. Johnson's heart almost stopped; the sealed envelope contained a series of threatening notes he intended to give to the crew throughout the flight.

Gambling that the flight attendants hadn't read the contents, Johnson opened the door, caught the attention of the stewardess holding the envelope, and, after quickly taking it from her hands, ducked back into the lavatory to continue adjusting his disguise.

Twenty minutes or so into the flight, Johnson handed stewardess Diane Surdam a white envelope with the words GRENADE—PIN PULLED PISTOL LOADED typed on the outside. His demands for the half a million dollars and four parachutes were listed inside, and to emphasize his seriousness he included a grenade pin and a live .45-caliber cartridge. He also claimed to have C-4 explosives.

Surdam carried the envelope to Captain Gerald Hearn, who radioed the instructions to Federal Aviation Administration executives and then set a course for San Francisco. FBI agents dressed as baggage handlers and maintenance workers waited for the plane but were unable to sneak on board. After the ransom money and parachutes were delivered, Johnson gave another handwritten note to Surdam ordering everyone off the plane except the flight crew. Efforts to stall the process long enough to stage a raid failed, and once all the passengers had disembarked, Johnson told the captain he was feeling "twitchy" and to get a move on. At approximately 7:45 P.M. San Francisco time, Flight 855 was airborne again.

About two and a half hours later, Johnson lowered the rear-exit stairwell and cautiously manueuvered his way down the steps with the duffel bag stuffed with $500,000 clipped to his flight suit. Captain Hearn had received Johnson's last note telling him precisely what altitude to maintain, and Johnson had warned the pilot that if he caught sight of any aircraft following them, he'd trigger the bomb after jumping. Two C-130s were already on their tail, but Johnson didn't see them. He suspected that the FBI would try to bug his parachutes, although he doubted they could have done so during the relatively short period the plane was in San Francisco. They had.

Johnson soon recognized Interstate 15's lights flickering into view. As freezing air whipped around him and turbulence caused the stairwell to shake, Johnson knew the time had come to jump, even though he wasn't as close to his home in Provo as he'd planned. With the highway now below him, he stood up, took one last look for any aircraft that might be trailing behind, and went feet first into the night. Seconds later he blacked out.

"Do any of these photos look familiar?" I ask a clerk at the first convenience store I come to on Interstate 15 in Springville. The pictures are from 1972 and show areas of Springville the way it looked back then.

She shakes her head.

"Is there someone around here who might know? Any old-timers?"

"I've only been here a few months, so I wouldn't even know who to tell you."

It's a Sunday, most of the town is closed, and I'd already called the old standbys, with no luck. This might actually be a bust.

With nothing to lose, I just start driving around Springville. As I'm going down South Main Street I pass the police station and decide to stop in.

The parking lot is almost empty, and the building looks deserted. I hit the intercom button near the front door.

"Can I help you?" a woman's voice asks.

I explain that it's not urgent but I'm trying to find a local landmark and was hoping one of the officers who's lived in Springville for a while could help me. I expect a curt reply, but she says: "I'm on dispatch duty, so let me get someone to cover for me and I'll come down there as soon as I can."

"Thanks," I say, "and again, no rush."

Jolted awake in midair, Johnson regained his equilibrium and determined that he was still thousands of feet above ground. He almost opened his chute but suddenly noticed the two C-130s prowling overhead, their massive spotlights hunting for him in the darkness.

Feeling weak and like he might pass out again, Johnson realized that at the risk of revealing his position he had to pull the rip cord. With as much energy as he could muster, he yanked the handle.

Nothing.

He jerked it harder, then tugged with both hands, but it was stuck. Finally his backup chute popped open, and Johnson scanned the ground for a soft patch of earth. He was descending fast, and he'd have to favor his left leg when he touched down to protect his sprained right ankle (from a recent ski injury), but he found a cow pasture and the landing went off without a hitch. He stashed the duffel bag and his parachute in a drainage ditch and, with military planes circling above and law enforcement agents and dogs on the ground, he strolled over to the Hi-Spot Drive-in as if nothing had happened. Using a crisp $20 bill, he bought a Coke and paid a young man for a ride into Provo.

When he walked into his house around 1:00 A.M., his sister-in-law Denise greeted him practically shrieking, "Have you heard the news? Some guy jumped over Provo with half a million dollars!"

"No," he said, "I haven't."

The next day he went back to the landing spot, retrieved the loot, and buried it in his backyard.

. . .

I'm arranging the black-and-white pictures I have of Springville when the police department's dispatcher, Ruth Bybee, enters the lobby, and after we exchange hellos I ask her how long she's lived in the area.

"My whole life," she says.

I hand her a series of photos that show the culvert where Johnson hid the money. "I know this was before your time, but do you remember anyone talking about where it all happened?"

She gives me a *That's sweet, but we both know you're fibbing* look (I really wasn't) and says, "I'm old enough to remember it myself. Here's what you need to do. Take a left out of the station lot and go up to Airport Road. Go right onto 1750 West, and then you'll come up to a construction site across from a bunch of restaurants, and the big empty field is it."

"I can't tell you how much I appreciate this," I say. "This morning started out a little rough, but you made my trip to Utah."

Ruth tells me to "stay out of trouble," and I promise her I'll try.

By the time I get to the site, which is now a construction zone just off I-15, dusk has settled. I don't mean to trivialize James Johnson's crime or the trauma he must have caused the flight crew, but as I stand here looking up at the star-dotted sky I'm a little in awe of his gutsiness. The logistics alone are staggering, and he did all of this, it was later revealed, despite having a fear of heights.

Only hours after Johnson hit the ground, Utah National Guard members were gathering in Provo to assist local and federal authorities in their search. One of the troops who arrived early that morning was pilot Richard Floyd McCoy, a twenty-nine-year-old Sunday-school teacher and decorated war hero who'd served two tours flying C-13 combat helicopters in Vietnam, earning the Army Commendation Medal, the Distinguished Flying Cross, and a Purple Heart. He'd lived in Utah off and on for ten years, seven of them with his wife, Karen. The two had met at Brigham Young University, where McCoy studied law enforcement.

McCoy had told friends he aspired to work for the CIA or the FBI, and the prospect of hunting Johnson would have been an exhilarating one to a man like McCoy—except that McCoy knew James Johnson would never be found. Or, at least, no one with that name would. The man who had boarded Flight 855 and jumped from the plane at thirty thousand feet was, in fact, Richard Floyd McCoy. When McCoy checked in that morning with his National Guard unit, he had slept only a few hours after his late-night adventures. But he figured that not making an appearance would have only raised suspicions, so he shuffled in, bleary-eyed and still nursing a sprained ankle.

FBI agents suspected that James Johnson was an alias, and the first name on their minds when news of Flight 855 lit up the wires was D. B. Cooper. Less than five months earlier, a passenger named Dan Cooper (somehow this got garbled in the media and became D. B.) got on board a Northwest Orient Boeing 727, which also had an aft exit, and handed the flight attendant a note saying he had a bomb in his briefcase. He demanded $200,000 in unmarked bills and four parachutes, all of which he received when the plane made an emergency landing in Washington State's Sea-Tac Airport. Once the other passengers were unloaded, the plane took off, and Cooper told the flight attendant to go into the cockpit. With the main cabin now empty, he lowered the rear stairwell and jumped, literally and figuratively, into thin air. He was never found.

Legend has it that Richard McCoy, after reporting for Guard duty the morning of April 7, flew a helicopter over Provo as part of the search team looking for, well, himself. It's a great story but, alas, not true. Based on tips from both the young man who'd given him a lift home from the Hi-Spot and a supposedly close friend who claimed McCoy had been plotting something suspicious, FBI agents began analyzing McCoy's Army records to compare handwriting samples with one of the hijacking notes. When agents raided McCoy's house they discovered a fairly incriminating $499,970 in cash, and McCoy was arrested before he had a chance to participate in any manhunt.

McCoy was tried and convicted, and he began his forty-five-year sentence in July 1973 at the U.S. Penitentiary in Lewisburg, Penn-sylvania. From prison he attempted to have his case overturned on grounds that his Fourth Amendment rights had been violated; accord-ing to McCoy, the FBI's search warrant, which enabled agents to find the ransom money, was improperly obtained. The courts tossed out the appeal, and McCoy would have to serve his full time. Up until that point, however, he'd been a model prisoner who worked quietly in the prison's dentistry. With no hope of an early release, he began to plot his escape. Wielding a dummy handgun composed of dental plaster, McCoy hijacked a garbage truck and crashed through the front gate on August 10, 1974. For three months he was a free man. On Novem-ber 9, the FBI tracked him down in Virginia Beach (purportedly on a tip from his estranged wife, who was dating an FBI man). Surrounded, McCoy fired at one of the agents, missed, and was cut down in a hail of shotgun blasts.

Since the time of McCoy's death, strong evidence has emerged that McCoy was, in fact, D. B. Cooper. Technically, Cooper's FBI file re-mains active, and every few years someone makes a deathbed confes-sion that he was the real D. B. Cooper. But a criminologist and former Utah parole officer named Bernie Rhodes teamed up with Russell Calame, the former bureau chief for the FBI's Salt Lake office, and together they've made a convincing case that McCoy and Cooper were the same man. There was speculation from the start based on the fact that the two men *looked* almost identical (granted, there's no known photo of Cooper, but his police sketch bears an uncanny resemblance to McCoy), and Cooper was described as about five-feet-ten, 160 to 170 pounds. McCoy was five feet ten, 170 pounds. What Rhodes and Calame have done so meticulously is compare how the hijackings were conducted, showing an almost identical modus operandi. Cooper had many copycats, but only McCoy's tactics matched Cooper's with such specificity—and many of these details weren't known until Rhodes and Calame used the Freedom of Information Act to access the case files.

Even if it turns out that McCoy wasn't Cooper, McCoy remains a significant figure. His midair robbery was one of several high-profile skyjackings that prompted the FAA to begin implementing vast improvements in airline security. Air marshals had already been placed on select flights following a spate of hijackings to Cuba, but starting in 1972 the government began cracking down in ways that seem obvious today. All carry-on bags had to be inspected. Passengers would be required to pass through a long, almost corridor-like machine modeled after what loggers used to detect nails and other pieces of metal embedded in timber. And planes with rear stairwells were equipped with devices that prevented them from being opened midflight.

Because of these and other systemwide measures, hijackings of major passenger airliners became increasingly rare in the United States— until September 1976, when Croatian separatists ordered Chicago-bound TWA Flight 355 out of New York's LaGuardia Airport to land in Paris. After commandeering the plane, they announced that, as proof of their seriousness, they had stashed explosives in a subway locker under Grand Central Terminal. Although their claim of having smuggled weapons aboard Flight 355 turned out to be a bluff, the Manhattan bomb was real; on Saturday, September 11, a police officer named Brian Murray died while trying to deactivate the explosives. There were no other hijacking-related fatalities within the United States for another twenty-five years. To the day.

HEIGHTS ARTS THEATRE

Looking back on the course of vice I had run, and comparing its infamous blandishments with the infinitely superior joys of innocence, I could not help pitying, even in point of taste, those who, immersed in gross sensuality, are insensible to the so delicate charms of VIRTUE. . . . Temperance makes men lords over those pleasures that intemperance enslaves them to: the one, parent of health, vigour fertility cheerfulness, and every other desirable good of life; the other, of diseases, debility, barrenness, self-loathing, with only every evil incident to human nature. . . .

If you do me then justice, you will esteem me perfectly consistent in the incense I burn to Virtue. If I have painted Vice in all its gayest colours, if I have decked it with flowers, it has been solely in order to make the worthier, the solemner sacrifice of it to Virtue.

—From Memoirs of a Woman of Pleasure by John Cleland. Notwithstanding the (insincere) tribute to virtue, even by present-day standards the 1749 book is an extremely graphic, XXX-rated tale of promiscuity. Considered the first pornographic English novel, it has been banned more than almost any other fictional work.

HAVING ALREADY IMMERSED myself in several divisive constitutional issues and on the verge of plunging into yet another, I'm ready for a nice noncontroversial diversion. Hence my detour, while driving to Cleveland, off Highway 80/90's exit 25 into beautiful Beatosu, Ohio.

Inside the "Every Day Is Christmas!" Candy Cane Christmas Shoppe in Archbold, I ask a sales clerk where Burlington and Elmira are because Beatosu is supposedly wedged between the two. "It should be right where you've marked it," she says, looking at the red *x* I've drawn on a regional map. "But I'm not familiar with the town. Bee-a-too-su. I'm from this area, and I've never heard of it before."

There's no reason she should have, since it's entirely made up. Beatosu is a "paper town," one of countless fictitious entries—along with fake roads, alleyways, streams, mountains, lakes—that lurk on various U.S. and foreign maps. Cartographers include these on road atlases as either boredom-killing pranks or, more legitimately, as "copyright traps" to catch competitors who've duplicated their information instead of doing original research. Beatosu was snuck onto the map I'm carrying by Peter Fletcher, chairman of the Michigan State Highway Commission and a proud University of Michigan alumnus who couldn't resist poking fun at the Wolverines' archrival, Ohio State University. Beatosu's more accurate pronunciation is "Beat OSU."

Since mapmakers are reluctant to compromise their product's overall integrity, they usually place the traps in remote areas or make only subtle manipulations to real geographical points, like giving an actual street some slight wiggles when in reality it's perfectly straight. Print and online reference editors have their own tricks to snare copycats. The *New Oxford American Dictionary* once included the word *esquivalience*—defined reproachfully as "the willful avoidance of one's official responsibilities." And years ago the *New Columbia Encyclopedia* profiled Lillian Virginia Mountweazel, a fountain designer and accomplished photo-essayist from Bangs, Ohio, whose life was tragically cut short "at the age of thirty-one in an explosion while on assignment for *Combustibles* magazine." Bangs was, at one time, a real Ohio town about forty miles northeast of Columbus, but Mountweazel herself never existed.

Although I'm not sure what to photograph, I take a few landscape pictures of where Beatosu should be, head back to Highway 80/90, and drive west for several hours to Coventry Village in Cleveland. Here I'm on the lookout for my main Ohio site, the former Heights Arts Theatre, a cinema once managed by a shrewd publicity hound named Nico Jacobellis. After Jacobellis showed a barely erotic 1958 French film about adultery called *Les Amants* (*The Lovers*), he caught the attention of the nation's nine most powerful film critics—the justices of the Supreme Court—and got himself a high-profile case that he knew, win or lose, would result in great media exposure for his business. *Jacobellis v. Ohio* became a significant milestone in America's ongoing struggle between protecting free speech and allowing communities to establish their own obscenity standards, and it also brought to my attention one of the federal government's most titillating secrets: "adult movie day" at the U.S. Supreme Court.

Located at 2781 Euclid Heights Boulevard with bright, multicolored bulbs lighting up its refurbished marquee, the old theater is easy to find. When I pull up at about 9:00 P.M., a steady stream of pedestrians stroll about, leisurely enjoying the warm night. Johnny Malloy's Sports Pub now occupies the building, and the owners have maintained the cavernous art deco interior well.

Les Amants, starring Jeanne Moreau and directed by Louis Malle, had its Coventry Village premiere here on November 13, 1959. Suspecting the film might violate Ohio's decency statute, Detective Earl Gordon attended the opening and told Police Chief Edward Gaffney the next morning that, in his opinion, *Les Amants* was indeed pornographic. Gaffney approved a follow-up raid, and on the evening of November 14, Gordon marched into the theater with two other officers, stopped a showing already in progress, confiscated the reels, arrested Jacobellis for "possessing and exhibiting an obscene film," and threw him into jail. (I watched *Les Amants* on DVD before visiting Ohio to better understand what all the fuss was about. By today's standards, it's hardly outrageous. Jeanne Moreau does express herself "enthusiastically" during one climactic moment, but I've seen shampoo commercials that are more risqué.)

Jacobellis was convicted and hit with a $2,500 fine. He took the case to the Ohio Court of Appeals, but they affirmed the judgment, as did the state's supreme court. "[We] viewed *Les Amants*," one peeved justice wrote.

> The film ran for ninety minutes. To me, it was 87 minutes of boredom induced by the vapid drivel appearing on the screen and three minutes of complete revulsion during the showing of an act of perverted obscenity. *Les Amants* was not hardcore pornography, that is, filth for filth's sake. It was worse. It was filth for money's sake.

Jacobellis appealed to the U.S. Supreme Court, but a similar, relatively recent decision suggested that he'd have an uphill battle. Two years before *Les Amants'* scandalous debut, the Court had ruled against Samuel Roth, a publisher of erotica who'd sent out unsolicited advertisements to random names on a mailing list. Some recipients complained, and Roth was arrested under the Comstock Act for transmitting "lewd, lascivious or filthy" materials through the postal service. This same law, originally passed in 1873, had initially prevented such literary classics as James Joyce's *Ulysses,* Ernest Hemingway's *For Whom the Bell Tolls,* and D. H. Lawrence's *Lady Chatterley's Lover* from being distributed. The justices upheld Roth's conviction, arguing that communities could restrict materials if "to the average person, applying contemporary community standards, the dominant theme of the material, taken as a whole, appeals to prurient interest" and if they were "utterly without redeeming social importance."

Among Jacobellis's staunchest defenders was the American Civil Liberties Union, which argued, "There is no evidence in the record that the motion picture film involved in this case presents a clear and present danger," referring to a criterion put forth by Justice Oliver

Wendell Holmes Jr. in a previous free-speech case, *Schenck v. United States.* "We believe that, under the current state of knowledge, there is grossly insufficient evidence to show that obscenity brings about any sufficient evil."

Leading the charge against Jacobellis was the Citizens for Decent Literature, an Ohio-based group founded by Charles H. Keating Jr. (the same Charles Keating caught up in the savings-and-loan scandals three decades later and sentenced to prison by a young Judge Lance Ito—of O. J. Simpson trial fame—for conspiracy, fraud, and rack-eteering). "By definition 'obscenity' appeals to lustful interests and emotions," Keating stated in his *Jacobellis* amicus curiae brief. "It does not contain ideas of value. It is not in the competitive market place of ideas. It contributes nothing in the search for truth or the development of civilization."

Jacobellis won, 6–3.

"We recognize the legitimate and indeed exigent interest of States and localities throughout the Nation in preventing the dissemination of material deemed harmful to children," Justice William J. Brennan wrote in the Court's judgment on June 22, 1964. "But that interest does not justify a total suppression of such material, the effect of which would be to 'reduce the adult population . . . to reading only what is fit for children.'"

Under *Roth v. United States,* obscenity had been defined as some-thing "utterly without redeeming social importance." In *Jacobellis,* Brennan latched onto "utterly" and used the word to make it consider-ably more difficult to ban *any* work, asserting that, if the material had even one iota of "literary or scientific or artistic value or any other form of social importance, [it] may not be held obscene." Brennan also stated that the words "contemporary community standards" set forth in *Roth* applied not to individual towns and cities but the "Nation as a whole."

Justice Hugo Black also sided with Jacobellis and affirmed his steadfast position that even the most vulgar material was protected by the First Amendment, and the Supreme Court had no business suppressing it. "If despite the Constitution," he contended, "this Nation is to embark on the dangerous road of censorship, . . . this Court is about the most inappropriate Supreme Board of Censors that could be found."

Justice Potter Stewart's opinion, also for the majority, was the shortest but by far the most famous. After briefly mentioning *Roth* and sympathizing with the Court's attempt to "define what may be indefinable," Stewart wrote:

> I have reached the conclusion, which I think is confirmed at least by negative implication in the Court's decisions since *Roth* and *Alberts*, that under the First and Fourteenth Amendments criminal laws in this area are constitutionally limited to hardcore pornography. I shall not today attempt further to define the kinds of material I understand to be embraced within that shorthand description; and perhaps I could never succeed in intelligibly doing so. But I know it when I see it, and the motion picture involved in this case is not that.

Chief Justice Earl Warren, joined by Justices John Harlan and Tom Clark, dissented. "We are told that only 'hard core pornography' should be denied the protection of the First Amendment," Warren wrote. "But who can define 'hard core pornography' with any greater clarity than 'obscenity'?"

Warren particularly bristled at Brennan's groundless (in his view) reinterpretation of *Roth* concerning local versus federal control: "It is my belief that, when the Court said in *Roth* that obscenity is to be defined by reference to 'community standards,' it meant community standards—not a national standard." Warren feared this "national" interpretation would turn the Court into the very "ultimate censor" other justices wanted to avoid becoming and precipitate a never-ending log of obscenity cases, each requiring an individual review. He thought it better to let the states handle it.

Elated, Nico Jacobellis ran a full-page advertisement in the *Cleveland Plain Dealer* after his victory announcing: "At Last You Can See the Most Controversial Motion Picture!" Once the hullabaloo surrounding the film petered out, however, Jacobellis left Cleveland for Hollywood to pursue a lucrative advertising and marketing career with 20th Century Fox.

As Chief Justice Warren predicted, *Jacobellis* prompted a surge in the number of movies the Court had to review, and adult movie day became a regular event. The films were shown in a large ceremonial room on the first floor. Justice Thurgood Marshall relished the screenings and particularly enjoyed when directors made gratuitous attempts to bestow an element of educational or artistic merit on their otherwise lurid movies. Near the end of a soft-core film called *Vixen,* one of the female leads is caught up in an attempted hijacking to Cuba, allowing another character to wax philosophical about the differences between communism and democracy. "Ah, the redeeming social value," Marshall joked. He also took pleasure in needling his fellow justices. After watching a graphic documentary about the dangers of sexually transmitted diseases, Marshall looked over at a visibly mortified Justice Harry Blackmun and deadpanned, "Well, Harry, I didn't learn anything, how about you?"

Also according to legend, Justice John Harlan would position himself next to his more conservative colleagues and ask them, because of his failing eyesight, to narrate—in meticulous detail—what was happening on-screen. During especially raunchy scenes he would exclaim, "By Jove!" or "Extraordinary!"

After the March 1966 ruling on the case *A Book Named "John Cleland's Memoirs of a Woman of Pleasure," et al., v. Attorney General of Massachusetts,* which lifted a ban on the unexpurgated 1963 reissue of Cleland's eighteenth-century novel, some justices (and many Americans) felt that the Supreme Court had unleashed a wave of smut on the nation. The Court took yet another stab at the obscenity test in *Miller v. California,* a lawsuit against porn distributor Marvin Miller, who'd sent out a mass mailing to hawk his sexually explicit wares. On

June 21, 1973, the Court ruled against Miller in a 5–4 squeaker that established the following obscenity "guidelines":

> (a) whether "the average person, applying contemporary community standards" would find that the work, taken as a whole, appeals to the prurient interest, (b) whether the work depicts or describes, in a patently offensive way, sexual conduct specifically defined by the applicable state law; and (c) whether the work, taken as a whole, lacks serious literary, artistic, political, or scientific value. We do not adopt as a constitutional standard the "utterly without redeeming social value" test of *Memoirs v. Massachusetts.*

The Miller test, as it has become known, still stands.

The Court also punted the issue of "community standards" back to local jurisdictions. Pornographic films have occasionally been screened at the Court since *Miller,* and after Justice Potter Stewart retired from the Court in 1981, clerks were known to yell out whenever the action started getting hot and heavy, "Yup, that's it, right there—I know it when I see it!"

As I'm taking a long-exposure shot in the dimly lit Johnny Malloy's bar, a young woman sitting close by with four friends asks me in a playful, slightly slurred voice, "Are you taking our picture, Mr. Cameraman?" She then flashes me a wide, snapshot-ready grin.

I smile back while adjusting my tripod and tell her I'm just shooting the bar.

"Oh, okay," she says, feigning a small pout. "Are you a reporter or something?"

I mention the trip and that there was a Supreme Court ruling based on something that took place here years ago.

The young woman pushes back an empty chair and without looking at me points to it. "Sit," she orders while grabbing a pitcher of beer to pour me a glass.

"I've got some driving tonight," I say, "so I can't drink, but that's very nice of you." I am a bit thirsty, though, and flag down the waitress for some ice water.

"Are you just starting your trip?" my new friend asks me.

I tell her I've been on the road for a while now.

"So you're like a historian?" she asks.

"Well," I say, never sure how to answer that question. "I don't have a degree or anything, but it's a subject I really love."

"I haaaaaated history."

"Me, too," I tell her, and we commiserate about how boring we thought it was growing up.

"What happened here again, like a crime or something?"

I summarize *Jacobellis* and go into greater detail about adult movie day at the Supreme Court.

"Oh. My. God," she says.

My sentiments exactly.

"What's your story after this?"

"Actually, it's about booze," I tell her, tapping my water glass against her beer.

"To history," she says, clinking back.

"To history."

NEAL DOW'S BIRTHPLACE,

H. H. HAY DRUGSTORE,

AND MONUMENT SQUARE

Rum, *n.* Generically, fiery liquors that produce madness in total abstainers.

—*From* The Devil's Dictionary *(1911) by Ambrose Bierce*

ANY HISTORICAL EVENT involving mass quantities of alcohol and rowdy mobs gets my immediate attention, and within minutes of reading about the Rum Riot of 1855 in Portland, Maine's Monument Square, I added the site to my itinerary. At the epicenter of the incident was Neal Dow, whose obsession with curing America of its licentious ways catalyzed two constitutional amendments and ushered in a new era of search-and-seizure procedures that fundamentally altered our judicial system. Plus, Dow was the embodiment of this country's early puritanical spirit, and no discussion of U.S. history would be complete without a mention of its Puritan-steeped legal foundations.

A quick summary: On November 11, 1620, two days before stepping onto the New World, the first Pilgrims (or "Separatists") composed the

Mayflower Compact, swearing "all due submission and obedience" to a soon-to-be-formed "Civil Body Politic." For sixteen years they—and the thousands of Puritans who arrived in Massachusetts after them— governed themselves under a hodgepodge of mostly English precedents and Old Testament edicts until finally organizing everything into the 1636 *Book of Lawes*. This, along with Jamestown's 1610 *Lawes Divine, Morall, and Martiall, etc.,* was the earliest legal code written in America. (Ironically, some of the Virginia Company's punishments were more draconian than those instituted by the early Pilgrims and Puritans.)

Also referred to as Plymouth Colony's "General Fundamentals," the *Book of Lawes* covered mundane matters such as bans on thatch roofing for new dwellings, curbs on selling "corne beans and pease" outside the colony to prevent food shortages, and the need to erect "a paire of stock[s]." (Purportedly, the first man placed in Boston's pillo-ries was the carpenter who built them, guilty of overcharging the town for materials.) Capital offenses included treason, murder, arson, "con-versing with the divell by way of witchcraft," and a host of sexual acts, some of which are still illegal. In 1642, Governor William Bradford recorded in his journal *Of Plymouth Plantation* a farmyard fling that would raise eyebrows if it appeared on a police blotter today. "Ther[e] was a youth whose name was Thomas Granger detected of buggery (and indicted for the same) with a mare, a cowe, [two] goats, five sheep, 2. calves, and a turkey," Bradford wrote. "He was first discovered by one that accidentally saw his lewd practise towards the mare. (I forbear perticulers.)"

H. L. Mencken famously defined Puritanism as "the haunting fear that someone, somewhere, may be happy," and its adherents have yet to shake their reputation as prudish, booze-hating killjoys. But Puritans did not, to be fair, abstain from alcohol entirely (one *Book of Lawes* entry involved price controls for beer; "two pence for a Winchester pint"), and they enjoyed unashamedly robust sex lives, so long as the sex was between married couples. They spurned the Calvinist notion that celibacy was purer than sexual union, and divorce was allowed if a spouse refused to fulfill his or her bedroom duties. Court proceedings from 1669 captured this emasculating grievance uttered by Middlesex County resident Hannah Hutchinson about her husband, Samuel: "Though he had a pen, he had no ink."

For Puritans, work was the primary indulgence, idleness their unforgivable sin. They outlawed theatergoing, gambling, dancing, and even Christmas celebrations. Attending church on Christmas was acceptable, but taking a day off to feast and relax in what smacked more of pagan reveling than religious worship was out of the question. (Long after the ban on Christmas was lifted in 1681, the Puritans' humbug attitude endured, and December 25 didn't become an official federal holiday until 1870.)

From this austere and pious New England stock sprang Neal S. Dow, born in Portland, Maine, on March 20, 1804. Though physically small, from childhood Dow manifested a headstrong, self-confident personality. In his otherwise staid autobiography, *The Reminiscences of Neal Dow,* he relates a surreal account describing his scuffle at about the age of seven with a local monkey penned up next to Portland's barbershop. "For what seemed to me a long time the monkey had most of the fun and I most of the pain," Dow recalled, "but at length the brute got tired and knew enough to give up." That tenacity only grew more emboldened once Dow found a larger cause to fight.

While employed by his father, a successful tanner, Dow interacted with numerous laborers and was shocked "not only by the prevalence of drunkenness among them, which indeed was more or less apparent in all classes of society, but by the evident inability of workmen to provide for the pressing necessities of their families when spending so much as was their habit for intoxicants." He went on to lament: "My indignation at the men who brought so much suffering upon their families for the gratification, as it then seemed to me, of a mere taste for liquor, softened into pity and sympathy when I found them apparently helpless victims of a controlling appetite that was dragging them to ruin."

. . .

"You have to understand what Portland was like in the early 1800s," Rob Quatrano tells me as we walk around the house Neal Dow built and inhabited until his death in 1897. Rob, now in his late forties, has been the live-in caretaker here for the past twenty years. "There were three hundred taverns in this small town, and some literally served drinks out of a trough. Every workday a bell would ring at eleven A.M. and four P.M., and that was rum time. Workers would stop and have a few drinks before going back to their jobs."

I confess to Rob that ever since childhood I've dreaded visiting colonial-era house museums like this one. Something about the stuffy atmosphere and mundane lectures on antique furniture always made me drowsy, and to this day I find them soporific. But Rob's enthusiasm is invigorating, and he's a font of stories unlike any I heard during my grade school field trips.

"Even firefighters got drunk on a regular basis back in the 1800s," Rob says. "And if your house was burning down, you could pay them with liquor. 'Water for the fire, rum for the fireman' was the saying." Rob goes on to explain that it wasn't uncommon for two engine companies to arrive, inebriated, at the same alarm and start brawling with each other.

"What drew me to Portland was the Rum Riot in Monument Square," I say to Rob, "but the more I learn about Dow, the more I'm interested in him and *any* unmarked places connected to his life."

Rob immediately thinks of two.

"If you look across the road where the Rite Aid is, that's Dow's birthplace, 778 Congress," he informs me as we peer out the living room window.

Rob then tells me that Dow's "rebirth" occurred in front of what was once the H. H. Hay drugstore, a few blocks from here, just off Congress.

"Dow was walking down the street," Rob says, "and right by the store he saw a child about nine or ten, drunk, stumbling around. The boy grabbed Dow's pant leg and begged for money. It was at that point,

Dow later said, that he was transformed. That's what put him over the edge."

As a member of Portland's volunteer Deluge Engine Company, Dow successfully persuaded his fellow firemen not to serve spirits at their anniversary bash. But after the incident at Hay's, he was convinced that encouraging people to abstain was no longer enough, and he sought to outlaw alcohol entirely. He helped establish the Maine Temperance Society and lobbied throughout the 1830s and '40s to enact statewide prohibition.

In 1851, Dow was elected Portland's mayor, and with his newfound political power he drafted a bill that, on June 2, 1851, made Maine the first state in America to ban the sale of alcohol, with strict punishments for noncompliance.

Dow's triumph garnered him national acclaim as "the Napoleon of Temperance," due to both his diminutive stature and his domineering personality. Between 1852 and 1855, about a dozen other states adopted what became known as the Maine Law. Dow's popularity began to falter back in Portland, however, and even he conceded in his *Reminiscences* that prohibition wasn't exactly "accepted in a spasm of excitement." Distillers, saloon keepers, liquor retailers, and other merchants financially devastated by Dow's crusade joined forces to defeat him, and Dow lost reelection in 1852. But over the next few years he made enough new allies to eke out a forty-six-vote win in April 1855.

Two months later, rumors started circulating that barrels of rum were being stashed under city hall, and on June 2 a horde of screaming, apoplectic townspeople surrounded the building. What most enraged the crowd was the rank hypocrisy of the man they believed to be stockpiling the rum: Mayor Neal Dow.

"How many visitors do you get here each year?" I ask Rob.

"On average about twelve," Rob says.

"A *year*? That's . . . not a lot."

"Even people who live in Portland don't realize how important Dow was."

Right on cue, the doorbell rings. Three women and a man, all of whom look to be in their sixties, are interested in taking a tour, and Rob is happy to oblige.

I ask what brought them here, and one woman says she heard Rob speak at a community AARP event. "He was very good, very dynamic. Afterward I told my husband, my sister, and her friend that we should stop by." (We all nod hello.) "We're from the area and go by this house all the time," she continues, "but we've never come inside before."

I've already heard a good portion of Rob's presentation, but I lag behind to eavesdrop. Before Rob can launch into his talk, one of the women walks over to a lamp and asks if it belonged to Dow.

"It did," Rob tells her. "Almost everything you see is original."

"Oh, look at this," the other woman says, tapping her finger on the expertly carved piecrust edging around a wooden table.

My hand instinctively goes to my mouth, stifling a Pavlovian yawn.

Pointing to an oil portrait of Dow over the fireplace, the first woman says, "Is that him? He looks like such a nice man."

"He was! People assume he was this elitist aristocrat," Rob says, taking a few steps and mimicking the stiff-spined walk of a pompous nobleman. "But he was a very compassionate and generous man. He was also active in the abolition and suffrage movements. And he was a tiny guy like me." (Dow was just over five feet tall, and Rob's not nearly that short.)

"What type of shutters are these?" someone asks, and I'm suddenly feeling woozy again.

"Those are Indian-massacre shutters," Rob says.

"Indian-massacre shutters?" I ask, reviving.

"If there were Indian raids on the town, these would be closed up for protection."

Just as I'm feeling reenergized, the women start inquiring about the dinnerware, and before I pass out on the carpet, I whisper to Rob that I'm going to meet up with Representative Herb Adams, who's been waiting for me to call. "But I'll stop back in before leaving," I say.

Herb is a lifelong Mainer and local legend, having served as a state representative off and on since 1989, and we'd arranged for him to take me to Monument Square.

It's surprisingly warm out, but Herb arrives at Dow's house wrapped up in a blue windbreaker underneath a thick, long scarf. He reminds me of Dr. Dennis Jenkins from my Paisley trip; there's a distinguished air about him coupled with a stout ruggedness.

Herb's knowledge of Maine is encyclopedic, and during our short stroll down Congress Street he's constantly alerting me to historic buildings and other points of interest.

"That, as you can see, is Henry Wadsworth Longfellow," he says, identifying a statue of the Portland-born poet.

"It looks restored."

"Yes, a few years ago. Workers cleaned it using high-power hoses that sprayed a blast of finely crushed walnuts. Water wasn't strong enough and sand was too abrasive, so crushed walnuts did the trick. The whole area was overrun with squirrels crazed *out of their minds* with joy."

Every twenty feet or so we're interrupted by a friendly "Hey, Herb!," and when one resident comes up to buttonhole him, I slip away for a moment to photograph 594 Congress Street, where the H. H. Hay & Co. drugstore used to be. Now it's a Starbucks.

Herb rejoins me and we walk a few blocks down to a massive square plaza with a giant monument in the middle. "This must be Monument Square," I observe astutely.

"Yes, but it was Market Square in Dow's day."

"Didn't the old city hall used to be in the middle?"

"That's right."

"And it was in the basement that Dow was storing the rum?"

"Right again."

For almost twenty years, Dow had antagonized no end of anti-prohibition businessmen, legislators, and residents who were rather fond of their spirits, so when word leaked that Dow himself had hidden below city hall an estimated $1,600 worth of alcohol, a hefty bar tab even today, it was retribution time. To rile up anti-Dow sentiment, his adversaries disseminated the following circular:

> While the city authorities are busy searching private houses for demijohns and jugs of liquor, it is, perhaps, not strange that they should overlook wholesale importations into the city of what are probably impure liquors intended for sale. . . . Where are our vigilant police, who are knowing to the above facts, and who think it their duty to move about in search of the poor man's cider, and often push their search into private houses, contrary to every principle of just law? . . . The old maxim reads: "*Fiat justitia ruat coelum,*" which means, "Let the lash which Neal Dow has prepared for other backs be applied to his own when he deserves it."

Hoisted by his own petard, as it were.

By the afternoon of June 2, 1855, more than one thousand men and women had amassed around city hall. A local judge issued a warrant for the alcohol's seizure, and the expectant crowd—many of whom hoped to intercept the bounty—started growing impatient. They were also growing in numbers, and the municipal police force was over-whelmed. Dow called in the militia, which only heightened tensions. When the mob threatened to rush city hall, both the local sheriff and Neal Dow read them the Riot Act and ordered everyone to disperse. They responded by hurling rocks, and that's when Dow instructed the militia to open fire. People ran screaming as bullets flew in every direc-tion. Minutes later the square was deserted, save for a lone dead body on the ground. Twenty-two-year-old John Robbins was killed in the mêlée. Seven other men were shot but survived.

Dow was hauled before a grand jury, accused of manslaughter. A lengthy investigation exonerated Dow of any responsibility for Rob-bins's death and further cleared him of wrongdoing for stockpiling the rum. The Maine Law explicitly allowed the sale of liquor for

medicinal and industrial uses, and an authorized municipal committee had approved the alcohol's importation and storage specifically
for these reasons. Once tempers cooled, nobody really believed that
Dow, the lifelong teetotaler, sought to create a bootlegging empire.
Self-righteous, uncompromising, and meddling, perhaps. But a greedy,
rum-dealing crook, no.

Dow's reputation nevertheless took a dive, and with it down went
the Maine Law, which was abolished in 1856. That same year Dow
wisely decided against running for mayor, and in 1857 he sailed
overseas for six months to rally his abstemious counterparts in Great
Britain. Dow rebounded in 1858 when he was elected to Maine's legislature, but in 1860 he had to weather another political firestorm when
a close associate he'd campaigned for turned out to have been embezzling state funds.

Redemption came again in April 1861; at fifty-six years of age, Dow
volunteered to fight for the Union during the Civil War. He was appointed a colonel, and his Thirteenth Maine (Temperance) Regiment
served under General Benjamin Butler and helped capture New Orleans. Dow was promoted to brigadier general in April 1862 and sustained multiple wounds on May 27 during the battle for Port Hudson.
Five weeks later, the still-recuperating Dow was nabbed by Confederate soldiers and held for well over a year in a prisoner-of-war camp. On
February 25, 1864, he was exchanged for one of the Union Army's
most prized POWs—General William Henry Fitzhugh Lee, son of
General Robert E. Lee.

"In mid-April 1861," Herb tells me, "a theater group was in town performing Shakespeare's *Hamlet*. One evening, people were gathered in
this square, buzzing about the attack on Fort Sumter, when the official announcement was made that the Union had declared war on
the South. Everyone burst into cheers—except a lone southern actor
who was conspicuous by his silence. And he was right here in Market
Square on that momentous night."

"Wow," I say. "That's incredible."

Herb and I stand there for a minute savoring the story.

Something occurs to me. I turn to Herb and ask, "We are talking about John Wilkes Booth, right?"

"Yes," he says.

"Just checking."

While Herb goes off to speak with another constituent, I wander Monument Square taking pictures and thinking about Maine's tumultuous five years banning spirits and how aptly they foreshadowed the capital-*P* Prohibition movement to come more than six decades later. Far from casting alcohol and its associated evils out of society, Dow's crusade made otherwise respectable folks feel like common criminals forced to sneak into secret "grog-taverns" and similar establishments. People feared being tattled on by their neighbors or having policemen barge into their homes in search of stockpiled liquor, fostering suspicion between citizens and resentment toward government and its agents. And violence ensued. Nothing like the street-fought tommy-gun battles that erupted during the 1920s and '30s, but enough to convince Maine voters in 1856 to repeal their law. (At least for a while; Mainers amended their state constitution twenty-seven years later to outlaw booze once again.)

Obstinate to the end, Dow ran for president in 1880 on the Prohibition Party ticket. He lost spectacularly but relished the opportunity to barnstorm the country preaching the gospel of sobriety and rallying apostles eager to wage holy war against Demon Rum.

Victory for the prohibitionists came in January 1920 with the enactment of the Eighteenth Amendment, followed one month later by the Volstead Act, which made it illegal to "manufacture, sell, barter, transport, import, export, deliver, furnish or possess any intoxicating liquor" in the United States. Neal Dow had died twenty-two years earlier, on October 2, 1897, having outlived his wife and five of their nine children. Venerated in his own day as the Napoleon of Temperance, Dow was all but forgotten when Prohibition became the law of the land. Better known to most Americans were Wayne Wheeler, de facto leader of the Anti-Saloon League; Carrie Amelia Nation, the hatchet-wielding barroom smasher who altered her name to Carry A. Nation; and federal agents Eliot Ness and Richard "Two Gun" Hart.

Genuinely good intentions drove many Americans to lobby for a dry USA, free of booze-related crimes. But this idyllic, sober paradise was not to be. In its wake, Prohibition left thousands dead, either burned alive in home-still explosions or poisoned by denatured alcohol. Drug use soared. Political corruption grew rampant, exacerbated by an increasingly formidable Mafia syndicate that was once little more than a loose affiliation of street thugs. And billions of dollars in potential tax revenues were lost. On the plus side, jazz flourished in speakeasies across the nation, and NASCAR was born on Appalachia's backcountry roads after bootleggers learned how to outrun Johnny Law in souped-up automobiles, and then later raced one another for kicks.

America's "Noble Experiment" ended in December 1933 with the Twenty-First Amendment, the only constitutional amendment passed to fully repeal a previous one.

Another of Prohibition's most enduring legal legacies—a watershed change in how law enforcement conducts investigations—is its most overlooked. A hint of this transformation is evident in the anti-Dow circular that grumbled about city authorities on a mission to hunt down "the poor man's cider, and [who] often push their search into private houses." This isn't how the system originally worked.

Up until the 1850s, police officers rarely initiated searches of a suspect's property or person. The victim did. (With murders, coroners often requested the investigation.) Authorities didn't start poking about until after the aggrieved party appealed to a judge or magistrate for a search warrant. Many American communities didn't even have a full-time police force, which, to a citizenry wary of centralized power, reeked of a standing army. And since selling or owning unlicensed alcohol was considered by most to be a victimless crime, constables didn't run around aggressively raiding establishments or individual homes.

Neal Dow set out to change all that. Five years before the 1851 Maine Law was passed, his state enacted a "prohibitory" bill that restricted alcohol sales. But it had no teeth, and Dow resolved to give the new legislation fangs. Along with hitting violators with stiff fines and prison terms, Dow inserted rules permitting the local "sheriff, city marshal or deputy" to "search the premises described in said warrant, and if any spirituous or intoxicating liquors are found therein he shall seize the same." So long as they were voters, any three individuals could stand before a judge and assert that they had "probable cause" to believe malfeasance was occurring. That's all it took. (To Dow's credit, he also changed the law so that at least one of the complainants had to attest that he'd actually witnessed a crime. He couldn't just say he *suspected* it, he had to swear under oath that he had seen it. This was a major change that raised the evidentiary standards in all search-and-seizure procedures.)

When other states modeled their prohibition laws after Maine's, they established similar measures, and police raids into private residences became standard practice nationwide. While this might seem to be a violation of the U.S. Constitution's Fourth Amendment, the Bill of Rights originally applied only to the federal government; states weren't bound by it. A series of U.S. Supreme Court rulings over the years gradually reined in local authorities, culminating with *Mapp v. Ohio* in 1961, when the Court firmly applied the exclusionary rule to the states.

Herb Adams and I head back to Neal Dow's house, and before hitting the road I say good-bye to Rob, who's still giving a tour to the folks from Portland.

From here it's off to North Carolina to see the correctional facility where a Prohibition-era moonshiner named David Williams was locked up after fatally shooting a sheriff's deputy who had charged onto his property. The crime itself wasn't particularly historic; deadly encounters between bootleggers and law officials were common during the 1920s. But while in prison, Williams invented a weapon that, according to General Douglas MacArthur, helped U.S. forces win the Pacific ground war in 1945. Williams created the patent-winning innovation under the noses of the prison's warden and security guards. He designed it, in fact, with their blessing.

PART V

SPARKS

Inventions and Technological Advancements

CALEDONIA CORRECTIONAL INSTITUTION

Dear John: I thought of writing you last Sunday, but did not. I have been studying up at odd times about Marshall. He has what is called paranoi[a]. . . .

He seems to have a particular grudge against his wife and against his father and the history of such cases are that the first person they kill, they go mad and try to kill everybody. He has certain paralysis of the head while I was down there and was very much worse Sunday than he was two or three days later.

He has an insane delusion of being a bandit and killing someone, and if he is not restrained in some way the result in the next two or three years can almost be predicted.

—From a letter written in October 1919 by the Reverend J. Mack Williams to John Williams about their brother David Marshall Williams. Less than two years later David was arrested for killing Deputy Sheriff Al Pate, and this letter was presented in David's trial—by his own defense counsel.

SEVERAL SHOTS SEEMED to come out of nowhere. One bullet whizzed past Sheriff N. H. McGeachy's face, almost nicking his nose, and another clipped Deputy Bill West's ear. McGeachy had seen at least three men with guns scurry toward a wooded area when he drove up to David Williams's moonshining operation in Godwin, North Carolina, but they had all disappeared into the trees before opening fire. As McGeachy and West dropped to the ground, Deputy Al Pate, still standing, suffered a direct hit and died within seconds. Later that night McGeachy found Williams's father, a respected and prosperous member of the community, and encouraged him to surrender his twenty-year-old son. David Williams denied shooting Pate but admitted to running the illegal still and gave himself up.

"Mr. Pate was about 60 years of age and leaves a widow and four children," the *Fayetteville Observer* wrote on July 23, 1921, the day after the evening raid. "One of the saddest features of his death is the fact that his daughter, who was married last week, is off on her honeymoon." Residents were grief-stricken and outraged, and they demanded swift justice for the deputy's murder.

Although the evidence fingering Williams as the shooter was weak and mostly circumstantial, his legal team felt the safest strategy was for him to plead insanity. They submitted the letter written two years earlier by his brother the Reverend J. Mack Williams, stating that David was clinically paranoid, and asked the reverend to testify in person. The Reverend Williams obliged, reiterating his fears about David's mental health and his "mania" for guns going back to his childhood days hunting in the backwoods of Godwin. It was a risky legal strategy (Williams himself wasn't too pleased about being called mentally unhinged), but a single juror remained stubbornly convinced that Williams was indeed insane, and the judge declared a mistrial. Williams agreed to lesser charges and received a thirty-year sentence. He maintained his innocence but knew that if he attempted a second trial and lost, he could face life in prison or the electric chair.

"[David Williams] was a sandy-haired, broad-shouldered youngster, his light-blue eyes hard and unsmiling," wrote Captain H. T. Peoples in a lengthy 1951 article about Williams and his time inside North Carolina's Caledonia Prison Farm. Peoples was the prison's superintendent, and he remembered Williams well. "In the first month I don't believe young Williams spoke more than twenty words to anyone." Williams kept mostly to himself, failing even to correspond with his parents. When Peoples nudged him to send a letter to his distraught mother, Williams opened up for the first time and told him that he "didn't want to write home from a prison postmark" and that he had "hurt them enough already." Peoples also recalled:

> He looked at me steadily, with those bright, intense eyes. After a moment he said: "I was a crazy kid to get mixed up in that moonshine business. I never killed anyone—never. But all of this could kill my mother and father. Somehow, I'm going to make it up to them."

A week later Williams requested a pencil and some paper, which Peoples gladly provided. When he caught Williams scribbling away after the other prisoners had gone to sleep, he saw that Williams was doodling instead of composing a letter. Peoples was disappointed at first but then noticed "the hard, bitter eyes were softening. Whatever he was doing, it was making him a little happier."

Williams's knack for fixing hopelessly broken-down machines earned him a coveted job running the metal shop. One night Peoples walked in on him slaving away with draft instruments, drawing boards, and sketches scattered everywhere. Williams made no effort to hide his handiwork, and the two men looked at each other for a moment.

"It's . . . a new kind of gun," Williams said. Then he broke into a rare grin. "Don't worry, this has nothing to do with an escape. I wouldn't try to escape now if the gate was wide open. I've got too much work to do, and this is a good place to do it."

Now called the Caledonia Correctional Institution, the prison is located about ninety miles northeast of Raleigh. While driving up to the facility, I might have thought a freak blizzard had recently swept through the rural county recently if it weren't for the 95-degree heat; I've never seen cotton fields this late in the harvesting season, and the soft white clumps dotting the brown earth look like patches of thawing snow.

Waiting for me at the main entrance is my escort for the afternoon, Lieutenant Daryl Williams.

"Nice to meet you," I say. "Are you related to David Williams?"

"Not that I know of."

"But that means you could be," I say.

"I'm pretty sure I'm not."

Daryl asks me if I want to go straight to the old metal shop or tour the whole facility.

"I'm up for the full deal."

Daryl tells me that about 560 inmates are incarcerated here, and the total property covers 7,500 acres. Having watched enough prison documentaries, I don't see anything at Caledonia that's totally unfamiliar—cell blocks, cafeteria, yard, visiting area, and so on—but what does surprise me is how relaxed the environment feels. This isn't to diminish the very real threats both the guards and prisoners face on a daily basis, but I expected the atmosphere to be more tense, vaguely hostile.

I mention this to Daryl, and he assures me that one has to stay alert at all times. "Just this morning we had an incident," he says but doesn't go into details.

We walk through the prison's canning factory and its adjoining warehouse, which is packed high with generically labeled cans of corn, collard greens, applesauce, and fruit punch.

"Most of this will go to prisons and other state institutions throughout North Carolina—*except* public schools," Daryl tells me while ducking out of the way of a small forklift hoisting pallets.

The facility seems clean and orderly, and I would confidently eat whatever's in these cans (except the collard greens, but only because my Yankee taste buds find them bitter). I can understand, however, parents being somewhat wary about their kids slurping down fruits and vegetables prepared by men incarcerated for rape, child abuse, drug trafficking, and premeditated murder.

We head back to the main building. "So this," Daryl tells me, opening a door to a steep, narrow staircase, "is where the old blacksmith shop used to be."

I follow him down, and we encounter about half a dozen prisoners in two adjoining rooms fixing the basement pipes. They all look over, and a few say hello.

"This used to be all one big space," Daryl says as we step into the smaller room. Both are empty now.

I ask Daryl what would happen today if an inmate, especially one sentenced for killing a law enforcement officer, were discovered constructing a "new kind of gun" in the metal shop. The answer isn't a surprise: He'd be locked up in a special disciplinary unit.

Back in 1921, Superintendent Peoples was less hamstrung by such regulations and not only encouraged Williams to keep at it but allowed him to pick through the prison junkyard for parts. Williams plunged in, collecting old tractor axles, Ford drive shafts, walnut fence posts, and other scrap items that he filed down, pieced together, and manipulated to construct half a dozen rifles. Guards stopped by to have Williams work his magic on their guns, too, whenever they needed repairs.

And it was at Caledonia that he constructed the prototype of what would become his most influential innovation: the short-stroke piston. In early models of semiautomatic carbine rifles, the entire barrel kicked back almost four inches to hit the breech mechanism. Williams cut that to one-tenth of an inch without losing substantial firepower. "You know how you can hit one croquet ball a long distance by holding your foot on another ball and transmitting the shock of the mallet?" Williams explained to Peoples. "It's the same idea." This alteration alone led to the production of a shorter, lighter, and more dependable rifle, the M1 carbine.

"I didn't know it then, of course, but what this young prisoner was telling me that night would one day be considered by firearm experts one of the most revolutionary advances since Browning's development of the machine gun," Peoples later wrote.

The notion of a cop-killing inmate assembling a small arsenal of handmade weapons behind bars didn't sit well with some folks, and Peoples was summoned before North Carolina's prison board in Raleigh to explain himself. According to one report, Peoples stated that he was so confident Williams wasn't plotting to break out that he offered to serve the remainder of Williams's sentence if he did.

That wouldn't be necessary. Newspaper articles and word of mouth soon transformed the young, self-taught engineer into something of a local hero. By the late 1920s, a number of influential names had joined Peoples in lobbying Governor Angus McLean to release Williams early: FBI director J. Edgar Hoover, Sheriff McGeachy, and reportedly even Deputy Pate's widow. On September 29, 1929, almost eight years after his conviction, David Marshall Williams was pardoned.

The Winchester Repeating Arms Company hired Williams after he was released, but corporate life proved almost more arduous to him than prison. Paranoid that his colleagues would steal his ideas and feeling stifled in the bureaucratic environment, Williams became a raving hothead who stormed out of meetings and threatened his colleagues when he felt ignored or underappreciated. Winchester considered firing him but recognized that, despite his tantrum-throwing antics, Williams was still a genius.

When the U.S. Ordnance Department requested designs for a "light rifle" prototype, Winchester submitted a semiautomatic carbine that incorporated Williams's short-stroke piston concept, making the rifle more compact and reliable. The military had already been impressed by Williams's floating chamber (another invention he conceived while inside Caledonia), which enabled weapons meant for .30- and .45-caliber ammunition to fire .22 ammo during training. This might not sound terribly exciting, but it saved the War Department millions of dollars, since the .22s were smaller and cheaper.

On October 1, 1941, Winchester officially received word that it had won the contract for the M1 carbine. An estimated eight million M1s were produced during World War II and the Korean War, more than any other American small arm. General Douglas MacArthur is quoted as heralding the M1 as "one of the strongest contributing factors in our victory in the Pacific."

By the time Williams died at the age of seventy-four, he had been credited with dozens of patents and earned numerous awards and tributes. In 1952 the feature film *Carbine Williams,* starring Jimmy Stewart, was released, and a state marker was erected near Williams's Ogden home that says: "1900–1975, 'Carbine' Williams, designer of short-stroke piston, which made possible M-1 carbine rifle, widely used in WWII." And in 1968 ex-felon Williams was made an honorary deputy U.S. marshal.

There may be more examples, but after an exhaustive search I could find only two other inmates in American history who created significant innovations while serving time. In the spring of 1921, a convict at Leavenworth's maximum-security penitentiary designed a new type of adjustable wrench (patent 1,413,121), and about sixty-five years later in a Texas prison, a convicted pot grower named Jason Lariscey developed a method for cutting Kevlar that facilitated the mass production of bulletproof helmets for U.S. troops.

Lieutenant Daryl Williams and I climb the stairs out of the old metal shop and return to the main entrance. I thank him for my tour and ask if, on the way out, I can pick some souvenir patches of cotton, which are beyond the gates but still technically on the prison's property. He doesn't see why it should be a problem. "I just don't want to get shot or anything," I tell him.

After visiting Caledonia, I had planned on passing through a town called Franklinton just outside of Raleigh to find the unmarked spot where the famed boxer Jack Johnson died. On June 10, 1946, Johnson was refused service at a local diner because he was black, and he sped off in a rage and skidded around a corner too fast, hurtling his car into a tree. Physically and historically, Johnson was a giant. Born to slaves, he became boxing's first African American heavyweight world champion in 1908. When he creamed former champion James Jeffries, who'd come out of retirement to (in his words) "demonstrate that a white man is the king of them all," race riots erupted in twenty-five states and caused at least two dozen deaths. In 1912, Johnson became the first person convicted under the Mann Act, which prohibited "transporting women across state lines for immoral purposes." The lady in question was Lucille Cameron, Johnson's soon-to-be-wife. That she happened to be white and a prostitute didn't help his case or public image. Cameron refused to testify, but an old flame named Belle Schreiber—also a white prostitute Johnson had traveled with—agreed to work with prosecutors, and Johnson fled the country. He returned seven years later and spent almost a year in prison after surrendering himself at the United States/Mexico border.

As epic as Johnson's life was, I've decided I'm not going to Franklinton. Right before arriving in North Carolina, I had a minor anxiety attack upon realizing that I'd burned through the majority of my allotted budget and estimated schedule, despite being only halfway through my itinerary. Time to pick up the pace and resist the urge to follow every potential lead. Franklinton will have to wait.

For the record, though, Jack Johnson's story wasn't entirely irrelevant. He was the guy who invented a new kind of adjustable wrench while imprisoned at Leavenworth.

ELISHA OTIS'S BIRTHPLACE

She took her place in the [elevator] car, with a super-intendent and the man who worked the apparatus. Instead of descending, the car began to mount with alarming rapidity. The casting which united the piston to the platform on which the car rested had broken. . . . [T]he piston darted downwards with fearful speed to the bottom, while counterweights, now much heavier than the car and its load, pulled the car up at a dizzy rate. Arriving at the top floor, the car was rammed against the top beam. The shock . . . broke the chains which held the counterweights, and the car went flying down to the basement. The weights fell with a report almost equal to a cannon shot. . . . The three occupants of the car were dead.

—From an 1877 American Architect and Building News article describing Baroness de Schack's death in a hotel elevator, which was not constructed by the Otis Elevator Company

ON APRIL 10, 1790, Congress passed the first U.S. Patent Act, granting inventors legal protection over their creations. All blueprints and, if possible, working models had to be approved by a three-man board, and the original members of this triumvirate were no run-of-the-mill bureaucrats: Secretary of War Henry Knox, U.S. Attorney General Edmund Randolph, and Secretary of State Thomas Jefferson reviewed every proposal.

Samuel Hopkins received America's first patent in 1790, and, somewhat naïvely, I'd hoped that his accomplishment had gone unmarked. No such luck. A tribute to him was erected long ago in Pittsford, Vermont. It reads:

> *To Samuel Hopkins who, in 1781,*
> *settled here on a farm*
> *about half a mile S.W. of this spot,*
> *was granted the first U.S. patent.*
> *Signed by George Washington,*
> *it covered the making of pearl-ash.*
> *On this ingredient of*
> *soap manufacture was founded*
> *Vermont's first main economy.*

Hopkins's innovation was regional in scope, and I was curious about inventions that had impacted society as a whole in even more dramatic and far-reaching ways.

Maybe, I thought, America's *second* patent would prove more scintillating. While futzing around on the U.S. Patent and Trademark Office's website, I typed (per their instructions) "0000002" into the database, and up cropped information about a loomlike mechanism for "manufacturing wool or other fibrous materials" that made pearl ash seem riveting in comparison.

Before signing off, I spotted something peculiar: the file date for patent number two was listed as July 29, 1836. That couldn't be right.

Certainly forty-six years hadn't passed between America's first two patents.

I called the USPTO to inquire about the gap and was told that, indeed, almost ten thousand patents had been issued during that period.

"Where'd they all go?" I asked.

Turns out, funny story. All applications and prototypes were *almost* lost in August 1814 when Washington was invaded by the British, who gleefully ran amok and incinerated the Capitol, Supreme Court, the White House (then called the President's Mansion) and every other federal building in sight except one—the Patent Office. Dr. William Thornton, the agency's recently appointed superintendent, implored British troops to spare the building because the records inside benefited all mankind, not just Americans. Torch-wielding mobs aren't known for making calm, rational decisions midriot, but the Brits found the argument persuasive and rampaged elsewhere. So far, so good. Then, on December 15, 1836, Patent Office employees were dumping fireplace ashes near stacks of kindling when a wayward spark ignited a blaze that swept through the building. Despite having averted catastrophe years earlier, staff members accidentally burned the whole place down all by themselves.

Reluctant to give up on Hopkins entirely—perhaps, I thought, he'd created another contraption later in life that had more pizzazz— I looped back to my original source on him (a general history of Vermont) to see if I'd missed anything.

I had, but what I'd overlooked wasn't about Hopkins. Mentioned elsewhere in the book were fellow Vermont inventors Thomas Davenport, Isaac Fischer, and Elisha Otis.

Otis.

I'd seen that name before and even had a mental image of its distinct lettering. Of course: I stepped over it several times a day going in and out of my apartment building's elevator. Up until that point I'd never thought about the person behind the company or, frankly, the history of elevators. They were a nifty convenience, like automatic doors and escalators, but little more. Otis, I learned, hadn't invented the elevator per se. References to various hoists date back to the first century B.C., and the Roman Colosseum had a lift for animals and gladiators around A.D. 80. Some European castles and monasteries atop steep mountains utilized pulleys and large rope-drawn baskets big enough to hold a person, and in the 1600s a similar contraption, called "the flying chair," was used by the French, who also employed dumb-waiters. Henry Waterman constructed an elevator-like mechanism in 1850, but its intended passengers were barrels and other bulky goods. What I later discovered, however, is that Elisha Otis came along and did more than just improve on the design. He transformed the world.

Otis hailed from Halifax, Vermont, right above the border with Massachusetts. Laura Sumner, the town clerk since 1967, sent me a map with a circle around the property where Otis was born and con-firmed for me that it was unmarked. She also promised to wrangle up a volunteer who could take me out to the site if she wasn't available when I came to visit.

After flying into Boston's Logan Airport several weeks later, I drive up to Halifax and find five people waiting for me inside Laura's of-fice, all of them hovering around a long work table and plotting what looks like a military incursion. They've unearthed early land deeds, grantee maps, Elisha's birth announcement, and nineteenth-century reminiscences about Halifax itself. Laura introduces me to our fellow enthusiasts: Douglas Parkhurst, president of the Halifax Historical So-ciety; Constance ("Connie") Lancaster, a local historian; Stephen Sand-ers, who lives in what some believe is the oldest house in Halifax and has been a resident for "only" twenty-five years (which, in New England terms, still makes him a newcomer); and Bernice Barnett, a freelance writer in her seventies whose ancestry traces back to the town's founding.

"Bernice is a direct descendant of Sally Pratt, the first female birth in Halifax," Connie says.

Stephen catches me leafing through his copy of *Born in Controversy: History of Halifax, Vermont* to see what's written on Elisha Otis (sur-prisingly, just a few lines), and I ask if there's a bookstore where I can buy a copy. "This is hard to find," he says. "You can have this one." I protest, but he insists.

"I appreciate that," I say, genuinely touched.

Looking over the book's cover, I inquire what the "controversy" regarding Halifax was. I'm imagining some juicy, long-forgotten scandal, but Stephen tells me it merely concerned the tug-of-war between New York and New Hampshire over the land that became Vermont.

Laura informs me that the area circled on the map she had given me is incorrect. "For all these years we had the home in the wrong place. But Connie researched the land records extensively, found more reliable information, and now we know where it is."

Bernice opts out of the hike, and the rest of us pile into Laura's minivan. From the parking lot we turn left onto Branch Road and then take a right onto Brook Road, which dead-ends after about two miles. We go right onto Green River and head four miles until we hit Perry Road and park. This is as far as we can drive.

"It's about a three-quarter-mile walk through a trail in the woods," Connie says.

I'm advised that there's poison ivy along the path, and while looking down, I notice weirdly shaped animal tracks.

"Those are moose prints," Laura tells me, "and they're fresh."

"I've never seen a moose before. I'm guessing they're pretty harmless?"

"They'll attack if they're in rut."

"In a rut? You mean, like, depressed?"

"In rut. It means they're looking to mate."

Connie is up ahead and yells back to say that the Otis property will be on the right-hand side.

Huge maples canopy the sky, and Laura cautions me: "Careful of the widow makers," referring to the large broken limbs dangling precariously above us.

As I'm simultaneously watching my step for poison ivy, remaining on the lookout for moose in heat, and staying alert for falling branches, I see Connie stop for a moment and check her map.

"Found it!" she calls out, and those of us lagging behind trot up to join her. From where we're standing, I can see a long, squat stone wall about forty feet away. We wade through a dense patch of ferns that my wildly arachnophobic imagination is convinced harbors entire spider colonies, and I shamelessly let the others go in front of me. Stone steps lead up to what would have been an entrance to the old house, and there's a hearth and central chimney with a root cellar several feet below. Laura notices shards of pottery and mocha ware (most likely *not* owned by Otis and his family but by residents who lived there after them), and I walk around to search for any other evidence of domesticity.

The youngest of six children, Elisha Graves Otis was born here on August 3, 1811. He mastered woodworking and engineering skills on the family farm and at nineteen started bouncing back and forth between New York and Vermont, dabbling in carpentry, operating his own gristmill, running a freight-hauling business, and manufacturing high-end carriages. In 1845 he settled in New York with his second wife (his first had died in 1842) and two young sons, Charles and Norton, and was eventually hired by a bedstead-manufacturing company to oversee the installation of all machinery in its new factory. To raise heavy equipment and lumber from floor to floor, Otis erected a Waterman-like hoist. Nothing fancy or unique at first. But he knew these lifts were inherently dangerous—ropes could break, sending workers plummeting to their deaths—so he jerry-built vertical safety brakes not unlike the horizontal ones he'd been developing for railcars. In 1852 his employer, Benjamin Newhouse, came to him for help after a lift holding two men dropped, with horrific consequences, at one of Newhouse's other factories. Otis built him two "safety hoisters," and a third for a neighboring company impressed by the concept.

When Newhouse announced that he'd be closing the bedstead operation, Otis incorporated the E. G. Otis Company to design and build safety hoists for lifting not only goods and supplies but people.

There were, alas, no takers, and by the end of 1853 he had a total inventory of $122.71, including two oil cans, a secondhand lathe, and the accounting ledger that recorded his measly earnings. Doubtful he could overcome the public's fear and distrust of the notoriously accident-prone mechanisms, Otis considered heading west to capitalize on the Gold Rush.

Enter P. T. Barnum, who was enthralled by Otis's innovation. In 1854, Barnum paid Otis $100 to stand on an elevator platform suspended by a single rope high above gathering onlookers inside the Crystal Palace, first constructed for the 1853 World's Fair in New York. Barnum's showmanship was infectious; the normally unpretentious Otis doffed a top hat and, after a short pause to ensure that he had the crowd's rapt attention, ordered an axe-wielding assistant to cut the rope. When it snapped, the platform plunged—about two feet. Spring-released brakes automatically locked into place, and Otis calmly assured the relieved spectators, "All safe, gentlemen. All safe."

At last he was in business. After fulfilling orders for about three dozen freight lifts during 1855 and '56, Otis installed the world's first safe passenger elevator on March 23, 1857, inside E. V. Haughwout & Company's chinaware and glass emporium at 488 Broadway (now a registered landmark) in Manhattan. Demand grew and Otis was finally seeing years of hard work come to fruition.

Then on April 8, 1861, forty-nine-year-old Elisha Otis died of diphtheria, leaving the company in the hands of his two sons. Fortunately they proved to be even more capable businessmen than their father. Charles and Norton weathered the economic slump during the Civil War and oversaw exponential growth in its aftermath.

Before the 1850s, buildings were no more than three or four stories tall, but within a decade they began shooting up two or three times that height with the installation of Otis's safety elevators. Tribute should also be paid to architects such as William Le Baron Jenney and George Fuller, who launched the mass construction of "skyscrapers" using steel skeletons instead of load-bearing masonry, and British engineer Henry Bessemer, who (with a little help from American William

Kelly) revolutionized steel production. But regardless of their design or material, nobody was going to hike up and down buildings more than four or five stories tall.

"Those who remember the Broadway of twenty years ago can hardly walk the street now without incessant wonder and surprise," *Harper's* magazine observed soon after Otis died. "For although the transformation is gradually wrought, it is always going on before the eye. Twenty years ago it was a street of three-story red-brick houses. Now it is a highway of stone, and iron."

By 1872 there were two thousand Otis Brothers & Co. elevators in service. It was the brand of choice in finer hotels, office complexes, high-rise apartments, and stores nationwide, although it did have competitors. One company believed that creating an airtight shaft would prevent an elevator from crashing more effectively than a braking system. Theoretically, the falling car would eventually slow to a halt on a cushion of air. Theoretically. When, during an early demonstration, the test car came screaming down to ground level carrying eight brave passengers, it blew out the first-floor doors, injuring—but thankfully not killing—everyone inside. The company quickly went out of business.

Otis expanded abroad, and an early assignment included the Eiffel Tower, scheduled to open before 1889 in celebration of the French Revolution's centenary. Otis was selected over European engineers because it could best solve the challenge of installing elevators within the tower's curved legs.

One by one other prestigious landmarks followed: the Empire State Building, the Kremlin, the Vatican, the United Nations, the World Trade Center, Rio de Janeiro's Christ the Redeemer statue, the Kennedy Space Center, the Shanghai World Financial Center, and Burj Dubai (currently the tallest building in the world). Steam and hydraulic-powered motors have given way to electric and computerized systems, and time- and life-saving features have appeared incrementally. In 1950, Dallas's Atlantic Refining Building featured the "do-it-yourself" autotronic elevator, which replaced attendants with buttons; and automatic reopening doors came soon after, to prevent passengers trying to dash in between them from getting squashed.

Fatal accidents happen, but very rarely. On average, twenty-six people are killed by elevators each year (car crashes account for the same number every seven hours), and repairmen are the most likely victims. When something does go wrong, however, it goes *hideously* wrong, as any online search using the keywords "elevator decapitation" will attest.

Laura starts rallying everyone back to her car so that I don't miss my flight from Boston tonight. I thank all of them for their help, and we discuss the need to get a marker placed somewhere in the vicinity of Otis's birthplace—maybe closer to Perry Road than way out in the woods where no one would see it.

With exactly two hours to make the two-hour trip, I race to the airport.

Having lived in Massachusetts as a kid, I've seen the Boston skyline countless times flying in and out of Logan, and I gradually lost that sense of awe when a plane rises over a city, especially after sunset. Not tonight. With my forehead pressed against the window, I'm newly transfixed by the expanding grid of blinking multicolored lights below and think of other favorite skylines—Manhattan, Chicago, Los Angeles, Dallas, Miami—I've seen on previous journeys. All of them, and hundreds more around the world, sprouted up because of Elisha Otis. A subsidiary of United Technologies since 1976, the Otis Elevator Company remains unmatched in size and reach, carrying the equivalent of the world's population every four days on 2.3 million products in two hundred countries and territories. No other form of public transportation comes close.

Embarrassed that I initially perceived his idea as a mere convenience, I take some comfort in knowing that Elisha Otis himself underestimated how drastically his work would reshape the global landscape; he didn't patent his innovation for *seven years*, an eternity in patent registration. (Lawsuits have been won and lost over whether an application was submitted days or even hours before a similar design was filed.) And Otis, having already received numerous other patents for railcar brakes, a steam plow, and a bake oven, wasn't ignorant of the process. But he was lucky. During those seven years, none of his competitors thought his automatic safety elevator idea was worth stealing, replicating, or patenting either.

WILLIAM MORRISON'S
LABORATORY

Topsy, the ill-tempered Coney Island elephant, was put to death in Luna Park, Coney Island, yesterday afternoon. The execution was witnessed by 1,500 or more curious persons, who went down to the island to see the end of the huge beast, to whom they had fed peanuts and cakes in summers that are gone. In order to make Topsy's execution quick and sure 460 grams of cyanide of potassium were fed to her in carrots. Then a hawser was put around her neck and one end attached to a donkey engine and the other to a post. Next wooden sandals lined with copper were attached to her feet. These electrodes were connected by copper wire with the Edison electric light plant and a current of 6,600 volts was sent through her body. The big beast died without a trumpet or a groan.

—From the January 5, 1903, Commercial Advertiser. *Thomas Edison promoted Topsy's execution, which used alternating current (AC) power, to scare Americans into thinking that AC was so dangerous it could kill a full-grown elephant. Edison was engaged in a propaganda war with Nikola Tesla and George Westinghouse, who favored AC over Edison's direct current (DC). Edison lost, and most electronics now use alternating currents.*

"THERE IS NOT the slightest doubt but that my [Morrison] buggy preceded every horseless carriage in the world, save only those cumbersome machines built on the order of tractor engines," Iowa inventor William Morrison boasted after the 1890 debut of his motorized surrey. "I will give $5,000 to any person who can show cuts [i.e., images] of any horseless carriage designed to carry passengers and which was successfully operated before mine was put on the streets of Des Moines."

While Elisha Otis doesn't have a historical marker at his birthplace— unlike Thomas Edison, Henry Ford, Alexander Graham Bell, and the Wright brothers, to name a few of his esteemed peers—there are at least tributes to him elsewhere, and his name graces the metal skims on the floorboards of elevators worldwide. William Morrison has nothing in his honor, anywhere, not even in downtown Des Moines, where he proved himself an automotive pioneer.

The general concept of a self-propelled vehicle wasn't new; Leonardo da Vinci had sketched out a model of one as early as the sixteenth century; German engineer Carl (also spelled Karl) Benz was puttering around Mannheim on his Motorwagen in the mid-1880s; and an attorney from Rochester, New York, named George Selden received the first American patent for the idea in 1895. But Morrison was indeed the first in the United States to actually build a real, working forerunner to the modern four-wheeled automobile.

Morrison warrants attention in his own right, but he also represents a host of geniuses whose groundbreaking work has either been crated up and left to gather dust in history's warehouse or been overshadowed by other innovators. About half a dozen European and American inventors, for instance, patented the incandescent lightbulb years before Thomas Edison. One of them, John Starr from Ohio, is believed to have beaten Edison by decades. Electrical engineer Elisha Gray submitted his telephone patent several hours before Alexander Graham Bell's attorney handed in Bell's application on February 14, 1876, but Bell became the more famous of the two. Gray's defenders argue that he lost out because an alcoholic Patent Office employee was bribed to ensure that Bell's claim received priority. (Bell was also accused of later coming to the patent office himself, perusing Gray's application, and then stealing concepts he later incorporated into his own design.) And more than two years before the Wright brothers briefly dipped and bobbed over the sands of Kitty Hawk on December 17, 1903, the *Bridgeport Herald* profiled a German-born immigrant named Gustave Whitehead who, according to the article, flew a motor-propelled airplane in Fairfield, Connecticut. Several witnesses later signed affidavits swearing that they, too, witnessed the August 1901 flight. Whitehead could have settled the question and possibly earned his chance at immortality had he, like the Wright brothers, captured his flight on film. (The true inventor of photography is also, of course, a matter of debate.)

William Morrison's old basement laboratory, or "the Cave," as he referred to it, used to be in the middle of Fifth Avenue, right between Locust Street and Grand Avenue in downtown Des Moines. I'm not complaining about my Vermont (or any other) hike, but every so often it's nice to visit sites that don't require contending with the threat of snakes, poison ivy, randy moose, or crashing tree limbs.

Joining me is local automobile historian Bill Jepsen, who self-published a terrific book titled *Iowa's Automobiles: An Entertaining and Enlightening History,* which he spent twenty years writing. Bill has driven about an hour in from Boone, Iowa, to show me around Des Moines and share his file on Morrison, which is invaluable because there's scant information on the man. Bill also deserves credit for actually finding the spot where Morrison worked.

"Were you always a car guy?" I ask Bill after he meets me outside of my hotel in his GMC truck.

"Well, I started out as a car kid," he says, "sitting on the front steps of our Davenport home in the 1950s at the age of five or so trying to name cars as they drove by."

Bill graduated from the University of Iowa in 1967, got drafted, and

served in Vietnam, he tells me, as a "Remington Raider." From my
blank expression he can see that I have no clue what that means. "I sat
behind a Remington typewriter and filled out reports and records," he
explains. On the GI Bill, he studied twentieth-century American history with plans of becoming a teacher, but he never got certified.

Bill and I approach Fifth Avenue, and there's strong evidence that
Morrison had an early model of his car up and running on this very
street years before he officially introduced it to the world on September 4, 1890, during the city's annual parade, Seni Om Sed. (Des Moines
spelled backward. Sort of.) Spectators—up to a hundred thousand in
all—clamored for a look at Morrison's homegrown four-horsepower
invention rolling down Walnut Street on steel-clad wooden wheels
under a surreylike carriage. By far the event's most popular attraction,
the buggy was greeted by cheers and applause for the entire length of
the route.

Scientific journals and gossip mags alike went dizzy over Morrison's
horseless carriage, prompting sixteen thousand letters to pour into his
office from both well-wishers and oddballs around the world questioning how it worked, inquiring if they could get their own, and asking if
he was married. (He was.) Overwhelmed by the onslaught, Morrison
tossed out the letters but saved two whole bushel baskets' worth of enclosed postage stamps.

What makes Morrison's car all the more noteworthy is that it was
electric. America's first automobile ran on batteries, not fossil fuels. And
the Morrison Electric, as he called it, wasn't some one-time wonder
constructed for his own driving pleasure; Morrison built a line of cars
and sold them for $3,600 each. To promote the power and durability
of rechargeable batteries, the American Battery Company bought one
to exhibit at the 1893 World's Fair in Chicago, sparking national interest. Two years later, ABC entered a Morrison Electric in this country's
first automobile race. Unfortunately, and in a sign of things to come, it
lost the fifty-four-mile contest to Frank and Charles Duryea's gasoline-
fueled automobile, the first of its kind in the United States. The Duryea
brothers were also first to set up a car-manufacturing plant, followed

by Ransom Olds, who patented the assembly-line process—not Henry Ford, as is commonly believed.

Ford considered producing electric cars, too, but his hero and (later in life) close friend Thomas Edison waved him off the idea after toying with it himself. "Electric cars must keep near to power stations," Edison told Ford. "The storage battery is too heavy. Steam cars won't do, either, for they require a boiler and fire. Your car is self-contained—carries its own power plant—no fire, no boiler, no smoke and no steam. You have the thing. Keep at it."

Initially, though, electric cars were all the rage. Some drove faster than their fuel-powered competitors, and they were less messy, quieter, and a cinch to start, requiring just the push of a button instead of a cumbersome hand crank. (Advertisers pitched these features to female drivers in particular.) The Electric Carriage and Wagon Company put an entire fleet of electric cabs on the streets of New York in 1897, and by 1899 electric vehicles were beginning to outsell cars with combustion engines. An electric taxi in Manhattan even earned the ignominious distinction of causing the first automobile fatality in America; on September 13, 1899, cabdriver Arthur Smith accidentally ran over a sixty-eight-year-old man named Henry Bliss at Seventy-Fourth Street and Central Park West in Manhattan. Bliss died at Roosevelt Hospital the next day.

Bill points out the spot we're looking for on Fifth Avenue, and, as he parks, I jog up ahead to take pictures. After a few moments, I realize that the light-gray concrete building with red trim now houses some sort of daycare or educational center, and a teacher starts to peer out the large windows and is clearly wondering what this strange man with a camera is doing outside.

There's no international hand sign for "I'm a history buff, not a weirdo," so I gesture to her as best I can that I'm not photographing the classroom or any students. The teacher's eyes narrow to a stern glare, and I slink off after snapping one more picture. I call over to Bill, "Okay, we should probably go."

"That was fast."

"Yup," I say, trying not to seem too suspicious as I hustle out of view of the school window. "Got everything I need."

Thomas Edison's counsel to Henry Ford proved right in the end, and electric cars ultimately couldn't beat out their fuel-guzzling competitors in the early 1900s for the same reasons they still haven't entirely caught on today—they're more expensive and they can't go as far on a single charge as gas-powered cars can travel on a full tank. Their failure a century ago partly accounts for why Morrison himself has been forgotten.

Not that he'd have cared. "I wouldn't give ten cents for an automobile for my own use," Morrison told a reporter from the *Des Moines Register and Leader* in 1907. Despite his $5,000 boast about being first (a wager he would have lost to a number of other Europeans but to no American), Morrison wasn't passionate enough about cars to go around embroiling himself in patent lawsuits. What interested him most were the batteries inside the vehicles, and before moving to California to try his hand at gold mining, he received eighty-seven patents, most of them related to battery storage. Little is known about his life out west except that he made a small fortune and then passed away in 1927. (The exact year of his birth isn't known, but Morrison was in his mid- to late seventies when he died, and he was buried back in Des Moines.)

Morrison's apathy about his accomplishments was the exception among early American inventors. All the rest seemed to be engaged in endless legal fights. Elisha Gray sued Alexander Graham Bell over the telephone. Bell got into a scrap with the Wright brothers over patented improvements to the airplane. Henry Ford duked it out with George Selden for hogging the automobile patent without putting it to use. And Nikola Tesla clashed with his former employer Thomas Edison over alternating and direct currents. Tesla also wrangled with Edison's friend Guglielmo Marconi about who invented the radio, and their feud is proof of how confusing these cases can be. In 1903 the Patent Office sided with Marconi—after having first awarded the radio patent to Tesla three years earlier. Then, in a decision that stands to this day, the U.S. Supreme Court reversed the Patent Office's reversal, giving Tesla final bragging rights. But he never knew of his victory, having died embittered and penniless in the New Yorker Hotel several months before the Court's ruling.

Few of these wars, however, can compare with Philo Farnsworth's David-versus-Goliath battle with RCA Communications concerning the patent for electronic television. That a lone, self-taught engineer from Rigby, Idaho—where I'm off to now—took on the world's most powerful broadcasting company and won isn't even the story's most remarkable angle. What's more compelling, I think, is that Farnsworth came up with the idea when he was only fourteen years old.

THE FARNSWORTH FARM

Nobody had it, nobody was close and lemme tell you nobody cared that much 'cause at best it was gonna be considered a nifty parlor trick. Nobody had it except a 14-year-old kid in Rigby, Idaho, standing in a field of potatoes. He rode a three-disc plow, drawn by a mule, making three parallel lines in the earth at once. Then three more. Then three more and three more until he was done with his work. He stepped off the plow, looked back at the rows and rows of parallel lines, and that's when he realized the key to the most influential invention in history. So he did what any world-class electrical engineer would do in that situation: He went to see his 9th grade science teacher.

—From David Sarnoff's monologue in The Farnsworth Invention (2007) by Aaron Sorkin. The character is based on the real RCA president and Farnsworth nemesis, David Sarnoff.

"JUSTIN TOLMAN WAS Philo Farnsworth's science teacher," Mike Miller tells me as we drive up to the newly renovated Rigby Junior High School, "and Tolman's classroom would have been in the old building, which was torn down long ago." The site is now an empty athletic field, with metal tackling dummies lined up on one end and soccer posts on the other.

Mike is a Rigby native and a sergeant in the sheriff's department. When I first contacted the local museum, then the library, and finally the public school to find out where Philo Farnsworth lived ninety years ago, nobody could pinpoint the location, and everyone said the same thing: Call Sergeant Miller. He'll know.

He didn't, actually. Not right away. But he promised me he'd find out, and he's come through.

Before we drive out to see where Farnsworth was raised, we pass by his old school. When the fall semester started in 1921, Farnsworth waited by the building's front entrance to badger Justin Tolman into allowing him to attend his senior-level science class. At first Tolman wasn't going to let a ninth-grader waltz into his honors course, but he finally relented, and after a few weeks he realized that Farnsworth had a better intuitive grasp of science than the older students, if not himself.

From the junior high school, Mike and I drive from downtown Rigby to our main destination—472 North 3700 East.

"I had to go through a lot of old records to verify the location," Mike says, "but here's where Farnsworth and his family moved to in early 1921. This is the farm where he had his revelation." There's no house there now, just an old feedlot.

Farnsworth's father had brought his family to Idaho in 1919 from Provo, Utah, where Philo was born on August 19, 1906. They first stayed with relatives on a 240-acre ranch a few miles outside of Rigby, and young Farnsworth was ecstatic to discover that the house had electricity, a rarity then in rural America. When he stumbled on a pile of technology magazines, he was practically beside himself. One, *Science and Invention,* was running a contest to improve the Model T, and Farnsworth zeroed in on a bedeviling security problem. Since all Fords used an identical key, whoever possessed one could start—and steal—any car. Farnsworth proposed a simple, cost-effective method of magnetizing each key to make it unique. He won first prize.

Antitheft ignition locks were kids' stuff compared with Farnsworth's primary obsession: solving the technological riddle that would make television a reality. Russian engineer Constantin Perskyi introduced the word *television* (same spelling and everything) during a lecture he delivered in French at the 1900 Paris World's Fair, and he referenced the German technician Paul Nipkow's idea of using hole-punctured spinning mechanical disks to convert images into electrical impulses and then send them through a wire to a second disk, which would project them onto a screen. Inventors throughout Europe and the United States tried to build on this "mechanical" model, but Farnsworth, who'd read about Nipkow, recognized its inherent limitations and knew that a radically different approach was needed.

During the summer of 1921, Farnsworth had learned that electrons could be beamed across a vacuum (or cathode) tube, undisturbed by air molecules that might otherwise cause distortion, and he wondered whether these rays, if properly manipulated, could project clear images onto a photoelectric screen at the other end of the tube. The problem was transmitting and capturing the pictures in their entirety, and this seemed technically impossible.

Like any restless and sensible young man, Farnsworth loathed the monotony of daily chores, but they did give him time to think. One morning before his fifteenth birthday, he was out plowing the family's potato field when he took a short break. While looking back over the rows of freshly tilled earth, inspiration struck.

Lines.

Lines of electron rays, guided by magnets, could zigzag across the screen rapidly enough to fool the eye into believing it was watching a continuously moving image. No mechanical or optical spinning discs could accomplish this, ever. "Mechanical" television was a technological dead end. "Electronic" television, Farnsworth realized, was the answer.

He rushed home and explained the still-percolating breakthrough to his father, who didn't have the faintest idea what Philo was talking about. But he gave his son memorable advice: "You need to keep this a secret, because everyone already thinks you're a bit odd. This would convince them for sure."

Six months later Farnsworth couldn't hold out any longer and confided in Justin Tolman his idea for an integrated electronic television system, which included a rudimentary camera that Farnsworth called an "image dissector" and a cathode-ray tube (or receiving set), which is why some of us still refer to a TV set as "the tube." Farnsworth breathlessly detailed to his science teacher how the components interacted, and he sketched the design on Tolman's blackboard, then drew more detailed schematics on a sheet of notebook paper. Farnsworth asked his teacher if he had any reason to believe the principles involved were scientifically unsound. Awestruck, Tolman shook his head and encouraged Farnsworth to just "study like the devil and keep mum."

Farnsworth's next major obstacle was more practical than theoretical. He was broke. While established inventors working on television prototypes oversaw entire teams of scientists and engineers in well-equipped, corporate-funded laboratories, Farnsworth labored alone in the family attic piecing together whatever odds and ends he could salvage from Rigby's junkyards and auto shops. And unlike his competitors, the teenage freshman had to ask his mom's permission to work past bedtime.

Money proved so tight for the entire family that Farnsworth senior moved his wife and younger children back to Provo. Philo dropped out of school, took correspondence courses, scraped by in various low-paying jobs, and joined the Navy in 1924. (Tired of "Fido" cracks, he dropped the *o* from his name and was henceforth Phil Farnsworth.) That same year his father passed away, and Farnsworth was granted an honorable discharge to care for his grieving mother in Provo.

Utah beckoned for another reason: Elma "Pem" Gardner, a spirited seventeen-year-old bombshell Farnsworth had fallen for who had a sharp mind and wasn't put off by his impromptu soliloquies about the beauty of electromagnetic-wave transmissions. Pem was the one bright spot in an otherwise bleak period when Farnsworth, working as a street sweeper, constantly worried that at any moment another inventor would steal his thunder.

That seemed ever more likely in 1925. On June 13, Charles Francis Jenkins showcased his Radiovisor, which transmitted synchronized sound and pictures from a radio station in the nation's capital. Jenkins had already established his engineering bona fides by helping to invent the Vitascope, a film projector marketed under Thomas Edison's name. (Predictably, there was a spat over patent rights, which resulted in a $2,500 settlement to Jenkins.)

Around the same time Jenkins was rolling out the Radiovisor in Washington, Scottish inventor John Logie Baird was introducing something similar in England. On January 26, 1926, Baird repeated for the media in his London laboratory a demonstration he'd given staff members months earlier, broadcasting live images on his Televisor. That Baird didn't harm anyone in the process was achievement enough; a one-man safety hazard, Baird had blown up a previous lab and nearly electrocuted himself in the process. As a young inventor, he reportedly caused a blackout in Glasgow after overwhelming the power supply by using large surges of electricity to convert graphite into diamonds. But despite their breakthroughs, Jenkins and Baird relied on a form of mechanical television that produced hazy images. Even Paul Nipkow had long abandoned the outdated technology.

Farnsworth's own luck changed in the spring of 1926 when two wealthy businessmen, George Everson and Leslie Gorrell, hired him as a temporary office boy. Impressed by his work ethic and intelligence, they asked Farnsworth his future plans. He entrusted them with his television idea, and after consulting with various engineers to confirm that the lad wasn't an absolute loon, they ponied up a $6,000 investment.

The day after their May 26, 1926, wedding, Phil and Pem Farnsworth left Utah for Los Angeles, where Phil could access the California Institute of Technology's superb research library and be close to Hollywood. From the get-go he recognized television's entertainment potential.

Phil and Pem's apartment doubled as home and lab. What, exactly, was going on in there baffled their fellow tenants. Farnsworth kept the curtains drawn, worked long hours, looked gaunt and mildly possessed whenever he emerged, and was constantly hauling strange coils, tubes, hoses, liquids, and glass bottles inside. Finally his neighbors came to the reasonable conclusion that the Farnsworths were bootleggers and alerted authorities, prompting a surprise visit by the LAPD. "They're doing somethin' kooky they call electric vision," one officer told another after searching the premises, "but they ain't got no still."

Of greater concern to Farnsworth was a visit from Everson and Gorrell inquiring how their money had been spent. After forewarning them that numerous kinks needed ironing out, Farnsworth began his presentation. He connected the image dissector to the reception tube, gathered everyone in the lab around for the historic moment, and flipped on the generator. The humming machine soon began to make alarming pops and hissing noises. Acrid-smelling smoke filled the room, and Farnsworth made a dash toward the generator, but it was too late. Months of work and possibly a life's dream sat in flames before him.

Everson and Gorrell didn't lose hope. Although unable to contribute more capital themselves, they eventually convinced a notoriously skeptical San Francisco banker named J. J. Fagan and his colleagues to offer $25,000 for 60 percent ownership in the enterprise. Farnsworth's elation was tempered only by the minor humiliation of needing Everson to serve as his legal guardian in the deal; Farnsworth, only twenty, wasn't old enough to sign the partnership contract on his own.

Fagan's investors gave Farnsworth a one-year deadline and requested he move closer to their offices, so in September 1926, Pem and Phil once more packed up their belongings and relocated to San Francisco.

They rented a home to live in and a loft at 202 Green Street, where Farnsworth and his two assistants—Pem and her brother Cliff— would work.

On January 7, 1927, Farnsworth filed a patent for his electronic "Television System" to protect the idea, but he still hadn't constructed a functioning model. With pressure mounting, he needed extra hands. He brought in his geologist cousin, Arthur Crawford, to find the perfect chemical element for the screen (cesium initially won out), followed by his sister Agnes and Pem's sister Ruth as part-time helpers.

That September they tested the entire system—but this time just for themselves, no audience. Cliff placed a drawing of a triangle in front of the image dissector in one room while the rest of the team watched the receiving tube in another. A line appeared. Not the whole figure, but one clearly defined side. "That's it, folks!" Farnsworth cried out. "There you have electronic television." He repeated the show for Everson, who then wired Gorrell in Los Angeles: THE DAMNED THING WORKS.

Everson recommended to Farnsworth that, for his demonstration to Fagan and others, he produce something slightly more advanced than a single straight line. Farnsworth obliged. When the eager bankers huddled around the television screen to see what image Cliff was holding in the other room, up popped a dollar sign, eliciting bursts of laughter.

The men felt the moment had come for a press conference, but Farnsworth insisted on more time. To the investors' dismay, the event wasn't scheduled until Saturday, September 1, 1928, and only a handful of reporters bothered to show. Monday's story in the *San Francisco Chronicle*, however, was picked up by newspapers across the country and later around the world. S.F. MAN'S INVENTION TO REVOLUTIONIZE TELEVISION, the headline proclaimed over a glowing article about the "young genius." Farnsworth's name was poised to become as famous as Ford, Edison, or Wright.

"Are you Farnsworth?" a policeman asked Phil the morning of October 28 while he and Pem were out playing tennis in a rare moment of relaxation. Phil said that he was.

"Well, you might want to get down to your laboratory right away," the officer told him. "The place is on *fire*."

The place was gone. What caused the blaze remains unknown, and fortunately the loft and equipment were fully insured. Farnsworth got the lab up and running again, but he lost months of time. His greater crisis was financial; just as his newly incorporated Television Laboratories was hitting its stride, Farnsworth's backers pulled the financial plug. They wanted a major corporation to step in and offer them a return on their investment.

Meanwhile, buzz was growing around Farnsworth's lab and a steady stream of celebrities and venerated scientists journeyed to 202 Green Street to see the wunderkind's miracle machine. Movie star Douglas Fairbanks Jr. caused quite a stir when he and his Oscar-winning wife, Mary Pickford, stopped by, but Farnsworth most enjoyed kibitzing with fellow inventors such as Lee De Forest, a pioneering figure in radio, vacuum tubes, and electronics. Guglielmo Marconi also paid a visit.

Few guests expressed more interest than Vladimir Zworykin, head of Westinghouse Electric Corporation's television research division, and Farnsworth believed that Westinghouse could be his savior. If the company agreed to a licensing arrangement, he would receive a percentage on every television camera and receiver set sold, netting him millions of dollars. Farnsworth hosted Zworykin for three days in mid-April 1930, answering every question and even inviting him to his house for dinner. Before Zworykin left San Francisco he picked up an image dissector in Farnsworth's lab and said, "This is a beautiful instrument. I wish I had thought of it myself." It was the highest compliment one inventor could extend to another.

No offer, however, was forthcoming. In fact, by the time Zworykin returned east, he was no longer employed by Westinghouse but had been hired by its sister corporation, RCA, at the behest of its president,

David Sarnoff. Sarnoff had promised Zworykin a million-dollar budget to bring television to the masses, just as RCA had done with radio, and he had sent Zworykin to snoop on Farnsworth.

Like Zworykin, Sarnoff was a Russian-born immigrant. He spoke only his native tongue when he left Minsk (now the capital of Belarus) for New York in 1900 at the age of nine. A quick study, he soon became fluent in English, shed his accent, and sold penny newspapers to support himself, his mother, and his ailing father. At the age of fourteen he had a chance encounter with Guglielmo Marconi, who admired the boy's pluck and made him his personal errand boy.

Years later Sarnoff was promoted, becoming a full-time wireless telegraph operator at the American Marconi Company. Along with providing Sarnoff invaluable experience working within a corporate structure, the job proved auspicious for placing Sarnoff at the center of—as he would recount throughout his life—a disaster of unprecedented magnitude.

Just before 10:30 P.M. on April 14, 1912, Sarnoff was manning American Marconi's telegraph station atop the Wanamaker Building at Ninth Street and Broadway in New York when an urgent message beeped over the wires: "S.S. *Titanic* ran into iceberg. Sinking fast." Twenty-one-year-old David Sarnoff was now the lone connection between Western civilization and the ships relaying updates about the doomed ocean liner and her 2,223 passengers. "I gave the information to the press associations and newspapers at once," Sarnoff later said,

> and it was as if bedlam had been let loose. Telephones were whirring, extras were being cried, crowds were gathering around newspaper bulletin boards. . . . President Taft ordered all stations in the vicinity except ours closed down so that we might have no interference in the reception of official news. . . . It seemed as if the whole anxious world was attached to those phones during the seventy-two hours I crouched tense in that station. I felt my responsibility keenly, and weary though I was, could not have slept. . . . We began to get the names of some of

those who were known to have gone down. . . . I passed the information on to a sorrowing world, and when messages ceased
to come in, fell down like a log at my place and slept the clock
around.

Terrific story. But, as it turned out, mostly false. Numerous operators worked that night (there's some speculation that Sarnoff wasn't
even on duty), and Wanamaker was actually one of the stations temporarily shut down. Worst of all, about two weeks later, newspapers
revealed that American Marconi had *withheld* names of the ship's
passengers to prolong the gripping account and boost its own publicity. And it worked. Even after the shameful ploy was exposed, the
company's stock and orders for their wireless services soared. (Ironically, Guglielmo Marconi himself considered traveling on the *Titanic*
but decided to leave Europe a few days earlier and sailed instead on
the British ocean liner *Lusitania*—the same ship that was sunk in
May 1915 by a German U-boat.)

Sarnoff began his rapid climb up the corporate ladder in 1919, when
he was brought on as commercial manager for the newly formed Radio
Corporation of America. Within about ten years he was running the
place. By then he realized that television, not just radio, was the future,
and RCA its rightful progenitor.

"Up for some lunch?" Sergeant Mike calls to me from the feedlot. I'm
standing out in the middle of the pasture, lost in thought.

"Sure," I say, and walk over to his car, still thinking about how im-
possibly young Farnsworth was when his eureka moment struck. On
our way into town, Mike and I pass several kids about Farnsworth's
age, reinforcing my incredulity that a gangly, intense teenager with
very few resources had set in motion such a major revolution in technology. There's a sense of heartbreak, too, in knowing what was in
store for him.

Nothing had ever come easily to Farnsworth, but starting in the early
1930s, he and Pem were hit with a series of Job-like tragedies. They

struggled, like millions in the Great Depression, to keep their noses above water. When a second wave of bank failures swept the country after the initial stock market crash, Phil and Pem were left with only $1.57 to their name. (An unexpected reimbursement check carried them awhile, but there were few other guaranteed payments on the horizon.) Then in March 1932 their eighteen-month-old son, Kenny, developed strep throat. This was the era before penicillin and other antibiotics, and only an emergency tracheotomy could stop the infection from ravaging his lungs. After the operation, the attending intern who was supposed to be watching Kenny fell asleep and didn't see Kenny's breathing tube begin to clog up. When a restless Farnsworth checked in on his son, he found the boy suffocating to death. Doctors rushed into the room after hearing Farnsworth call for help, but there was nothing they could do. Phil and Pem watched helplessly as baby Kenny gasped uncontrollably and then passed away right before their eyes. Farnsworth's business partners were so anxious about his company's financial straits that they wouldn't let him travel to Utah to bury his son. Pem went alone. Overwhelmed with grief and stress, the couple barely spoke to each other when she returned.

David Sarnoff, meanwhile, was thriving. One by one his competitors plunged into bankruptcy, and when Sarnoff was named president of RCA in 1930, he had nearly unfettered control over an entire media empire. Three years later, RCA opened its massive new headquarters in Rockefeller Center, with a sculpture of Prometheus erected out front signaling to the world that RCA, like the Greek god, would bring the fire of knowledge to mankind.

And bustling away in RCA's massive lab in Camden, New Jersey, Vladimir Zworykin and his team were perfecting electronic television, with Zworykin maintaining all along that he had conceived of it well before Farnsworth.

Farnsworth wasn't confrontational by nature, but on this matter he'd exhausted all patience and filed suit with the Patent Office to officially answer the question: Who invented electronic television, him or Zworykin?

RCA lawyers hit back with a two-pronged line of attack. First, they claimed Zworykin had patented a television-like device in 1923, making him the true inventor. Second, they insisted it was preposterous to believe that some kid with "only a grade school education" conceived in 1922 an innovation that had eluded "great men of science and skill" for years.

Honor, not just money, was at stake, and Farnsworth and his lawyer, Donald Lippincott, took particular umbrage at RCA's accusation that Farnsworth's teenage brainstorm in the potato field was pure fantasy. As tangible proof of Farnsworth's veracity, Lippincott produced one Justin Tolman, in the flesh. By then Tolman was retired, but he well remembered his "brightest student" and had brought with him the aged but still legible piece of notebook paper containing Farnsworth's original sketches from early 1922.

To vindicate Farnsworth's claims, Lippincott had one more stellar witness—Vladimir Zworykin, who had said in Farnsworth's Green Street lab that he wished he had invented the image dissector himself. Zworykin admitted to making the statement but claimed that he was just being polite. Lippincott scoffed at this, along with the notion that Zworykin's 1923 patent resembled electronic television in any meaningful way.

The Patent Office's ruling came in at almost fifty pages. Farnsworth began reading it line by line but eventually gave up, lost in the dense legalese, and skipped to the end. There, in the nine-word conclusion, was all he needed to see: *Priority of invention is awarded to Philo T. Farnsworth.*

"How many kids in Rigby do you think know who Farnsworth is?" I ask Sergeant Mike as we grab lunch at the deli in Broulim's supermarket.

"Most of them have a general idea. They learn about him in school, and the local museum is named after him."

I tell Mike that I'd recently been browsing through my old high school U.S. history textbook to see if Philo Farnsworth was mentioned. He wasn't. Nor was fifteen-year-old Claudette Colvin (from the Civil

Rights Movement) or nineteen-year-old Ridgely Whiteman, who discovered the Clovis archaeological site.

"It's amazing when you think of how many young people have had an impact on history," I say to Mike, "and yet in textbooks meant for the very same age group, they're ignored."

While we're eating, one kid after another comes up to say hi to Mike. At first I think they're wisely paying deference to the officer who might one day be pulling them over for speeding or some other infraction, but their affection seems genuine. A boy about sixteen or seventeen plunks down next to us and leans his head against Mike's shoulder.

"How you holding up?" Mike asks.

"I'm all right," he says, clearly not.

They talk for a few minutes, and after he leaves, Mike turns to me and says, "That poor kid. His brother was killed last week in a terrible accident."

"Drunk driving?"

"No, he was climbing a metal fence at the baseball field when the top of his head hit a wire dangling from a light pole, and it electrocuted him."

"Jesus."

Another teenage boy walks by and, playing it cool, gives Mike a high five without stopping.

Mike and I get into a deeper conversation about history, and I learn that it's a lifelong passion of his. When I ask why it matters to him, he surprises me by speaking of history in practical terms.

"I think the more that people, especially young people, know about where they live, the more pride and ownership they feel about the place, and the less likely they are to disrespect or vandalize it."

"History as crime fighter," I say. "I like that."

And I think he's right. Even though I'm only a tourist, I've become a little possessive about the towns I've visited after immersing myself in their past.

As far as anyone can determine, Phil Farnsworth himself never returned to Rigby, Idaho. One calamity after another kept him scrambling just to stay solvent. A year after his patent win over RCA, he and Pem sailed to England to meet with the business partner most responsible for Farnsworth's financial survival—John Logie Baird. Baird had given up on mechanical television, and he coordinated with the BBC to license Farnsworth's electronic model for $50,000. Together, they would take on EMI/RCA, which was also hoping to dominate the European market, and they planned to showcase their superior system at London's Crystal Palace exhibition in December 1936. (The architectural wonder was inspired by New York's Crystal Palace, where Elisha Otis presented his safety elevator in 1854.) But Farnsworth was once again the victim of unbelievably bad luck: on November 30, 1936, the exhibit hall caught fire, reducing his high-tech cameras and monitors, all of them irreplaceable, to globs of melted plastic and glass. The BBC ended its agreement with Baird and Farnsworth and opted to partner with EMI/RCA instead.

RCA was moving aggressively back in the States, too. At the 1939 World's Fair in New York, David Sarnoff "introduced" commercial television to the masses and went on to publicly crown himself the Father of Television. Despite securing a licensing arrangement with RCA in the aftermath of his lawsuit, Farnsworth knew that within a few years the deal would be irrelevant once his major patents expired and became fair use. The already high-strung inventor became so anxious that his doctor suggested he start smoking just to calm down.

Farnsworth did find some measure of solace whenever he returned to the old farmhouse in Brownfield, Maine, that he'd bought in 1938 and had spent long hours restoring. In October 1947, two days before he was scheduled to meet with his insurance agent to make certain the property was fully covered after all its renovations, the place burned down. "That's enough," Phil said to Pem while walking through the charred remains of his home and laboratory. "Let's get out of here."

They moved to Fort Wayne, Indiana, and then to Salt Lake City, where Brigham Young University gave Farnsworth an underground bunker lab to pursue his research in nuclear fusion. Crippling depression and ailments plagued Farnsworth for the rest of his life, and he died of pneumonia on March 11, 1971. By the time of his death at age sixty-four, he'd been awarded three hundred U.S. and foreign patents that led to advances in electron microscopes, radar, peaceful uses of atomic energy, and air-traffic control.

Regarding his most famous invention, television, Farnsworth was decidedly mixed. When he was younger and idealistic, Pem later recalled, her husband believed it could be "a marvelous teacher" that allowed viewers "to see and learn about people in different lands. . . . Differences could be settled around conference tables, without going to war." Later he referred to it more dismissively, saying that "there's nothing on it worthwhile." On this matter, Farnsworth and Vladimir Zworykin were in agreement. Zworykin was asked by an interviewer what he most liked about TV, and the elderly scientist responded in his thick Russian accent, "Da svitch, so I can turn the damn theenk off."

Only once did Farnsworth appear on national television himself. In July 1957 he was the mystery guest—introduced as "Dr. X"—on CBS's hit game show *I've Got a Secret*. Celebrity panelists asked him a series of questions to try to guess his identity as the inventor of electronic television.

Farnsworth went home victorious, having earned the top prize of $80 and a carton of Winston cigarettes. He won, though, because none of the show's famous panelists had a clue who he was.

ROBERT GODDARD'S
BACKYARD

We cast this message into the cosmos. It is likely to survive a billion years into our future, when our civilization is profoundly altered and the surface of the earth may be vastly changed. Of the 200 billion stars in the Milky Way galaxy, some—perhaps many—may have inhabited planets and spacefaring civilizations. If one such civilization intercepts Voyager and can understand these recorded contents, here is our message: "This is a present from a small, distant world, a token of our sounds, our science, our images, our music, our thoughts and our feelings. We are attempting to survive our time so we may live into yours. We hope someday, having solved the problems we face, to join a community of galactic civilizations. This record represents our hope and our determination, and our good will in a vast and awesome universe."

—*Message carried by the Voyager 1 and 2 spacecrafts, launched in 1977. Also inside were gold records featuring greetings in fifty-five languages and music by Mozart, Beethoven, Bach, and Chuck Berry. (During an April 1978 Saturday Night Live sketch, Steve Martin reported that aliens had received the records and transmitted a four-word reply: "Send more Chuck Berry.")*

WERNHER VON BRAUN is often referred to as the father of America's space program, and the National Aeronautics and Space Administration's official biography of von Braun praises him for being "without doubt, the greatest rocket scientist in history." To his credit, von Braun redirected the spotlight onto the man he considered more worthy of such acclaim. "In the history of rocketry, Dr. Robert H. Goddard has no peers," von Braun remarked.

> He was first. He was ahead of everyone in the design, construction, and launching of liquid-fuel rockets which eventually paved the way into space. When Dr. Goddard did his greatest work, all of us who were to come later in the rocket and space business were still in knee pants.

Goddard was practically in knee pants himself when the idea for space flight came to him at his boyhood home at 1 Tallawanda Drive in Worcester, Massachusetts.

"On the afternoon of October 19, 1899, I climbed a tall cherry tree and, armed with a saw which I still have, and a hatchet, started to trim the dead limbs," Goddard later wrote of his epiphany. Historical anecdotes involving cherry trees tend to be apocryphal, but this one at least is taken from a primary source—Goddard's autobiography. "It was one of the quiet, colorful afternoons of sheer beauty which we have in October in New England," he went on to relate, "and as I looked towards the fields at the east, I imagined how wonderful it would be to make some device which had even the possibility of ascending to Mars. I was a different boy when I descended the tree from when I ascended for existence at last seemed very purposive."

"Unfortunately the tree is gone," Barbara Berka tells me as we're standing in front of Goddard's old house on Tallawanda Drive, "but the home is the original." Barbara, a Worcester resident and nationally recognized expert on Goddard, knows the current owner and was able to secure permission for us to come by.

"It's big," I say. Not ostentatiously so, but I wouldn't define the white clapboard colonial as modest, either.

Barbara points to a corner window and says, "There's the second-floor room where Robert was born."

Robert Hutchings Goddard came into the world on October 2, 1882, and, after the family moved to neighboring Roxbury for several years, they came back to this house when his mother required treatment for a nearly fatal case of tuberculosis. Goddard also suffered from a host of illnesses, causing his father to pull him out of high school. Young Robert occupied his time conducting homemade science experiments (an explosion here and there rattled his parents, but no lasting damage was done), flying kites, sky-gazing through a telescope, and reading stacks of books. Jules Verne and H. G. Wells were favorites.

Goddard went back to school in 1901, graduated as the valedictorian, and then enrolled in Worcester Polytechnic Institute. During his senior year at WPI he submitted an article, "On the Possibility of Navigating Inter-Planetary Space," to *Popular Science Monthly*, *Scientific American*, and *Popular Astronomy*. All three rejected it. After attending WPI he earned his master's degree and Ph.D. at Clark University, also in Worcester. In 1912 he taught physics at Princeton while spending his nights theorizing about rocket propulsion. His teaching came to an abrupt halt a year later when Goddard came home after catching tuberculosis. His doctors predicted he'd be dead within two weeks.

Instead, during his convalescence he completed the two patents (1,102,653 and 1,103,603) for liquid-fueled, multistage rockets that would revolutionize space travel and influence rocket design to this day.

Shooting large objects high into the air was not, Goddard would have been the first to admit, a novel idea. Fireworks date back a thousand or two years (no one knows exactly when), and in the thirteenth century, Chinese warriors launched lance-tipped bamboo stalks and other projectiles packed with gunpowder at invading Mongols—who, impressed, created and unleashed their own "fire arrows" while marauding through Asia, Europe, and the Middle East. By the 1800s virtually every major army was employing some type of crude missile in battle, and U.S. soldiers of course were on the receiving end of the "rockets' red glare" in September 1814 when British forces pounded Baltimore's Fort McHenry.

In November 1918, Robert Goddard himself demonstrated to top Army brass at the Aberdeen Proving Ground in Maryland a shoulder-held "rocket-powered recoilless weapon" that would enable an individual soldier to blow up a tank or blast through bunker walls. World War I ended days after Goddard's presentation, so the military shelved his invention. (Twenty-three years later, a talented young engineer named Lieutenant Edward Uhl was tasked by a special ordnance unit to revive the idea. After troops finally got ahold of the M1 rocket launcher, as it was officially called, they nicknamed it "the bazooka" due to its shape and the hollow *thwump* it made when fired.)

Early on, Goddard paid for much of his research out of his own pocket. A $5,000 grant from the Smithsonian in 1917 floated him for two years, but by 1919 he had resumed teaching at Clark to pay the bills. On January 11, 1920, the Smithsonian published reprints of Goddard's *A Method of Reaching Extreme Altitudes,* outlining in sober, technical prose how multistage "cartridge rockets" could escape Earth's atmosphere and reach the moon.

Only if Goddard had insisted that the lunar surface were made of Vermont cheddar could he have provoked more ridicule from U.S. and foreign media. *The Graphic,* a well-respected British weekly, blasted Goddard's idea as demonstrably preposterous for several reasons. First, to achieve the necessary thrust for the roughly 240,000-mile journey, the rocket would disintegrate before even leaving the atmosphere. Second, since the planet Earth is hurtling through space at the fantastic speed of 67,000 miles per hour, there'd be no possible way to accurately line up a moon shot. This would be like firing a bullet from a jet plane to hit a cannonball whizzing through the air. And if in Goddard's fantasy universe these and other impossibilities could be miraculously overcome, the whole effort would be pointless because the rocket could never return to Earth in one piece, so there'd be no scientific data to be gathered.

The Graphic's editorial was a gentle, condescending pat on the head compared with the wallop Goddard received from the *New York Times* on January 13, 1920. "That Professor Goddard with his 'chair' in Clark College and the countenancing of the Smithsonian Institution," the newspaper wrote sarcastically,

> does not know of the relation of action to reaction, and the need to have something better than a vacuum against which to react—to say that would be absurd. Of course he only seems to lack the knowledge ladled out daily in high schools.

The idea of a rocket propelling itself through space is what the *Times* found most laughable:

> After the rocket quits our air and really starts on its longer journey, its flight would be neither accelerated nor maintained by the explosion of the charges it then might have left. To claim that it would be is to deny a fundamental law of dynamics, and only Dr. Einstein and his chosen dozen, so few and fit, are licensed to do that.

Some of Goddard's colleagues at Clark also thought he was a few planets short of a solar system, and one professor delighted in asking him whenever they met in the halls, "Well, Robert, how is your moon-going rocket?" Humiliated, Goddard was reluctant to publicize himself or his theories ever again.

He nevertheless hunkered down and continued his research in and out of the lab. "One day Goddard came into Clark after a rainstorm and walked down the corridors still holding the umbrella over his head," Barbara tells me, emphasizing how absentminded he'd become.

Goddard did allow for one "distraction"; since 1919 he'd been courting Esther Kisk, the tall, shy blue-eyed secretary for Clark University's president. Goddard was initially drawn to her beauty and intelligence, but what sealed the deal, they both later joked, was that she could read his almost indecipherable scrawl. The couple married in June 1924.

Two years later, after endless experiments testing powder- and liquid-based propellants, calculating nozzle dimensions to maximize thrust efficiency, burning self-oxidizing fires in vacuum tubes to ensure that booster engines would indeed function in an oxygen-deprived environment, and trying out different-sized combustion chambers and motors, Goddard was finally ready to bring three-dimensional life to his one-dimensional blueprints.

On March 16, 1926, he trudged through the snow-crusted fields of his aunt Effie's farm in Auburn, Massachusetts, and at 2:30 P.M. launched a ten-foot liquid-powered metal tube into the air. Later that night Goddard wrote in his diary: "It rose 41 ft, & went 184 ft,. in 2.5 seconds." The next day he added, "It looked almost magical as it rose, without any appreciably greater noise or flame, as if it said 'I've been here long enough; I think I'll be going somewhere else, if you don't mind.'"

Other attempts, using larger frames, failed, and three years passed before Goddard's next historic liftoff. On July 17, 1929, he built the first rocket to carry a payload. Packed into the rocket's 11½-foot body was a thermometer, a camera, an aneroid barometer, and a parachute. None of them ultimately performed their respective duties, but Goddard was tickled that the rocket flew twice as high as its 1926 predecessor.

Aunt Effie's neighbors did not share his excitement, and while hunting around for the scattered pieces of his creation, Goddard heard sirens off in the distance. Moments later a patrol car pulled up, followed by ambulances (there'd been reports of a plane crash) and two journalists tagging along to investigate what all the commotion was about. "[You're] the moon-rocket man," one reporter realized, sniffing a scoop. "How close did you get this time?" It was exactly the sort of attention Goddard loathed. Several days later the Massachusetts fire marshal branded Goddard a public menace and prohibited him from conducting any more rocket tests in the state.

Through his contacts at the Smithsonian, Goddard was granted access to a patch of federally owned property at Camp Devens in Middlesex County, Massachusetts, to continue his experiments. And while the newspaper accounts predictably painted him as a local laughingstock, they caught the attention of one admirer who believed Goddard was a visionary genius. "Esther," Goddard told his wife at dinner that night, "I had an interesting call from Charles Lindbergh."

"Of course," she said. "And I had tea with Marie, the Queen of Romania."

The world's most famous aviator was sincere in his desire to help, and Lindbergh used his connections to secure for Goddard a $100,000 grant from the business tycoon and philanthropist Daniel Guggenheim.

With a staff of assistants, Goddard set up shop on a sixteen-thousand-acre ranch near Roswell, New Mexico, where a stable climate and sprawling desert free of prying reporters and noise-sensitive neighbors made for ideal conditions. The dry, warm air also kept his dormant tuberculosis in check.

Launch after launch, Goddard's rockets got bigger, sailed higher, and became more advanced. His first major Roswell flight climbed 2,000 feet in the air at 500 miles per hour, and a year and half later he sent up the world's first rocket stabilized by an internal gyroscope.

On April 20, 1938, Goddard and his team gave their first public demonstration. Officers from the New Mexico Military Institute, who were serving as official witnesses, watched in awe as Goddard's rocket flew, from their perspective, what looked to be more than a mile (or 5,280 feet) into the sky. Goddard reported the actual height to be 4,215 feet.

Also in 1938 came sad news from Massachusetts. A massive hurricane had barreled down on Worcester and destroyed something of great personal value to Goddard. Taciturn as always, he recorded in his diary two short but sorrow-filled sentences: "Cherry tree down. Have to carry on alone."

At the outset of World War II, Goddard traveled to Washington to offer every branch of the armed forces full use of his rocketry patents and research. They all rebuffed him.

Years later the Navy did enlist his assistance on a peripheral project dealing with jet-assisted variable thrust engines, but by then German engineers, using slave labor from concentration camps, had bounded far ahead of the Allies in rocket production. They built the world's first long-range ballistic missile, the V2, in 1944, and more than three thousand of these 14-ton behemoths rained down on cities throughout Great Britain and Belgium, killing 7,000 civilians. At the helm of the undertaking was Wernher von Braun, one of 350 former Nazi scientists rounded up after Germany surrendered and sent to America as part of a secret U.S. government program dubbed Operation Paperclip. Von Braun eventually led the team that built the Saturn V booster rockets for the Apollo 11 moon mission.

Goddard died from throat cancer on August 10, 1945, less than a week before World War II ended. His patents and experiments continued to influence von Braun and NASA engineers, and to this day every multistage, liquid-fueled rocket is based on Goddard's designs.

After Barbara Berka and I spend some time walking around Goddard's old home, we drive several miles away to see the Robert Goddard Monument, which wasn't unveiled until May 12, 2006. Barbara was instrumental in getting the Worcester memorial built, and the eight-paneled polygonal structure features a ten-foot-high stainless steel rocket standing side by side with the American flag. Barbara wrote the accompanying text on each panel, and Clark University and WPI helped with funding. I ask Barbara if NASA chipped in, too.

"No," she says.

"I guess they did name the Goddard Space Flight Center in Maryland after him."

"They did that as part of a patent-infringement settlement!" Barbara says. "NASA had been using many of Goddard's inventions without permission, so Esther had to sue. She won a million dollars and an agreement from NASA to name the Center for her husband. She ended up giving most of the money to the Smithsonian because they believed in him from the start."

Barbara, a retired science teacher who serendipitously got involved in the Goddard Memorial Association back in 1998, can't understand why Goddard is so underappreciated considering his contributions to the space program and society at large.

"When I speak at schools, I make a point of telling the students how much their lives are influenced by Goddard," she says. "Along with his more than two hundred patents, you have all of the spin-offs from the space program." These include everything from conveniences like scratch-resistant lenses, the DustBuster, and Tempur-Pedic foam mattresses, to more critical innovations such as GPS, self-righting life rafts, and flame-retardant fabrics.

NASA's crowning triumph, of course, wasn't a particular invention so much as an event in the summer of 1969 partially inspired by Goddard's foresight. Throughout the late 1960s, America had been reeling from the assassinations of Martin Luther King Jr. and Bobby Kennedy, race riots, Vietnam War protests, and an overall sense that the country was splitting apart at the seams. Then, on Sunday, July 20, at 10:56 P.M. eastern standard time, astronaut Neil Armstrong hopped off the *Eagle* lunar module and was followed nineteen minutes later by Edwin "Buzz" Aldrin, becoming the first human beings to walk on an extraterrestrial surface.

For those of us born after the moon landing, it's hard to comprehend fully how breathtaking the endeavor was. This was the pinnacle of human achievement, a merging of individual courage and technological genius unlike anything the world had ever seen. I myself hadn't grasped its risk and significance until, while researching Goddard, I stumbled on one of the most important presidential speeches *never* given.

Unbeknownst to the public, White House speechwriter William

Safire had prepared a statement for President Richard Nixon to read in the event that Armstrong and Aldrin were unable to lift off from the moon and rejoin Michael Collins, orbiting above them, for the return trip to Earth. Since no rescue mission was planned (or possible) and their oxygen supply was limited, the two astronauts would have slowly suffocated to death.

"Fate has ordained that the men who went to the moon to explore in peace will stay on the moon to rest in peace," President Nixon would have told a grieving world in this chilling alternate scenario.

> These brave men, Neil Armstrong and Edwin Aldrin, know that there is no hope for their recovery. But they also know that there is hope for mankind in their sacrifice.
>
> These two men are laying down their lives in mankind's most noble goal: the search for truth and understanding.
>
> They will be mourned by their families and friends; they will be mourned by their nation; they will be mourned by the people of the world; they will be mourned by a Mother Earth that dared send two of her sons into the unknown.
>
> In their exploration, they stirred the people of the world to feel as one; in their sacrifice, they bind more tightly the brotherhood of man.

And this is exactly what they did, but, thankfully, without having lost their lives in the process. More than five hundred million men, women, and children (out of three billion people) across every continent watched the landing live on television that night, awestruck by what we—humanity—had achieved. Never before had the world been so united, so uplifted. Whether it ever will be again remains to be seen.

Sadly, two of the men most responsible for this moment were no longer alive to witness it themselves. President John F. Kennedy was killed two and a half years after he'd stood before a joint session of Congress on May 25, 1961, and declared that "this nation should commit itself to achieving the goal, before this decade is out, of landing a man on the Moon and returning him safely to the Earth." On the morning of July 21, 1969, a note was found on Kennedy's grave at Arlington National Cemetery that read simply: "Mr. President. The Eagle has landed."

There's no account of any message being left at Robert Goddard's final resting place 450 miles away in Worcester's Hope Cemetery. But Goddard did receive a long-overdue public vindication the day after Apollo 11 sailed into space. Under the headline A CORRECTION, the *New York Times* ran a three-paragraph editorial that owned up to its January 1920 comments mocking Goddard's intellect and belief that a rocket could reach the moon.

The paper amended its earlier criticisms and humbly concluded: "It is now definitely established that a rocket can function in a vacuum as well as in an atmosphere. The *Times* regrets the error."

PART VI

BITTER PILLS AND MIRACLE CURES

Medical Pioneers and Discoveries

HARTFORD UNION HALL

A grand exhibition of the effects produced by inhaling NITROUS OXIDE, EXHILARATING or LAUGHING GAS! will be given at UNION HALL, on *Tuesday evening*, December 10, 1844.

Forty Gallons of Gas will be prepared and administered to all in the audience who desire to inhale it.

Twelve Young Men have volunteered to inhale the Gas, to commence the entertainment. . . .

The Effect of the Gas is to make those who inhale it either Laugh, Sing, Dance, Speak or Fight, &c., &c., according to the leading trait of their character. They seem to retain consciousness enough to not say or do that which they would have occasion to regret.

—*Advertisement placed by Gardner Colton in the* Hartford Daily
Courant *to promote his nitrous oxide road show in Connecticut*

FROM WORCESTER, MASSACHUSETTS, the spot in downtown Boston where Dr. John Webster killed and dismembered Dr. George Parkman in 1849 isn't exactly on the way to my next site in Hartford, Connecticut, and I promised myself to limit these side trips. But Parkman's death is linked to my Hartford story about the invention of anesthesia, so it's not entirely off topic. Plus, I'm already in Massachusetts, and I can knock this off lickety-split.

What most shocked Bostonians about Parkman's murder wasn't its barbarity but that both Webster, a distinguished Harvard professor, and Parkman, a respected physician and wealthy landowner, hailed from the gilded class. Hacking a former acquaintance to pieces just wasn't done in polite society. And over money, no less. Webster had borrowed a substantial sum from Parkman and then became evasive whenever Parkman broached the subject of repayment. Fed up with constant excuses, Parkman marched up to Webster's office in the Massachusetts Medical College (its name before becoming Harvard's med school) on November 23 to collect the loan in full. He was never heard from again.

After Parkman's frantic loved ones combed local neighborhoods, posted sizable rewards for information leading to his whereabouts, and convinced authorities to drag the Charles River for his body, a suspicious janitor chiseled into the brick-lined privy under Webster's basement laboratory and, much to his horror, fished out a human pelvis, thigh, and lower leg. He summoned the police, who arrested Webster and searched his workplace from top to bottom. Inside a tea chest they uncovered a headless carved-out torso stuffed with another thigh, and at the bottom of a furnace they removed charred viscera, bones, and a jaw fragment with several teeth attached. Webster had so thoroughly mutilated the corpse that prosecutors had to call in renowned doctors and dentists to identify the remains.

Webster's court case exploded into an international media event. The British were especially enthralled by the trial, and when Charles Dickens toured the United States in 1867, he purportedly told his Boston hosts that the first place he wanted to see was the room inside the medical college where Parkman met his grisly demise.

That building is gone now, but it would have been here at North Grove and Cambridge Streets, close to Massachusetts General Hospital. After parking in a short-term lot, I scout around and talk with security guards familiar with the area. As I suspected, there are no plaques or markers about the historic incident anywhere. There is, however, a slight nod to George Parkman, and it's actually where I left my car. This is either an insensitive joke or a feeble tribute, but the one structure named after the murdered doctor on Mass General's grounds is the Parkman Parking Garage.

Boston to Connecticut is an easy shot across the Mass Pike and down I-84. Heading into Hartford, I haven't the slightest idea what my destination looks like now, only that it's on the northwest corner of Pearl and Main Streets.

Like many major New England cities, downtown Hartford today is an architectural jumble, with gleaming skyscrapers towering over colonial churches and upscale shopping centers abutting seventeenth-century cemeteries. Upon driving to the corner where Union Hall used to be on Main, I find a humongous concrete-and-black-glass office complex with BANK OF AMERICA emblazoned on top. I park a few blocks away and then walk back to circle the building on foot. More than 165 years ago the spot was occupied by Union Hall, a three-story concert space that hosted choirs, symphonies, recitals, lectures, plays, and, on December 10, 1844, Gardner Colton's "Laughing Gas!" exhibition.

Although potentially life-threatening to audience members, Colton's show triggered a series of events that brought an end to one of humanity's most feared torments: surgery without anesthesia, which—up until the mid-1800s—was how all operations were conducted. The prospect of having a tumor removed or a limb amputated was so terrifying that otherwise reasonable men and women chose to die slowly from whatever infection or cancer afflicted them rather than face the doctor's scalpel or bone saw.

"When the dreadful steel was plunged into the breast—cutting through veins, arteries, flesh, nerves—I needed no injunctions not to restrain my cries," the English author Frances Burney wrote to her sister on September 30, 1811, to describe what a mastectomy felt like. While fully conscious.

> I began a scream that lasted unintermittingly during the whole time of the incision—& I almost marvel that it rings not in my Ears still! so excruciating was the agony. When the wound was made, & the instrument was withdrawn, the pain seemed undiminished, for the air that suddenly rushed into those delicate parts felt like a mass of minute but sharp & forked poniards.

That was only the exploratory part of her procedure. Next came slicing out the tumor. "I concluded the operation over—Oh no! presently the terrible cutting was renewed—& worse than ever," Burney wrote. "I then felt the Knife tackling against the breast bone—scraping it! This performed, while I yet remained in utterly speechless torture."

Burney was fortunate that she survived at all. If the crude, improvised butchery of early surgery didn't kill patients right away, operating room infections often finished them off. Most physicians didn't bother to clean their instruments or even wash their hands until the 1870s, when England's Dr. Joseph Lister finally convinced the medical establishment that good hygiene and sanitation practices saved lives. Decades earlier, Dr. Oliver Wendell Holmes Sr.—the esteemed poet and father of U.S. Supreme Court justice Oliver Wendell Holmes Jr.—had also suggested that certain diseases were contagious and advocated that doctors should sterilize their equipment, but his peers laughed off both ideas as ludicrous. (They were more impressed when he showed them a handy new device called a stethoscope, which, invented by Dr. René Laënnec in 1816, Holmes helped popularize in America.) An outspoken critic of his own profession, Holmes once remarked that if most of contemporary medicine "could be sunk to the bottom of the sea, it would be all the better for mankind,—and all the worse for the fishes."

Numerous palliatives were attempted before anesthesia came along, all to little or no effect. Ice and tourniquets desensitized targeted areas but could only be used on certain extremities, and the numbness wore off quickly. Adults and occasionally children were plied with laudanum, opium, liquor, and similar intoxicants, but each of these had potentially unpleasant side effects (for example, vomiting, seizures, death). Some doctors tried hypnotism, while others resorted to "bleeding to *deliquium animi*," a technique that induced fainting through bloodletting. Both patients and doctors were eager to find a panacea, but one of the most obvious solutions hadn't received serious attention until 1844.

On December 10 of that year, hundreds of Hartford residents streamed into Union Hall at 7:00 P.M. to see Gardner Colton's "one night only!" laughing-gas performance. Local press had raved about his previous exhibitions in other cities, and the turnout was excellent. "Mr. Colton gave the same entertainment last spring to an immense audience of ladies and gentlemen in the Broadway Tabernacle, New York—the papers stated that there were four thousand present," the *Hartford Daily Courant* reported on December 9. "From the conversation we have had with Mr. C. and from the good reputation he brings among us, we have no doubt but he will meet a liberal support." Unmentioned in the article was that Colton, a thirty-year-old Vermont chair maker by trade, had recently dropped out of medical school after less than two years.

Colton took the event seriously, though, and began by discussing the chemical properties of nitrous oxide. He then invited audience members to inhale a whiff of gas for themselves. Among those in attendance was a local dentist named Horace Wells, who, to the embarrassment of his wife, dashed onstage without hesitation and proceeded to get high. Minutes later, Wells bumped into his friend Sam Cooley and noticed blood dripping down his trousers. Cooley had somehow smashed his knee after taking a few tokes of gas but, despite the injury, kept hopping about giddily, oblivious to the pain. Right at that moment, Wells realized that nitrous oxide could be the presurgical anodyne doctors had been looking for. Why anyone else in the audience, which included dentists and physicians, didn't make the same connection is a mystery. But no more so, I guess, than with every other innovation that seems obvious in hindsight.

After the performance, Wells approached Colton and asked him if he'd be willing to bring a bag of nitrous oxide to his office for a more formal experiment. Colton agreed, and the next morning they were joined by Dr. John Riggs, a former student of Wells's and an accomplished dentist in his own right. Not wanting to risk anyone else's health, Wells volunteered to have one of his own teeth extracted. After Wells inhaled the gas and conked out, Riggs clamped his forceps around a wisdom tooth and jerked it free, root and all. When Wells revived and his tongue instinctively probed the empty space, he exclaimed, "I didn't feel it so much as the prick of a pin!" This was the first documented case of an American undergoing a medical procedure while anesthetized.

Wells began offering nitrous oxide to patients and taught other dentists, including his competitors, how it should be used. Demand was so great that he looked to expand his practice throughout New England. During a January 1845 visit to Massachusetts, he called on Dr. John C. Warren, the chief surgeon at Mass General and a member of Boston's Brahmin elite. (Warren's father had founded Harvard's medical school, and his uncle had died a hero on Bunker Hill.) Wells requested permission from Warren to demonstrate nitrous oxide in front of an audience of students and doctors at the hospital, and Warren agreed.

Originally, Wells planned an amputation for his presentation, but the patient never showed. A student volunteered to let Wells remove a nagging tooth, and what should have been a cinch for the seasoned dentist turned into a disaster. Perhaps nervous or distracted handling the nitrous oxide and prepping for the extraction simultaneously, Wells failed to provide a strong enough hit of gas, and when Wells plucked out the young man's molar, he awoke with a start. Humiliated, Wells was practically hissed out the door, and he slunk back to Hartford the next morning broken in health and spirit. "The excitement of this adventure," he remarked, "brought on an illness from which I did not recover for many months."

Less than two years later another dentist, Dr. William Morton, asked Dr. John C. Warren if he could attempt a similar demonstration, and Warren reluctantly consented—but only on the condition that he (Warren) perform the actual operation after Morton had administered the gas. On October 16, 1846, Morton entered Mass General's domed proscenium wheeling beside him a fragile, clinking contraption of tubes and glass globes that, he announced to the skeptical audience, would finally make all surgeries painless.

No one, it's safe to assume, was rooting for Morton's success more than Gilbert Abbott, the twenty-year-old human guinea pig about to have a walnut-sized growth excised from under his jaw. Morton held a rubber hose up to Abbott's lips and instructed him to breathe in the fumes. Within moments, he was out cold.

As soon as Warren began cutting into Abbott, those in attendance fully expected the young patient to leap shrieking from his chair. But no, he continued to doze peacefully. After the tumor was removed and the incision stitched up, Abbott woke up as if nothing had happened. The once doubtful audience sat thunderstruck, then burst into cheers and applause.

Until that day, major medical advances had, with rare exception, originated overseas and migrated by way of scientific journals and word of mouth to the States. This time, Americans were at the forefront of a revolutionary development. The Brits had come close decades earlier but, inexplicably, dropped the ball. In 1799, English doctor Thomas Beddoes was utilizing nitrous oxide for medical purposes—but mostly to treat respiratory illnesses. Humphry Davy, a twenty-two-year-old chemist who worked with Beddoes, proposed in 1800 using the gas as a means of "destroying physical pain . . . during surgical operations," but no one paid much attention to the idea, and Davy himself didn't push it. Nitrous oxide was a notoriously temperamental substance, and dosages needed to be calibrated just right. Large quantities could easily kill a person, while smaller amounts offered only a fleeting high. Davy was well familiar with this, having developed an addiction to the stuff. No laws prohibited using nitrous oxide for personal enjoyment, and Davy delighted in hosting for friends and acquaintances frequent "snorting parties."

These had become something of a fad in Britain and then America, particularly among stressed-out college students. "I drank tea at Aunt Warren's yesterday," Anne Warren wrote to her mother from school on March 20, 1825. "Cousin Abby and Edward made some gass [sic] . . . and Cousin Edward [took] it all alone. It had but little effect upon him. It only made him laugh and walk about the room." Anne Warren was Dr. John C. Warren's niece.

On October 17, 1846, William Morton returned to Mass General and repeated his demonstration from the day before, this time on a female patient. Tabloids and scientific journals alike praised Morton for ridding mankind of an age-old terror, and he was inundated with congratulatory messages. "Everybody wants to have a hand in the great discovery," read one flattering note from an eminent colleague who advised Morton to decide on a name for his "agent." And this should be done expeditiously, since it was destined to *"be repeated by the tongues of every civilized race of mankind"* (emphasis in the original). The letter writer was Dr. Oliver Wendell Holmes Sr., and he offered his own recommendation: "[It] should, I think, be called *anæsthesia*."

Not everyone shared in the celebration. After learning of Morton's "discovery," Horace Wells became literally sick to his stomach, and he had reason to feel sucker punched. Years earlier, Wells had taken William Morton on as an apprentice, befriended the young man, and helped him establish a dental practice in Boston. And it was there, in January 1845, that he had told Morton and his associate, Dr. Charles Jackson, how gases such as nitrous oxide and ether could knock out patients long enough for a dentist to painlessly extract teeth or fill cavities, which, in the 1840s, were hollowed out using hand-cranked drills. Wells had already administered nitrous oxide more than a dozen times with auspicious results, and he believed its use could be expanded to other procedures. Upon hearing this, Morton became uncharacteristically quiet, apparently taking it all in.

Of the two, Morton was usually the effusive one, bustling with energy and ideas. Wells was reserved and sensitive, almost shy. Though four years older than Morton, he appeared more boyish, his soft, plump face framed incongruously by mutton chops. Morton attired himself extravagantly and exuded a charming, bon vivant air. Wells was a deeply religious man, dedicated to his faith and family. He was educated in the finest academies but was naïve. Morton, who had dropped out of high school to tend bar, was street-smart and able to manipulate friends, business partners, and romantic interests into believing whatever he wanted. At least for a while.

Wells remained in a funk that only worsened when he learned of Morton's triumphant demonstration at Mass General. Adding insult to injury, Morton sent Wells a letter on October 19, 1846, wondering if he'd be interested in hawking, in exchange for a percentage of sales, Morton's new compound, "Letheon," a mixture of sulfuric ether and oil of orange (to mask ether's offensive odor).

For Morton to treat Wells like a potential door-to-door salesman after stealing the idea from him was galling enough, but even more stunning to Wells was that Morton had obtained a patent for anesthesia. Traditionally, advances in the healing arts were freely shared for society's benefit. Morton went further, demanding $100,000 in compensation from Congress after hearing that Army surgeons were using ether while operating on U.S. soldiers wounded in the Mexican-American War.

As Congress debated paying Morton, Morton's former associate and now archenemy, Charles Jackson (the two had a falling-out over money), challenged Morton publicly. Jackson insisted that *he* had formulated Letheon.

From out of nowhere came yet another petitioner, Dr. Crawford Long, a Georgia pharmacist who presented credible but not absolute proof of having employed ether for medicinal purposes in March 1842. Long's contention is possibly true, but he didn't publish his findings until 1849 (five years after Wells had begun using it regularly), and whatever experiments he might have done in the spring of 1842 didn't set in motion the widespread adoption of anesthesia.

Charles Jackson's lawyers began a withering assault on William Morton's personal character after discovering that in his youth he had left behind a trail of jilted fiancées and bilked creditors. Even before arriving in Hartford to study under Wells, Morton had been accused of counterfeiting, embezzling, forgery, and theft. He'd managed to stay ahead of the law, however, bouncing from one state to the next— Massachusetts, New York, Ohio, Missouri, Louisiana, Maryland, Massachusetts again, and eventually Connecticut—all by the age of twenty-four. Wells had known none of this when he accepted Morton as a student in 1844.

Exasperated by each party's charges and countercharges, Congress dropped the matter entirely. Morton took to the courts and sued the New York Eye Infirmary for patent infringement, hoping to establish a legal precedent. Instead he only succeeded in confirming what most medical institutions already knew by then: Morton's patent was worthless and should probably never have been granted in the first place. "It was only the extended use of a previously well-known principle," the judge declared, ruling against Morton.

Wells, still distraught by Morton's betrayal, floundered financially. He patented an improved shower bath and traveled throughout New England pitching his invention. When that sputtered out, he tried to launch a business that imported high-end reproductions of fine art.

On January 17, 1848, two days after his thirty-third birthday, Wells returned to his true calling and opened a dental office in New York City. His practice offered patients a bouquet of vapors to choose from: nitrous oxide, ether, and chloroform, the buzz du jour. Wells got hooked on the latter and swiftly descended into madness. "My brain is burning," he wrote to his beloved Elizabeth in what would be his last letter home. "I am becoming a deranged man. My dear wife and child, if I am to live, I would be a maniac."

By Friday, January 21, Wells was locked up in jail, having been arrested for wandering lower Manhattan's streets in a stupor and hurling sulfuric acid at prostitutes. Racked with shame, the once devout family man stuffed into his mouth a chloroform-soaked silk handkerchief, which he had snuck into his cell, and slashed the femoral artery in his left leg with a razor blade. Guards found Wells's cold, bloodless body the following Monday.

After Wells's death came the recognition and accolades that had so eluded him in life. Among other prestigious organizations, the American Dental Association and the American Medical Association judged Wells to be the true inventor of anesthesia. In 1875, Hartford erected a towering bronze statue of Wells in Bushnell Park with HORACE WELLS / THE DISCOVERER OF ANESTHESIA carved below. Wells's grave marker in Hartford's Cedar Hills Cemetery says the same.

As does William Morton's headstone, which sits under a tall, fluted Greek column in Massachusetts's famed Mount Auburn Cemetery:

> *Inventor and Revealer of Anaesthetic Inhalation*
> *Born August 9, 1819*
> *Died July 15, 1868*

Not to be outdone is Dr. Charles Jackson, who passed away twelve years after Morton and also rests in Mount Auburn. Jackson continues the dispute across the graves by concluding his long-winded epitaph with these words:

> *Through his observations of the peculiar*
> *effects of sulphuric ether*
> *on the nerves of sensation*
> *and his bold deduction*
> *therefrom, the benign*
> *discovery of painless surgery was made.*

Dr. Crawford Long's grave, in his native Georgia, alludes only to his faith, but residents from his birthplace in Jefferson rallied to honor their local hero with a statue that proclaims:

In memory of
Doctor Crawford W. Long
the first discoverer of anesthesia

(Personally I think Gardner Colton, whose presentation at Union Hall inspired Horace Wells, deserves a similar tribute. At this point, why stop with four?)

A year after Horace Wells committed suicide, William Morton and Charles Jackson faced each other in one final feud. On March 21, 1850, Jackson was invited to provide his expert opinion in a highly publicized spectacle—the trial of Harvard professor John Webster, who had been accused of murdering Dr. George Parkman. After carefully reviewing the evidence, Jackson testified that the bone and teeth fragments unearthed in Webster's stove were undoubtedly those of Parkman.

To rebut Jackson, defense attorneys called in their own heavyweight, William Morton. Whatever ambivalence his professional peers held about Morton's personal character, he was still one of Boston's most prominent dentists. On the stand he seemed to relish undercutting Jackson's conclusions, pointing out that dissections frequently occurred in the medical school building and, thus, the remains found in Webster's office could have belonged to any number of anatomical corpses. The teeth weren't unique, either, Morton declared, and only an overactive imagination would think otherwise.

Persuasive though he was, jurors were more convinced by Jackson and another star witness, Dr. Nathan Keep, George Parkman's personal dentist. In a dramatic courtroom moment, Keep produced a plaster mold of Parkman's gums used to construct his dentures, and the recovered teeth fit inside perfectly.

Webster was found guilty and, despite offering a posttrial confession to lessen his punishment, sentenced to die. Webster's trial was historic not because of his or George Parkman's social standing, though that certainly spiced things up, but because Webster was the first American convicted of murder based on forensic science. In this case, odontological evidence.

After Webster was hanged on Boston Common on August 30, 1850, friends established a fund to support his grieving wife and their three children. The close-knit New England community proved generous and sympathetic, regardless of their feelings about Webster. One of the largest contributions was sent in by a local woman who, through tragic circumstances, had recently been widowed herself. The donor was Mrs. George Parkman.

MINNESOTA RIVERBANK

Ruth Sprague,
dau. of Gibson
& Elizabeth Sprague,
died Jan. 11, 1846 aged
9 years, 4 mos & 18 days.
She was stolen from the grave
by Roderick R. Clow & dissected
at Dr. P. M. Armstrong's office
in Hoosick, New York, from which place
her mutilated remains were
obtained & deposited here.
Her body stolen by fiendish men,
Her bones anatomized,
Her soul, we trust, has risen to God,
Where few physicians rise.

—Epitaph on a gravestone in Maple Grove Cemetery,
Hoosick Falls, New York

WITH THIRTY-EIGHT prisoners set to drop from the wooden platform simultaneously, there was some concern as to whether the scaffolding would hold. Initially, more than three hundred Dakota Sioux Indians were condemned to hang in Mankato, Minnesota, on December 26, 1862, for their actions in the Dakota Uprising earlier that year, but upon reviewing each case personally, President Abraham Lincoln issued 263 pardons. What has brought me to Mankato isn't just the execution of the thirty-eight men, it's what happened to their bodies afterward, a grim fate that denotes a larger, more neglected chapter in the annals of medical history.

Up until 1862 relations between Minnesota's approximately seven thousand Dakota Indians and the U.S. government had been peaceful, albeit strained. Eleven years earlier tribal members had acquiesced to living on reservations in exchange for guaranteed payments from Washington. Many, however, chafed under federal authority and resented being wards of the state. Hostilities escalated in August 1862 when Congress, preoccupied with the Civil War, went months without paying its promised allotment. Starvation loomed, and some Dakota began hunting in "white" territory, aggravating tensions with local farmers. After a violent confrontation on August 17, the tribe's warriors rampaged across the Minnesota River valley, torching barns and homes, slaughtering livestock, and killing hundreds of white settlers. Rounded up by U.S. soldiers and militia, the Dakota accused of committing the most egregious crimes were sentenced to die (whether they were actually guilty is another matter altogether), with the hanging scheduled for the day after Christmas.

An "air of cheerful unconcern marked all of them," a *St. Paul Pioneer Press* reporter observed of the prisoners as they prepared themselves on the morning of their execution. They carried "little pocket mirrors and before they were bound, employed themselves in putting on the finishing touches of paint, and arranging their hair according to the Indian mode." They marched to the gallows, heads high, and rushed the steps almost in "a race to see which would get up first." As white cloths were draped over their faces, the men started singing.

"The tones seemed somewhat discordant, and yet there was a harmony to it," the reporter continued.

> Save the moment of cutting the rope, it was the most thrilling moment of the awful scene. And it was not their voices alone. Their bodies swayed to and fro, and their every limb seemed to be keeping time. The drop trembled and shook as if all were dancing. The most touching scene on the drop was their attempt to grasp each other's hands, fettered as they were. They were very close to each other and many succeeded. . . . [An] old man reached out each side, but could not grasp a hand. His struggles were piteous, and affected many beholders.

The scaffolding didn't break, but one rope did snap, sending a body crumpling to the ground. Soldiers rushed over to the shaken prisoner, gently helped him to his feet, and then returned him to the platform, where he was strung up for a second and final time.

Most died within seconds, but after ten minutes one man kept twitching and his raspy, labored breathing could be heard faintly under the white cloth. Finally a soldier tightened the noose with a hard jerk and the spasms stopped.

Declared "extinct" by Army doctors after half an hour, the thirty-eight bodies were cut down, piled onto mule-drawn wagons, taken down to the Minnesota River, and hastily buried in a sandbar. With the show over, Mankato began emptying out as most of the spectators drifted off. Most, but not all; lagging behind were a group of men, spades in hand, waiting for nightfall. Once the sun set, they hiked down to the riverbank, found the shallow graves, disinterred the corpses, and hauled the prized but cumbersome human loot back home.

"They even drew lots to determine who got the best cadavers," Professor Bill Lass tells me as we pass Mankato's public library, where the gallows had been erected. "Everyone wanted Cut Nose. He was six feet four inches and considered a magnificent specimen."

Bill, now in his eighties, taught for forty-two years at Minnesota State University and is an expert on local history, particularly the Dakota.

Near the library is a statue called *Winter Warrior* depicting a gaunt, pensive Dakota, resting on one knee and gazing into the distance. Next to him is a bronze plaque that describes the December 26 hanging—the largest mass execution carried out by the government on American soil—but there's no mention of its aftermath.

As we walk along Riverfront Street toward the Minnesota River, Bill points to a long patch of dark, wet sand below. "The river has changed since 1862, but the Dakotas were buried right around there."

When I ask why in the sand, Bill says that, in late December, the ground anywhere else would have been frozen.

"Do you think I could walk on that?" I ask, unsure of how firm it is.

"I can't tell from this distance."

"Any interest in joining me?"

"I'll wait up here," Bill says.

Maneuvering cautiously down the steep riverbank and through thick brambles, I try to keep my balance without picking up too much speed. No use. Gravity takes over and my shuffle turns into a trot and then a full run. I hit the ground with a thud (yup, it's solid) and regain my footing. Strewn along the sandbar are small piles of ash-white driftwood that look eerily like discarded bones.

The men who came to this same spot to steal the Dakotas were all respected citizens from Mankato and neighboring towns. Had they been caught—and authorities most likely knew and turned a blind eye to what they were up to—they would have justified their actions as benefiting the common good. They were all doctors in search of corpses for anatomical study, and as gruesome as their actions no doubt were, "body snatching" was common practice in America and had been for two hundred years. In other countries it had been going on much longer.

"A beautiful prostitute, taken by the students from a tomb in the church of San Antonio of Padua, was employed for the public dissection, the last one held by me in Padua," Andreas Vesalius wrote in a 1546 letter. "Her body was slightly emaciated and therefore [ideal]." Vesalius is considered the father of modern anatomy and authored *De humani corporis fabrica* (*On the Fabric of the Human Body*), a beautifully illustrated book that was unprecedented in depth and detail. Vesalius believed that nothing could replace that fingers-in-the-gristle experience of an actual dissection, and doctors throughout Europe and America were of a similar mind.

With the proliferation of medical schools in the 1800s, the demand for cadavers surged. Amputated legs and arms discarded by hospitals went only so far. Doctors wanted heads, necks, and torsos, preferably attached. The most committed and apparently least sentimental among them even rolled their own dead loved ones onto the dissecting slab. Dr. William Harvey, who mapped out the human circulatory system in the 1620s, famously took a scalpel to his sister and father after they died.

In 1744, Massachusetts enacted a law, the first of its kind in the colonies, allowing physicians to acquire corpses from county coroners—but only of men shot dead in duels or executed for having killed someone while dueling. Legislators weren't so much interested in furthering scientific knowledge, however, as they were in adding a mark of shame to dueling, a tradition that increasing numbers of religious and political leaders deemed uncivilized. To be carted off after dying and cut up by a bunch of students was, to many, a great indignity, and this stigma made it all the more difficult for medical schools to acquire bodies.

"No occurrences in the course of my life have given me more trouble and anxiety than the procuring of subjects for dissection," one of America's most distinguished nineteenth-century surgeons wrote while reflecting on his career. "Executed criminals were occasionally procured," he continued,

> and sometimes a pauper subject was obtained, averaging not more than two a year. While in college I began the business of getting subjects in 1796. Having understood that a man with-

out relations was to be buried in the North Burying-Ground, I formed a party. . . . When my father came up in the morning to lecture, and found that I had been engaged in this scrape, he was very much alarmed, but when the body was uncovered, and he saw what a fine, healthy subject it was, he seemed to be as much pleased as I ever saw him. This body lasted the course through.

That doctor was John C. Warren, who had allowed both William Morton and Horace Wells to demonstrate anesthesia at Mass General and whose father had helped establish Harvard Medical School. Warren went on to recall his youthful adventures:

With the cooperation of my father, I opened a dissecting-room at 49 Marlborough Street [in Boston]. Here, by the aid of students, a large supply of bodies was obtained for some years, affording abundant means of dissection to physicians and students. In the meantime, however, schools began to be formed in other parts of New England, and students were sent to Boston to procure subjects. The exhumations were conducted in a careless way. Thus the suspicion of the police was excited; they were directed to employ all the preventive measures possible, and watches were set in the burying-grounds. Thus the procuring of bodies was very diminished, and we were obliged to resort to the most dangerous expedients, and, finally, to the city of New York, at great expense of money and great hazard of being discovered.

Warren's reminiscence abounds with euphemisms. Here's how "subjects" were, in fact, often "obtained": Body snatchers, and these included both eminent doctors and first-year med students, secretly cased cemeteries for recent burials or bribed groundskeepers for the locations. Then they would return past midnight, dig a hole near the tombstone (where the head would be), break open the top half of the coffin with a crowbar, loop a rope around the corpse's neck or underarms, yank it out, and leave behind clothes, valuables, and whatever small tokens of affection had been tenderly placed with the departed. To ensure that no one recognized the body later, any unique scar or birthmark—and sometimes the entire face—was cut off. Not all physicians, it should be noted, engaged in such deeds. Many hired professional "resurrectionists" to handle their dirty work for them.

Body snatchers embraced a peculiar sense of honor and haughtily disassociated themselves from grave robbing, which was stealing from the dead. To them, while only a low-life thief would swipe rings or jewelry from the deceased, the whole corpse was fair game. And the law was on their side; in most states body snatching was a misdemeanor or no crime at all.

The 1788 Doctors' Riot had a hand in changing that. Details are hazy, but according to the most intriguing version, on April 13 a young boy peeked into a New York Hospital window and saw several Columbia College medical students and their teacher carving up a dead woman. Either in jest or to scare him off, someone waved a severed arm at the boy and said that it had belonged to his mother. Coincidentally, the lad's mom *had* just passed away, and he went off screaming to his father. Word spread, and within hours an angry rabble descended on the hospital and ransacked the dissecting room. The students who had instigated the ruckus were locked up—for their own safety—and the horde, now numbering in the thousands, surrounded the jail hollering for justice. (Founding Father John Jay got smacked in the head by a brick while trying to calm the situation.) Governor George Clinton called in state militia troops, who opened fire on the crowd, killing seven people and wounding eight. Within a year New York passed "An Act to Prevent the Odious Practice of Digging Up and Removing, for the Purpose of Dissection, Dead Bodies Interred in Cemeteries or Burial Places," which imposed on body snatchers stiff fines, corporal punishment, and imprisonment. But legislators acknowledged that corpses were necessary for anatomical study, and they granted doctors a whole new crop of bodies to dissect, including executed arsonists, murderers, and burglars.

Legislation in America was also influenced by events abroad, particularly the misdeeds of two Irish immigrants in Scotland named William Burke and William Hare. From November 1827 to November 1828, Burke and Hare had been providing the respected anatomy lecturer Dr. Robert Knox with a steady supply of fresh corpses. A bit too fresh, police later realized. Burke and Hare, authorities discovered, had been killing residents at an Edinburgh lodging house run by Hare's wife. It began (somewhat) innocently enough. The first tenant had died of natural causes and he was overdue on his rent. Hare thought it only fair to sell the body for what was owed, plus maybe a few extra pounds for his troubles. Victim number two was deathly ill, and Burke and Hare hurried him along in the process. Then, tired of waiting for people to get sick and die, they started offing people willy-nilly. Thirteen murders later they got nabbed, and Hare testified against Burke for immunity. Burke was hanged in January 1829, and his corpse was publicly dissected before a standing-room-only crowd at the Edinburgh Medical College.

Outrage over the Burke and Hare murders prodded Massachusetts legislators in 1831 to outlaw body snatching, but they didn't want to deprive the medical community entirely of corpses, so they permitted doctors to take, with some restrictions, the unclaimed bodies of those who would otherwise have been buried "at the public expense." Dead paupers, transients, African Americans (enslaved or free), and anyone else considered down and out had already been plundered on a regular basis from city-run cemeteries, but with this new act they could be acquired legally.

Tougher laws notwithstanding, bodies continued to be stolen from church graveyards and family lots, and those who could afford it hired armed guards and invested in massive stone sepulchers, crypts, and iron fences to thwart intruders. One company in the Midwest even sold "torpedo" coffins rigged to blow up when tampered with.

Neither money nor status, however, guaranteed protection. When the Honorable John Scott Harrison was laid to rest in North Bend, Ohio, Harrison's family secured his casket in a brick-lined vault buried under heavy stones and paid a night watchman to patrol the area. Incredibly, Harrison's body was found days later—during a search for another corpse—at the Ohio Medical College. Harrison's posthumous reappearance made a few headlines, considering that he was a former congressman and the son of U.S. president William Henry Harrison. (John Harrison's own son Benjamin also became president.)

VIP corpses were usually avoided, but on rare occasions a high-profile name proved too irresistible. In 1859 students from the medical college in Winchester, Virginia, rushed to Harpers Ferry when they heard that Watson Brown had been mortally wounded during the failed raid led by his father, John, the legendary abolitionist. After stealing and dissecting Watson's body, the students proudly exhibited his remains in their school's laboratory. Three years later Union troops marching through Winchester discovered Watson's skeleton on display and burned the college down in retaliation. It was never rebuilt.

More states followed Massachusetts and New York's lead, ratcheting up the punishments for body snatching while also allowing medical schools to lawfully obtain the "friendless dead" from hospitals, prisons, almshouses, asylums, and other public institutions. Faced with mounting risks and declining profits, most resurrectionists went out of business by the early 1900s.

During the mid-twentieth century, as Americans benefited from miraculous advances in medicine, they became more willing to donate their bodies for scientific research. Today, medical schools rely primarily on plastic models and virtual cadavers instead of real ones. In 1993, under the auspices of the National Institutes of Health, scientists created the first digital representation of a human body, inside and out, from scalp to toe. Within hours of dying, a thirty-eight-year-old man named Joseph Jernigan was flown to a Denver laboratory, where his still-warm corpse was dipped and frozen solid in a −100 degree Fahrenheit gel and then sliced into more than eighteen hundred sections. Each millimeter-thin sliver was photographed and scanned into a computer, creating a seamless three-dimensional image.

Obese and lacking an appendix and one testicle, Jernigan wasn't considered physically ideal, but there were logistical factors in his favor. He had willed his body to the Texas State Anatomical Board, and the Denver lab knew, months in advance, exactly when to expect him: August 5, 1993. This was the day that Jernigan, a convicted murderer, died by lethal injection.

"It's very difficult to find an intact, non-traumatized, non-pathologic cadaver," the project's director, Dr. Vic Spitzer, later remarked, echoing a centuries-old lament. "I'm not condoning execution. But I don't believe in wasting resources either." What was left of Jernigan was cremated and disposed of locally.

Where each of the thirty-eight Dakotas ended up after being hanged and dissected isn't recorded. There's a strong possibility that some of their remains were sold or donated by the Mankato doctors to museums and other scientific institutions. Native American bones and relics had been highly sought out ever since the discovery of a Virginia burial mound in the 1770s containing one thousand skeletons of Monacan Indians. This was America's first major archaeological dig, and the man credited with finding and excavating the barrow was Thomas Jefferson. (There's just nothing this guy didn't have his hands in.)

"We do know who got Cut Nose," Bill Lass tells me as we leave the riverbank. "Dr. William Worrall Mayo."

This, actually, I had read, and I'd also heard a coda to the story that even Bill wasn't familiar with.

Before Cut Nose's corpse began to putrefy, the doctor who acquired him boiled and cleaned the bones so that he could educate his young sons about human anatomy. Far from frightening the boys, it nurtured their passion to become doctors. After attending medical school and working with their father, Charles and William Mayo helped establish a clinic in Rochester, Minnesota, that has since grown into one of the most respected and emulated health facilities in the world.

RANKIN FARM

The next year, 1915, was the very devil of a year for pellagra, and 1,535 souls in Mississippi are down in the records as having died from it—and who can tell how many perished forgotten? . . .

And who blames the eminent medical men, the celebrated scientific authorities of our American land for shaking their heads, maybe even pointing their fingers at their foreheads when they heard the wild notions of [Dr. Joseph] Goldberger? He was a man of excellent reputation, the name of the Public Health Service was back of him, and they'd been waiting for him to send news from the southland of some horrible microbe, or a spoiled-corn poison, or a bug like the buffalo gnat, or some drug with an unpronounceable name that would cure pellagra. . . . [But he] hadn't even given a letter to a new vitamine that might be the answer. . . .

Goldberger for all his kind brown eyes and his gentle speech—that oddly keeps just the faintest touch of the New York East Side—was mulish. No laboratory slave he, just because it was the fashion to do all science in laboratories. And now he went, this bad pellagra year of 1915, to Governor Brewer, of the State of Mississippi, and asked him a most unreasonable, ticklish, and dangerous favor.

—From Hunger Fighters (1928) by Paul de Kruif

RIGHT ON THIS spot where I'm standing, just beside the train tracks across from the Mississippi State Hospital, a tribute was erected to Dr. Joseph Goldberger after his death in 1929 for finding "the cause and cure for pellagra near here at the Rankin Farm." Years ago, however, the sign—which, by then, had been riddled with bullet holes—was torn from its foundations and vanished. According to the staff members at the Mississippi Department of Archives and History who provided me with a copy of the tribute's full text, no one knows for certain who knocked it down or why, but regardless, due to budget constraints it won't be replaced anytime soon. Except for a portrait of Goldberger that hangs in the National Institutes of Health (NIH), the agency he worked for back when it was called the U.S. Public Health Service (PHS), this marker was the last tangible memorial to a doctor responsible for eradicating an entire disease from the United States.

Goldberger's official NIH biography was my first introduction to the man and a joy to behold. Here, at last, was a medical pioneer whose professional career seemed as inspirational as his personal life. In 1883 the nine-year-old sheepherder's son from the Austro-Hungarian Empire landed in New York with five brothers and sisters. He then bootstrapped his way through school, wooed and wed an attractive high-society southern belle from New Orleans named Mary Farrar, and helped rid the United States of pellagra, a disease that was killing thousands of Americans each year. And he managed to accomplish all of this without murdering and chopping up any of his colleagues, claiming credit for medical breakthroughs that weren't his own, or absconding into the night with Native American corpses.

Well, it turned out there was one small matter that both the NIH and the missing marker glossed over, and it concerns what happened during the summer and fall of 1915 at Rankin Farm here in Whitfield, Mississippi.

In February 1914, Surgeon General Rupert Blue personally asked Goldberger to head up the government's war against pellagra after another PHS doctor quit the post in frustration. Thirty-nine years old at the time, Goldberger was a living legend within the PHS for having risked life and limb to investigate other deadly epidemics. He nearly died from yellow fever in 1902 while tracking the virus in Mexico, fought a less serious though still agonizing bout of dengue fever five years later in Texas, and, during a return trip to Mexico in 1910, contracted typhus and teetered on the brink of death for several days. He rebounded and then gleefully wrote to his wife about the professional "notches" he was accumulating for having suffered through these "quarantinable diseases." Mary, pregnant with their second son and tired of raising the first one alone, was somewhat less thrilled by it all.

Goldberger readily accepted Surgeon General Blue's offer to combat pellagra and was eager to solve the epidemiological riddle that had bedeviled scientists for almost two hundred years. Nothing about the disease made sense. In the United States, pellagra attacked every age, race, and gender but hit the poor and African Americans the hardest. It struck year-round and in all parts of the country but primarily in rural southern towns where cotton fields dominated the landscape. Outbreaks seemed to increase after major flooding as well.

Its symptoms were also uniquely grotesque. Pellagra marked its victims with a painful, bright-red, butterfly-shaped rash across the face and caused the lips to dry up, crack, and bleed. Inflammation spread across the hands and forearms, like formal long gloves, and encircled the neck (a condition called Casal's necklace, named after the Spanish doctor, Gaspar Casal, who discovered pellagra in 1735), creating a macabre, costume-like appearance. The lesions eventually crusted over and sloughed off, leaving the skin hard and scaly. Internally the disease ravaged the intestines and brought on acute diarrhea and nausea. Many pellagrins, as the victims were called, slipped into comas or developed dementia, and approximately one out of three died.

Goldberger crisscrossed the South inspecting hospitals, group homes, orphanages, insane asylums, and prisons where pellagra was rampant. He probed water sources for bacteria, scrutinized bathroom facilities and sleeping quarters for their sanitary conditions, and checked for bug and mold infestations in kitchens, food pantries, and grain-storage bins. Many southern doctors believed that, because pellagra cases abounded in areas where people ate mostly corn-based diets, some microbe or parasite was infecting the kernels. Other health officials insisted that the disease was contagious. No obvious answers came to light, but Goldberger did conclude his whirlwind tour with one critical question: At all of these institutions, why weren't the staff members coming down with the disease?

On a hunch, in May 1914 Goldberger began cataloging the food served at both the Methodist Orphans' Home, where approximately 30 percent of its children were afflicted, and at the Mississippi Baptist Orphanage, whose administrators so feared the stigma attached to pellagra that they insisted their orphans were suffering only from severe sunburns. Goldberger estimated that about 50 percent had pellagra.

Cornmeal, beets, rice, cabbage, and other low-cost fare represented the bulk of the children's meals, while staff members were fed higher-quality foods. Goldberger soon suspected that the problem wasn't what the orphans were eating but what they were *not* eating. With funding from the PHS, Goldberger supplied each facility with large quantities of quality meats, eggs, fresh milk, beans, and other protein-rich foods. The results were overwhelming. Within days, virtually everyone improved and no additional cases emerged.

None of this shed light on why pellagra cruelly disfigured its victims or spared some but not others (although the same could be said of countless disorders), but if Goldberger's diet-related theory were true, it would explain other mysterious aspects of the disease. Pellagra was disproportionately affecting impoverished communities because sharecroppers, who were scraping by only marginally better than the slaves who had worked the land before them, subsisted mostly on corn bread, grits, and the occasional slab of fatback, washed down with coffee. Fruits and vegetables had been crowded out by cotton, a more lucrative crop, and floods wiped out harvests and cattle, causing farmers to further restrict their already meager diets.

Goldberger was guardedly optimistic about his findings but realized that they ran counter to the conventional wisdom. His premise, however, wasn't entirely without precedent; goiter and scurvy were two other known "deficiency diseases" cured by simple nutritional changes. Goiter, identified by swollen thyroid glands, could be prevented by ingesting iodine (hence the reason we iodize table salt), and scurvy was easily treated with foods rich in vitamin C. British sailors earned the nickname "limeys" for consuming large quantities of limes and other citrus fruits on long voyages.

Dr. James Hayne, South Carolina's public health director, wasn't buying Goldberger's theory. Hayne and numerous other southern doctors were convinced that pellagra was transmitted through some contaminating agent, and they took particular umbrage at Goldberger's insinuation that the South's entrenched poverty was responsible for exacerbating the disease. Hayne also dismissed Goldberger's orphan studies as scientifically lacking.

On this last point Goldberger didn't disagree. He himself realized that, to prove his thesis, he needed to perform a long-term trial under controlled conditions that could be verified by other doctors. And this time it wouldn't be enough for him to simply alleviate the disease, as he'd done at the orphanages. He would have to induce it.

Pellagra was excruciating to endure under the best of conditions, and no one, Goldberger assumed, would voluntarily sign up for such an ordeal out of pure selflessness. So in January 1915 he devised a plan and met with Mississippi's governor, Earl Brewer, to outline what he intended to do. Despite the political risks involved, Brewer gave Goldberger his blessing, and Surgeon General Rupert Blue signed off on the proposal, too. Pellagra cases were on the rise, and the three men believed urgent measures were required.

On April 19, Goldberger started feeding a group of twelve white men, all of whom worked on Rankin Farm and ranged in age from twenty-four to fifty, a carbohydrate-based diet that would "hopefully" give them pellagra within six months. Goldberger and his colleague

Dr. George Wheeler carefully supervised the men's food intake and checked them daily for symptoms.

May, June, and July passed with no results.

Once August came, Goldberger began to fear that he might have been wrong about the disease. Then in late September the first rashes sprouted, and by October, Goldberger's subjects started coming down with full-blown pellagra. Goldberger brought in a group of dermatologists to corroborate, and they all agreed with his diagnosis.

That Goldberger had selected for his Rankin Farm study only Caucasians—which he did to dispel the stereotype that African Americans were more predisposed to pellagra—is not what most troubled later generations of medical ethicists and historians. What has stained Goldberger's otherwise stellar reputation is that all of his subjects were prisoners.

Before the Mississippi State Hospital was built on this site, the property belonged to the Mississippi State Penitentiary. About five hundred feet away from MSP's main detention complex but still part of the prison was a screened-in cottage surrounded by fields and animal pens. That was Rankin Farm, home to Goldberger's sequestered "pellagra squad." He had considered other penal facilities, but the Rankin setup was ideal because the inmates could be isolated and yet still remain within the same general environment of the control group—that is, the rest of MSP's inmate population. Goldberger did not want his subjects smuggling in food or becoming infected (if indeed pellagra turned out to be contagious) by anyone beyond their cluster. This was the whole point of using prisoners; they were, by definition, contained, allowing Goldberger to confirm to the scientific community that no outside influences had made them sick.

In exchange for participating, the men were granted their freedom. Goldberger had convinced Governor Brewer that the public health benefits of curing pellagra outweighed the political repercussions of releasing the inmates, some of whom were murderers serving life sentences. When the experiment was over and the men were allowed to resume a wholesome diet, Brewer held a small ceremony in his office for the pellagra squad and gave each one of them his pardon along with a new suit and $5 in cash.

"Dr. Jos. Goldberger," a *Jackson Daily News* editorial proclaimed on November 2, 1915, the day after the study ended, "[has] robbed pellagra of its terrors [and] is entitled to rank with the men of medical science who developed the mosquito theory of yellow fever transmission, the antitoxins for diphtheria and typhoid, the cure for hookworm disease and the eradication of the bubonic plague." Newspapers in other cities gushed with similar praise. Some Mississippi citizens did protest, angry that convicted killers had been let back into society for doing little more than consuming a diet barely worse than their own. None of their indignation, however, concerned doctors from a federal agency performing, for the first time in our nation's history, prolonged and potentially lethal medical experiments on prisoners.

American prisoners, to be specific. In November 1906, while stationed in the Philippines (a U.S. territory then), Army doctor Richard Strong infected thirty-four Filipino inmates with a cholera vaccine tainted with plague organisms. Thirteen died. Strong was investigated but cleared of any criminal wrongdoing. Six years later he was researching the deficiency disease beriberi and ended up killing several more Filipino inmates. Unlike Goldberger's squad, however, Strong's subjects were not pardoned but paid off in cigarettes. Strong returned to America in 1913 and became Harvard University's first professor of tropical medicine.

More than three decades later the same German doctors who quoted from Madison Grant's *The Passing of the Great Race* during the Nuremberg trials to try to prove that Americans had acted no differently than the Nazis, also cited Richard Strong's experiments in the Philippines. And Dr. Joseph Goldberger's at Rankin Farm.

"Goldberger, every now and again, comes [to Rankin] fagged, gray-faced from his incessant prowling up and down through the asylums, mill villages, orphanages, wherever this death of the poor and lowly may call him," Paul de Kruif wrote in his best-selling book *Hunger Fighters,* excerpts of which were submitted by Hitler's top physicians at Nuremberg. "Goldberger and [Dr. George] Wheeler," de Kruif continued,

> look at the knuckles of those their experimental animals, at the backs of their hands and the backs of their necks, and see— nothing. And the weeks are passing, and where's the pellagra? Together these two companions in this criminal research for the good of humanity hold secret council about the ticklish business that goes on here in this little prison house. What if these doings leak out? What if the American nation were to get up on its ear at the news that Government doctors were actually trying to give helpless convicts—human beings after all—the deadly malady of pellagra?

The fact that Nazi doctors obscenely exploited Goldberger, the "hawk-faced" Jew (de Kruif's words), as an involuntary witness in their defense, does not of course make his actions comparable to theirs. But this depiction of Goldberger engaging in "criminal research" has gained traction over the years. Most of the scholarly works and references I've found on the history of medicine in America either ignore him entirely or lump him in with Richard Strong and Leo Stanley, the unscrupulous chief surgeon at California's San Quentin State Prison. Beginning in 1918, Stanley implanted testicular glands and entire testicles—originally from executed inmates, and later from rams, goats, boars, and deer—into the scrotums of living prisoners. An early devotee of eugenics who believed that hormonal imbalances were linked to criminality, Stanley experimented first on senile inmates, followed by those he deemed of "moron intelligence." His ghoulish operations ended not due to any public outrage but because Stanley decided to retire from San Quentin and practice medicine in more posh conditions as a cruise-ship physician.

Medical ethics aren't my forte, but considering that there were no established guidelines for human experimentation in 1915, I do think Goldberger's actions deserve to be put into some context. Goldberger enlisted only volunteers and warned them of the risks involved. He gave the men written consent forms and encouraged them to talk with family members and attorneys before signing up. He monitored their health constantly to make certain no one was at risk of suffering long-term effects, and when one prisoner became seriously ill early on (from an unrelated ailment, it turned out), Goldberger immediately released him from the study. The man still received his freedom.

Goldberger's inmates were unquestionably enticed by the promise of a full pardon, a reward that wouldn't be allowed today. Current regulations prohibit giving prisoners in federal studies *any* "possible advantages," not even a more spacious cell or tastier meals, that might influence their decision to participate in medical tests. They must be motivated solely by a desire to further scientific research. Some ethicists argue that this policy is itself unfair because nonprison (or, "free-world") subjects almost always receive incentives, and prisoners shouldn't be denied the same opportunities. Goldberger's true motivations are impossible to know, but by all accounts he treated his pellagra squad with respect and secured their freedom because he believed they deserved compensation for their hardship.

In the aftermath of the Rankin experiments, several prominent southern doctors refused to accept Goldberger's dietary-deficiency hypothesis and clung stubbornly to the idea that pellagra was communicable. Undaunted, Goldberger conducted a series of tests on himself that if nothing else underscored his personal dedication to bringing the deadly scourge to an end. On April 28, 1916, Goldberger mixed the dried, flaky scabs from various pellagrins with their urine, nasal secretions, and liquid feces, and then, as colleagues looked on, swallowed the concoction whole. He repeated the process several more times and never developed pellagra or any other illnesses except light indigestion and, I'm guessing, a staggering case of bad breath.

Many of Goldberger's skeptics *still* remained unconvinced and continued to denounce his theory, and they were joined by southern politicians who resented a Yankee from New York lecturing their citizens on how to adopt better eating habits. Frustrated that regional pride was undermining public welfare, Goldberger nevertheless recognized how costly it would be, with or without federal help, for southern states to overhaul their agricultural system and ensure that every individual received enough fresh milk, eggs, meat, vegetables, and bread to stave off pellagra. Finding a cheap, readily available preventative became Goldberger's obsession, and after years of trial and error he was able to isolate which foods were most effective. The results defied common sense. Buttermilk did the trick, but butter did not. Beef and canned salmon were a yes, gelatin and cod-liver oil a no. Baker's yeast proved only moderately successful, but brewer's yeast worked wonders. It appeared, in fact, to be the panacea Goldberger had been searching for. Just two teaspoons three times a day were necessary, and it cost only pennies to purchase and distribute. (Biochemists learned eight years after Goldberger's death that niacin was the active nutrient, and in 1943 the War Food Administration mandated that all commercially made white bread be enriched with niacin and other vitamins.)

Whatever scorn Goldberger had endured from his southern critics all but dissipated after the Great Mississippi Flood of 1927, which covered an estimated 16.5 million acres across seven states, killed hundreds, and destroyed $100 million worth of crops, countless livestock, and more than forty thousand homes and farms. The flooding began in mid-April, and by summer, pellagra cases were rising again. Surgeon General Hugh Smith Cumming ordered Goldberger to the South, and this time he was embraced like a conquering hero. "Delta in Grip of New Menace from Pellagra," exclaimed the *Jackson Daily News* on July 25, 1927. "Poor Diet Causes Wide Spread of Disease, Goldberger Coming." And with him came 12,000 pounds of brewer's yeast to be doled out across the region, followed by another 350,000 pounds to avert future epidemics. The aid was accepted with open arms.

During the fall of 1928, Goldberger was recommended for the Nobel Prize in Physiology or Medicine. "It is not an exaggeration to say that many competent observers believe that no more important piece of medical research work has been accomplished in this generation than has been done by Doctor Goldberger," the official nominating statement read. "It has put in our hands knowledge which when applied may be expected to lead to the eradication of pellagra. In addition to this immediately practical outcome of his investigations, there has come a broader understanding of human nutrition and diet by the definite establishment of pellagra as one of the deficiency diseases."

Christiaan Eijkman, the Dutch doctor who discovered what caused beriberi, and Sir Frederick Hopkins, a pioneer in vitamin research, ultimately received the 1929 Nobel award. But even if Goldberger had won, he wouldn't have been alive to accept the prize; a malignant kidney tumor had metastasized throughout his body in December, and he passed away on January 17, 1929. Before he died, Goldberger offered up his body for scientific study.

Goldberger had also instructed that his memorial service be a simple affair. Having dedicated his entire career to public service and raising four sons, he had no life savings to leave his wife, and an elaborate funeral would have been one more financial burden Mary couldn't afford. After his death, Goldberger's friends and admirers—including the Mayo brothers—successfully lobbied Congress to provide Mary with a pension. She would have been destitute otherwise.

Not until 1946, in the wake of the Nuremberg trials, did the American Medical Association formulate its "Rules of Human Experimentation," which stated that "(1) the voluntary consent of the person on whom the experiment is to be performed must be obtained, (2) the danger of each experiment must be previously investigated by animal experimentation, and (3) the experiment must be performed under proper medical protection and management." (Goldberger didn't initially use animals because he thought only humans contracted pellagra. He later realized that the canine disease "black tongue" was similar, and he began conducting dietary tests on dogs. It was during these trials that he discovered the efficacy of brewer's yeast.)

Ironically, experimentation on human subjects in the United States only got worse after Nuremberg. Cold War hysteria prompted an almost "anything goes" mentality among government scientists, and thousands of ghastly tests were performed on inmates and unsuspecting members of the general public.

In 1946 scientists with the U.S. Atomic Energy Commission collaborated with Quaker Oats and the Massachusetts Institute of Technology to feed breakfast oatmeal spiked with radioactive calcium to mentally retarded children and teenagers at the Walter E. Fernald State School outside of Boston. (MIT and Quaker Oats paid a $1.85 million settlement to the test's adult victims in 1998.) And when the arms race escalated in 1949 after the Soviets set off their first nuclear bomb, U.S. troops bore the brunt of early, large-scale radiation experiments. On November 1, 1951, some three thousand military personnel were trucked to the Frenchman Flat basin in the Nevada desert, and a bomb more powerful than "Fat Man," which wiped out Nagasaki, was detonated seven miles away. Given no shelter or protective gear, the men were exposed to the shock waves, intense heat, and radioactive fallout. During a similar exercise the next year, troops were positioned four miles from a nuclear blast, and in 1953 they were placed a mere seven thousand feet away. Sailors aboard U.S. warships were also anchored downwind of nuclear explosions in the Pacific, and the Veterans Administration has since designated 210,000 Americans "atomic veterans" from Cold War–era tests like these, many of whom have reported increased rates of thyroid disease, leukemia, and terminal cancers.

In 2003 the Pentagon admitted that between 1962 and 1974, Army scientists based out of the Dugway Proving Ground—my original Utah site until I was nearly arrested for taking pictures of the Deseret Chemical Depot—were infecting service members on land and sea with nerve agents such as sarin gas to better understand how various toxins affected the immune system. (Not well, they discovered.)

President Bill Clinton offered a formal apology on October 3, 1995, for the government's radiation experiments after a Department of Energy report laid bare the agency's earlier transgressions. Both his statement and the DOE exposé on its past actions were unprecedented, and they would have been major news if both the media and the American public hadn't been distracted by a more pressing story that broke just hours later: football legend O. J. Simpson was found not guilty following an eight-month murder trial.

After I walk the perimeter of the Mississippi State Hospital to make sure I haven't missed anything, I circle back to the front gate and ask the security guard if he remembers seeing Goldberger's tribute or has any knowledge of its fate.

He answers no to both questions and offers his own anticlimactic theory on why it's gone: "Someone probably just wanted it for the scrap metal."

When I mention that the sign had been shot up pretty badly, indicating, I think, some element of displeasure with the intended target, the guard looks at me like I'm from Neptune.

"Around here folks shoot at signs all the time, just for the hell of it," he tells me. "They don't need a reason."

On that note I thank him for his time and scoot off to the airport. The National Center for Agricultural Utilization Research in central Illinois is my next stop—thanks, indirectly, to Joseph Goldberger.

Dr. Alexander Fleming's discovery of penicillin at St. Mary's Hospital in London is probably the most oft-cited "accidental" medical discovery in history, and ever since I heard about how Horace Wells practically stumbled over his nitrous-oxide idea at Union Hall, I've been on the lookout for similar fortuitous scientific advances here in the States. While studying up on Goldberger in a tattered secondhand medical textbook, I inadvertently flipped past the pellagra section and landed midway into the chapter on penicillin. One word floated off the page: *Peoria.*

I read more carefully and learned that, although Fleming was indeed responsible for the initial find, it was a team of American scientists in Illinois who transformed penicillin into a wonder drug that has since saved millions of lives. And they, too, had good fortune on their side.

USDA NATIONAL CENTER

FOR AGRICULTURAL

UTILIZATION RESEARCH

The most exciting phrase to hear in science, the one that heralds new discoveries, is not "Eureka!" but "That's funny. . . ."

—*Author and former biochemistry professor Isaac Asimov*

SERENDIPITY HAS LONG been one of medicine's most steadfast collaborators. I don't say this to demean in any way the scientists who've made groundbreaking discoveries by mistake; their genius was recognizing what others might have ignored or tossed into the garbage. "In the fields of observation," the French chemist and microbiologist Louis Pasteur remarked, "chance favors only the prepared mind."

Pasteur spoke from experience. While studying a particular strain of cholera in 1879, he and his assistant Charles Chamberland forgot to infect a brood of lab chickens with the disease before they headed out on vacation (Pasteur and Chamberland, not the chickens). Upon returning to Paris weeks later, Pasteur injected the birds with the now weakened culture and found that instead of dying, they became immunized. From this research Pasteur invented several lifesaving vaccines.

As evidence that scientists should probably take more holidays, when Alexander Fleming got back from his summer break in 1928, the notoriously untidy doctor noticed mold growing in a Petri dish containing *Staphylococcus aureus* that was inhibiting the bacteria's growth. Fleming wondered if the furry blue-green lump, later identified as *Penicillium notatum,* could possibly be a new germicide, and after further testing, it indeed turned out to be an extremely effective antibiotic.

Fleming announced his find in February 1929 at the prestigious Medical Research Club, but none of his colleagues showed much interest. His June 1929 article on penicillin, published in the *British Journal of Experimental Pathology,* met with similar apathy. Painfully shy, Fleming didn't push the topic and eventually immersed himself in other projects.

Almost a decade later, England was bracing for war and British scientists urgently sought out new treatments for battlefield infections, which they knew from past conflicts often killed more troops than bombs and bullets combined. Thirty-three-year-old Dr. Ernst Chain, a Jewish refugee from Hitler's Germany who resembled a young Albert Einstein, stumbled across Fleming's 1929 article by "sheer luck," he later said, and showed it to Dr. Howard Florey, his boss at Oxford University's Sir William Dunn School of Pathology. Florey agreed that it warranted more study, and the two men, along with Dr. Norman Heatley and Dr. Margaret Jennings, secured a Rockefeller Foundation grant to research penicillin's medical applications. Funding appeals to their own government's Medical Research Council, British pharmaceutical companies, and Oxford University were all rejected.

Time was running short. In July 1940 the Luftwaffe launched a ferocious six-month bombing campaign over England that ultimately killed more than twenty thousand civilians. Like many parents who had the means, Florey sent his children overseas, and they ended up staying in Connecticut with his friend Dr. John Fulton. Aside from possibly losing their own lives, Florey and his team feared that a direct strike on their lab would wipe out irreplaceable research; a single batch of Fleming's original *Penicillium notatum* was all they had to work with. In case of a full-on German invasion, they planned to rub the penicillin spores, which were extremely resilient, into their coat pockets and flee to a neutral country.

On February 12, 1941, police constable Albert Alexander became the first person treated with penicillin. Alexander had scratched his face on a rose thorn, causing an infection to flare across his cheeks and into his eyeballs, which started to swell up hideously. The right eye had to be lanced right away before bursting, and the left one was extracted entirely. Soon Alexander's entire body was under attack. "He was oozing pus everywhere," Heatley recorded in his diary. Then, less than twenty-four hours after Alexander received penicillin, his condition improved noticeably, and by February 22 he had rebounded almost completely.

Almost. Just as he was on the verge of a full recovery, doctors exhausted their penicillin stock. Despite his dramatic turnaround, Alexander's now defenseless body was unable to repel the last lingering microbes, and they multiplied with a vengeance. Within days he was dead.

Florey and Heatley had frantically tried to grow penicillin in anything they could get their hands on—Petri dishes, bedpans, pie tins, cafeteria trays—but purifying the low-yield mold was maddeningly slow. If one patient could so rapidly drain their supplies, they realized, there was no hope of providing mass quantities for injured troops and civilians in the years to come.

Still unable to persuade the British government or private companies to underwrite their efforts, Florey decided he would have to approach a partner outside of war-torn Europe, a partner with the resources, manpower, and scientific wherewithal to produce this new wonder drug on a massive scale. He knew just whom to call.

. . .

"Good morning, USDA, how may I help you?" a lovely Scottish voice asked when I first contacted the Department of Agriculture's National Center for Agricultural Utilization Research (NCAUR) in Peoria. I told the receptionist, Jackie Shepherd, what I was doing and briefly recapped my understanding of NCAUR's role in manufacturing penicillin after English doctors had discovered it. Jackie verified that, yes, I had the right place, and connected me to their communications officer, Katherine O'Hara, to schedule a visit. But before patching me through, Jackie playfully admonished me. "I don't believe that Fleming was English," she said, her native lilt sounding stronger than before. "He was a Scotsman."

When I arrive weeks later at 1815 North University Street I'm pleased to find Jackie manning the front desk, and she's as gracious in person as on the phone. Jackie buzzes Katherine O'Hara, and while I'm waiting, I peruse the lobby display cases about NCAUR and its three sister labs in Louisiana, California, and Pennsylvania. They were all built during the Depression to devise new ways of putting surplus crops to good use, and their accomplishments are both impressive and eclectic. They've created frozen concentrated orange juice, lactose-free milk, dehydrated potato flakes, biodegradable plastics, and a silicone emulsion that preserves antique books. Peoria, specifically, came up with the idea of using infrared lamps to make french fries crispy, designed an ingenious method of cleaning Navy warplanes by air blasting them with ground corncobs, and produced the blood plasma substitute dextran.

Katherine, a warm and welcoming host, takes me up to her office, where she hands me a packet of penicillin-related materials from NCAUR's archives.

"Here's what started it all," she says, pulling out the historic July 9, 1941, telegram from Department of Agriculture administrator Dr. Percy Wells to NCAUR director Dr. Orville E. May:

HEATLEY AND FLOREY OF OXFORD, ENGLAND, [ARE]
HERE TO INVESTIGATE PILOT SCALE PRODUCTION
OF BACTERIOSTATIC MATERIAL FROM FLEMING'S
PENICILLIUM IN CONNECTION WITH MEDICAL DEFENSE
PLANS. CAN YOU ARRANGE IMMEDIATELY FOR
SHALLOW PAN SETUP TO ESTABLISH LABORATORY
RESULTS IN METAL [CONTAINERS].

Heatley and Florey's journey to the United States was exhausting and dangerous, requiring cloak-and-dagger measures to get them from London to Lisbon, where they scurried onto a Pan Am Clipper with blacked-out windows. From Portugal they flew directly to New York City. America wasn't yet at war, but with the Luftwaffe patrolling the skies over Europe and German warships prowling the Atlantic, no mode of transportation to the States was safe. (Before leaving, Heatley and Florey went out for a much-needed night of entertainment and decided to catch the new Alfred Hitchcock thriller *Foreign Correspondent.* They were unaware that in the movie's climactic scene, a plane identical to theirs is shot by a German destroyer and plunges into the ocean. "The sinking of the 'Clipper' in the film struck [Florey] & me as rather a bad thing to see," Heatley noted dryly in his diary.) Throughout the entire trip, Florey held on tightly to a briefcase packed with notebooks and carefully wrapped vials of freeze-dried penicillin.

They landed at LaGuardia Field on July 2 wearing thick wool suits more appropriate for England's cooler climate than Manhattan's sweltering heat. But summer humidity or not, neither man let go of his jacket; smeared into the coat pockets were the "backup" spores they would use in the event that Florey's briefcase was heisted.

From the East Coast, the doctors made their way to Peoria, and on July 14 they met with Dr. Robert Coghill, director of NCAUR's fermentation division, and Dr. Andrew Moyer, an expert on the nutrition of molds.

"Clete here is going to take you to Moyer and Coghill's old labs," Katherine says as she introduces me to Dr. Cletus Kurtzman, one of Moyer's successors. Clete's been working at NCAUR for forty-two years and oversees a collection of 100,000 different microbes. After we talk for several minutes I can sense that his passion is undiminished, and I ask him what first got him interested in science.

"I've been fascinated since I was a child. I'd go down to the pharmacy and buy powdered sulfur, potassium nitrate, and sulfuric acid, then come home and do experiments. Looking back on it, I'm surprised they'd sell those things to a boy, but it sure was fun." He adds wistfully, "Those were the good old days."

"And you never got hurt or anything?" I ask, thinking of how a young Robert Goddard nearly blew himself to pieces playing with similar chemicals.

"Let's just say I'm very lucky to have all ten digits and a face."

Clete and I start walking over to the building's center section, and along the way he tells me, "I'm afraid the laboratories won't look like they did originally."

"No worries," I say. "I just want to see where it all happened."

Within forty-eight hours of Heatley and Florey's arrival at NCAUR, Moyer and his team were hard at work cultivating the samples smuggled over from Oxford. After an initial scare, when the spores that had blossomed so quickly in England didn't take to NCAUR's balmy, 80-degree-plus temperatures (the new air-conditioning system wasn't operational until that September), the Peoria scientists were finally able to grow the first tiny batch of mold by July's end.

To mass-produce penicillin, which was the whole reason the Oxford doctors had come to Illinois, Moyer first suggested utilizing corn-steep liquor in the fermentation process. The idea was as much practical as it was scientific; the thick, syrupy liquid was rich in nitrogen, and it could be acquired easily because nobody wanted the stuff. A by-product of cornstarch, it was often just dumped into the Illinois River.

Adding corn-steep liquor alone, they discovered, upped the yield a stunning 1,000 percent.

Florey left Peoria to embark on a hat-in-hand tour of America's pharmaceutical giants, begging them to mobilize their resources behind penicillin. Drug companies were familiar with its potential but also its production-related drawbacks and, like their British counterparts, doubted they could make a profit. Cultivation tanks the size of swimming pools, some scientists estimated, would be needed in order to skim off enough mold from the culture fluid's surface, and that investment alone was calculated to be prohibitively expensive.

The Peoria crew was working to tackle this very problem, and they believed that "submerged growth" was the solution. If penicillin were brewed up in large drums—not just on the surface but throughout the mixture—production could be boosted exponentially. Moyer recommended adding lactose to the corn-steep liquor and aerating the broth with a constant supply of sterile oxygen in ten-thousand-gallon vats.

This, too, increased yields substantially.

Moyer realized, however, that to truly maximize results they needed a more resilient mold. Leading the hunt for this new, tougher strain was another NCAUR mycologist, the unfortunately named Kenneth Raper, who instructed members of the U.S. Army Transport Command to bring him mold extracts and soil samples from wherever they traveled around the world.

Any reluctance the pharmaceutical industry had initially shown in the summer of 1941 vanished on December 7. After the attack on Pearl Harbor, Lederle Laboratories, Merck, E. R. Squibb, and Charles Pfizer (more companies came aboard later) all agreed to join forces to mass-produce penicillin, and they received special dispensation from the government to work together without violating antitrust laws.

Having been on the sidelines for so long, the drug corporations struggled initially. By the early spring of 1942, they had collectively whipped up a mere 5.5 grams—barely more than a teaspoon's worth—of pure penicillin, which at best could treat only a single individual.

The opportunity to do just that came in mid-March at Connecticut's New Haven Hospital, where thirty-one-year-old Anne Miller was dying of blood poisoning brought on by a severe bacterial infection. Doctors had tried transfusions, surgery, and sulfanomides (the first antimicrobial drugs), but nothing worked, and Miller was deteriorating fast. Coincidentally, Miller's doctor, John Bumstead, was also caring for a fellow physician, John Fulton, who had mentioned in passing that his English friend Dr. Howard Florey had developed a powerful new antibiotic called penicillin. Bumstead implored Fulton to get a dose for Miller, and Fulton was able to pull a few strings. The medicine was rushed to New Haven on Saturday, March 14, and Miller recuperated fully. She was the first American treated with penicillin and, it is believed, the first person anywhere saved by it.

At NCAUR there was further cause for celebration. After working seventy-hour weeks sifting through a malodorous array of decaying fruits, old cheeses, breads, meats, and clumps of dirt contributed by U.S. aircrews and scientists from around the globe, Raper had finally isolated the "super" mold he'd been searching for. Approximately fifty times more potent than anything previously tested, the strain eventually became the primogenitor for almost all of the world's penicillin. And it was found, by chance, on an overripe cantaloupe purchased at a Peoria grocery store. (The exact location, alas, isn't recorded. Robert Coghill only noted the source in NCAUR's records as a "fruit market" near the lab.) The miracle melon itself was neither preserved for posterity nor disposed of with any kind of ceremonial pomp befitting its historic significance. After cutting the mold off the rind, staff members sliced up the cantaloupe and ate it.

By June 1944, right in time for the D-Day landings at Normandy, drug companies were churning out an estimated 100 billion units of penicillin per month, enough for an estimated forty thousand U.S. and British combatants. Hitler's forces had to rely on less effective sulfa drugs and, consequently, experienced higher fatality rates, more amputations, and longer recovery times for injuries, diminishing their overall troop strength. Thousands of German soldiers were also incapacitated by sexually transmitted diseases such as syphilis and gonorrhea, which penicillin would have easily treated. On and off the battlefield, penicillin cured an ever expanding range of afflictions—pneumonia, strep throat, gas gangrene, septicemia, spinal meningitis, scarlet fever, puerperal sepsis, to name just a few—and with virtually no side effects. It became as indispensable to the Allied war effort as any weapon.

In late October 1945, Alexander Fleming, Howard Florey, and Ernst Chain jointly won the Nobel Prize for Physiology or Medicine. Only three people, at most, can receive the award for the same discovery, and fairly or not, Heatley was shut out. (Moyer wasn't even in the running, but he was the second microbiologist inducted into the National Inventors Hall of Fame. The first was Louis Pasteur.) That same fall NCAUR stopped manufacturing penicillin and licensed all production to private pharmaceutical firms. After the war, demand shifted from military to civilian applications, and penicillin became wildly profitable. In 1951 drug companies were producing approximately 30 trillion units a month, and within three decades that number skyrocketed to 385 trillion units.

Clete opens the stairwell door to the third floor, and we walk into a bright fluorescent-lit hallway.

"All of this has been newly renovated since the 1940s, and even the walls have been offset by the new construction, but Moyer's lab would have been around here," he says in front of Room 3118.

We peek inside, and Clete explains that this is where they now store NCAUR's one hundred thousand cultures. "About eighty thousand of the microbes are fungi," he says, "and the other twenty thousand are bacteria." Large double-door steel refrigerators, like those found in any modern household kitchen, line both sides of the laboratory, and down the middle are liquid-nitrogen containers the size of industrial drum barrels.

We step back into the corridor, and before we return to Katherine's office, Clete starts talking about a medical innovation developed during the early 1950s by Dr. Allene Jeanes in the lab right across from Room 3118. As Clete goes into detail about its chemical properties—something about polysaccharides and carbohydrate structures—my scientifically challenged brain begins to shut down, and I stand there nodding reflexively.

Then he mentions the word *dextran* and I realize he's describing the blood plasma substitute I'd read about in the lobby. Originally intended for U.S. troops fighting on the front lines in Korea, it's commonly used in hospitals today and has prevented countless patients from bleeding to death.

The lifesaving blood extender was created out of a "slimy bacterium," Clete tells me, that wasn't exactly drawn from the lab's official collection of microbes. Another NCAUR scientist had shown the mold to Dr. Jeanes after spotting it inside a half-empty bottle of old root beer that someone, fortuitously, had neglected to throw away.

DR. MAURICE HILLEMAN'S

BIRTHPLACE

If I had to name a person who has done more for the benefit of human health, with less recognition than anyone else, it would be Maurice Hilleman.

—Dr. Robert Gallo, *director of the Institute of Human Virology and the codiscoverer of the human immunodeficiency virus (HIV)*

When my birth was registered at the County Court House, it was spelled Hilleman. The second "n" had been deleted because of anti-German sentiment in which our Church had been smeared with yellow paint.

Nothing else happened on August 30, 1919, except that on that day, Charles Guiteau was hanged for the murder of President James E. Garfield.

—From Dr. Maurice Hilleman's unfinished autobiography, "Out of the Kingdom." (Guiteau was actually executed thirty-seven years earlier.)

DR. MAURICE HILLEMAN'S widow, Lorraine, generously shared with me a copy of the autobiography her husband was struggling to complete while dying of cancer. Before meeting with his nephew Art Larson, here in Miles City, Montana, I was curious to read what Hilleman had written about his birthplace and its influence, if any, on his later achievements. "I consider it fortunate to have been born into modest means without a silver spoon in the mouth," Hilleman recalled in rushed and uncorrected prose (understandable, considering the circumstances). "Work on the farm began at age 5 years of age [*sic*] where working with plants, animals, soil, mechanics and electricity gave a practical introduction into the workings of the biological and physical sciences." Sadly, Hilleman had only made it up to the section about his high school years when he passed away at the age of eighty-five on April 11, 2005.

After he died, every major obituary echoed Dr. Robert Gallo's sentiments about Hilleman's contributions to global health and also noted that his research has possibly saved more lives than any other scientist's. Some dropped the "possibly" altogether. "Among scientists, he is a legend," Dr. Anthony Fauci, director of the NIH's National Institute of Allergy and Infectious Diseases, said of Hilleman. "But to the general public, he is the world's best-kept secret." He's a bit of a secret in Miles City, too.

Having spoken with half a dozen local residents before coming here to find the house where Hilleman was born, I already knew that there were no memorials or tributes to him anywhere in his hometown. This is all the more perplexing to me now as I'm driving down Main Street because I can't help noticing that *every other house* appears to have its own historical marker. I've never seen anything like it. Most are mounted near the sidewalk on top of thin, waist-high stanchions shaped like a conductor's stand, and the rest are bolted next to front doorways. I pull over to investigate. CARPENTER ERNEST ANDERSON BUILT THIS LOVELY ONE-AND-A-HALF STORY BUNGALOW IN 1916, notes one. A few lawns down: CONSTRUCTED IN 1913 FOR DR. CURTIS N. RINE-HART, A PROMINENT MILES CITY DENTIST, THE HOME REFLECTS THE

TOWN'S SECOND GROWTH SPURT. And for another doctor: RENOWNED
MONTANA ARCHITECT CHARLES S. HAIRE DREW THE PLANS FOR PROMI-
NENT LOCAL PHYSICIAN DR. FRANCIS GRAY, WHO WAS A CHARTER STAFF
MEMBER OF HOLY ROSARY HOSPITAL.

I pass the Montana Bar, which boasts a bronze plaque from the
National Register of Historic Places, and continue on toward the local
museum to check out what information it has on Hilleman. I'm scan-
ning homes and business fronts for additional markers en route, and I
almost swerve into an older man slowly puttering along the shoulder
on a John Deere rider mower.

Inside the museum I ask the only staff member present, a gentleman in his sixties, if they have any memorabilia or exhibits related to
Dr. Maurice Hilleman.

"That name doesn't sound familiar," he says, reaching for a thick
binder. He flips through the pages and traces his finger down an alpha-
betical list of noteworthy residents. I look over his shoulder.

No Hilleman.

"You need to talk to Bob Barthelmess. He's pretty much the town
historian."

"Do you know where I can find him?"

In walks the guy I almost clipped a few minutes ago.

"That's him right there."

Fortunately, Bob doesn't seem to recognize me.

I say hello and explain that I'm in town to locate the birthplace
of Dr. Maurice Hilleman and learn more about his early years in
Miles City.

"Never heard of him," Bob says gruffly. "What's so special about him?"

"Well, among a number of things, out of the fourteen or so vaccinations that most people receive in their lives, Hilleman developed, like,
half of them."

"If that's true, and he's from here, how come I don't know who he
is?" Bob's tone is more befuddled than accusatory, but there's a hint of
suspicion that I'm pulling his leg.

"I had no idea who he was either until a few months ago," I say. "I've been talking with Art Larson here in Montana, who's going to take me to—"

"Yeah, I know Artie. Used to be involved with the museum."

"He's Hilleman's nephew."

"His *nephew*? He never mentioned that to me."

"I'm seeing him later today. Anyway, I hear you're the expert on Miles City, but is there someone else you think I should talk to, someone who knows as much about the town as you do, if that's possible?"

"Yes," Bob says. "But he's dead."

"Ah."

"Where was this Hilleman fellow born?" Bob asks me.

"I think right down the street from here."

"Looks like somebody's been asleep at the post," Bob says, finally sounding convinced that this required further investigation. We exchange contact details, and I promise to update him on whatever else I find.

Art and his wife, Nancy, live an hour north of Miles City and are driving down to show me exactly where Hilleman was born. In the meantime, I'm meeting with the town's mayor at a coffee shop called Kafé Utza.

Not that I've hung out with a lot of mayors—in fact, I believe this is a first—but I can't imagine any of them being cooler than Joe Whalen. Bored working as the manager of an Internet provider company in North Dakota, Joe hopped on his motorcycle in May 2000 and headed west. While passing through Miles City en route to his native California, he stopped at the Montana Bar, had a cold beer, and right then and there decided he had found his new home. Joe opened up a bookshop in 2002 and, four years later, filled a vacant seat on the city council. Two months after that he was asked to serve out the previous mayor's term, which he did, and since then he's been "properly" elected.

In his early to mid-forties, I'm guessing, and ruggedly good-looking, Joe is friendly and approachable but not in a slick, political way. Just laid-back and personable. He's well familiar with Maurice Hilleman and wants to see him honored. "I think we can get the town to do something," Joe says, "and he certainly deserves the recognition." After we chat for a good thirty minutes or so, Art and Nancy pull up in their Ford Bronco and Joe comes out to say hello before returning to work.

Art, a seventy-eight-year-old rancher, had a stroke earlier this year and doesn't say much as we drive through town. "He wasn't the chattiest person before the stroke," Nancy tells me, "but this has been a hard couple of months. He's doing better though." Nancy is an accomplished local artist, and she, too, was born in Miles City. I ask them both where they lived, and Art chimes in: "My old house used to be the town brothel. *Before* our family lived there."

"What do you all remember of Dr. Hilleman, as a person?" I ask.

"He was extremely modest," Nancy says, "and serious, although he had a kind of wry sense of humor. Obviously he was very smart, but he never talked about his work."

Art nods and adds, "He also knew how to hypnotize chickens."

We drive along Main Street for a few minutes and, five hundred or so feet past the museum, turn onto Water Plant Road, which curves to the right for three-quarters of a mile and dead-ends directly in front of a dilapidated, light-blue two-story house.

"That's it," Nancy announces."That was Maurice's first home."

I ask them if they want to walk around the property with me for a few minutes, and Art shakes his head.

"That's okay," Nancy tells me. "We're fine right here. Take your time."

Art and Nancy don't know when the Hilleman residence was last occupied, and from the outside it's hard to gauge. Much of the exterior paint has been worn away by rain and frigid winds, exposing patches of brown wood. Waist-high weeds poke through broken planks that were once a front porch. Half the windows are shattered, and yet a mysteriously clean white curtain flutters gently in and out of a front window. Behind it there's a white metal birdcage hanging from the ceiling. Otherwise the interior looks forlorn and empty. I step back and notice cinder blocks neatly stacked near a side door. On a tree about ten feet from the house is a rusted shovel blade nailed into the bark about six feet off the ground.

Maurice Ralph Hilleman was born in this house on August 30, 1919, the eighth child of Gustav and Anna Hillemann. There was a ninth, Maurice's twin sister, but she was stillborn. Gustav buried the baby girl hours later, followed by Anna the next day; during labor, she had developed eclampsia, a swelling of the brain, and died on September 1. Per his wife's final request, Gustav dug up their infant daughter, tucked her into Anna's arms after she passed away, and laid them both to rest in a single grave.

"I always felt that I cheated death," Hilleman later said of his birth, and, by all accounts, he kept cheating throughout his childhood. Before reaching the age of ten, he had come close to drowning in the roiling currents of the Yellowstone River, getting crushed by a freight train on a railroad trestle (he leapt to safety with half a second to spare), and suffocating to death after a diphtheria infection puffed up his throat. "I was proclaimed near dead so many times as a kid," Hilleman recalled. "They always said I wouldn't last till morning."

Hilleman attended Montana State University, graduated first in his class, and won a full University of Chicago scholarship to earn his microbiology doctorate. The skinny, perpetually broke young student who had to get by on one meal a day made medical history at Chicago with his doctoral thesis. Hilleman discovered that chlamydia—which infects several million Americans a year and can make women infertile—wasn't a virus, as most scientists believed, but a unique bacterium, and his research enabled doctors to treat the disease more effectively.

The New Jersey pharmaceutical company E. R. Squibb recognized Hilleman's brilliance and hired him right out of school. For four years he worked on creating flu vaccines, and in 1948 he joined the team of scientists at the Walter Reed Army Medical Center in Washington, D.C., tasked with studying influenza and preventing future outbreaks.

Hilleman, almost single-handedly, did just that in the spring of

1957. On April 17 he read a short newspaper article about a nasty influenza bug racing through Hong Kong. As a precautionary measure, Hilleman cabled an Army medical post in Japan and told them to track down an infected U.S. soldier, collect a saliva specimen, and rush it to Washington. He regrew the sample and identified it as similar to the Asian flu strain that had swept the globe in 1889. Hilleman immediately alerted the World Health Organization, the U.S. Public Health Service, and the Army's own Commission on Influenza about the potential threat, but all of them thought he was being hasty. In defiance of protocol, Hilleman issued a press release declaring that another pandemic was imminent and encouraged several vaccine manufacturers to get a jump on production. He also instructed them to advise their chicken farmers not to destroy their roosters at the end of hatching season, a standard practice Hilleman remembered from his Montana youth. Hundreds of thousands of additional eggs would be needed, he told them, to incubate millions of vaccine doses.

Critical time was lost when the health agencies initially dragged their feet, and seventy thousand Americans were killed by the Asian flu, but the numbers could have been dramatically higher were it not for Hilleman's rapid response. "Many millions of persons, we can be certain, did not contract Asian flu because of the protection of the vaccine," Surgeon General Leonard Burney later said. For his efforts Hilleman was awarded the Medal for Distinguished Public Service by the secretary of defense.

In 1957, Hilleman and his wife, Thelma, moved to Pennsylvania so he could accept a position heading up all virus and cell biology research at Merck. Thelma died of breast cancer in 1962, leaving a distraught Hilleman to care for their young daughter, Jeryl Lynn, by himself. On March 23, 1963, Hilleman's little girl came down with epidemic parotitis. Better known as the mumps, the painful infection usually passes after a few weeks without inflicting any long-term harm, but in extreme cases the virus can cause deafness, diabetes, and brain damage.

After swabbing Jeryl Lynn's throat, Hilleman returned to his lab and injected the culture into chicken embryos. From this he produced the "Jeryl Lynn" mumps vaccine, which continues to be administered to this day. (There's still no cure for the mumps, and the best "treatment" remains getting immunized and not coming down with it in the first place.)

Emboldened, Hilleman began tackling one vexing disease after another—but, thankfully, without relying on his daughter to be stricken with each one.

Next came measles, a virus that was killing and blinding tens of millions of children a year. In 1968, Hilleman invented a vaccine that, within the United States alone, brought the number of infections down from four million to approximately one hundred. He followed up with a three-in-one measles/mumps/rubella shot that has made the vaccinations less expensive and more accessible, especially to children in poorer nations.

During the mid-1970s, Hilleman pushed Merck to mass-produce vaccines for pneumonia and related illnesses. Since these could be treated with penicillin, other pharmaceutical companies deemed the research a waste of resources. But as Hilleman accurately predicted, the overuse of antibiotics made it necessary to expand the medical arsenal, and the pneumococcal vaccines were eventually put into wide use.

When Hilleman reached Merck's mandatory retirement age of sixty-five in 1984, he refused to stop working. For him, Merck made an exception. By the time he died in April 2005, Hilleman had helped to develop more than forty vaccines, including for chicken pox; *Haemophilus influenzae* type b, or "Hib," a bacterium that can lead to meningitis and paralysis; hepatitis A; and hepatitis B (with crucial assistance from Baruch Blumberg and Irving Millman), thereby cutting liver disease by 99 percent in some countries. His measles vaccine alone is estimated to have saved, at a minimum, more than 100 million lives over the past four decades.

After taking one last look at Hilleman's childhood home, I walk back to Art and Nancy's truck, climb in, and ask them why they think Hilleman has been so overlooked. Nancy mentions that, as far as Miles

City goes, Montana folks are reserved by nature, so his family wouldn't have campaigned for any kind of tribute, lest it seem like they were bragging about one of their own.

"A lot of folks didn't even know all that he had done until after he died," Nancy adds. "He never boasted about it."

According to his coworkers, Hilleman demonstrated that same reticence for self-promotion at Merck. He shied away from publicity whenever the company announced another of his breakthroughs, and he never named any of his vaccines after himself, which other scientists have done. (He did call the mumps vaccine "Jeryl Lynn" for his daughter, but he intentionally left off their last name.)

"You want to know why Hilleman's not more popular?" Art pipes up from out of nowhere, just as we're about to say our good-byes. "Nobody likes gettin' those damn shots."

Actually, I think he's on to something. They may not hurt as much as they did in the old days, when the needles were bigger, but vaccinations are still an inconvenience. And when they work, which they overwhelmingly do, the result is—nothing. We can't see or feel the payoff. No aches and pains have been alleviated, no inflammations relieved, no sores healed. It's easy to take for granted something whose benefits can only be left to the imagination.

Which is why I thought it might be worthwhile to find a site associated with the world's deadliest plague, a pandemic caused by a virus that scientists could neither cure nor restrain. Known as "Spanish influenza," the disease is commonly thought to have kicked up first in Europe during World War I and then run riot across the globe, killing tens of millions of people in a matter of months.

Only in recent years has it come to light that a county doctor from Sublette, Kansas, treated the first documented victims of the Spanish flu in 1918, and they were most certainly not from Spain. They were his neighbors.

DR. LORING MINER'S HOUSE

Waving good-by in the Seattle depot, we had not known that we had carried the flu with us into our drawing rooms, along with the presents and the flowers, but, one after another, we had been struck down as the train proceeded eastward. We children did not understand whether the chattering of our teeth and Mama's lying torpid in the berth were not somehow part of the trip. . . . We began to be sure that it was all an adventure when we saw our father draw a revolver on the conductor who was trying to put us off the train at a small wooden station in the middle of the North Dakota prairie. On the platform in Minneapolis, there were stretchers, a wheel chair, redcaps, distraught officials, and, beyond them, in the crowd, my grandfather's rosy face, cigar, and cane, my grandmother's feathered hat, imparting an air of festivity to this strange and confused picture, making us children certain that our illness was the beginning of a delightful holiday.

—From Memories of a Catholic Girlhood (1946) by Mary McCarthy. (Both of McCarthy's parents died from the Spanish flu soon after arriving in Minneapolis.)

WHILE WALKING THROUGH the airport in Liberal, Kansas, I notice a flyer pinned to the community bulletin board that cautions visitors to "please avoid the following acitivity" and, underneath, shows an adorable blond toddler kissing the wet, mud-splattered snout of a caged pig. Next to this tongue-in-cheek warning is a more somber government advisory about the swine-flu virus that recently swept through the country. Thankfully, the outbreak didn't explode into the epidemic initially predicted (fewer people, in fact, died from this strain than from the regular seasonal flu), and after the threat petered out, there was a lot grumbling on radio call-in shows and cable news that the whole campaign needlessly frightened the public and wasted millions of dollars in unused vaccines. Pig farms, including those in this Kansas community, were hit hard financially because many consumers feared they could become ill by eating bacon or ham and stopped buying pork products altogether. Here in the airport, someone has apparently expressed frustration over the whole situation, having scrawled "Hogwash!" above the two swine-flu alerts.

But if health officials were overcautious, it wasn't without reason; they knew full well what can happen when society is caught off-guard by a lethal, highly contagious influenza strain that, once unleashed, can't be stopped by all the medicine in the world. Foremost in their minds was the Spanish flu of 1918, which killed more people than any pandemic in history. And it did so with unrelenting ferocity. Symptoms included fevers that spiked up to 104 degrees; excruciating muscle aches; vomiting; profuse bleeding from the nose, ears, and eyes; and coughing fits so violent and prolonged that even the strongest victims tore rib cartilage hacking up a red, frothy sputum that constantly filled their lungs. Those unable to fight the virus or its accompanying complications, such as pneumonia and tuberculosis, usually died within ten days. There were anecdotal reports that some people got sick in the morning and were dead by nightfall, while others languished in agony for more than two weeks. Oddly, the disease killed otherwise healthy young men and women at almost the same rate as infants and the elderly. This had never occurred before with an influenza strain. (Nor has it since.)

Other mysteries about the Spanish flu puzzled scientists for decades, including the simple question of where, on earth, it had started.

Spain would seem the obvious answer, but the country has been unfairly linked with the disease since May 1918. France, Great Britain, Germany, and other warring European nations had experienced outbreaks a month earlier, but their governments were censoring the media and prohibited news about a growing plague because it was too depressing. The Spanish press, unencumbered by such restrictions, covered it extensively, and so to the rest of the world the flu had apparently originated in Spain.

After the war, epidemiologists intent on locating the true epicenter focused initially on France's west coast. From there, the disease had clearly expanded across Europe beginning in April 1918. But further investigation revealed that this was exactly when the first influx of American doughboys had disembarked en route to the Western Front, and many of the U.S. soldiers had been herded off crowded troopships already sick. The disease, it seemed, had come from the United States. Scientists backtracked the virus west to Fort Riley, Kansas, where in early March several soldiers at Camp Funston were hospitalized with the flu. More than five hundred of their fellow troops were bedridden within a week, and by the end of the month the number had jumped to eleven hundred. Private Albert Gitchell, admitted to the infirmary on March 4, is frequently cited as "patient zero." But there are some minor disparities about this, too; according to some reports, his name might have been Mitchell, and he checked in sick on March 11, not a week earlier. Regardless, in 1998 a bronze historic marker was erected at Fort Riley stating that the "first recorded cases of what came to be the worldwide influenza epidemic were first reported here in March 1918."

Now it appears that *this* information is off by a month and several hundred miles. A lengthy state-by-state account of the pandemic produced only a few years ago by the U.S. Department of Health and Human Services contains this small update:

In late January and early February of 1918, a local physician in Haskell County noticed a rash of severe influenza cases.

Although the physician had seen many cases of influenza throughout his career, these cases were extraordinary. Influenza, usually a mild disease, had suddenly become a killer. Over the course of the next two months, influenza ran rampant through Haskell County, cutting a swath among the county's residents. . . .

By mid-March, Camp Funston was in the throes of an influenza epidemic.

That local physician was Dr. Loring Miner from Sublette, Kansas, the seat of Haskell County, and he was the first person in America to sound the alarm about what was later referred to as "the Spanish flu." Miner appealed in writing to the U.S. Public Health Service for advice and assistance but received neither. The agency did, however, print in its spring 1918 issue (vol. 33, no. 14) of *Public Health Reports* Miner's letter concerning "the occurrence of 18 cases of influenza of severe type . . . [in] Haskell, Kans." This particular edition of *PHR* particularly caught my attention because its lead article was "PELLAGRA— Its Nature and Prevention" by Joseph Goldberger.

Miner's *PHR* warning somehow went overlooked for almost ninety years, as did several February 1918 notices in a Haskell County newspaper listing the names of local residents sickened by influenza. Unknowingly, the paper also foreshadowed the epidemic's expansion, mentioning Fort Riley servicemen home on leave and Haskell County citizens spending time with relatives at the Army post; "Ernest Elliott left Sublette," one article stated, "to visit his brother at Funston," and an earlier item had noted that Elliott's young child was among those stricken with influenza. With an incubation period of one to three days, it leapt from host to host before carriers even knew they were sick themselves. And as the virus fanned out from town to town, state to state, country to country, it was growing stronger.

Since Loring Miner documented this potent new strain before anyone else and treated its first victims, I contacted the Haskell Township Library in Sublette to find out where he had lived and worked.

"You wouldn't happen to know where Miner's old home is or who owns it now?" I asked librarian Helen Hall.

"I do," Helen replied.

"Oh, great," I said, grabbing a pen to write down the name. "Do you think they'd be okay with me stopping by to see it and take some photographs?"

"No," Helen clarified, "*I* live in it."

A few seconds passed in silence before Helen asked, "Are you still there?"

"Sorry," I said, "I'm just thrown by the coincidence."

"It's a small town."

(Indeed. Less than one square mile in size, I later found out.)

Helen said she'd be happy to show me around, and in the meantime she'd collect some additional materials about Miner.

That was weeks ago, and as I'm driving out of the Liberal airport now, I stop at a gas station to use the restroom and get my bearings.

"How far up is Sublette?" I ask the attendant.

"About thirty miles."

"Any landmarks I should look for? I don't want to whiz past it by mistake."

"You won't."

"I'm pretty good at getting lost."

"Trust me," he says. "Out there you can see a can of tuna from six miles away, and if you walked up and stood on it, you could see for another ten." (Best line of the trip, so far.) Then he adds: "If you're really that worried, keep an eye out for the giant grain elevators."

Half an hour later, and sure enough, there they are, a row of one-hundred-foot-tall silos across from the Sublette water tower. I turn off the highway and drive around for a few minutes before finding the library.

Inside, I meet with Helen Hall and Jamie Wright, the library's director who also went out of her way to locate biographical material on Miner for me. There isn't much about him, but what's known is that Miner had migrated to Kansas from Ohio in 1887 and didn't move to

Sublette until 1913. Although he'd bought an automobile in 1910, he often made his rounds on horseback because cars were notoriously unreliable and most roads were unpaved and often muddy. A single house call could take up to two days, and a solid meal was sometimes Miner's only payment. Apparently the good doctor wasn't averse to having a drink—or several—on or off the job, but the consensus seems to be that residents liked him immensely and would rather have had a slightly inebriated Dr. Miner treating them than a sober anyone else.

"Did you ever find anything of his in your home?" I ask Helen, who's offered to drive me over to the house.

"Nothing that I'm aware of," she says. "But other people had lived there before me."

From the library we go east on Chouteau Avenue about six short blocks and turn right onto South Inman, just past the elementary school. We park a few doors down in front of a cozy-looking "four-square, prairie home," as Helen describes it, with a wraparound porch and cedar-and-rock siding. A cheerful garden gnome and two stone angels stand on the lawn.

I don't want to impose on Helen by asking to go inside, so I stay on the front walkway and take some pictures.

"Didn't Ernest Elliott live around here?" I ask, referring to the man who visited his brother at Camp Funston after his child—and, most likely, he, too—had been infected in February 1918.

"Right there," Helen says, pointing to a house across from hers.

Of the three dozen largest Army posts in America, twenty-four of them were overrun with influenza cases by May 1918. The close quarters proved a perfect breeding ground for the virus, and from these bases it spread swiftly to neighboring towns.

President Woodrow Wilson's administration, like its European counterparts, refused to acknowledge the mounting health crisis lest it dampen the country's wartime morale. Early proposals to quarantine troops were rejected, and massive patriotic gatherings went on as planned, despite evidence that the disease was highly transmissible.

On September 28, 1918, some 200,000 people came together for a Liberty Loan rally in Philadelphia. Within three days, every hospital bed in the city was full.

Surgeon General Rupert Blue (the same man who enlisted Joseph Goldberger to defeat pellagra years earlier) dithered as fatalities surged. In September, after tens of thousands of Americans had died, Blue finally acknowledged that there might be an epidemic at hand, but his response was underwhelming; instead of galvanizing doctors and scientists across the country in a single, coordinated effort, Blue offered the public a short list of schoolmarmish dos and don'ts to prevent further infections, including "Avoid tight clothes, tight shoes, tight gloves"; "Your nose not your mouth was meant to breathe thru"; and "Food will win the war . . . Help by choosing and chewing your food well."

Newspapers followed the White House's lead, or lack thereof, and took a similar head-in-the-sand approach. "Do not even discuss influenza," the *Philadelphia Inquirer* instructed. "Worry is useless. Talk of cheerful things." Other papers downplayed the so-called plague as part of a "Hun plot" to stir up national hysteria. They nonetheless ran advertisements that capitalized on their readers' growing sense of unease. "Spanish Influenza! Can you afford sudden death?" one ad asked ominously. "If not, protect your Family and Business by Life Insurance." Car dealerships warned the public to stay off crowded street trolleys and buy an automobile instead.

When the government and media could no longer suppress that a full-fledged epidemic was raging, they took a new tack and claimed that the whole thing had been *caused* by the Germans. One high-ranking U.S. military officer suggested that enemy agents had released "Spanish influenza germs in a theatre or some other place where large numbers of persons are assembled," and a Public Health Service representative announced that there were "authenticated cases" of this biological warfare. No proof was ever given.

With the medical community stumped on how to stem the disease, an increasingly scared and confused public ingested every conceivable home remedy, from red-pepper sandwiches and raw garlic to shots of kerosene and sugar cubes sprinkled with turpentine. Only one real cure existed: bed rest and luck.

October 1918 was the epidemic's deadliest month. October 1918, in fact, remains the deadliest month in American history. Influenza killed two hundred thousand men, women, and children in thirty days, and the population in 1918 was a mere third of what it is today. Never before had the United States confronted so many dead and dying in such a short period. Family members too weak or terrified to remove their deceased loved ones left them locked in bedrooms or covered in blankets on front porches. Bodies stacked up outside of funeral homes and morgues unable to process and bury the corpses. In Pennsylvania, steam shovels were brought in by the Bureau of Highways to dig mass graves. Hospitals couldn't keep up with the parade of victims staggering into their emergency rooms. "There was a man lying on the bed," one nurse recalled, "[and] he had stopped breathing. I don't know whether he was dead or not, but we wrapped him in a winding sheet and left nothing but the big toe on the left foot out with a shipping tag on it to tell the man's rank, his nearest of kin, and hometown." Orphanages, overrun with boys and girls who'd lost both their parents, had to turn children away.

Cities hit early on by the plague tried to brace other communities for what was to come. "Hunt up your wood-workers and set them to making coffins," one distraught sanitation worker on the East Coast implored colleagues in California. "Then take your street laborers and set them to digging graves. If you do this you will not have your dead accumulating faster than you can dispose of them."

But until they experienced it firsthand, many city officials initially doubted the doomsayers. "If ordinary precautions are observed," the chief health officer of Los Angeles stated in late September 1918, "there is no cause for alarm." Forty-eight hours later, with infection rates surging, the L.A. government started shutting down schools, movie houses, churches, and synagogues.

Around the same time, San Francisco began quarantining flu

victims—but also carrying on with patriotic events. On October 11 more than fifty thousand citizens gathered in front of the Chronicle Building to hear the celebrated French tenor Lucien Muratore sing "La Marseillaise" and "The Star-Spangled Banner" in a show of French and American solidarity. By October 18 flu cases in San Francisco had quadrupled.

Basic services collapsed in city after city as police officers, firemen, and garbage collectors failed to show up for work. Factories emptied out and schools closed their doors. Local governments banned citizens from attending dance halls, theaters, and roller rinks, efforts that most citizens understood. Riots nearly erupted, however, when saloons and brothels were boarded up.

Some small towns warned would-be visitors to keep their distance. In Meadow, Utah, the lone public health officer drove out to the borderline and erected a makeshift sign that declared THIS TOWN IS QUARANTINED—DO NOT STOP. But ultimately his efforts were futile; the postman had already been infected and unknowingly spread the virus throughout Meadow.

With the threat of death ever present, people went insane with grief. A Chicago man who could no longer bear the sight of his wife and four children suffering from influenza was overheard raving, "I'll cure them my own way!" before slitting their necks.

Throughout it all President Wilson remained silent. On October 12 he personally led a war-bond parade in Manhattan, attracting a cheering throng of twenty-five thousand. Within a week, an additional two thousand New Yorkers were dead.

After cresting in October, infections began to dip nationwide in November and then rise again one month later. Another, less punishing wave swept the country in March 1919, and then, as suddenly as the disease had appeared almost a year earlier, it was gone.

Determining with absolute certitude where, down to the square foot, influenza attacked its first victim isn't possible. Nor is it likely that the real patient zero will ever be identified, though in all probability it was a local farmer infected by a sick bird. But what strikes me while standing in the middle of South Inman Street and looking at this small oasis of homes surrounded by corn, milo, and wheat fields is that, within two months of Miner's report to the Public Health Service, the virus had left Haskell County in rural Kansas and was decimating countries half a world away. Spanish flu went on to kill 675,000 Americans and at least 50 million people overseas. Other estimates put the global tally at twice that, but the final number won't ever be known because the doctors, nurses, and coroners who normally recorded fatalities were either overworked to the point of exhaustion or dead themselves.

There's no mention in anything I've read to indicate if Dr. Loring Miner ever got sick from the Spanish flu, but he definitely didn't die from it; Miner was killed on September 30, 1935, when his car swerved off the road and struck a power-line pole outside of Sublette.

Back at the library I ask Helen and Jamie where Miner is buried, and Jamie says, "The Valley View Cemetery in Garden City, thirty miles up the road." I hadn't planned on going there, but I figure that while I'm in the area, it's worth a visit.

"You can easily make it to Garden City before it gets dark," Jamie tells me.

I thank her and Helen for all their help and head back onto U.S. 83, stopping only once to see where Miner had his car accident.

Inside Valley View's main office a very nice woman named Tabitha gives me a cemetery directory and marks where Miner is buried. Valley View has thirteen thousand graves spread out over forty-seven acres, and within seconds of exiting the door, I'm already turned around but too embarrassed to go back in and ask which way I was supposed to walk. A truck pulls into the parking lot and, hallelujah, out steps one of the groundskeepers.

"Hey, can I ask you a quick question?"

"Sure," he answers.

"I'm trying to find Dr. Loring Miner, and he's supposed to be here," I say, pointing to the highlighted section. "But I'm not sure which direction that is."

As he looks at the map, I casually mention Miner's small but historic role in being first to report on the influenza pandemic of 1918. "I'm traveling the country to find people and places neglected by history."

"If you want, I can drive you over. It's not far, and there's something else that might interest you."

"That'd be great, if you have the time."

"Won't take long. Jump in."

When I introduce myself, he says, "Nice to meet you," but doesn't volunteer his name.

He asks me where I'm from.

"Washington, D.C.," I say.

"Most people from out of state come here to see the Clutters, the family killed up in Holcomb that Truman Capote wrote about in his book," he tells me, referring to *In Cold Blood*. From what I recall, the two murderers slashed Herb Clutter's throat after shooting his two teenage children and his wife.

"They're over in the northwest section of the cemetery. People have traveled from as far away as Japan and Australia just to see their graves."

We slow down after a series of short turns, and he points to a red marble gravestone and says, "Miner's right over there. I'll drop you back here in a minute." We then drive past a large memorial that, from the map, I'm guessing is Monument Grounds.

"That's essentially our tomb of the unknown soldiers," my guide says. "And see those bushes at the base? Under those are the amputated limbs of veterans. But that's not what I wanted to show you."

I'm still processing that piece of trivia when we come to the southeast corner of the B section and pull over. We get out and walk past a row of graves, and I take note of the names and dates: OSCAR CLIFTON CLAMPITT DEC. 16. 1916–JULY 25. 1918, HILDA DAU OF GUST & FANNIE PETERSON AUG. 17. 1917–AUG 11. 1918, and IN MEMORY OF LOUIDA V. REDWINE 1895–1918. One headstone is for two members of the same family who died within a day of each other: Alpha A. Jones on November 10, 1918, and Jephthah L. Jones on November 11.

"Are these people all flu victims?" I ask.

"It's against Kansas law to list the cause of death on a headstone, but it's a good possibility."

He keeps walking and then stops a few feet ahead of me in the middle of a large rectangle of grass, about fifteen by forty feet.

"Under here," he tells me, "are the remains of thirteen people who were definitely killed by the influenza. They all worked at the local sugar beet factory, and nine of them died in a single day."

"And there's no marker or anything for them?"

"Nothing. That's a lot of folks for a small community to lose so quickly, and the townsfolk were probably overwhelmed and buried them as fast as they could."

I stand there for a moment taking it all in, and he asks me if I want a ride back to Miner's plot.

"I think I'm going to stay and linger," I say, "but I really appreciate your bringing me here. I'd never have known about this if you hadn't pointed it out."

"Few people do," he says, heading back to his truck. "It's like it never happened."

This is what's so bewildering to me. No war or disaster has killed as many Americans, and yet the pandemic's imprint on our national psyche is so faint as to be nearly imperceptible. College and high school history textbooks give it short shrift, at best tacking on a sentence or two about it at the end of their chapters on World War I, and relatively few works of literature have focused on it either. This is especially remarkable considering how many extraordinary writers—William Faulkner, Edith Wharton, Robert Frost, Eugene O'Neill, Jean Toomer, William Carlos Williams (the doctor/poet who treated flu victims), F. Scott Fitzgerald, and Ernest Hemingway, to name a few—lived through it. Katherine Anne Porter's own bout with the virus inspired her novella *Pale Horse, Pale Rider* (Porter came so close to dying that the local newspaper had already typeset her obituary); Thomas Wolfe fictionalized his brother's death from influenza in *Look Homeward, Angel;* and William Maxwell described surviving the flu as an eight-year-old boy in *They Came Like Swallows.* But these authors, along with Mary McCarthy, are the notable exceptions, and they all touched on it only briefly.

One reason the plague has mostly been forgotten, I assume, is—despite claiming more lives than the Civil War (and in considerably less time)—there wasn't a larger cause at stake. Societies understandably glorify their wartime dead, even on the losing side, by memorializing their courage and sacrifice in context of a greater struggle. Tragically, but to be perfectly blunt, victims of the Spanish flu died for nothing.

And while diseases such as smallpox and polio scarred or crippled their victims, Spanish influenza didn't leave behind any marks or disabilities as lasting reminders of its existence. The dead were buried and the survivors went on with their lives, physically unscathed by their brush with mortality.

Nor was there any great medical breakthrough that would lend the story a climactic moment of triumph. Doctors frantically tried to produce a vaccine, but their efforts were doomed from the start because they mistakenly believed that Spanish flu was caused by a bacterium. In actuality the culprit was a virus, which is much smaller and attacks the body differently, and scientists weren't able to examine and categorize different viruses until the invention of the electron microscope in the 1930s. Even then, the precise nature of Spanish influenza remained elusive because nobody could find a live sample of it to analyze. Viruses, unlike bacteria, can't survive for long outside of their human (or animal) hosts, and Spanish influenza had burned itself out more than a decade earlier. Any chance of unlocking its secrets seemed futile.

Virologists nevertheless persisted in searching for some remnant of the disease, and a Swedish-born University of Iowa graduate student named Johan Hultin was particularly tenacious in attempting to track it down. After hearing an impromptu remark by a visiting professor in 1950 about where the virus might still possibly be found, Hultin was inspired to travel three thousand miles from the Midwest to a remote Eskimo village in Alaska. After reading about what he eventually discovered there, so was I.

PART VII

BURIAL PLOTS

Forgotten Graves, Cemeteries,

and Stories About the Dead

BREVIG MISSION

Science advances one funeral at a time.

—Max Planck, recipient of the 1918 Nobel Prize in Physics

"I WOULDN'T BE alive today if it weren't for the Spanish flu,"
Lisa Fallgren, my seatmate on Flight 870 from Nome to Brevig Mission,
Alaska, says to me after I mention the reason for my traveling to Kan-
sas and then here.

That's certainly a different take on the pandemic, I think to myself.

"My grandfather's first wife died from the flu in 1918," she explains,
"and if he hadn't gone on to marry my grandmother, my mother never
would have been born, and then, of course, I wouldn't have either."

A U.S. Census Bureau representative based out of Seattle, Lisa has
visited Brevig Mission multiple times to conduct one-on-one interviews with residents who don't have easy access to phones or e-mail.
And because no roads lead to the isolated village on Alaska's Seward
Peninsula, flying is her—and my—most reliable way to go. Once we
touch down, we'll have only five hours until our afternoon departure,

and I was strongly advised by the Bering Air reservations agent not to miss the 4:35 flight back to Nome. There's no lodging in town, and if a storm blows in this evening, I could be stranded indefinitely. "The plane might come early," the representative also instructed me, "so be there by four o'clock."

Our nine-seat puddle jumper begins its descent over a narrow Bering Strait inlet and lands in Brevig Mission on a short runway by the water's edge. After we deplane, I ask Lisa where we're supposed to wait later today, since there doesn't seem to be a building or any type of shelter close by except for a small hangar that's locked up.

"You just stand outside," she says.

"Really? What do you do when it rains or snows?"

She shrugs. "I guess you get used to it."

Before Lisa starts down a dirt road leading into town, I ask her if she knows where the cemetery is. She points off to the left and tells me it's less than ten minutes from here.

"It's hard to get lost," she says.

This I can understand. From the "airport," I can make out most of the village about three-quarters of a mile away. Roughly four hundred Inupiat Eskimos live in Brevig Mission, but except for two men zipping along the main road in all-terrain vehicles, there doesn't appear to be much human activity. Whale-hunting Eskimos were the first to settle here almost two centuries ago, followed in 1900 by a rather hardy and determined group of Lutheran missionaries from Norway. A post office was named after one of their pastors, Reverend T. L. Brevig, and it's been Brevig Mission ever since.

Instead of setting out directly for the cemetery, I decide to meander a bit. There's no town center, just clusters of gray single-story wooden houses topped by blue or red corrugated metal roofs. I walk down to the shoreline and see half a dozen kids splashing around in the ocean. For Alaskans, the 40-something degree temperature is practically a heat wave, but I'm shivering in my thin windbreaker and can't imagine how frigid the water must be.

Not far from the young bathers, I notice hanging from an exposed wooden framework rows of bright red chili peppers, a striking burst of color that contrasts vividly with the overcast sky and dark gray sea. I approach to within about twenty-five feet and realize that they're not peppers but plump red strips of salmon meat turned inside out, drying in the crisp air. As I move closer, several dogs suddenly rise up out of nowhere and charge toward me, barking like crazy. Chains tighten with a hard *thunk,* and the huskies, stopped midlunge, whine and growl, infuriated at the unfairness of it all. Instinctively I step backward with my hands raised and, in a hushed tone, say, "Sorry, guys, sorry." Apology not accepted; they continue to snarl, whimper, and circle about. I have no desire to add to their torment or, frankly, be anywhere near them if a restraint breaks, so I make a beeline for the main road.

Brevig Mission's cemetery is about an acre in size, and as I walk up to the graves, it appears that all of the markers are wooden crosses. Names, dates, and an occasional Bible verse have been hand carved into the painted slats, and only the more recent additions are legible. Many are splintered and weather-beaten. Some are nothing more than short gray stubs jutting out of the ground.

Bordering the southwest perimeter of the cemetery and demarcated by two large white crosses is a patch of land about thirty feet long. Buried under here are the seventy-two Brevig Mission residents killed in late November 1918 by Spanish influenza. Despite quarantines and travel restrictions into Alaska, somehow the virus reached this secluded outpost and wiped out 90 percent of the local population within five days, leaving alive only eight children and teenagers.

In the summer of 1951, Johan Hultin traveled to this exact spot next to the cemetery in search of long-dead victims of the Spanish flu. And their bodies still needed to be relatively intact; bones would not suffice. Hultin wanted lung tissue, in particular, and he hoped that the frozen tundra had prevented the corpses from deteriorating entirely over the previous thirty-three years. Village elders were persuaded by Hultin's argument that his research might lead to lifesaving vaccines and permitted the excavation. Three of the council members who granted their approval were among the eight survivors from 1918.

Hultin got the idea to come here after the eminent virologist William Hale had made an offhand comment during a brief visit in January 1950 to the University of Iowa, where Hultin was studying microbiology. "Everything has been done to elucidate the cause of [the Spanish influenza] epidemic," Hale remarked at an informal luncheon with half a dozen students and faculty members. "But we just don't know what caused that flu. The only thing that remains is for someone to go to the northern part of the world and find bodies in the permafrost that are well preserved and that just might contain the influenza virus."

After obtaining a government map that identified areas in North America covered with permafrost, Hultin marked three Alaskan towns that he knew had been devastated by the pandemic: Nome, Wales, and Brevig Mission. When the National Institutes of Health rejected his funding appeal, Hultin was able to secure a $10,000 grant from the University of Iowa. (Hultin later learned that the NIH had decided to organize its own search, a $300,000 expedition to Nome led by scientists and doctors from the Walter Reed Army Medical Center. A principal participant in the classified and ultimately unsuccessful venture was a young Dr. Maurice Hilleman.)

Hultin spent more than a year and a half planning his trip and flew to Alaska in the summer of 1951. He was joined by his faculty advisor, Albert McKee, and two other professors, Jack Layton and Otto Geist. The three senior scientists all waited in Fairbanks until Hultin sent word that he had uncovered something promising in one of his targeted towns.

Nome and Wales were both a bust, leaving Brevig Mission as the last chance. Hultin slept on an air mattress at the local school and toiled up to eighteen hours a day struggling to break through the concrete-hard earth covering the mass grave. On the fourth day he came across his first body—a small girl, about six to ten years old, with red ribbons in her hair. Hultin contacted McKee, Layton, and Geist in Fairbanks and told them to head over.

Aided by warmer weather, the four men were able to clear a hole seven feet deep and ten yards long within two days. They exhumed four well-insulated adult bodies, cracked through their sternums, and extracted chunks of soft tissue from each lung, which were then put in sterilized screw-cap jars and placed, for further protection, inside large thermoses.

Mission halfway accomplished.

Back in Iowa, and under conditions that would be considered shockingly unsafe today, Hultin attempted to find and revive a hibernating specimen of Spanish influenza by injecting cultures made from the infected lung tissue into live mice, ferrets, and other lab animals normally susceptible to the virus. Every test came up negative, and after almost two months of experimenting, Hultin ran out of tissue. The disease appeared, indeed, to be dead, with little hope of ever being regrown.

Hope emerged four decades later in the form of a self-described LSD enthusiast and California surfer dude named Kary Mullis, who also happened to be (and still is) a brilliant biochemist. In 1993, Mullis won the Nobel Prize in Chemistry for developing the polymerase chain reaction (PCR), a technique that enables scientists to replicate DNA sequences ad infinitum and with perfect consistency. This means that even if they have only a single droplet of blood, strand of hair, or cell to work with, they can make limitless copies of an individual gene. And since virtually all DNA research and advances—from tracing family genealogy to finding cures for cancer and other diseases—now depend on PCR, the procedure is considered one of the most revolutionary scientific breakthroughs of the twentieth century. (In his autobiography, *Dancing Naked in the Mind Field*, Mullis describes exactly how and where his brainstorm occurred: While driving to dinner with his girlfriend on California's Highway 128, the basic idea came to him in a flash, so he pulled over at mile marker 46.58, reached into his glove compartment, and scribbled down PCR's essential framework on the back of an envelope.) Hultin eagerly followed Mullis's progress, recognizing that PCR might one day help solve the Spanish influenza riddle.

Hultin wasn't alone. In 1996 a team of scientists led by Dr. Jeffery Taubenberger at the Armed Forces Institute of Pathology in Washington, D.C., had begun analyzing bits of lung tissue taken from American servicemen killed by Spanish influenza in 1918. The Institute had grown out of the Army Medical Museum, established during the Civil War by President Abraham Lincoln and the U.S. Army's surgeon general, William Hammond. Military doctors were instructed to remove pathological samples from patients afflicted with life-threatening ailments and send them to the museum, and the repository—which has become sort of a national archive of death and disease—now holds more than 7.2 million tumors, lesions, growths, and skin graphs. Later moved to an annex of the Walter Reed Army Medical Center, the gruesome inventory was warehoused for twenty-one years at Ford's Theatre after the playhouse was shut down following President Lincoln's assassination.

Nobody had thought to check the Institute's vast collection for influenza-infected specimens until Taubenberger submitted a request in early 1995. Information on one promising sample popped up in the database right away: lung tissue excised from the body of Roscoe Vaughn (also spelled Vaughan in some records), a twenty-one-year-old private killed by Spanish flu at Camp Jackson, South Carolina. On September 26, 1918, Vaughn literally drowned to death in an infirmary hospital bed when his chest cavity filled with fluids. Army doctors cut out several fingertip-sized pieces from Vaughn's lungs, encased them in candle wax, and forwarded them to Washington, where they sat, untouched, for seventy-eight years. After eighteen months of exhausting work, Taubenberger and his indefatigable lab technician, Ann Reid, were able to tease out a partial genetic sequence of Spanish influenza from the specimen. Although incomplete, this was closer than anyone else had come to decoding the virus.

Johan Hultin learned about Taubenberger's work in the March 21, 1997, issue of *Science* magazine and promptly wrote to him, indicating that he knew where additional and possibly better specimens could be found. Taubenberger had never heard of Hultin but was intrigued. Soon the two men connected by phone, and Hultin expressed his eagerness to return to Brevig Mission. Expeditions like these required considerable planning and years simply to secure funding, so Taubenberger tempered his enthusiasm. He thought it worth exploring, though, and asked Hultin for an approximate timetable.

"I can't go this week, but maybe I can go next week," Hultin answered, and then further stunned Taubenberger by saying he'd use his retirement savings to underwrite the whole thing himself. Taubenberger assured Hultin that the Institute's labs would dedicate the necessary staff time and resources to thoroughly analyze whatever he brought back from Alaska, and the two men also agreed not to tell anyone what they were up to. Hultin didn't want the publicity, especially if his second try also proved fruitless, and somewhat in jest he told Taubenberger that he thought it best to give him deniability in the event that he (Hultin) uncovered a dormant strain of Spanish influenza and unleashed another pandemic on mankind.

True to his word, Hultin departed for Alaska a few weeks later, and he left without even having first requested permission from Brevig Mission's town council to exhume the mass grave one more time. "When it comes to digging in cemeteries and dealing with dead ancestors, one can't do that by phone," Hultin recalled. "You have to go up in a very quiet, low-profile way, and talk to them about it."

The 1918 survivors had long since passed away, but many of the older villagers remembered Hultin from his 1951 visit and how respectfully he had conducted himself. The elders allowed him to proceed and provided him with four young men to help with the excavation, a welcome relief to the seventy-two-year-old retiree, who assumed he'd have to do the backbreaking work himself. Once again he slept on an air mattress at the local school.

After three days of arduous picking and shoveling, Hultin and his team came across human remains. All skeletons, no soft tissue, and therefore no flu virus. Hultin was facing the prospect that this attempt was also for naught, but the grave went deeper, into still-colder ground, and the men kept digging.

The next day, August 23, 1997, Hultin found a female body seven feet down that was remarkably preserved. He estimated the woman to have been in her late twenties or early thirties when she died.

"I sat on a pail—turned upside down—and looked at her," Hultin later said of the moment.

> She was an obese woman; she had fat in her skin and around her organs and that served as a protection from the occasional short-term thawing of permafrost. Those on the other side of her were not obese and they had decayed. I sat on the pail and saw this woman in a state of good preservation. And I knew that this was where the virus [sample] has got to come from, shedding light on the mysteries of 1918. I gave her a name. Lucy. Donald Johanson had sat in Ethiopia in 1974 and looked at a skeleton that shed light on human evolution. He had named her Lucy. I also thought of Lucy, lux, Latin for light. She would help Taubenberger shed light on that pandemic.

With an autopsy knife, Hultin sliced out most of her lungs and immersed the sections in a chemical solution. Thinking it might be inappropriate to store Lucy's organs in the school refrigerator, Hultin burrowed a hole in the ice-cold ground and placed the container there overnight. The next day he and his crew shoveled all the dirt back into the grave and replaced the sod exactly as it had looked before.

Hultin added something, too. In 1951 there were wooden crosses at each end of the burial site, but they had both rotted away to almost nothing over the years. Before rushing back to San Francisco, Hultin went into the school's workshop and constructed two new crosses, which he mounted where the originals had stood. They were his tribute to the dead and his thank-you to the community that had shown him such hospitality.

. . .

Once he returned to San Francisco, Hultin still had the logistical matter of getting the prized specimens safely to Taubenberger. Flying to Washington, D.C., and personally delivering them would have been the quickest and most dependable option, but it was too expensive, and Hultin had already personally sunk $4,100 into the Alaska trip. He feared that if he shipped the package, though, it could get lost or ruined. Hultin divided the lungs into four pieces and, hedging his bets, sent one by UPS, one through the regular postal service, and two using Federal Express, from two different towns.

Taubenberger received all four parcels in perfect condition. Within a week he and Ann Reid verified that Lucy's lung tissue contained Spanish influenza, and it was the same viral strain that had killed Private Roscoe Vaughn at Fort Jackson. More testing confirmed that the virus was dead, just as Hultin had found almost half a century earlier. But this time it didn't matter. By using PCR they were able to decode its entire genetic sequence, a historic achievement in itself. Taubenberger wasn't satisfied, however, and decided to go one step further. He wanted to bring Spanish influenza back to life.

This raised obvious ethical and security issues, since the virus—which is twenty-five times more deadly than the regular seasonal flu—could conceivably be used as a biological weapon or accidentally released. But Taubenberger believed that the benefits of re-creating the virus, publishing its genetic code, and allowing other scientists to study its makeup outweighed the dangers. To do all of this required the approval and participation of numerous government agencies, including the National Institutes of Health, the Centers for Disease Control and Prevention, the Department of Defense, and the National Scientific Advisory Board for Biosecurity. Authorization was granted, and the experiment took place in the CDC's Biosafety Level 3 laboratory, a highly secure airtight facility reserved for "indigenous or exotic agents which may cause serious or potentially lethal disease after inhalation."

In October 2005, Taubenberger and his team finally announced that, after reconstructing Spanish influenza's complete gene sequence, they had also successfully regrown the virus, a feat never before accomplished with an extinct disease. Mice exposed to the virus died within three days, and when it was injected into human lung tissue (in a Petri dish; nobody was actually infected), it rapidly destroyed the cells. Based on Taubenberger's findings, some pathologists have theorized that the reason healthy people in their twenties and thirties succumbed to Spanish influenza at a higher rate than children and the elderly was precisely *because* these young men and women were strong and robust; their immune systems overreacted to the extremely aggressive virus, causing their lungs to flood with bodily fluids rich in white blood cells.

"It's clear that the 1918 virus remains particularly lethal," Taubenberger said after bringing about its Lazarus-like resurrection, "and determining whether pandemic influenza virus strains can emerge via different pathways will affect the scope and focus of surveillance and prevention efforts." Deciphering how a specific virus operates opens up insights into other viral strains and reveals how they grow, mutate, jump from animal to animal, and attack their hosts. Research based on Lucy's lung tissue has already led to improved flu vaccines that have prevented larger epidemics, and ideally, someday scientists will build on Hultin and Taubenberger's work to uncover a genetic Achilles' heel in one strain that will make it possible to wipe out all of them.

Here in Brevig Mission, the temperature has dipped noticeably and the sky is darkening. I check my watch and see that it's almost 4:00 P.M.

I walk to the hangar and wave at Lisa, who's already waiting and looks like she's engrossed in her notes. I plunk down on the gravel and pull the "Lucy/Brevig Mission" file out of my backpack. While passing through Nome on my way here I stopped in the city's lone historical museum to see what information it had regarding the pandemic's impact on Alaska. A staff member kindly photocopied for me magazine articles, newspaper clippings, and personal correspondences describing how swiftly and unexpectedly Spanish flu had descended on this region.

"You had hardly gotten out of sight when the whole town came down with the epidemic," a Nome banker named Levi Ashton wrote to his neighbor Joe (no last name is given) on February 9, 1919.

> In many cases the little babies suffered terribly. Houses were broken open and the babies found in bed with their dead mother, sometimes the children were alive and sometimes they were not. A woman who lived a short distance below Chinik called there for provisions and left again for home. The Chinik people forgot about her for about a week and then someone thought to look her up and see how she fared. A man went to the cabin but was driven away by the dogs, that were starving and showed a desire to attack him. He went back to Chinik and got a gun, killed the dogs and broke into the cabin. He found the four grown natives dead and four small children huddled up in the fur robes trying to keep warm without any fire. The older two had taken what milk they had under the robes with them and to keep it from freezing to feed the babies on and had frozen their feet and legs and hands in their endeavor to keep the smaller ones warm. One child had its feet frozen to the floor. They brought them to Chinik and then to Nome. One child had to have its feet cut off, and later it died.

Ashton also mentioned several Alaskans who took their own lives rather than risk becoming infected.

> During the epidemic there were but three suicides. Two natives hung themselves over in Baldwin's gymnasium. One of them hung himself to a hat and coat hook on the wall which was too low to do the job properly and he had to kneel down to accomplish his ends. When he had expired a friend took him down and removing the noose from his neck placed it on his own and repeated the stunt.

I finish reading the six-page typewritten letter and just sit for a moment trying to figure out why Ashton felt compelled to write such a graphic and detailed account. Partly, I guess, there was the practical matter of sharing information with an old friend at a time when newspapers had been shut down and other forms of communication were limited. (Ashton refers to the letter itself as "this bulletin.") With respect to the more explicit descriptions, there must be something cathartic about getting images like those out of one's head and down on paper. It's a coping mechanism, especially in the aftermath of such an immense tragedy. I also wonder if, maybe subconsciously, Ashton hoped that his letter would be passed down over the years—which, in the end, it was—as evidence of how horrific a disaster like this truly can be. Societies are forgetful, and with forgetting comes complacency. Ashton's recollections are a warning to anyone who might question, at the outset of a potentially similar epidemic, whether all the government alerts and preventive measures are worth the time, expense, and effort. Yes, the letter says, emphatically. More so than we could ever imagine.

A faint buzz grows louder over the horizon, and from behind a bank of clouds a small plane bursts cinematically into view. Our ride is here. Lisa and I make small talk in the minute or so we have to wait before walking to the airstrip.

I ask her where she's off to after Nome.

"Back to Seattle. And you?"

"South Carolina, to see the grave of a guy named Henry Laurens," I tell Lisa right before the roar of propellers drowns out our conversation.

Laurens served as president of the Continental Congress in 1777, and was imprisoned by British troops in the Tower of London after being captured during a secret diplomatic mission to Europe. What especially interests me about Laurens, however, is not his life but his death, which marked the beginning of the most significant shift in burial practices in American history. And this posthumous angle is what's determining which graves I'm visiting for the penultimate leg of my journey. An extraordinary biography is not enough; any number of fascinating individuals lie buried and forgotten throughout the United States. For my purposes, each story, like Lucy's here in Brevig Mission, must center on the corpse itself. Or, in the case of Henry Laurens, the lack thereof.

HENRY LAURENS'S GRAVE

Love. Life's single greatest risk. Life's single greatest reward. Love captures your heart in a second and holds it for eternity. You have experienced a love without equal.

You have had someone truly special in your life and mere words simply will not do.

Your very own LifeGem diamond(s) can be created from the carbon in cremation ashes, a lock of hair, or both. Of course, not only do we turn ashes into diamonds and hair into diamonds, we also have a full line of cremation jewelry, rings, and pendants to accent your beautiful LifeGem cremation diamond. . . .

If you have just lost a loved one, your loved one can be cremated at one of our certified facilities across the nation, or at the facility of your choice. . . . **You do NOT need to send the deceased to our location.**

—*From an advertisement for LifeGem, which sells its .90- to .99-carat blue diamonds for $19,999 (the cost dropping to $18,999 for orders of two or more)*

TO DESCRIBE MEPKIN Abbey in eastern South Carolina as heavenly is far too easy, but goodness is this place gorgeous. Thirty miles north of Charleston, the three-thousand-acre estate was given as a gift to the Catholic Church in 1949 by publishing magnate Henry Luce and his wife, Clare Boothe, and it's now run by Trappist monks.

"No matter how stressful my day has been," Thomas Ashe Lockhart tells me while making a turn off Dr. Evans Road into a long, tree-lined driveway, "the moment I come through these gates, all of my cares go away."

Lockhart is the great-great-great-great grandson of Henry Laurens, a South Carolinian aristocrat who owned Mepkin for thirty years during the latter part of the eighteenth century. Laurens's funeral here in December 1792 might have been more symbolic than consequential, but it represented the beginning of a trend that has fundamentally altered how Americans dispose of their bodies and choose to be memorialized.

We park near the gift shop, and Tom, a spry eighty-one-year-old attorney originally from North Carolina, guides me across lush, rolling lawns bordered by giant oaks draped in Spanish moss. We pass through a small forest and up a hill to the brick-walled enclosure where Henry Laurens and his family are buried. Along the way, Tom has been sharing with me a biographical sketch of the man he refers to as "one of America's most overlooked Founding Fathers."

"Did you know that Laurens kept George Washington from being fired during the Revolution?" he asks me.

I did not. I knew that Washington had his critics, but I wasn't aware that he came close to being removed as commander. Leading the charge, Tom tells me, was Thomas Conway, an Irish-born general serving in the Continental Army who became peeved at Washington for delaying his promotion to major general. He and other officers, including Washington's former aide-de-camp Thomas Mifflin, questioned Washington's leadership abilities after the Army had suffered a string of early defeats, and they pushed for General Horatio Gates to replace him when Gates's troops beat the British at Saratoga. (Gates received all the glory, but Major General Benedict Arnold, in his pre-traitorous days, also deserved credit for the win, and this lack of recognition was one of many slights that turned Arnold against his country.) Henry Laurens helped quash the mini rebellion with assistance from the Marquis de Lafayette, and Conway was demoted. He continued badmouthing Washington until General John Cadwalader challenged him to a duel to shut him up once and for all. Cadwalader did so literally, shooting Conway in the mouth.

"Imagine the war without Washington," Tom says, "or if he'd never been president. Laurens saved him."

The third of six children, Henry Laurens was born on March 6, 1724, in Charleston, South Carolina. At age twenty-three he launched what became a lucrative import/export company that bought and sold everything from furniture, dyes, and rum to animal pelts, white indentured servants, and African slaves. Tom emphasizes to me that Laurens withdrew from the slave trade before the Revolution.

In the summer of 1750, Laurens married nineteen-year-old Eleanor Ball. None of their first three children lived past infancy. John Laurens, born in 1754, was the first to survive into maturity. Five years later came Martha, who was stricken with smallpox during an epidemic in 1760 and pronounced dead. But while preparing her body for burial, Martha's doctor made the astonishing discovery that she was in fact still conscious, and, after several days of vigilant care, she recovered fully. Henry Laurens was elated but also shaken by how close Martha had come to being buried alive, and the experience left a deep impression on him.

Laurens entered public life in 1757, serving first in South Carolina's Common House Assembly. He was initially cool to the idea of America breaking from the Motherland and pushed for reconciliation, but after British troops attacked South Carolina and the Declaration of Independence was signed, his support for the Revolution became unwavering. In January 1777 he was voted into the Continental Congress, and later that year his fellow representatives unanimously elected him president.

Laurens resigned as president of the Continental Congress in December 1778 and accepted a diplomatic assignment to solicit $10 million (and those are eighteenth-century dollars) in war funding from the Dutch. He was also responsible for negotiating a long-term treaty of "amity and commerce" with the Netherlands. While rounding the coast of Newfoundland en route to Europe, Laurens's ship was captured by the British. Laurens stuffed sensitive documents into weighted sacks and pitched them overboard, but English sailors easily fished the bobbing bundles out of the sea. Inside they found a list of prominent Dutchmen sympathetic to American independence, along with the proposed treaty. Great Britain declared war on the Netherlands and accused Laurens of high treason. Fifty-six years old and suffering from gout, he was shipped to England and confined to the Tower of London.

"The 'Constable of the Tower,'" Tom says to me, "was officially the British general Lord Cornwallis. When Cornwallis surrendered at Yorktown in 1781, the man he handed his sword to was Lieutenant Colonel John Laurens, Henry's son. Cornwallis was swapped for Laurens in a prisoner-of-war exchange, and he came back to Mepkin in 1784 after spending some time in Paris."

"Laurens led quite a life," I say to Tom, who nods in agreement.

And it was a life made even more historic by how it ended. "Having settled all affairs which relate to my estate and provided for the different parts of my family in a manner which appears to me to be just and equitable, I come to the disposal of my own person," Laurens wrote in his will. "I solemnly enjoin it upon my son as an indispensable duty that as soon as he conveniently can after my decease, he cause my body to be wrapped in twelve yards of town cloth *and burnt until it be entirely and totally consumed*" (emphasis added). These instructions aren't remarkable today, but in the 1700s they were unprecedented; before Laurens, no American had been cremated per his—or her—request, and on December 8, 1792, Laurens became the first.

This distinction is often bestowed on Joseph De Palm, an elderly New Yorker cremated in Pennsylvania on December 6, 1876, but Laurens remains the real trailblazer, so to speak. De Palm, it's true, was the first to be incinerated by a crematorium (Laurens went up in smoke atop an outdoor pyre), and his send-off is better documented because it was viewed by a gaggle of doctors, clergymen, scientists, and several dozen reporters, some of whom had traveled from Europe. Laurens's cremation was held privately here at Mepkin and attended solely by loved ones. Whether family members felt that the spectacle was too dreadful to relate or were embarrassed that Laurens had picked a burial rite normally associated with pagans and Native Indians isn't clear, but apparently not one witness wrote about the cremation. His daughter Martha refrained from mentioning it in an otherwise detailed letter she sent her husband after the funeral, although she later referred to it, once, as "that awful ceremony."

The only contemporary account I could find describing it was printed in a London newspaper:

> A few days since departed this life Henry Laurens, Esq., about seventy years of age, and his corpse was burned the Thursday after his decease. This was done by his son at the request of his father, who made this reserve in his will, that unless his son complied with this he should be cut short in any of his estate, which is worth £50,000. The ashes remaining from the body were taken up and put into a silver urn for that purpose.

Squinting to see if there's a cross or some other religious icon on Laurens's faded headstone and finding none, I ask Tom if Laurens considered himself a religious man.

"Absolutely," Tom says. "He was a devout Episcopalian from a long line of Huguenots."

I thought Laurens might have been an atheist or agnostic only because Americans' long-standing aversion to cremation was based primarily on their Christian beliefs. Many feared that it was eternally irrevocable and would prevent their corporal resurrection on Judgment Day, and the whole idea of having one's body cast into flames evoked unsettling thoughts of hellfire. Orthodox Jews deemed the practice sacrilegious and still reject it, as do most Muslims.

European attitudes began to shift during the 1870s, roughly 1,550 years after Rome's first Christian ruler, Constantine I, had banned cremations throughout the empire. In 1873, Queen Victoria's personal surgeon, Sir Henry Thompson, was roaming the World Exhibition in Vienna when he came upon a crematorium displayed by an Italian professor of anatomy named Bruno Brunetti. Convinced that corpses emitted "deleterious" gases and leaked infectious fluids into wells and groundwater, Thompson had already been pondering ways to hygienically dispose of human bodies after death, and Brunetti's brick-encased furnace seemed to offer the perfect solution. Thompson returned to England and wrote a lengthy treatise advocating for the widespread use of crematoriums as a public health measure, and he suggested that there would be an economic bonus, too: Not only would funerals be less expensive, but the ashes could be sold as fertilizer. Thompson's 1874 essay garnered international attention and helped kick-start the cremationist movement in England and America.

Among those influenced in the States was a Washington, Pennsylvania, philanthropist and doctor named Francis Julius LeMoyne, who shared Thompson's conviction that rotting corpses caused "the graveyard pollution of air and water." Wealthy but frugal, LeMoyne believed that funerals and their accompanying expenses (coffins, flowers, undertaker's fees, et cetera) were becoming unnecessarily extravagant and wasteful, and he was drawn to cremation's simplicity and cost-effectiveness. So, during the summer and fall of 1876, LeMoyne spent $1,500 of his own money to construct America's first crematorium. He originally wanted to place the thirty-by-twenty-foot red-brick structure inside Washington's main graveyard, but town trustees dismissed the idea out of hand, leaving him with no other option but to build it on his personal estate.

An article about LeMoyne caught the attention of Henry Steel Olcott, a well-known Manhattan lawyer and U.S. Army colonel who had served on the commission responsible for investigating Abraham Lincoln's assassination. Raised Presbyterian, Olcott had turned to Eastern faiths in his early forties and found special comfort in the idea that cremation freed one's soul after death. Olcott didn't care that LeMoyne's intentions were based more on health and economical reasons than religious ones. What mattered to him most was that once LeMoyne finished his crematorium he would need a body to burn, and Olcott, as luck would have it, already had one on hand.

Baron Joseph De Palm was over seventy years old and ailing when Olcott first met him in 1875. The two New Yorkers held similar views on religion and became such close friends that De Palm made Olcott executor of his will, which stipulated that his funeral would be organized "in a fashion that would illustrate the Eastern notions of death and immortality" and would culminate in his cremation. De Palm passed away on May 20, 1876, and Olcott had his body injected with arsenic, a short-term preservative, until LeMoyne was ready for him. That took longer than expected, so Olcott brought in a mortician named August Buckhorst to keep De Palm from wasting away. Embalming was a relatively new practice in the States, with no set standards or regulations, and undertakers pretty much winged it. Buckhorst smeared De Palm's skin and replaced most of his innards with a potter's clay and carbolic acid mixture that proved surprisingly effective.

Six and a half months after De Palm died, LeMoyne's crematorium was at long last finished, and on December 5, 1876, Olcott escorted his old friend's withered but still presentable corpse by train to Washington, Pennsylvania. The next morning, invited guests crammed into the viewing room as Olcott meticulously prepared De Palm for the furnace. First he doused the white sheet around De Palm's body with water and alum to keep the fabric from instantly burning off and exposing anything that might scandalize the more genteel folks in attendance. Then, to mask the inevitable stench of burning skin, he sprinkled De Palm with spices, flowers, and evergreen sprigs. With the aid of four other men, Olcott and LeMoyne carried De Palm across the room and placed him headfirst into the retort. No eulogies or prayers were offered, but to show their respect the gentlemen did doff their hats.

For all intents and purposes the event went off without a hitch. Olcott and LeMoyne didn't set the building on fire. Nobody fainted, freaked out, or tried to disrupt the proceedings. And De Palm's body didn't explode (as one *New York Times* correspondent predicted) or end up as a grotesque clump of unevenly cooked flesh, bone, and hair.

Journalists on the scene were, nevertheless, unanimously critical. The kindest dubbed the affair a "disappointment" and "folly," while the harshest blasted it as a revolting desecration of everything holy, more "pig roast" than civilized ceremony. The story generated ample coverage but had to compete with the news that two hundred Manhattan theatergoers burned to death in a fire that same day. "The greater cremation weakened public interest in the lesser," Olcott later pouted in his journal.

Henry Laurens's cremation eighty-four years earlier didn't exactly prompt a craze of copycats (Laurens was, however, an inspiration to nineteenth-century cremationists), but De Palm's actually threatened to derail the movement for years. Despite their respectable titles, Dr. LeMoyne, Colonel Olcott, and Baron De Palm were depicted in the press as a bunch of wackos. LeMoyne had already been pegged an "eccentric" and "radical" for his progressive social positions—for example, his belief that women and African Americans deserved the same rights as white men—but he did have his peculiarities. Ironically, the man who espoused cremations on public health grounds wasn't big on personal hygiene himself. LeMoyne abhorred taking baths and purportedly cleaned his body by gently scraping it with a table knife.

Olcott and De Palm were considered crackpots for their unorthodox spiritual beliefs and because of their association with New York's Theosophical Society, which Olcott had cofounded to promote interest in paranormal and mystical phenomena, particularly mediumistic communication—that is, conversing with the dead. There's no word, alas, on whether or not Olcott tried to chat with De Palm in a post-cremation séance.

De Palm remains the most mysterious of the three. He introduced himself as Baron Joseph Henry Louis Charles De Palm, an affluent Austrian-born nobleman. Whatever wealth and status he once enjoyed in Europe, if any, apparently did not survive the journey to America; reporters discovered that he died bankrupt and nearly homeless. Although De Palm's aristocratic persona was probably nothing more than a harmless exaggeration, it further linked all cremationists, in the eyes of the public, with foreign kooks and practitioners of "black magic."

More than a year passed before LeMoyne had any other takers. Then, on February 15, 1878, he burned the body of Jane Pitman from Cincinnati, making her the first American woman to be cremated. Another cremation had occurred since De Palm's, but Lemoyne wasn't involved. Utah doctor Charles Winslow had been incinerated in a small crematorium hastily erected on a vacant lot in downtown Salt Lake City on July 31, 1877. Builders assembled the temporary structure in a matter of days and tested it by tossing a forty-pound bag of calf meat into the flames. It worked and, with the scent of cooked veal still lingering in the air, Winslow's corpse went next.

Except for Henry Laurens, the first American to incorporate Christian rituals and readings into his cremation was Dr. Julius LeMoyne himself. Two days after he died from diabetes-related complications on October 14, 1879, LeMoyne became the third individual (out of an eventual forty-two) cremated in his own facility. To those already opposed to cremation, LeMoyne's more traditional ceremony was undone by his request to have his ashes sprinkled under a rosebush. "The great difficulty [with] this reform," the *Philadelphia Inquirer* editorialized with unabashed elitism after LeMoyne's death, "has been the impracticable character of those persons who have been foremost in urging its adoption. . . . They [are] the very last class of men and women who should have been picked out to introduce a reform of any kind among a sober and intelligent people."

The *Inquirer* might have been more impressed with Dr. Samuel Gross, cremated on May 8, 1884. The name wasn't ideal from a publicity standpoint, but Gross was an eminent surgeon and past president of the American Medical Association. That same year the nation's first public crematorium was built in Lancaster, Pennsylvania, and by the end of the century, two dozen were up and running in fifteen states.

Other highly regarded Americans began offering their support, although not always their bodies, to the cause, including Massachusetts senator Charles Sumner, Harvard president Charles William Eliot, William Waldorf Astor and Andrew Carnegie (two of America's richest men), sculptor Daniel Chester French, Rabbi Stephen Wise, and Thomas Wentworth Higginson, the abolitionist minister and literary mentor to Emily Dickinson. Distinguished religious leaders also stepped forward to present a theological defense of cremation, noting that there wasn't one Bible verse forbidding it and that if being incinerated prevented resurrection, then every Christian martyr who had been burned at the stake was doomed as well. They also pointed out that God, being omnipotent and all, could just as easily reassemble a cremated body as he could a putrid corpse infested with worms and maggots.

Both religious and secular proponents harped on the relative tidiness of cremation compared with nature's messier and more prolonged process. "Shall [bodily decay] be done in sixty minutes or less, through the influence of, and with all the grandeur, and beauty, and brilliancy, of the cumulative heat of an imprisoned and condensed sunbeam, with harmless and beneficial results," one cremationist, C. N. Peirce, asked rhetorically, "or shall [a corpse] through a period of fifteen or twenty years moulder in the earth, polluting everything with which it comes in contact[?]"

This line of reasoning also resonated increasingly with Sanitarians, a formidable citizens group whose passion for encouraging public and personal cleanliness bordered on the obsessive-compulsive. These self-described preachers of purity crusaded against spitting in public, launched community-awareness campaigns on the importance of washing oneself with soap and water, and lobbied for better trash-removal services, street sweeping, and improved sewer systems.

And nineteenth-century America, to be honest, was in need of a good scrubbing. Horse and human waste streamed down city gutters. Rancid garbage piled up on sidewalks. Slaughterhouse butchers dumped bloody animal carcasses in open lots. And many urban cemeteries were run-down and emitted a revolting stench from improperly interred corpses. Sanitarians became convinced that this foul-smelling miasma, as they called it, harbored diseases and spread epidemics, a position that LeMoyne and his fellow cremationists had pushed for years. (Sanitarians probably would not, however, have allowed the pungent, bathtub-averse LeMoyne into their ranks.)

Frightening the masses with warnings about poisonous graveyard vapors was just one of several scare tactics used by cremationists. In speeches, letters to the editor, and their own publications, *The Urn* and *Modern Crematist,* they highlighted the many indignities suffered by those who opted for a regular burial. Stray dogs had been known to dig up and chew off limbs of the newly dead. Body snatchers and resurrectionists prowled cemeteries for fresh cadavers they could sell to medical schools. Ex-slaves, according to one (almost certainly apocryphal) story in *The Urn,* had chopped up the bones from a white corpse and carved them into gambling dice. Women also had to consider the possibility that their dead bodies might be defiled in unspeakable ways. Perhaps the most fearful specter raised by cremationists was premature burial, and a surprising number of people who chose to be cremated—including Henry Laurens—cited this as their primary reason for doing so.

"Wasn't Laurens afraid of being buried alive ever since Martha was mistakenly pronounced dead as a child?" I ask Tom.

"Yes," he says. "That experience haunted him his entire life, so he put it in his will that he had to be cremated."

The logic of this escapes me. I can appreciate how terrifying it would be to wake up in a casket six feet underground and realize that you're trapped and about to die a slow and agonizing death, but opting to be roasted as a precautionary measure seems extreme. I can think of any number of less drastic alternatives I'd like to have tried on me first— several hard slaps to the face, smelling salts, a good tickling—before being set on fire. To each his own, I guess.

Cremations in the States surged from 16 in 1884 to 1,996 in 1899, a 1,250 percent increase. This represented a tiny sliver of Americans overall, but it was progress nonetheless. At the turn of the century, prestigious cemeteries such as Mount Auburn in Massachusetts started building columbaria for urns and setting up their own crematoriums.

In 1913 a small band of crematorium operators joined together and founded the Cremation Association of America, further legitimizing the movement, and by the early 1940s, 3.7 percent of the U.S. population was electing to be cremated, up from about 1 percent in 1920. That number held steady for twenty years but then dipped during the 1950s economic boom, as a "bigger is better" mentality prompted Americans to splurge on everything from fin-tailed Cadillacs to lavish burial arrangements. In an age of conspicuous consumption, few people wanted to be packed inside a measly coffee-can-sized urn for eternity when there were polished steel nuclear-bomb-proof coffins with plush satin interiors to be had.

That mind-set began to change in 1963, when Jessica Mitford, a British-born author living in California, published *The American Way of Death*. Mitford exposed how funeral homes guilted emotionally vulnerable family members into making excessive purchases well beyond their means. Some undertakers were committing outright fraud, charging for a host of services that were wholly unnecessary or never provided, such as "grief counseling." Mitford also condemned the bereavement business for so overcommercializing death that it had cheapened the mourning process. Simplicity wasn't just less expensive, she argued, it was more authentic.

Also in 1963, and this was the real watershed moment, Pope Paul VI reversed the Vatican's ban on cremations. With conditions. Priests could not perform funeral masses for cremated remains (in 1997 this restriction was itself rescinded) or conduct services at crematoriums.

Although not exactly a full about-face, the change represented a huge shift that, virtually overnight, made it possible for millions of practicing Catholics in America to choose cremation over a traditional burial.

From the mid-1960s to the late '70s, when the nation sank into a deep recession and thriftiness prevailed over profligacy, the trend line in cremations popped up dramatically. Today, approximately 40 percent of Americans are cremated. (To put this in a global context, it's 69 percent in Canada, 72 percent in England, and 99 percent in Japan, the highest among industrialized nations.) The numbers vary widely within the United States; for Hawaii, Alaska, and Arizona, the rate is over 50 percent, while in Alabama and West Virginia it's closer to 5 percent. The overall percentages are increasing every decade.

As are the number of businesses offering Americans unique and imaginative ways to transform their ashes or "cremains" into something memorable. Along with being pulverized into diamond jewelry by LifeGem, one can be mixed with concrete to create a realistic-looking coral rock and placed undersea by Eternal Reefs, ground up with gunpowder and packed into a shotgun shell by Canuck's Sportsman's Memorials, or "baked" inside vinyl plastic and pressed into a set of 33-r.p.m. records by the British company And Vinyly, which will also personalize the albums with whatever music or audio its customers request.

"I hope this isn't too personal," I say to Tom, "but have you decided, you know, when the time comes, if you're going to be buried or—"

"Cremated," he says. "It's in my will. I'm dividing up my ashes into thirds, and some will be placed here and the rest in North Carolina and Teffont Evias, England, where my ancestors are from."

That's another advantage of cremation. You can spread yourself around. People have had themselves strewn along hiking trails, scattered in sand traps on their favorite golf course, or spread across the fifty-yard line of their college football field. Ten years ago the ashes of scientist John Kotowski were exploded over San Francisco Bay as part of a fireworks display, and the gonzo journalist Hunter Thompson went a similar route when his ashes were blown out of a cannon near his home in Aspen, Colorado. Another writer, Mark Gruenwald, convinced his colleagues at Marvel Comics to stir his ashes into the ink used for a special printing of *Squadron Supreme.* Dr. Timothy Leary, the Harvard professor fired for promoting the psychological benefits (in his opinion) of LSD back in the 1970s, had his ashes distributed among family and friends, one of whom worked for a company that launches cremains into space. On April 21, 1997, seven grams of Leary's ashes, along with bits of *Star Trek* creator Gene Roddenberry, were placed in a Pegasus rocket and shot into orbit, where they circled the earth for six years before burning up in the atmosphere. Planetary geologist Eugene Shoemaker one-upped them all when some of his ashes were sent to the moon aboard NASA's unmanned Lunar Prospector probe. Sixty-nine years old when he died in a car crash, Shoemaker was a beloved figure in the space community for having helped train the Apollo astronauts. He is, to date, the only person whose remains are on the moon.

A light rain begins to fall, and I tell Tom I'm ready to leave whenever he is. Tom has been the epitome of a southern gentleman, ever since my first phone call to him months ago, and I especially appreciate his time because I've sensed from the start that he's not thrilled I'm concentrating on this narrow aspect of Laurens's biography. He hasn't said this outright, but I'm guessing he'd prefer that Laurens be mentioned alongside America's other Founding Fathers instead of some guys who had their ashes launched from a cannon or blended into comic-book ink.

I finish packing up my camera gear, and Tom says to me, almost as an aside, "You know there's some question as to whether Laurens's ashes are even here."

"You're kidding!" I exclaim.

"No, I'm not," he says. "That's the family lore at least."

Far from disappointing, this is a welcome bit of trivia.

"That's awesome," I say.

Tom seems surprised by my response, and admittedly it was a poor choice of words. I quickly explain that I'm intrigued by the whole subject of missing remains not due to some morbid fixation but because it relates to the accuracy of grave markers. Some sites claim to be the final resting place of prominent historical figures, when in truth that might not be the case. Laurens makes the sixth distinguished American I've now heard about who, possibly, isn't buried where he's supposed to be.

Number five is the whole reason I'm off next to Kentucky.

DANIEL BOONE'S GRAVE

The often repeated saying that those who forget the lessons of history are doomed to repeat them has a lot of truth in it. But what are "the lessons of history"? The very attempt at definition furnishes ground for new conflicts. History is not a recipe book; past events are never replicated in the present in quite the same way. Historical events are infinitely variable and their interpretations are a constantly shifting process. There are no certainties to be found in the past.

—Historian Gerda Lerner

ALL I WANTED, just to establish a basic understanding of Daniel Boone's life, was to first nail down when and where the man was born. Timothy Flint's 1833 *Biographical Memoir of Daniel Boone, the First Settler of Kentucky* is the earliest biography about the famed frontiersman and seemed a trustworthy resource to start with. "Different authorities assign a different birth place to Daniel Boone," Flint writes in his book's opening sentence. "One affirms that he was born in Maryland, another in North Carolina, and still another during the transit of his parents across the Atlantic. But they are all equally in error. He was born in the year 1746, in Bucks county, Pennsylvania."

Flint's confidence was encouraging—and misguided; he got the county right (although Bucks was originally called Berks) but was way off on the year. In *My Father, Daniel Boone,* which features historian Lyman Draper's extensive interviews with Nathan Boone, Nathan states categorically: "I have shown you the family records, which in my father's own handwriting show his birth to have been October 22, 1734."

Every other major biography confirms that this is the more accurate date, with one slight caveat. In the middle of the eighteenth century, colonial America, following Europe's lead, altered its calendar, and all dates before this modification can be referenced in two different ways. In 1582, Pope Gregory XIII replaced the "Old Style" Julian calendar, created by Julius Caesar six hundred years earlier, with the "New Style" Gregorian calendar to make up for an eleven-minute discrepancy between the Julian year and the solar year—that is, the time it actually takes our planet to orbit the sun. (An eleven-minute lag doesn't sound like much, but it adds up, and the months were falling out of sync with the seasons.) Predominantly Catholic countries switched immediately after the papal decree, while Protestant nations were slow to implement Pope Gregory's somewhat complicated system. Great Britain and the colonies didn't adopt the New Style until 1752, and many Americans born before then chose to have their original birth date put on their grave, followed by the initials O.S. for Old Style.

So, ultimately, the consensus is that Daniel Boone came into the world on October 22, 1734, in Berks County, Pennsylvania. Or on November 2, 1734, in Bucks County. Or any combination thereof.

"There's a lot of folklore and misinformation surrounding Boone's life, and separating fact from legend has always been a challenge," Steven Caudill, a professional eighteenth-century reenactor who specializes in portraying Boone, says, commiserating with me as we drive through Frankfort, Kentucky.

"I grew up outside of Boonesborough, was raised on stories about Boone, and I've always been interested in him," he says. Almost fifty years old, Steve served in the Army and then in the Winchester, Kentucky, police department before parlaying his fascination with Boone into a full-time job that keeps him on the road year-round. During a brief trip back home he's agreed to accompany me to Boone's grave in the Frankfort Cemetery at 215 East Main Street.

Incorporated in 1844, the cemetery was proposed by a local judge named Mason Brown who had visited Mount Auburn Cemetery in Massachusetts, returned home, and encouraged his fellow Kentuckians to create a burial ground equally as picturesque. I'd say they succeeded. Overlooking the Kentucky River, Frankfort Cemetery is one hundred acres of beautifully landscaped hills and gardens connected by winding paths and walkways. More than twenty thousand people are buried here, including an impressive assembly of statesmen, artists, writers, and war heroes. On our way up a sloping macadamized road, Steve and I pass the marker for Presley O'Bannon, the young Marine lieutenant who was the first American to raise a U.S. flag on captured foreign soil. This happened during the April 1805 Battle of Derne at Tripoli and inspired the lyrics in the Marines' Hymn:

> From the halls of Montezuma,
> To the shores of Tripoli;
> We fight our country's battles
> In the air, on land, and sea.

Farther up the rolling lane, Steve points to a fifteen-foot-high obelisk on our right surrounded by a black wrought-iron fence.

"That's Boone's grave."

Once we get closer, I can make out carvings on each side of the memorial that appear to be scenes from Daniel Boone's life.

"He never would have worn that," Steve says, shaking his head, as he sees me examine one panel featuring Boone in his famed coonskin cap.

"Daniel was originally raised a Quaker, and like other long hunters he wore a Quaker-style felt hat." This is more than a nitpicky sartorial critique on Steve's part. "Wearing a coonskin cap would have been foolish for a number of reasons. For one, if you're loading your rifle in the rain," he says, mimicking a man holding a gun close to his chest and filling it with gunpowder, "you want to keep the inside of the barrel and your powder dry, and Quaker-style hats had larger brims to protect them from getting wet."

Steve isn't bothered by the panel that shows Boone slaying a deer or the one of his wife, Rebecca, milking a cow, but he's peeved by the last image, of Boone fighting a Native American. "He's always portrayed as this Indian killer," Steve says. "If anything, he was a peacemaker, despite the fact that his brother and two sons were killed by Indians." According to Nathan Boone, Daniel did kill at least one Indian during the Battle of Blue Licks at the end of the American Revolution, and Steve tells me there are two other instances in which Boone took an Indian's life.

"Both times in self-defense," he adds.

Perhaps the most persistent Boone misconception is that he founded Kentucky. Steve knocks down that myth instantly. "He founded Boonesborough and did more than anyone else to lead people into these parts, but others had been settling here before he did."

"What's so important about him, then?" I ask Steve. That came out harsher than I intended, and I already have an idea of Boone's significance anyway. I'm just curious about Steve's take, and I rephrase my question. "I mean, in your opinion, what would you say is his real legacy?"

Steve proceeds to emphasize how much Boone shaped the way our country came to see itself. Before Davy Crockett, Kit Carson, or Lewis and Clark, Daniel Boone represented the iconic American frontiersman. His roving, adventurous life in the woods influenced generations of artists and authors, from Thomas Cole and Frederick Church to Ralph Waldo Emerson, Henry David Thoreau, and Walt Whitman.

James Fenimore Cooper modeled Natty Bumppo in his Leatherstocking series partly after Boone, and the real-life abduction of Boone's daughter by a Shawnee-led war party inspired a dramatic plotline in *The Last of the Mohicans*. (Boone famously rescued his daughter and two other teenage girls in a daring raid on their captors.) Cooper's books were among the first novels out of America to become international bestsellers, and this further boosted Boone's fame overseas. Throughout the late 1700s and early 1800s, a time when our national identity was being forged, Boone—more so than presidents Washington, Adams, and Jefferson, or any other political figure back then—symbolized in the United States and abroad the quintessential American: self-made, rugged, independent, frugal, lacking pretense or pride, forever on the move, always exploring.

"Boone is a part of who we are," Steve says.

No dates, quotes, Bible verses, or mortuary symbols of any kind appear on Boone's memorial. Perhaps erring on the side of caution, whoever designed the obelisk had only two words engraved in the stone: DANIEL BOONE. But even this is in doubt; Daniel Boone's remains might not actually be here.

"Boone was originally buried in Marthasville, Missouri, next to his wife, Rebecca," Steve says, "and there's a grave marker for him there, too. About twenty-five years after Boone's death, the founders of this cemetery pushed to have his body put here. A host of dignitaries met with members of Boone's family and told them it would be a great honor to have Daniel and Rebecca back in Kentucky, and they agreed. Fifteen to twenty thousand people attended an elaborate parade when the remains were brought to Frankfort."

"At least what they *thought* were his remains, right?"

"That's the problem. Eyewitnesses in Missouri, who were at Daniel's and Rebecca's graves when they were dug up, later claimed that everything was so decayed and jumbled together, including the bones of other relatives and slaves, that the representatives from Kentucky took the wrong ones. A plaster cast had been made of Boone's skull before he was reburied, and in 1983 an anthropologist named Dr. David Wolf looked at it and said it wasn't the skull of a Caucasian male."

"A lot of what I've read suggests that whoever's here is really an unnamed slave."

"Well, that's what the Missouri folks say."

Steve reveres Boone, and I assure him that my intention isn't to make light of Boone's fate or malign those who insist he's buried in Kentucky—or in Missouri. The uncertainty over Boone's final whereabouts, not to mention his date of birth, relates to the more fundamental question about what we can learn from history when so many basic facts turn out to be mistaken or fabricated. Historical sites are hardly alone. Biographies often have their biases, either demeaning or inflating their subjects through the selective use of material; memoirs are notoriously self-serving; film footage and historic photographs have been staged or doctored; paintings tend to be even more unreliable; and history textbooks sometimes contain glaring whoppers overlooked by review panels and boards of education.

Getting back to physical places, I've noticed throughout my research a pattern of errors and irregularities even within the narrow context of historic grave sites. Starting with Amelia Earhart's. Her name came up while I was delving into the whole Wright brothers versus Gustave Whitehead controversy and stumbled across pictures of Burbank, California's Valhalla Memorial Park Cemetery. WELCOME TO THIS SHRINE OF AMERICAN AVIATION, a sign reads at the entrance of the massive vault dedicated to our country's greatest pilots. THE PLAQUES HEREIN MARK THE FINAL RESTING PLACE OF PIONEERS OF FLIGHT. Another photograph shows a plaque for Earhart, which surprised me because her remains were never recovered after she crashed somewhere in the Pacific on July 2, 1937. I called Les Copeland, president of the Burbank Aviation Museum (located at Valhalla), to inquire about this discrepancy. Les, who couldn't have been nicer, said they were accurate but agreed that a visitor could be led to believe that Earhart was entombed there. "Keep in mind, though," he added, "that her plaque is on the wall, and the others, for the pilots actually buried here, are on the floor." That's a fair point, and I don't mean to imply an intentional deception, but the "final resting place" wording is somewhat confusing.

More baffling is the squat marble tombstone in Granbury, Texas, for "Jesse Woodson James." The outlaw's full name is given correctly, and his birthday, September 5, 1847, matches up with the historical record. The date of death, however—August 15, 1951—does not, and a line at the bottom grudgingly acknowledges the more accepted date: SUPPOSEDLY KILLED IN 1882.

Most Jesse James experts agree that James was fatally shot in the back of the head on April 3, 1882, by fellow gang member Robert Ford for a $5,000 reward. James was laid to rest outside his family's farmhouse in Kearney, Missouri, under a headstone with an epitaph dictated by his mother: IN LOVING MEMORY OF MY BELOVED SON, MURDERED BY A TRAITOR AND COWARD WHOSE NAME IS NOT WORTHY TO APPEAR HERE. James's body was later disinterred and reburied next to his mom's at Kearney's Mount Olivet Cemetery.

The pro-Granbury crowd contends that James faked his death to evade a lifetime of manhunts and, after changing his name to J. Frank Dalton, moved to northern Texas, where he earned his living as a railroad contractor. Dalton "confessed" to being James at the age of 101, and when he died three years later, the local sheriff examined his body and reported it was missing its middle fingertip and had burn marks on its feet (apparently from when Union soldiers tortured James, a Confederate guerrilla in the Civil War) as well as other distinguishing scars consistent with injuries James had sustained earlier in life.

To resolve the decades-long quarrel, scientists exhumed the Kearney remains in 1995 and conducted a mitochondrial DNA test (using, of course, PCR), which indeed showed a positive link to relatives on James's maternal side. Not to be outdone, folks in Granbury dug up *their* Jesse James in 2000 to perform a genetic analysis, but when they opened the coffin they found not the corpse of a 104-year-old J. Frank Dalton but of a younger man with only one arm. The headstone had apparently been placed over the wrong spot. Nevertheless, it's still there, proudly proclaiming to be where the real Jesse James is buried.

Like Boone and James, Chief Sitting Bull has two graves in different states. After his Lakota warriors helped crush General George Armstrong Custer's Seventh Cavalry Regiment at Little Bighorn, Sitting Bull laid low in Canada for five years. He returned to America in 1885 and toured briefly in Buffalo Bill's Wild West show, earning $50 a week. In 1890, Indian Service agents feared that Sitting Bull was inciting a potentially violent Native American movement to regain territorial lands, and on December 15 police at the Standing Rock Reservation shot him dead while serving out an arrest warrant. Sitting Bull was unceremoniously buried by U.S. soldiers on the North Dakota side of Fort Yates, and the obscure and mostly unvisited grave site gradually fell into disrepair. His nephew, Clarence Grey Eagle, and a contingent of businessmen from Mobridge, South Dakota, hatched an elaborate plan to exhume Sitting Bull and bury him on a river bluff near Mobridge. After digging up his skeleton during an early-morning snowstorm on April 8, 1953, they loaded it into a hearse and used a decoy car to fool any North Dakota officials intent on trailing them. They crossed into South Dakota without incident and interred Sitting Bull under tons of steel-girded concrete to prevent anyone from stealing him back. Echoing the Boone saga, some historians and descendants of Sitting Bull insist that Grey Eagle and his cohorts dug up the wrong bones.

Last but not least is the story of poor Thomas Paine, the British-born immigrant turned ardent American patriot who has only one grave to his name, and he barely got that. Paine was so reviled by the end of his life for having disparaged all organized religions in his writings that no church would allow his body to be buried on their grounds. He was eventually laid to rest on his farm in New Rochelle, New York, and only six people attended the funeral. (Twenty-thousand mourners, by comparison, showed up at Ben Franklin's.)

A historical marker in New Rochelle reads:

ON THIS SITE WAS BURIED
THOMAS PAINE
1737–1809
AUTHOR OF
COMMON SENSE
THE PAMPHLET THAT STIRRED
THE AMERICAN COLONIES TO INDEPENDENCE

John Adams Said:
"Without the pen of Paine the sword of
Washington would have been wielded in vain."
AND
"History is to ascribe the American Revolution
to Thomas Paine."

That first line alone is both wrong and outdated. The marker does *not* stand over the original grave site, and while Paine indeed "was buried" near here in 1809, his remains were stolen ten years later by an English journalist named William Cobbett and never recovered. Paine's grave has been empty for two hundred years, and how this came to be is a tale worthy of elaboration.

A former critic of Paine's turned fanatical admirer, Cobbett was appalled that his newfound hero had been treated so shabbily at life's end by the very nation Paine had helped rouse to freedom decades before with the January 1776 publication of *Common Sense,* Paine's impassioned call to arms against the British. The pamphlet sold 500,000 copies during the Revolution, a mind-blowing number considering that the country's entire population was only 2.5 million and many folks were illiterate. No other book except the Bible has been read by a larger percentage of Americans. And when the Continental Army edged perilously close to defeat in December 1776, Paine churned out a series of publications titled *The Crisis* to lift the country's spirits. "These are the times that try men's souls," he famously proclaimed in the first essay, which was composed in the shivering cold at Fort Trenton. (Paine had enlisted as a soldier, but George Washington personally decided that the thirty-year-old pamphleteer would better serve his country by writing, not fighting. Paine donated his substantial profits from *The Crisis* to buy clothes and supplies for the Army's ill-equipped and hungry troops.) Washington rallied his embattled men with Paine's words and credited him with helping to turn the tide of the war in America's favor.

In 1781, Congress appointed Paine to complete Henry Laurens's diplomatic mission to Europe after Laurens was captured at sea and imprisoned in the Tower of London. Accompanied by Laurens's son, Colonel John Laurens, Paine helped convince France to lend the colonies $10 million and provide troops and warships, which proved indispensable in forcing Cornwallis's surrender at Yorktown.

In 1794 and '95, Paine released a withering two-volume critique of organized religion titled *The Age of Reason*. "All national institutions of churches, whether Jewish, Christian or Turkish [i.e., Muslim]," Paine wrote, "appear to me no other than human inventions, set up to terrify and enslave mankind, and monopolize power and profit." Whatever goodwill Paine had earned during the Revolution evaporated instantly. Congress refused to fund his pension, he was denied the right to vote, and former allies ostracized him entirely.

During a visit to the States, William Cobbett made a pilgrimage to Paine's grave in New Rochelle and couldn't believe what he found. "Paine lies in a little hole under the grass and weeds of an obscure farm in America," he reported in his journal. "There, however, *he shall not lie, unnoticed, much longer.* He belongs to England. His fame is the property of England; and if no other people will show that they value that fame, the people of England will."

So, in October 1819, William Cobbett dug up Thomas Paine's remains, packed them in a crate, and shipped them to Great Britain. He hadn't even bothered to backfill the grave, apparently figuring no one would care. He was right. Local authorities noticed the mound of dirt, launched a halfhearted search, and then dropped the investigation altogether.

Upon returning home, Cobbett announced his intention to build an extravagant memorial for Paine and organize a lavish funeral in his honor, which he would finance by parading Paine's bones around England and charging the public a fee to glimpse them. The plan was ill conceived from the start. Paine was more despised in his native country than in America, and some towns were still burning him in effigy once a year. The British poet Lord Byron summed up the public mood when he chided:

> In digging up your bones, Tom Paine,
> Will Cobbett has done well;
> You visit him on earth again,
> He'll visit you in hell.

Stuck with these very bones, Cobbett eventually stashed them inside a trunk under his bed. In 1835, Cobbett passed away, bankrupt, and left his family in dire financial straits. His son tried to auction off Paine's remains to the highest bidder, but the estate auctioneer refused to sell human bones on principle, and no one knows what happened to them next. Possibly they were buried in a nearby churchyard. Or piece by piece they ended up in different hands. A Unitarian clergyman insisted in 1854 that he had Paine's skull and finger bones, and Benjamin Tilly, Cobbett's secretary, is said to have extracted part of Paine's brain. The hardened, puttylike matter made its way back to America in 1905 and was placed inside a statue of Paine erected in New Rochelle. As to where the rest of Paine ended up, it's anyone's guess.

Were John Adams alive today, he'd be appalled to see two laudatory quotes attributed to him inscribed on Paine's memorial. There's no proof that Adams ever wrote or uttered the comment exalting Paine's pen over Washington's sword, and the second quotation is taken wholly out of context. Factually speaking, Adams did state, in a June 1819 letter to Thomas Jefferson, that "history is to ascribe the American

Revolution to Thomas Paine." In truth, far from praising him, Adams was *complaining* that Paine would be remembered so fondly. Three sentences earlier in his letter, Adams had referred to *Common Sense* as an "ignorant, malicious, short-sighted crapulous mass." That somehow didn't make it onto the memorial.

While Steven takes pictures of Daniel Boone's grave and circles the iron fence to inspect the site, making sure everything's in good condition, I wander off to check out the neighbors. A few rows away is old Mason Brown, whose visit to Mount Auburn inspired this cemetery. Farther up, my eye zeroes in on a name that practically leaps off its headstone: BLACKBURN.

Maybe it's not the same Blackburn I'm thinking of, I say to myself, but upon approaching the grave, I see that, yes, indeed, it's Luke P. Blackburn, former governor of Kentucky. His granite marker is more elaborate than Boone's, with four miniature Doric columns carved in the middle, all sorts of architectural flourishes, and a decorative "roof" on top that looks like a hybrid of Roman and Asian influences. Underneath that is a bronze bas-relief of the Good Samaritan parable.

Associating Blackburn with such charity is either a suitable homage or an inexcusable abomination, depending on one's perspective, and it reinforces how vexing it can be to render an opinion on a historical figure's life and legacy. Before entering politics, Blackburn had earned a medical degree at Kentucky's Transylvania University and went on to gain national praise for treating, on a pro bono basis, yellow-fever victims in the South between 1848 and 1854. He also contributed his own money to build a hospital in an impoverished area of Mississippi and successfully lobbied Congress to fund additional ones throughout the state. In 1854 he traveled to Philadelphia to secure an apprenticeship for his teenage son with the renowned Dr. Samuel Gross (the same Dr. Gross whose request to be cremated gave the cremationist movement an air of respectability). Later that year yellow fever hit Long Island, and once again, Blackburn volunteered to care for the afflicted without compensation. He was elected Kentucky's governor in 1879 by a political landslide but quickly grew unpopular because he instituted sweeping reforms that improved living conditions for prisoners. Nicknamed "Lenient Luke," Blackburn issued more than a thousand pardons and was literally booed off the political stage at the end of his term for being too compassionate.

That was Luke Blackburn, the humanitarian.

Then there's Luke Blackburn, the terrorist.

During the Civil War, Blackburn was the Confederate sympathizer who gathered up contaminated bedsheets and garments from yellow-fever victims in Bermuda and tried using them to spread an epidemic throughout Northern cities. He failed solely because the disease is not, as he'd assumed, contagious (again, mosquitoes are the vectors), a blunder that doesn't negate his desire to kill thousands of innocent civilians.

How do we remember such a man? In all of Kentucky there's only one major public tribute to Blackburn I'm aware of, and it's a prison outside of Lexington called the Blackburn Correctional Complex. Considering his record, that seems rather fitting.

Steve and I meet up at his truck, and after we drive out of the cemetery I realize I've yet to get his personal verdict on where Daniel Boone is buried.

When I ask him, he smiles at first. "That's a tricky question," he says. "I have to be careful because I'm friends with Boone's ancestors and there's disagreement among the family members."

Steve considers his reply carefully and finally says to me, "Well, it's not an answer that will make everyone happy, but I think Boone is in both places."

"Hmm," I say, giving the mental machinery a moment to process this. "So when the Kentucky folks took his remains, they mistakenly left some behind?"

"Exactly. Everyone agrees he was dug up pretty quickly, and there were hundreds of bones mixed together in that plot. Odds are that some were picked up and some stayed in Missouri."

"Nothing I've read about Boone has mentioned this. But . . . that definitely makes a lot of sense."

Steve concedes it's just a theory and the debate will probably never be resolved. DNA tests are exorbitantly expensive, and by now Boone's bones are probably too degraded to offer any conclusive results. Regional pride and, to be frank, tourist dollars also make it doubtful that either state would allow a disinterment and risk losing its claim to being Daniel Boone's *true* final resting place. The folks who dug up "Jesse James" in Granbury, Texas, discovered that the hard way.

"At the beginning of this whole journey," I say to Steve, "I had expected to find these grand 'lessons of history' everywhere I went, but in a lot of cases it seems that there's little we can really know for certain, like with Boone. We can't even confirm when he was born and where he's buried, and it casts doubt on everything in between."

"I wouldn't say that at all," Steve replies. "Maybe we can't verify every detail, but Boone's life speaks for itself, for the kind of man he was. He didn't swing from tree vines like Tarzan, the way Flint writes in his book, but he was a skilled pioneer who blazed the Wilderness Road and traveled thousands of miles over dangerous lands throughout his lifetime. From this alone we can assume he was an incredibly brave and resourceful man."

Steve's admiration for Boone, I realize, is no different from mine for the paleo-Indians Dr. Dennis Jenkins has been studying in Paisley, Oregon, and we know less about them than about Boone. On a broader level, I also understand that history can be recorded and relayed only in shorthand. We can't qualify every statement with "Now, this might turn out to be false" or "As far as we know . . ." The effect would be maddening. And second-guessing everyone who tries to share a historical anecdote by constantly interrupting, "What's your source on that?" is probably an excellent way of getting punched at a cocktail party.

But when historical references become more than just grist for idle conversation, when they are cited to influence public policy or shape legislation, they deserve to be scrutinized and challenged. While our inquiries might not always lead to perfect answers, they help us to ask better questions and keep us alert to how easily facts can be twisted,

ideas taken out of context, and legendary figures manipulated to promote a particular social or political cause.

What specific guidance the past offers us has been debated since
the time of Herodotus and Thucydides in the fifth century B.C., and
for every George Santayana–like sentiment proclaiming that historical
knowledge will lead us away from repeating the mistakes of yesteryear,
there's an equally persuasive argument cautioning that it might also
present us with false beacons.

"Historians are left forever chasing shadows, painfully aware of their
inability ever to reconstruct a dead world in its completeness however
thorough or revealing their documentation," historian Simon Schama
wrote in *Dead Certainties,* a book I recently read because it includes
a novella inspired by George Parkman's murder at Harvard. "We are
doomed," Schama concludes, "to be forever hailing someone who has
just gone around the corner and out of earshot."

I'm keeping an open mind and still seeking out those larger lessons,
but for now, Schama's observation sounds about right. I would only
add that the chase itself is half the fun.

THOMAS "PETE"
RAY'S GRAVE

When Batista was dictator of Cuba, he was of course a thorn in our sides. . . . So when Castro started fighting in the hills, we were very much in favor of his success. . . .

We of course watched developments very carefully and as quickly as Castro succeeded in driving Batista out of the country, we found that he was turning into a vindictive and almost irrational type of man that we would have to watch very closely indeed. Within a short time his selection of assistants who were known Communists and his establishment of close and friendly ties with the Soviets convinced us that we had a real problem on our hands.

—From a private letter written on April 24, 1961, by former president Dwight D. Eisenhower to his old friend John Hay Whitney

"A LOT OF people like the quiet and stillness of cemeteries," Janet Ray said to me before I came to visit her father's grave here at Forest Hill Cemetery, which presses up against Birmingham, Alabama's

Shuttlesworth International Airport. "But I find it comforting to hear the planes coming and going. My dad flew out of that airport in April 1961, and this was the last time I saw him alive." There is no question that Thomas "Pete" Willard Ray is buried at Forest Hill. Several FBI agents, a Birmingham coroner, and members of his own family, Janet included, all positively identified his body before it was laid to rest on December 8, 1979. Why Ray's corpse had gone missing since April 19, 1961—the day his B-26 bomber crash-landed in Cuba during one of America's worst Cold War crises—is the real story.

And it begins two years earlier, in 1959.

Near the end of President Dwight D. Eisenhower's final term in office, the Central Intelligence Agency began recruiting Cuban exiles and refugees to form a clandestine paramilitary unit that would invade their former homeland, stir up popular support against Fidel Castro, and overthrow his regime. Ranging in ages from sixteen to sixty, the men called themselves Brigade 2506 in memory of a comrade, Carlos Santana, accidentally killed during training exercises; 2506 was his enlistment number.

Their success would hinge on wiping out Cuba's air power before the main ground assault, and CIA planners recommissioned old B-26 Douglas Invaders for the attack. The World War II–era bombers had been mothballed for years, but with a new paint job and some minor adjustments they could be made to resemble Cuban B-26s left over from the Batista era. By using these planes, the CIA gambled that Brigade 2506's "Liberation Air Force" (LAF) could catch the Cubans by surprise and convince Castro's people that his own military had turned against him. And once the LAF pilots controlled the skies, they would be able to cover amphibious forces coming ashore off freighters disguised as merchant vessels. The CIA proposed an early-morning invasion near the city of Trinidad, where anti-Castro sentiment was still strong. Also close by were the Escambray Mountains, a potential hiding spot for Brigade 2506 forces in case their mission unraveled.

Since Alabama's Air National Guard was the last unit to fly and maintain the B-26s, Alabama guardsmen were enlisted to teach LAF crews how to master the vintage aircraft and assist with mission planning. Under no circumstances, however, would Americans be allowed to fly the bombing raids. They were to remain on base and help rearm and repair the B-26s when they returned from Cuba. Although our government was providing all of the ships, planes, weapons, and funding for the invasion, as well as training Brigade 2506 members in Florida, Texas, Virginia, and Louisiana, the CIA didn't want anyone to suspect that the United States was involved in any way.

Training camps were later moved to a coffee plantation in Guatemala owned by the brother of the Guatemalan ambassador to the United States, and another base was later set up in Puerto Cabezas, Nicaragua, to serve as the primary staging area. "I'm willing to support you, but be sure you get rid of that son of a bitch," President Anastasio Somoza of Nicaragua told his CIA contacts, referring to Castro, "or you are going to live with him for the rest of your life." (Somoza was also a dictator, but having been raised in America for much of his youth, the West Point–educated strongman was "our" dictator.)

Pete Ray, a twenty-nine-year-old Air Force veteran and Alabama guardsman who'd joined the Army in 1960 to fly helicopters, enthusiastically volunteered for the assignment when the CIA came calling. "My father loved his country and loved flying," Janet told me. "As a boy he went to the Birmingham airport to watch the planes and hang out with the pilots. He enlisted in the Air Force when he was seventeen, and he had to forge his mother's signature on the application form because technically he was too young." (I asked Janet where the nickname Pete came from, and she said she didn't know. "That's just what everyone called him.") Ray had married his high school sweetheart, Margaret Hayden, in 1952, and they built a house together in Center Point, a leafy suburb just outside of Birmingham.

Eisenhower's successor, John F. Kennedy, had received briefings about the covert operation before assuming the presidency and, after giving it his full attention once in office, worried that the undertaking would be too "noisy." On March 11, 1961, Kennedy ordered a smaller invasion and nixed Trinidad as the landing area. He directed the CIA to find, within a matter of days, a less populated spot that also had an airstrip nearby so the B-26s could continue their flights from within Cuba. Sleep-deprived intelligence analysts came back to the president with a new beachhead along the Zapata Peninsula that met his approval: Bahía de Cochinos, the Bay of Pigs.

According to Operation Zapata, as it was then being called, sixteen B-26 bombers would strike on April 15 and 16, followed the next day by ground forces and paratroopers. A lone LAF pilot pretending to be a Cuban defector would land his B-26 in Miami and declare that he was part of a larger coup. CIA operatives would broadcast the story, along with fake radio bulletins detailing the government's collapse, into Cuba to incite public uprisings. Finally, after the Brigade 2506 troops had either captured or assassinated Castro, a provisional, pro-American government would be installed.

That, at least, was the plan.

Until, with hours to go, it changed again. Further hoping to lower the operation's decibel level, President Kennedy cut the number of B-26s in half, from sixteen to eight. When the order was relayed to Puerto Cabezas, the LAF airmen were furious. Even before the reduction they felt undermanned and outgunned; every bombing run would require seven hours of nonstop flying (six for the round-trip journey alone), and their planes carried no air-to-air missiles, leaving them vulnerable to enemy jets. With the odds already stacked against them, the pilots insisted that they needed all sixteen bombers, if not more. Their entreaties fell on deaf ears, and they were commanded to suit up and get ready.

At daybreak on April 15, the tiny squadron of eight B-26s skimmed over the Atlantic, staying below radar, and caught the Cuban Air Force off-guard. They inflicted massive damage on three airfields before antiaircraft guns blew one B-26 out of the sky and punched holes into two more, forcing the planes to land in Key West, Florida, and the Cayman Islands. Hastily patched up and refueled, they hobbled back to Puerto Cabezas.

Around seven o'clock that same morning, LAF pilot Mario Zúñiga made a dramatic emergency landing at Miami International Airport and announced that he and other members of Castro's military were in revolt. Almost nobody believed him. His B-26 looked like it had recently been pulled out of storage and repainted, and one keen-eyed reporter observed that "dust and undisturbed grease covered [the plane's] bomb-bay fittings, electrical connections to rocket mounts were corroded, [and] guns were uncocked and unfired." Others noted that, though Zúñiga's bomber certainly appeared similar to those in Castro's Air Force, the nose of his B-26 was metal, while theirs were made of Plexiglas.

From photographs taken by U-2 reconnaissance planes, the White House learned that only half of Cuba's warplanes were destroyed in the first assault. Recognizing that the element of surprise was now gone and not wanting to lose additional bombers, President Kennedy and his advisors postponed further raids until the main invasion, when Brigade 2506's approximately fourteen hundred troops would be going up against tens of thousands of Cuban soldiers.

Frogmen and demolition experts disembarked from the cargo ships just before midnight on April 16 and were quickly spotted by Cuban militia, who then ran off after the two sides briefly exchanged gunfire. Word of the invasion reached Castro at his headquarters, but he and his senior officers couldn't determine if there were multiple attacks across the island or just one major thrust at the Bay of Pigs. Adding to their confusion were reports of landings along the northern coast near Bahía Honda. This, in fact, was a feint conducted by CIA operatives motoring around on small rafts outfitted with large speakers broadcasting sounds of crackling radio transmissions, men yelling orders, and heavy equipment being moved.

Due in part to the CIA's diversionary ploys, most Brigade 2506 members made it ashore by dawn on April 17. Later that morning, however, Castro directed the bulk of his troops to the Bay of Pigs and ordered his remaining T-33s and Sea Furies into the air. The jets descended on the incoming forces and sank or scared away the cargo ships offshore carrying much-needed munitions and supplies. As the LAF crews predicted, the Cuban warplanes outmaneuvered them handily, and four B-26s were quickly shot down. Without cover from above and surrounded by an advancing army, hundreds of Brigade 2506 members became mired in the swamps around the bay and were easily killed or taken prisoner.

Fearing an even greater bloodbath, the White House approved the one measure it had most wanted to avoid from the beginning. "Following is for your guidance," CIA headquarters cabled its station chief at Puerto Cabezas, Nicaragua, on April 18:

> AMERICAN CONTRACT CREWS CAN BE USED. B-26
> STRIKES BEACHHEAD AREA AND APPROACHES ONLY.
> EMPHASIZE BEACHHEAD AREA ONLY. CAN NOT ATTACH
> SUFFICIENT IMPORTANCE TO FACT AMERICAN CREWS
> MUST NOT FALL INTO ENEMY HANDS.

Americans Doug Price and Connie Siegrist were airborne hours later and joined by several other B-26s flown by their Cuban comrades, including Mario Zúñiga, who had already slipped out of Miami and returned to Puerto Cabezas. The sortie scored a direct hit on a convoy of Soviet-made trucks and tanks bearing down on Brigade 2506 ground forces, but while the strike served as a short-term morale boost, it had minor tactical significance.

Castro was mobilizing his troops for a decisive, all-out offensive on April 19, and Alabama guardsmen were eager to jump into the fray. At this point Washington was willing to extend further military support and authorized A-4D Skyhawk fighter jets from the USS *Essex* to cover the next wave of B-26s, although only for a designated one-hour window of time.

Eight Americans—pilots Joe Shannon, Riley Shamburger, Billy Goodwin, and Pete Ray, accompanied by crewmen Leo Baker, Nick Sudano, Wade Gray, and James Vaughn—volunteered for a final, last-ditch air raid to assist Brigade 2506's surviving members. Zúñiga, despite having barely slept in four days, insisted on going, too.

Six B-26s left Puerto Cabezas before sunrise on April 19, expecting to rendezvous with their faster and better-armed escorts as they neared Cuban airspace. None of the Skyhawks showed. (A simple time-zone-related miscalculation was said to be responsible for the mix-up.) Wade Gray and Riley Shamburger were first to come under attack. A T-33 swooped in from out of nowhere and blasted them from the side, killing both men and sending their plane straight into the ocean.

With a T-33 trailing them, Pete Ray and his flight engineer, Leo Baker, made a dash for the sprawling sugar refinery that doubled as Castro's field headquarters several miles north of the Bay of Pigs beachhead. A burst of antiaircraft fire struck their plane, and Ray transmitted a "Mayday, Mayday, Mayday" distress call before crash-landing in a cane field. They were never heard from again.

Janet Ray was six years old when her father disappeared, and yet her memories of that time remain vivid. "We were living at my grandmother's, right across the street from my school," she told me. "I remember being on the playground at recess, and I watched through the chain link fence as this fancy black car drove up to the house and three men in suits got out. I knew something was wrong, and when I got home my mother was barely able to speak. The men had said that my father was 'missing,' but that's all."

More men in suits came the next week. One, a lawyer connected to the CIA named Thomas McDowell, informed Margaret that her husband was probably lost at sea and the chance of finding him was slim. McDowell returned on May 3 with Alex Carlson, a lawyer representing the "Double-Chek Corporation," to tell Margaret that her husband was dead, and they instructed her not to discuss with *anyone* what he may or may not have been doing in Cuba. They would take care of that.

The next day Carlson held a press conference in Birmingham and announced that the four Americans were private mercenaries who died while flying noncombat cargo missions to aid anti-Castro freedom fighters. An anonymous group of affluent Cuban exiles, Carlson said, had paid the men through Double-Chek and would financially support the widows.

Carlson's statement infuriated the families. "My dad wanted to serve his nation and fight for what he believed was right," Janet told me. "He wasn't a soldier of fortune out to make a buck. One newspaper article even ran a picture of him with the words 'A nice nest egg' underneath. It made me physically ill."

Janet's mother started receiving payments twice a month purportedly from Double-Chek, and this went on until 1976, when she remarried. Double-Chek was clearly a CIA front, and even Carlson had trouble keeping his details straight, sometimes spelling the company's name Double Check, among other variations, in letters to the widows.

President Kennedy claimed "sole responsibility" for the Bay of Pigs fiasco, but behind the scenes he angrily blamed the CIA for giving him flawed intelligence. After a full review of the failed invasion, he forced the agency's director, deputy director, and chief of operations to resign. Unquestionably the lowest moment of his presidency, the Bay of Pigs undermined U.S. credibility around the world and transformed Fidel Castro into a communist hero who had defeated the "Yankee imperialists." It also exacerbated tensions with the Soviet Union, culminating in a near exchange of atomic weapons in October 1962 after the Russians were caught putting medium-range nuclear missiles in Cuba.

(In one of history's greatest "what if?" moments, at the height of the Cuban Missile Crisis, the president's senior circle of military advisors *unanimously* recommended bombing Cuba, and Kennedy might well have followed their counsel if he hadn't recently read *The Guns of August,* Barbara Tuchman's Pulitzer Prize–winning book about the events that led up to World War I. Kennedy became convinced that launching air strikes would provoke a Soviet response and cause a domino effect resulting in another world war. Against the advice of his Joint Chiefs of Staff, Kennedy ordered a naval blockade around Cuba to prevent additional missiles from being installed and proposed a secret deal to take U.S. warheads out of Italy and Turkey if the Soviets removed theirs from Cuba. Premier Nikita Khrushchev consented but added one more condition: Kennedy had to promise that the United States would never, ever, try to invade Cuba again. Kennedy readily agreed.)

Questions about the fate of Pete Ray, Leo Baker, Riley Shamburger, and Wade Gray reemerged in January 1963, when Attorney General Robert F. Kennedy publicly denied that any U.S. servicemen were killed at the Bay of Pigs. On March 6 a reporter pressed President Kennedy during a live, televised news conference to admit that the missing Americans had been "employees of the government or the CIA." Walking a verbal tightrope, Kennedy praised the airmen but remained vague about their mission. "Let me just say about these four men: They were serving their country. The flight that cost them their lives was a volunteer flight and while because of the nature of their work it has not been a matter of public record, as it might be in the case of soldiers or sailors, I can say that they were serving their country."

For the next ten years the CIA, the State Department, and the White House continued to stonewall the families, and Janet's mother gave up hope of ever finding out what happened to her husband.

"We had a memorial service for my dad," Janet told me, "but it's hard when there's no body to bury. It doesn't seem real."

At the age of fifteen, Janet figured she might have more luck with the Cuban government than her own, and she began writing to Castro himself. "I really did expect him to respond, but no one ever answered my letters."

Once Janet got her driver's license, she started going to local libraries and reading every book and newspaper article she could find on the Bay of Pigs.

"This was before the Internet," Janet said to me, "and it was much harder to gather information. I would also go through trash cans in our home to look for names and addresses of relatives or anyone I thought might have been friends with my father. I'd write to them or, if they lived close by, drive over and interview them. I also eavesdropped on the conversations my mom had with other adults in our home and recorded what was said in a spiral notebook. There was a lot of speculation, but no one really knew anything."

I asked Janet if other family members were working as diligently as she was to uncover the truth about her father.

"I think my mother was too traumatized to pursue it, and keep in mind that this was the era before Vietnam when Americans were more trusting of their government. I remember one time at my Uncle Bill's house, my cousin Debra Ann kept going on and on about Watergate. Uncle Bill couldn't take it anymore and finally said, 'Debbie, you're sitting at my table, and if you keep talking about the president of the United States that way, I'm going to break your plate.' That's how people were back then."

"So why were you so persistent?" I asked.

"I don't know. I was very tomboyish as a child. I didn't play with dolls. I preferred to be out exploring with my dog. My dad called me his Little Lulu, based on the old comic-strip character, always getting into trouble. He also said I was a fighter, and I guess that's part of it."

During college, Janet began visiting Miami's Little Havana to track down anyone who had flown with her father.

"How did you do that? I can't imagine you just walked up and down the streets asking random strangers if they knew Pete Ray."

"That's not far from the truth," Janet said. "I'd go into coffeehouses and barbershops or talk with people playing dominos, and a lot of them were related to the Cubans who took part in the invasion. It was a very close community."

Janet eventually did find Brigade 2506 veterans, and they spoke very highly of her father, but the trips offered no concrete information, only rumors.

Back in Alabama, Janet was gaining allies, including her father's first cousin Tom Bailey, who was also a *Birmingham News* reporter; a historian named Peter Wyden; Alabama's junior U.S. senator, John Sparkman; and Congressman John Buchanan. Buchanan and Sparkman lobbied the CIA to acknowledge in some capacity the heroism of Ray and his fellow Americans, and in 1977 the agency awarded the four airmen its highest honor, the Distinguished Intelligence Cross. Old habits die hard, however, and after presenting the medals, the CIA representatives told the families not to mention them to anyone. And they continued to refuse Janet's request for their files on her father.

Janet's big break came on April 19, 1978, exactly seventeen years after her father disappeared. "I was living at the Hahn Air Base in Germany with my husband, an Air Force pilot, and I'll never forget that moment," Janet told me. "I had picked up our mail, and there was a large envelope from Peter Wyden that contained a black-and-white photograph of my father's body that Peter had come across while doing research in Cuba."

"That must have been awful," I said.

"I had asked Peter to find whatever he could on my father's death when he went down there, but yes, it was still a shock. I was in my car parked behind the post office, and when I opened the package and saw the picture I just started screaming at the top of my lungs. Fortunately, an F4 had just taken off from the base, and I don't think anyone heard me."

Numerous details were still unclear; Janet didn't know, for instance, if her father had died in a shoot-out with Castro's soldiers after his plane went down or from the crash itself, but at a minimum she knew that he hadn't been a prisoner of war.

Armed with the photo, Janet redoubled her efforts to pressure Cuban and American officials to bring her father's remains back to the United States. Through Tom Bailey, Janet was also learning more about the incident, and by 1979 a clearer picture of her father's fate was coming into focus.

Pete Ray had survived the crash landing on April 19, 1961, and quickly extricated himself from the smoking wreckage of his B-26. Cuban troops hunted Ray down within hours and executed him with a point-blank shot to the head. (Leo Baker was either killed in the crash or shot by Cuban troops. And because of his olive skin, the soldiers assumed he was Cuban and tossed him into a pit with other dead rebels.) Ray's body was taken to a Havana morgue, where it was put on ice. For eighteen years Castro kept Ray's corpse in cold storage and proudly displayed it like a war trophy to other communist leaders when they visited Cuba.

Finally, in the winter of 1979, the Cuban government agreed to relinquish Ray's body.

"After all those years, why do you think Castro decided to return your father?" I asked Janet.

"I don't know for certain, but I was told he wanted to earn brownie points with the Carter administration," Janet said. "He wasn't doing it to be nice. There was an ulterior motive."

On December 8, 1979, Pete Ray was buried at Forest Hill Cemetery by the Alabama Air National Guard with full military honors, and the Air Force provided a flyover in Ray's memory. He now rests on a small hill overlooking the airport that had played such a central role in his life. Janet had informed me ahead of time that her father's headstone contains two errors. Under his name, he's identified as a "1ST LT US ARMY," when he was really a captain, and the actual date of his death was April 19, 1961, not April 18, as the marker states.

"I think my grandmother was so distraught when she filled out the paperwork that she was off by a day," Janet told me.

Daniel Boone comes to mind, and I asked Janet if there was any chance whatsoever that the Cubans had intentionally or mistakenly sent back the wrong body.

"No," she said. "Because of the condition he was in and the fact that he'd been shot in the head, the coroner discouraged me from looking at him, but I was adamant. I knew I wouldn't have believed he was really home until I saw him myself, and it was definitely my dad." The FBI also confirmed his identity using dental records and fingerprints.

Before Pete Ray was buried, Janet slipped a five-page handwritten letter into his uniform, telling her father how proud of him she was.

"Giving him a real funeral helped us to grieve properly," Janet said. "I also came to know him as a person through this whole process, and I just wanted to bring him home with honor."

Since there's no chance of ever retrieving the remains of Leo Baker, who was dumped in an unmarked mass grave, or of Shamburger and Gray, the two airmen lost at sea, Pete Ray is the only American killed at the Bay of Pigs whose body has been recovered, or ever will be.

I asked Janet, who now lives in Miami, if she's ever been to Cuba, and she told me she had no interest in going until the country was liberated from communism.

"Do you hold any ill will toward Cuba because of what Castro's regime did to your father?"

"I think I was actually angrier at our government," Janet said. "They led these men into harm's way and then turned their back on them."

There was, however, one final insult from Castro that rankles Janet to this day. Before releasing her father's body, the Cuban government (unsuccessfully) tried to bill the Ray family $36,000—for eighteen years and eight months of "refrigeration" costs.

HART ISLAND

During the last year of the War, I became aware from letters received from various parts of the country, that a very large number of our soldiers had disappeared from view without leaving behind them any visible trace or record. . . .

The heart-broken friends appealed to me for help, and by the aid of surviving comrades, I gained intelligence of the fate of nearly one half the number of [80,000] soldiers. . . . [These were men] who fell in the stern path of duty on the lonely picket line, perhaps, or [were] wounded, and left in some tangled ravine to perish alone, under the waters in some dark night, or, crazed with fever, to lie in some tent or hut, or by the wayside, unknowing and unknown, with none to tell his fate.

—*From the personal papers of Civil War nurse Clara Barton*

"THIS CAN BE a heavy experience," Melinda Hunt advises me as we're heading up the FDR Drive toward City Island in the Bronx.

From there we're renting a boat and venturing out to see Hart Island, the 101-acre cemetery where New York disposes of its unclaimed dead. "Even if you don't have a personal connection to anyone buried there," Melinda says, "it can still be emotional."

No one lives on Hart Island now, and the only people allowed onto it are the Rikers Island inmates who dig the graves and the armed officers guarding them. Under very strict circumstances, immediate relatives of the deceased are granted access, but they're closely observed at all times. Before connecting with Melinda, I had contacted New York City's Department of Correction (DOC) for approval to tour the island myself, under supervision, and the request was promptly denied.

"They reject almost everyone these days," I'm told by Melinda, the foremost expert on the place and founder of the Hart Island Project. The nonprofit organization's mission is to make the island "visible and accessible" and to create a single, searchable database containing the names of the dead, something the DOC itself doesn't have (everything is on paper). Slender and in her early forties, Melinda is an accomplished artist and photographer whose interest in all of this was sparked twenty years ago when she came across nineteenth-century pictures of Hart Island taken by the social reformer and photojournalist Jacob Riis. Along with compiling the names, Melinda helps people navigate the DOC's byzantine bureaucracy to find lost family members, a process that can be both complicated and intimidating. Between 1991 and 1994, she was frequently allowed onto Hart Island to take photographs or to accompany the relatives she had assisted so they could pay final respects to their loved ones or retrieve remains. Not anymore.

"The DOC won't let me go back out there and just freely walk around," Melinda says to me. "They've become much more restrictive."

"Since it's not a prison cemetery, why does the DOC run it?" I ask. "Why not the health department or some other social services agency?"

"Because it's cheaper to have inmates bury the dead."

At Jack's Bait & Tackle on City Island, where we're renting our little motorboat, I ask Jack's teenage son for a maritime map of the area that includes Hart Island. Melinda knows the location, but I still want a better sense of where exactly in Long Island Sound we're headed.

"You're not going on it, right?" the kid says, not really asking but telling me.

"No, only around."

"Good, 'cuz you'll get arrested if you do."

"I've heard that," I say.

With damp orange life vests hanging loosely around our necks, Melinda and I board the single-engine Yankee dory and putter out of the harbor, maneuvering through medium-sized yachts and small sailboats. Rain or black rumbling clouds would have been fitting for our somber journey, but the weather is discordantly cheerful. Bright blue sky, 70 degrees Fahrenheit, gentle winds.

"How long to get there?" I ask Melinda.

"About ten minutes."

For several of those minutes, I play out in my mind various scenarios that involve our "accidentally" running aground on the island, but when I mention this to Melinda, I get the impression that she's opposed to the idea.

Looking at the map Jack's son gave me, I'm reminded of the ambiguity over how Hart Island got its name. One suggestion is that eighteenth-century British cartographers thought the land was shaped like a heart and then later dropped the *e*, either inadvertently or for brevity's sake. This would make perfect sense except for the minor detail that Hart Island looks nothing like a heart—neither the organ nor the Valentine's Day icon. With its thick, angled top tapering off into a thinner, more crooked bottom, it resembles the rough outline of a horse's hind leg. Months ago Melinda sent me an excerpt from William Styron's 1951 *Lie Down in Darkness*, which offers this etymological theory:

> The island is named Hart's, after a deer which, in the later days
> of the English settlement, was seen to swim out to the place
> from the mainland and apparently to establish residence there,

among the scrub-oak and willow groves. The hart was later shot, so the legend goes, by a man named Thwaite who rowed out to the island in a skiff, with a big gun and a hankering for venison. It was this person, a gentleman of preternatural modesty, who named the island Hart's, rather than Thwaite's, and it was also he who made a tidy living for years by rowing picnickers out to the place; at that time there were sandy beaches there, woods, gentle groves—a perfect place, in short, to rest yourself.

Melinda believes there's a ring of truth to this, since *hart* is the archaic English word for "stag" and deer have been spotted there.

Any valiant notions on my part to go ashore, legal consequences be damned, dissipate the moment billboard-sized warnings on Hart Island loom into view: RESTRICTED AREA/NO TRESPASSING/NO DOCKING/NO ANCHORING/VIOLATORS WILL BE PROSECUTED. I tell Melinda I'll definitely stick to our original plan of just circling the island, and she nods in agreement.

If the signs weren't menacing enough, more than a dozen boats are marooned, some upside down and rotting, along Hart Island's thin, rocky shoreline. I'm guessing they've been left here simply because the DOC lacks the funds and manpower to remove them and not to intimidate potential trespassers. Nevertheless, they certainly amplify the DOC's message to stay away.

The land itself still looks like the peaceful, bucolic setting William Styron described six decades ago. I'm surprised, though, that the trees aren't bigger, having been left alone for so many years.

I mention this to Melinda, who replies: "Mass graves don't yield tall trees."

We hug the coast, and I notice dozens upon dozens of what appear to be round white markers pressed into a large grassy knoll at least several acres in size.

"That's where the infants are," Melinda says. "Each marker represents one thousand babies."

God, there must be tens of thousands of children buried here. And this is a relatively small parcel of land.

The DOC estimates that there are approximately 850,000 bodies interred on Hart Island, each one of them unclaimed or unwanted. The island's ledger is a catalog of forgotten lives and tragic deaths. Suicide victims pulled from the Hudson River. Homebound elderly found dead of starvation or heatstroke in their apartments. Stillborn infants whose parents couldn't afford to bury them. Teenage runaways beaten to death. Homeless addicts who overdosed in condemned buildings. New York is where they all happened to die, but they came from across this country and around the world. Although owned and managed by the city, Hart Island is a cemetery of national significance. It is the largest potter's field in the United States.

"I think the number might actually be closer to one million, if not more," Melinda says, "and almost half of them are children under five years of age. It's incredibly sad." An estimated twelve hundred interments take place each year. Adults are buried in pine boxes stacked three high, twenty-five across, two rows per trench. For babies, the coffins are five high and roughly twenty across in a single row.

Jacob Riis was also particularly moved by the number of children who ended up here. "The stormier the night, the more certain is the police nursery to echo with the feeble cries of abandoned babes," he wrote in *How the Other Half Lives*.

Often they come half dead from exposure. One live baby came in a little pine coffin which a policeman found an inhuman wretch trying to bury in an up-town lot. But many do not live to be officially registered as a charge upon the county. Seventy-two dead babies were picked up in the streets last year. Some of them were doubtless put out by very poor parents to save funeral expenses. In hard times the number of dead and live foundlings always increases very noticeably. But whether travelling by way of the Morgue or the Infants' Hospital, the little army of waifs meets, reunited soon, in the trench in the Potter's Field where, if no medical student is in need of a subject, they are laid in squads of a dozen.

Saint Matthew's Gospel contains the first written reference to a "potter's field." After Judas, in a fit of shame, threw the thirty silver coins he'd earned for betraying Jesus onto the Temple floor, the head priests looked at the money and debated what to do with it. "And the chief priests took the silver pieces," Matthew writes in chapter 27, verses 6 through 7, "and said, 'It is not lawful to put them into the treasury, because it is the price of blood.' And they took counsel, and bought with them the potter's field, to bury strangers in." The name stuck.

Every large metropolis grapples with how to handle its unclaimed dead. For smaller towns it's less of an issue because the deceased are usually known by someone. Melinda tells me that New York is the only major U.S. city to maintain a separate potter's field, and until 1869 there were several of them spread around Manhattan. Madison Square Garden, the New York Public Library, Washington Square Park, and the luxurious Waldorf-Astoria hotel were all built over "paupers' burial grounds," as they were also called. Today, most cities have contracts with local mortuaries and cemeteries to cremate unclaimed corpses after a designated period of time. In Los Angeles and Washington, D.C., it's a mere thirty days. At Hart Island, bodies are buried for twenty-five years, and then the bones are dug up and bunched together to make room for the newcomers.

Hart Island, Melinda has also taught me, is more than a potter's field. It's a time capsule of America's past. Siwanoy Indians sold the territory to a wealthy physician named Thomas Pell in 1654, and in the 1700s it was purchased by the DeLancey family, a French-born clan of aristocratic Huguenots. (They also owned an elaborate mansion at 54 Pearl Street in lower Manhattan that was later converted into Fraunces Tavern. New York's Sons of Liberty met and conspired there in the years before the Revolution, and, after the war, George Washington famously bid his troops farewell from the building's Long Room.)

The federal government used Hart Island as a military training ground in 1861 and then as a prisoner-of-war camp for Confederate troops. Disease, coupled with the North's icy winters, cut down the captured rebels faster than Union bullets. Mortality rates for POWs on Hart Island were among the worst in the nation.

When New York acquired the island in 1868, it allocated forty-five acres for burials on a low-lying section of land on the north side, and saved the southern portion for other city institutions and programs. Hart Island has been home to an infirmary for quarantined victims of the 1870 yellow-fever epidemic, an insane asylum, a women's hospital, a tubercularium, disciplinary barracks for unruly sailors and Marines during World War II, an alcohol- and drug-treatment center, and prison annexes.

"This was a perfect testing ground for pilot social programs because it's isolated and in a natural setting," Melinda says.

In the late nineteenth century young inmates were sent here to be rehabilitated, not just punished. This was all part of a growing penal-reform movement in America promoted by Edward Livingston, a New York lawyer and U.S. congressman who recommended that prisoners earn rewards for good behavior and, instead of remaining shackled behind bars all day and night, be allowed to go outside—on the condition that they performed meaningful labor. The first inmates on Hart Island were put to work, from the very start, digging graves.

As we round the northeast corner of the island, we pass another cluster of trees. "Through there is the missile silo," Melinda says.

This I had also heard about. Along with everything else, Hart Island functioned as a miniature Nike launch base during the Cold War. Installed in 1955, the missiles represented the last line of defense against a potential Soviet strike on New York City. They were removed in 1961.

"Has there ever been any commercial development on the island?" I ask Melinda. Spruced up, it would make for an ideal weekend retreat.

"No," Melinda says, "but it's been tried." In 1925 an African American businessman named Solomon Riley, she tells me, attempted to build an amusement park billed as "the Negro Coney Island" on Hart

Island's southern tip. Riley had already spent a sizeable chunk of change on the plan before city administrators shut him down, claiming that such a resort would be inappropriate so near the prison dormitories. "The main reason they stopped it," Melinda says, "is because the surrounding white communities didn't want an influx of black tourists."

We've come full circle. Had we not stopped or slowed down, we probably could have rounded the whole place in about three minutes. I cut the engine and we bob in the choppy water.

So far, nothing I've seen indicates that Hart Island is a burial ground swollen with remains or, as it's been referred to, the densest graveyard in America. Even if I had gone ashore, I wouldn't have spotted much evidence that I was walking across a cemetery. Grass and vegetation grow quickly over the trenches, masking them within a season, and on the entire island there's only one individual grave. Situated deep in a wooded area, its headstone reads SC-BI, 1985. That's it. Underneath lies New York's first infant victim of AIDS. Its placement is unintentionally symbolic of the disease's early years, when sufferers were feared and ostracized. I can't imagine a more friendless grave than this one, hidden away on an island that is itself all but unknown and out of sight.

Three monuments stand on Hart Island. One is for indigent Civil War veterans, and another was constructed by inmates after World War II, and it's an austere, thirty-foot-tall rectangular block of concrete inscribed with the word PEACE and nothing else.

And near the center of the cemetery is a ten-foot stone cross, also very minimalist, with an excerpt from the Gospel according to John engraved on its squat base: HE CALLETH HIS OWN BY NAME. Priests from Saint Benedict's Parish in the Bronx have occasionally been allowed to bless this site on Ascension Thursday and pray for those buried here. Otherwise, no other funeral rites or official ceremonies are regularly performed on the island.

Which doesn't mean there aren't ongoing efforts to remember the dead when they're laid to rest. During Melinda's visits to the island in the early 1990s, she interacted with prisoners who'd signed up for the grave-digging detail and was moved by their heartfelt gestures to memorialize these total strangers. Although prohibited from bringing any personal items or gifts to the island, the men placed at the graves offerings of food, fresh flowers they'd found nearby, and small improvised crosses.

In March 1992, Melinda had encouraged inmates, with the DOC's permission, to write about Hart Island and its impact on them. Far from responding with reluctance, the men were eager to open up, and Melinda shared with me several of the testimonials before we met.

"I've been on Hart Island, working now for almost two months," an inmate named Charles Yarborough recalled, "and in my opinion the hardest thing I find about being here is putting down the little ones. . . . No one knows where they are, what happened to the kids. That makes me think about my kids, about what and how they're doing."

"One thing I've learned from Hart Island is that I don't want to die [a] nobody with nothing or no one to care about me," another inmate wrote anonymously. "Hart Island is the best rehabilitation I've ever had and is something I'll never forget. I guess it's the loneliest place in the world and I pray and will always pray for the lonely and lost souls of Hart Island."

Nobody is on the island at the moment. Today's a Sunday and burials take place only during the week. I wouldn't be surprised if the NYPD Harbor Patrol or DOC officers conducted random sweeps every so often, but it's empty now, and I haven't spotted any police boats patroling the Sound either. Part of me is still tempted to sneak ashore, at the very least to say I'd set foot on Hart Island.

Ultimately, though, I'm content and ready to call it a day. I scan the island's length one last time, still overwhelmed by the knowledge that within this rustic, unremarkable patch of land, upward of one million men, women, and children are entombed.

As we motor back to City Island, I ask Melinda when Hart Island is expected to fill up.

"It's hard to say exactly," she says. "The numbers, I learn, are actually going down, from about three thousand a year in the 1980s to two thousand in the 1990s to twelve hundred now."

I would have assumed the numbers would be growing, simply because the general population is constantly expanding, but Melinda tells me that technology has made it easier for families to locate dead relatives, and social programs have cut mortality rates among the homeless, individuals with mental illnesses, and addicts.

"The most dramatic reduction in the past two decades has been in the number of stillborns," Melinda says. "You can track the decline starting in the mid-1990s, when New York began offering comprehensive prenatal care for poor women."

No one has studied these numbers more than Melinda; she and her volunteers have typed into the Hart Island Project's computerized database the names of sixty thousand people, along with information about when, where, and how they died. DOC administrators refused at first to give Melinda copies of Hart Island's records, but she eventually acquired them through New York's Freedom of Information Law. The documents, all handwritten, covered only 1977 to 2007; everything before 1977 had been stored in the warden's house on Hart Island, and vandals set the building on fire earlier that year, probably unaware of what they were destroying. Several hundred thousand names went up in smoke, forever erased.

"Are you familiar with Clara Barton's work to gather the names of Civil War soldiers who didn't return home?" I ask Melinda before we say our farewells.

"I'm not," she replies.

"It's a lot like what you're doing."

Barton is best remembered for risking her life during the war to nurse and comfort wounded soldiers under fire (at Antietam a bullet sliced through her blouse and killed the young man she was treating). But "the Angel of the Battlefield," as she was nicknamed, also earned her wings by helping family members of dead and imprisoned troops find out what had become of them.

She began this grueling chore, unofficially, after receiving letters from grief-stricken wives, mothers, and fiancées desperate to hear if Barton had possibly seen or cared for their loved ones. Similar appeals were flooding into the White House, and in March 1865, President Abraham Lincoln personally asked Barton to head up a government bureau that would locate these men and notify relatives of their fate. Lincoln's murder threw Washington into chaos, and neither Congress nor the War Department gave Barton the funding necessary to run the agency effectively. Undaunted, she paid for it all herself, spending more than $15,000 to hire a staff of twelve and set up an office in Annapolis, Maryland. (She was later partly reimbursed.) Over the next four years, Barton corresponded with thousands of anxious family members and traveled the country collecting and sharing information. One Union private, a former prisoner of war named Dorence Atwater, provided her with a register of thirteen thousand fatalities from the notorious Confederate POW camp in Andersonville, Georgia. A teenager when he was imprisoned there, Atwater had hidden the list inside his coat lining and smuggled it out when he was released. That list is why there are now thirteen thousand distinctly marked graves at Andersonville, a sight "mighty in [its] silence," Barton wrote after the last reburial was completed, "teaching the world a lesson of human cruelty it had never learned."

While New York City could never replicate on Hart Island what has been done at Andersonville, Melinda's database of names represents a unique and expanding memorial in itself, built with as much care and labor as any physical monument, and as moving as any public tribute to the dead.

Melinda was right about today's experience being an intense one, and it's discouraging to consider overall how many historical records and treasures have been destroyed or stolen by vandals, thieves, fires, and decay. For all that is taken from us, however, much is recovered—thanks to the Melinda Hunts and Clara Bartons of the world, who do the heavy lifting and hard work to salvage and restore the past. They give us reason to be hopeful. Not only about history, but about ourselves.

PART VIII

ALL IS NOT LOST

Finding and Preserving

History

LEARY'S BOOK STORE

[A]t this very time they are permitting their chief magistrate to send over not only soldiers of our common blood but Scotch & foreign mercenaries to invade and deluge us in blood. [T]hese facts have given the last stab to agonizing affection, & manly spirit bids us to renounce forever these unfeeling brethren. [W]e must endeavor to forget our former love for them and to *hold them, as we hold the rest of mankind, enemies in war, in peace friends.*

—*From the earliest known draft of the Declaration of Independence. The fragment was found accidentally after having been misfiled in the Library of Congress's archives. (Only the last fifteen words of the excerpt, italicized above, were included in the final version.)*

BEFORE THE PLACE was closed down in 1969 and wrecking crews later reduced it to rubble, Leary's Book Store stood at 9 South Ninth Street, between Chestnut and Market, in downtown Philadelphia.

Sentimental bibliophiles (such as myself) might consider Leary's alone worth recognizing because it was the nation's oldest continuously operating bookstore, but what has drawn me to its former location isn't Leary's history per se; rather, it was the discovery inside the building of a rare, nearly two-hundred-year-old parchment found by staff members packing up leftover inventory. Two centuries ago the one-page document apparently wasn't considered important enough to safeguard with due diligence, and it has since come to represent countless historic items that, although once abandoned or neglected, have been rediscovered and are now deemed irreplaceable.

I'm well aware that we cannot, as a society, preserve everything. Our cities would be overcrowded with storage warehouses if we tried to save and catalog every official record, piece of correspondence, manuscript, and artifact from our past. But the national heirlooms and relics that earlier generations have tossed out, misplaced, or sold off is mind-boggling. Plymouth Rock suffered three centuries of abuse from hammer-happy souvenir hunters before it was finally enshrined in its current memorial at Plymouth Harbor; cartloads of letters written by Thomas Jefferson, George Washington, and John Hancock were hauled out of government buildings in Washington, D.C., and dumped into the Potomac River to make room for Union Army munitions during the Civil War; and more recently, NASA administrators sheepishly announced in 2006 that they had lost the original video footage of Neil Armstrong and Buzz Aldrin's Apollo 11 landing, images shot with a special camera on the moon that were much crisper and more detailed than anything broadcast live on television. A NASA spokesman later conceded that they might have accidentally taped over it.

Not even original copies of the Declaration of Independence have been spared mistreatment. After Second Continental Congress delegates approved the final wording on July 4, 1776, the handwritten manuscript was rushed to John Dunlap's print shop on Second and Market Streets here in Philadelphia. Dunlap, a twenty-nine-year-old Irish immigrant, labored into the wee hours of July 5 to roll out an estimated two hundred copies, which were then carried by messengers throughout the colonies to be reprinted in local newspapers, distributed to state assemblies, and read aloud in taverns, churches, and town squares. Only about two dozen of these first, official versions of the Declaration—known as "the Dunlap broadsides"—have been recovered in the States, and three of them are mere fragments. Two copies intercepted by British officers during the Revolution are currently housed in England's Public Record Office, and the rest are mostly in various historical societies, universities, museums, and libraries throughout the United States.

In 2000 television producer Norman Lear and Silicon Valley entrepreneur David Hayden bought one Dunlap broadside at a Sotheby's auction for $8.14 million and, quite generously, toured it around the country at their own expense. Purportedly, the document was found behind an oil painting acquired for $4 at an antiques market in Adamstown, Pennsylvania. The buyer claimed that when he returned home and dismantled the frame, which appealed to him more than the artist's ho-hum pastoral scene, out dropped the Dunlap broadside from between the canvas and the wood backing.

Purportedly is the key word because manuscript experts are skeptical. It's not the document's authenticity that they doubt, just the story of how it turned up. The more likely scenario, they contend, is that someone swiped the broadside from a small historical society or library whose staff members were unaware that they'd even had it in their possession. (This isn't uncommon; manuscripts that were misfiled centuries ago or bundled up with other, unrelated materials are serendipitously discovered every so often by researchers going through an archive, usually while looking for something else.) The individual who supposedly bought the cheap painting has never been publicly identified, and no antiques dealer in Adamstown has stepped forward to verify the story.

As further evidence of the poor handling Dunlap broadsides have suffered since 1776, the copy now owned by the University of Virginia was uncovered inside an attic in Albany, New York, being used as wrapping paper. And about thirteen years later, a Dunlap broadside was found stuffed in an old wooden crate by employees of a soon-to-be-demolished Philadelphia bookstore. That would be Leary's.

Texas businessman Ira G. Corn Jr. and attorney Joseph Driscoll purchased the Leary's copy in May 1969 for $404,000 and later donated it, with financial assistance from fellow community and corporate leaders, to the city of Dallas. Now exhibited inside the J. Erik Jonsson Central Library, this is the only Dunlap broadside—and therefore one of the oldest existing copies of the Declaration anywhere in the world—freely displayed to the public on a permanent, year-round basis.

Contrary to popular perception, the elegantly handwritten Declaration of Independence showcased inside the National Archives rotunda is not the Declaration finalized on July 4. Called "the engrossed copy," this version was commissioned by Congress in mid-July 1776 and signed by most of the representatives on August 2. The actual document that Congress promptly handed to John Dunlap on July 4 has disappeared and was most likely cut up and destroyed in the printing process.

Several early, incomplete drafts of the Declaration have also been preserved, and they exemplify why original manuscripts are so valuable, especially those composed in an era when Delete buttons didn't exist; through every handwritten strike-through and careted addition, one can follow a document's evolution and the thought process of its author.

In what Jefferson himself labeled "Independence-Declaration original Rough Draught," he initially wrote:

> We hold these truths to be sacred and undeniable; that all men are created equal & independent, that from that equal creation they derive rights inherent and inalienable, among which are the preservation of life, liberty, and the pursuit of happiness.

Right on this document we can see how, at the behest of Jefferson's fellow delegates, "sacred and undeniable" were crossed out and "self-evident" was scribbled above. There's also a line through "& independent" and "preservation of," the phrasing about "equal creation" was reworked, and a reference to God was inserted. In the end, the Declaration's most vital pronouncement is made bolder and more memorable: "We hold these truths to be self-evident, that all men are created equal, that they are endowed by their creator with certain unalienable rights, that among these are life, liberty & the pursuit of happiness."

(It's a minor point, but Jefferson consistently used the word *inalienable*, not *unalienable*, and there's speculation that Dunlap inadvertently changed the word.)

Congress made about eighty edits—or, in Jefferson's words, "mutilations" and "acrimonious criticisms"—to the Rough Draft, as the copy is now referred to. Among the most vociferously debated passages was Jefferson's denunciation of the slave trade. "He has waged cruel war against human nature itself," Jefferson wrote accusingly of King George III,

> violating its most sacred rights of life & liberty in the persons of a distant people who never offended him, captivating & carrying them into slavery in another hemisphere, or to incur miserable death in their transportation thither. This piratical warfare, the opprobrium of *infidel* powers, is the warfare of the CHRISTIAN king of Great Britain. Determined to keep open a market where MEN should be bought & sold, he has prostituted his negative for suppressing every legislative attempt to prohibit or to restrain this execrable commerce.

How Jefferson, who owned hundreds of slaves himself, could have composed such a diatribe is a whole separate topic for discussion, but suffice it to say that certain southern representatives refused to sign the Declaration if this language remained. The section was excised, representing the largest single cut from Jefferson's Rough Draft.

Since Dunlap's broadsides represented the final product of Congress's edits and were printed on a movable-type press, they contain no handwritten marks or alterations. But because more than two dozen have been salvaged, it's still possible to compare them and find discrepancies. Many, including the Leary's copy, are slightly crooked, and at least eleven have faint overlapping text, indicating that the paper had been folded in preparation for distribution before the ink was completely dry. These and other imperfections accentuate the urgency of the moment.

No laws regulate what private collectors can or can't do with Dunlap broadsides as long as they're obtained legally. Fortunately, most buyers—such as Norman Lear, David Hayden, Ira Corn, and Joseph Driscoll—have put theirs on public display or donated them to reputable institutions. But there's nothing stopping a crazed millionaire from purchasing a copy and burning it to make a political statement or turning it into a papier-mâché hat for kicks.

Concerted efforts to safeguard documents of national importance didn't begin in earnest until 1933, when Congress established the National Archives. That same year, Robert D. W. Connor, the first archivist of the United States, delivered this mortifying assessment of our federal government's "system" to retain and catalog historic manuscripts:

> [Everything is] scattered throughout the country, stored wherever space can be found for them, in cellars and sub-cellars, under terraces and over boiler-rooms, in attics and corridors, piled in dumps on floors and packed into alcoves, abandoned carbarns, storage warehouses, deserted theaters, or ancient but more humble edifices that should long ago have served their last useful purpose. Typical is the case of valuable records relating to Indian Affairs which were found in a depository in Washington piled on dust-covered shelves mingled higgledy-piggledy with empty whisky bottles and with rags and other highly inflammable trash. In another Washington depository packed with documents the most prominent object which meets the eye as one enters the room is the skull of a cat protruding from under a pile of valuable records.

Although the cornerstone of the National Archives was laid in 1933, construction lagged due to the Depression and World War II, and the engrossed copy of the Declaration of Independence didn't settle into its permanent home until 1952.

That it hadn't been lost or ruined in the meantime, as had the great majority of Dunlap broadsides, is a miracle in itself. After the signing ceremony on August 2, 1776, the engrossed copy was repeatedly rolled up and unrolled as it accompanied Continental Congress members dashing from city to city, trying to keep one step ahead of British soldiers who would have loved to get their hands on the treasonous parchment.

In 1801, President John Adams ordered that key government manuscripts be moved from Philadelphia to the nation's new capital in Washington. The Declaration and its priceless companions were loaded onto a ship that sailed down the Delaware River, out to sea, through the Chesapeake Bay, and finally up the Potomac.

The State Department served as the Declaration's primary custodian, and the document's well-deserved rest was abruptly interrupted during the War of 1812, when British troops stormed Washington on August 24, 1814, and torched every federal building in sight (except the Patent Office, which, in 1836, we proved perfectly capable of burning down on our own, thank you very much). The day before the attack, a quick-thinking State Department clerk named Stephen Pleasonton crammed the Declaration and other official materials into coarse linen sacks and hid them in an abandoned gristmill just outside of Georgetown. After borrowing a wagon from local farmers, he hurried to Leesburg, Virginia, some thirty-five miles away, and kept the Declaration in a private home. It returned to the capital several weeks later.

Secretary of State Daniel Webster transferred the Declaration in 1841 to the new "fire-proof" Patent Office, a seemingly secure choice. Unfortunately, though, the document was hung opposite a large window in a bright hallway, where it stayed—exposed to direct sunlight—for thirty-five years, causing permanent discoloration and fading. The Declaration was returned to the State Department in 1877 and just in time; months later the Patent Office once again went up in flames. (The damage was extensive but not nearly as bad as in 1836.) The State Department entrusted the Declaration to the Library of Congress in 1903, and by then the document was deemed too fragile to be displayed and remained out of view for twenty-one years.

As conservation techniques improved over the decades, curators felt confident that the Declaration could be showcased publicly again, and on February 28, 1924, it was placed in the Library of Congress's Great Hall between double-paned, hermetically sealed glass. Three weeks after America declared war on Japan and Germany in December 1941, the Declaration was scuttled out of Washington and taken by train to the Bullion Depository at Fort Knox, Kentucky. It came back to the Great Hall in October 1944.

When the Declaration was finally delivered to the National Archives on December 13, 1952, the military pulled out all the stops. A twelve-man team of the U.S. Armed Forces Special Police carried both the Declaration and the U.S. Constitution, which were enclosed in a special helium-filled glass case, down the front steps of the Library of Congress and into an armored Marine Corps personnel carrier. The vehicle and its cargo were then escorted by machine-gun-toting soldiers and two light tanks along a parade route lined with Air Force, Army, Coast Guard, Marine, and Navy service members. This was a far cry from the days when the engrossed copy was tossed into burlap bags and carted around on rickety horse-drawn wagons.

Remodeled in 2003, the National Archives Rotunda for the Charters of Freedom currently holds the Declaration of Independence, the Constitution, and the Bill of Rights, all shielded behind bulletproof antiglare glass, framed by pure titanium and gold plating. Inside the airtight casing, argon gas maintained at 67 degrees Fahrenheit (give or take 2 degrees) prevents further deterioration, and the encasement can be lowered into a bomb- and earthquake-proof vault at a moment's notice. Each year more than a million people, Americans and foreigners alike, view the Charters of Freedom.

. . .

Nine South Ninth Street in Philadelphia has been paved over and is now a street-level parking lot. I will say, this certainly makes visiting the spot a breeze. There's no need to rent a boat or helicopter, no permissions have to be secured, it's visible twenty-four hours a day in good weather or bad, and photographing a bunch of parked cars doesn't elicit the same censure that snapping pictures of a prison, a military base, or a hospital does. A few passersby have looked at me quizzically, wondering what exactly I find so fascinating here, but mostly I'm met with indifference.

That Leary's was destroyed in the name of urban expansion isn't particularly shocking. It was not, after all, as historic as other local sites such as Congress Hall just a few blocks away, where the First United States Congress met in 1790 and the Bill of Rights was ratified; the President's House on Sixth and Market Streets, which was inhabited by George Washington and then John Adams before the White House was built (and this was the same mansion Ona Judge fled from in 1796); or, venturing out of Philadelphia, Thomas Jefferson's Monticello in Virginia, Fraunces Tavern in New York City, or Ford's Theatre in Washington, D.C.

What did surprise me, prior to coming here, was learning how many iconic American landmarks—*including* Congress Hall, the President's House, Monticello, Fraunces Tavern, and Ford's Theatre—have either been slated for destruction in the interest of commercial development or come irreparably close to utter ruin due to apathy and neglect. The President's House actually was torn down, and the other buildings would have been razed or condemned if preservationists hadn't jumped to their defense.

A U.S. Navy officer named Uriah Levy almost single-handedly saved Monticello in 1836, when he bought Jefferson's crumbling and forlorn estate in order to restore its former grandeur. The Colonial Dames of America prevented the demolition of Congress Hall in 1870, and thirty years later the Daughters of the American Revolution spared

Fraunces Tavern from being flattened to make room for a parking lot. Ford's Theatre had fallen into such disrepair by the end of the nineteenth century that on June 9, 1893, twenty-two government clerks inside the building (which, by then, had become a War Department annex after serving as a glorified warehouse) were crushed to death when the entire front section collapsed. Today, all of these sites are well-maintained and protected national landmarks.

Rescuing old structures is tedious, unglamorous work that often involves tangling with local bureaucracies, filling out endless paperwork, getting petitions signed, and mastering arcane city ordinances and zoning laws. On rare occasions, though, these efforts explode into dramatic clashes, and in the history of the preservation movement, no battle has become more of a public spectacle than the fight to save a former Spanish mission deep in the heart of Texas, my next destination.

Its name, appropriately enough, is synonymous with defiance against overwhelming odds.

It is, of course, the Alamo.

THE MENGER HOTEL AND
ADINA DE ZAVALA'S
RESIDENCE

Colonel Bowie will leave here in a few hours for [San Antonio de] Bexar with a detachment of from thirty to fifty men. Capt. Patton's Company, it is believed, are now there. I have ordered the fortifications in the town of Bexar to be demolished, and if you should think well of it, I will remove all the cannon and other munitions of war to Gonzales and Copano, blow up the Alamo and abandon the place, as it will be impossible to keep up the Station with volunteers, [and] the sooner I can be authorized the better it will be for the country.

—*General Sam Houston to Henry Smith, governor of the Texas territory, in a January 17, 1836, letter. After Colonel James Bowie arrived at the Alamo, he wrote to Smith directly and said the fort was worth defending. Smith agreed.*

BARRICADED IN A freezing, rat-infested room inside the Alamo, the lone defender had gone almost three days without food, water, or sleep after armed men had positioned themselves around the compound. Word of the standoff ricocheted across America, prompting a deluge of supportive messages for the fatigued but tenacious holdout. WIN OR LOSE, WE CONGRATULATE YOU UPON YOUR SPLENDID PATRIOTISM AND COURAGE, read one telegram from New York signed by John B. Adams, a descendant of President John Adams. Editors from the *St. Louis Post-Dispatch* wired San Antonio: COMMANDANT OF THE ALAMO:—WILL YOU SEND THROUGH THE POST-DISPATCH A MESSAGE TO THE WOMEN OF ST. LOUIS, WHO ARE WATCHING WITH GREAT INTEREST YOUR OWN GALLANT DEFENSE OF THE ALAMO?

The "commandant" was no military officer but a twenty-five-year-old Texas schoolteacher named Adina De Zavala, who had commenced her one-woman siege on February 10, 1908. De Zavala replied to the *Post-Dispatch*:

> My immortal forefathers suffered every privation to defend the freedom of Texas. I, like them, am willing to die for what I believe to be right.
>
> The fight is more than for the possession of the Alamo. Like every battle for its custody, the immortal principle of liberty and right is involved. In these days many people fear to fight for their rights, owing to the notoriety. I am not that kind. . . .
>
> The officers cannot starve me into submission.

De Zavala's impassioned statement echoed the urgent message William Barret Travis had dashed off seventy-two years earlier on February 24, 1836, when his two hundred Texian and Tejano rebels were fortified inside the old mission, surrounded by several thousand Mexican troops serving under President General Antonio López de Santa Anna. (Anglo Texans originally called themselves Texians; Tejanos were settlers of Mexican ancestry.) Travis, a twenty-six-year-old lieutenant colonel, had assumed command of the garrison after Colonel James Bowie was stricken with an incapacitating illness.

"To the People of Texas and All Americans in the World," Travis wrote:

Fellow citizens & compatriots

I am besieged, by a thousand or more of the Mexicans under Santa Anna—I have sustained a continual Bombardment & cannonade for 24 hours & have not lost a man—The enemy has demanded a surrender at discretion, otherwise, the garrison are to be put to the sword, if the fort is taken—I have answered the demand with a cannon shot, & our flag still waves proudly from the walls—<u>I shall never surrender or retreat</u>. Then, I call on you in the name of Liberty, of patriotism, & every thing dear to the American character, to come to our aid, with all dispatch—The enemy is receiving reinforcements daily & will no doubt increase to three or four thousand in four or five days. If this call is neglected, I am determined to sustain myself as long as possible & die like a soldier who never forgets what is due to his own honor & that of his country—

<u>Victory or death</u>

William Barret Travis
Lt. Col. Comdt

Carried past the Mexican lines by Captain Albert Martin, Travis's plea was copied and widely disseminated. The *Texas Republican* published a version of the letter on March 2, and the *Telegraph & Texas Register* reprinted it on March 5.

Reinforcements did come, but the support was too little, too late. Before sunrise on March 6, General Santa Anna ordered his troops to invade, and they caught Travis's men by surprise; Mexican soldiers had snuck up on the fort's sentinels, exhausted after nearly two weeks of constant bombardment, and stabbed them to death before they could sound an alarm.

Awakened by crackling gunfire and cries of "Viva Santa Anna!" the Alamo's defenders grabbed their loaded rifles and scrambled into position. Travis was shot dead early on after exposing himself to enemy fire while leaning over one of the main walls. Santa Anna's troops first breached the Alamo's north side, and when the Texians and Tejanos tried to repel the swarming invaders, the southern end became vulnerable and within minutes the defenders were being hit from every direction. Most retreated into the small church and long barracks and, in their haste, failed to spike the cannons, enabling Mexican soldiers to swivel them around and blast the buildings at close range. According to legend, Davy Crockett remained in the courtyard and, when his ammunition ran out, swung his rifle like a club and fought hand-to-hand before being overpowered. Colonel Bowie, delirious and barely able to move, was reportedly shot in his bed.

The battle was over by sunup, and Santa Anna's men methodically walked the grounds ramming their bayonets into any body that showed a flicker of life. Wives and children of the Texians and Tejanos, who had survived by hiding in the church's sacristy, were spared, and Santa Anna instructed them to return home and spread the word about his victory.

They did, but far from inciting fear, as Santa Anna had hoped, stories about the slaughter sparked an uproar and brought in droves of new volunteers eager to fight for Texas's independence. "[Had Santa Anna] treated the vanquished with moderation and generosity," the *New York Post* declared, "it would have been difficult if not impossible to awaken that general sympathy for the people of Texas which now impels so many adventurous and ardent spirits to throng to the aid of their brethren."

Hollering "Remember the Alamo!" 900 soldiers led by General Sam Houston descended on Santa Anna's 1,400 troops encamped along the San Jacinto River outside of what is now La Porte, Texas, on April 21, 1836. Santa Anna knew that Houston's men were nearby but never expected an attack in broad daylight from a numerically inferior force. The Battle of San Jacinto resulted in one of the most lopsided triumphs in American history; approximately 650 of Santa Anna's men were killed, while Houston, who led the infantry charge and was himself wounded, lost only 9.

More than 700 Mexicans, including Santa Anna, were taken prisoner as well. The self-anointed "Napoléon of the West" had valiantly tried to evade capture by stripping down to his silk underwear and hiding in a local marsh. Though urged by his men to sling a rope around Santa Anna's neck and hang him from the nearest tree, Houston chose to spare his life, and the two men signed a treaty that called for the withdrawal of Mexican forces from Texas.

(Between 1837 and 1855, Santa Anna became president of—and was exiled from—Mexico three times. He temporarily retired to Staten Island, New York, where he imported a sweet, sticky substance from the Mexican sapodilla tree that inventor Thomas Adams turned into a popular confection called Chiclets. Before dying in 1876, Santa Anna, conqueror of the Alamo, helped introduce chewing gum to America.)

Throughout Sam Houston's April 1836 negotiations with Santa Anna at San Jacinto, one of Houston's interpreters and most trusted advisors was a forty-seven-year-old Tejano named Lorenzo de Zavala—Adina De Zavala's grandfather. (And yes, the *de* in his name is generally lowercase, while hers is spelled *De*.) Elected governor to one of the largest territories in Mexico in 1832, he was appointed by President Santa Anna to be the first Mexican plenipotentiary to France in 1833. De Zavala resigned his post in protest, however, when Santa Anna revealed himself to be a vainglorious dictator. De Zavala moved to Texas, fell in love with the territory, and fervently advocated for its right to be an autonomous nation. He signed the Texas Declaration of Independence on March 3, 1836, and participated in drafting Texas's constitution two weeks later. Impressed by his loyalty and political acumen, de Zavala's fellow delegates picked him to be the republic's first vice president. After assisting Houston at San Jacinto, he returned to his home in Buffalo Bayou, less than a mile from the battlefield (his house, in fact, had served as a makeshift hospital for the wounded). While out rowboating that November, he tumbled into the bayou's chilly waters and later succumbed to a fatal case of pneumonia.

Adina De Zavala was born on November 18, 1861, in the same house where her grandfather had died, and she had grown up hearing stories about the Alamo, San Jacinto, and the Texas revolution. After studying history at Sam Houston Normal Institute, she accepted a teaching post in San Antonio and was dismayed, upon arriving in the city, to find the Alamo crumbling and vandalized. Graffiti marred the church's walls, statues of saints had been smashed, and the floors were slick with bat guano. A mercantile company, Hugo & Schmeltzer, had converted what remained of the long barracks into a grocery-and-supplies store.

In 1893, De Zavala founded the De Zavala Chapter—named after her grandfather, not herself—of the Daughters of the Republic of Texas (DRT), a group formed one year earlier to protect historic sites throughout the state. De Zavala's primary mission was to save the Alamo, and she was especially concerned that Hugo & Schmeltzer would sell the long barracks building, leaving its fate vulnerable to the whims of the next title holder. She secured a promise from Gustav Schmeltzer himself to give her organization first dibs on the property before another business or developer acquired it. Schmeltzer alerted De Zavala in 1903 that a prospective buyer had approached him about tearing down the structure and erecting an upscale hotel in its place, but he offered the DRT a preemptive bid of $75,000.

That was an astronomical price for the tiny all-volunteer group, so De Zavala marched over to the Menger Hotel, right beside the Alamo, hoping to convince the owners to purchase the neighboring property for both patriotic and self-interested business reasons.

The owners were away, but De Zavala was introduced to a guest named Clara Driscoll, the twenty-two-year-old heiress to the Driscoll family oil and real estate fortune and a staunch preservationist in her own right. Two years earlier, after touring cathedrals and holy sites overseas, Driscoll castigated her fellow Texans in the *San Antonio Express* for all but abandoning the Alamo, a sacred shrine in itself, she believed. "There does not stand in the world today a building or monument which can recall such a deed of heroism and bravery, such sacrifice and courage, as that of the brave men who fought and fell inside those historic walls," she wrote. Like De Zavala, Driscoll came from noble Texas lineage (both of her grandfathers had fought at San Jacinto), and the two women hit it off instantly. Together they plotted to rescue the Alamo and headquartered their efforts in the Menger Hotel.

Founded in 1859 by a stocky five-foot-tall German brewer and tavern owner named William Menger, the inn began as a modest rooming house built next to Menger's saloon so that drunken cowboys had a place to sleep off his notoriously potent ale. Today it's a five-story, 316-room hotel that takes up the entire block. (Not coincidentally, this is where I'm staying.)

Hugo & Schmeltzer held firm to their $75,000 asking price but agreed to let the DRT pay incrementally. Driscoll and De Zavala launched an aggressive fund-raising campaign, confident that once Texans became aware of the Alamo's precarious condition, they would flock to its aid. "Today its grim old walls, scarred and battered in that heroic struggle of liberty, stand threatened by vandalism and menaced by the hand of commercialism," they proclaimed in a letter to potential contributors. "So [we] ask you one and all to join us in rallying around the Lone Star flag as it floats over the Alamo."

The financial cavalry never arrived. Donations were paltry, and with hours to go before their option with Hugo & Schmeltzer expired on April 17, 1903, Driscoll dipped into her personal savings and covered the initial down payment of $5,000.

They now had until April 1904 to come up with $20,000, followed by five yearly installments of $10,000 each. In early May 1903, De Zavala and Driscoll persuaded the Texas legislature to allot $5,000 to the cause, but Governor Samuel Lanham vetoed the bill, claiming that the funds were not a "justifiable expenditure of the taxpayers' money."

By February 1904 the DRT had drummed up less than $6,000. With time running out, Clara Driscoll agreed to pay not only the

$14,000 but the five annual installments totaling $50,000. Driscoll's extraordinary act of charity earned her wide praise, and De Zavala was able to shame the state legislature into reimbursing her generous friend. This time the governor signed the bill, and, in return for recouping her money, Driscoll agreed to transfer the Alamo's title to the DRT, which would serve as the property's official custodian. At long last the Alamo was in safe hands, and De Zavala was elated.

Her joy, however, was short-lived; within months, a powerful new group formed solely to thwart her vision of seeing the long barracks resurrected to its former glory. Naming themselves the Alamo Mission Chapter, they demanded that what remained of the long barracks be destroyed entirely, leaving only the small church to represent the battle, even though many of the defenders had died inside or around the long barracks. De Zavala assumed the issue had been resolved, but the real showdown—which would become known as "the second battle for the Alamo"—was only just beginning.

"Is there a specific part of the hotel where Adina De Zavala worked or stayed?" I ask Ernesto Malacara, who was employed by the Menger for thirty years and is now the hotel's in-house historian. "I know she lived here in the early 1900s."

"The hotel has changed a lot since Miss De Zavala's time, so it's hard to say. This lobby is the same one built in 1859, but the rest of the hotel has gone through major renovations."

"And there's no mention of De Zavala anywhere in the hotel?" I ask.

"No," Ernesto says, "but I'm going to talk with the manager, because there should be."

Clara Driscoll deserves recognition, too, but a joint De Zavala–Driscoll tribute would probably send both women whirling in their graves. Sadly, despite their fast friendship in 1903 and combined efforts to rescue the Alamo from developers in 1905, by 1906 tensions between the women were escalating and within a year's time they were outright enemies.

Clara Driscoll had never liked the Hugo & Schmeltzer building and bought it, she later conceded, only to raze the "eyesore" completely and create a spacious plaza that focused attention on the church. De Zavala insisted that the long barracks' foundations needed to be maintained and that a museum and library should be added to educate visitors about the Alamo's history. As both women dug in their heels, Driscoll and her supporters seceded from the De Zavala Chapter of the DRT and created the Alamo Mission Chapter. De Zavala fired back, excoriating Driscoll for "pandering to the rabid desires of the money-getters, who for business reasons only, want to tear down 'unsightly walls.'" Each side claimed to be the Alamo's true protector, and the clash spilled into the courts.

With the legal situation in limbo, pro-Driscoll members inside the DRT recommended leasing out the Hugo & Schmeltzer building commercially. If they weren't allowed to knock it down anytime soon, they figured, why not profit from it in the interim?

Upon hearing that the new renters might be vaudeville performers, an outraged De Zavala hired several men to guard the building around the clock. Sheriff's deputies shooed them away but then realized that they had a larger problem on their hands: De Zavala was already hunkered down inside. "The [deputies] threw my men out bodily, expecting to take possession," she recalled.

> They did not know I was in an inner room, and when I hurried out to confront them, demanding by what right they invaded the historic building, consternation reigned. They withdrew outside the building for whispered consultation. The instant they stepped out, I closed the doors and barred them. That's all. There was nothing else for me to do but hold the fort. So I did.

Sheriff Dan Tobin was within his powers to remove De Zavala by force, but spectators and reporters had started to gather, and Tobin decided against smashing open the Alamo doors and dragging De Zavala outside kicking and screaming. She'd made it quite clear that she wouldn't go quietly.

Tobin did, however, order his men to prevent anyone from bringing De Zavala food or drink. He also shut off the interior electricity. A sleepless night in a dark, frigid building crawling with rodents and spiders would, he assumed, bring De Zavala to her senses.

He guessed wrong. De Zavala only became more obstinate, and media accounts were transforming her into a national hero. (She communicated with journalists mostly by speaking through keyholes and cracks in the walls.) Public sympathy forced Sheriff Tobin to relax his quarantine, and De Zavala was given a single glass of water and two oranges.

Her recalcitrance was a growing source of unease in the Texas capital, and the new governor Thomas Campbell finally announced that the Alamo would be put back under state control and the demolition of any buildings postponed indefinitely. That was good enough for De Zavala, and she ended her protest. Again, newspapers far and wide gushed about her actions. The *Denver Post* declared that she had "risk[ed] her life to hold [the] Alamo," the *Cincinnati Post* determined that "red-blooded Americans" would have agreed with her stance, and the *Baltimore American* referred to her as a "Joan of Arc in these modern commonplace times, ready to serve through patriotism and full of the spirit of her fighting sires." She was proof, the editors wrote, that "all the romance and heroism of the world is not dead yet."

San Antonio developers fumed. Tearing down the long barracks, they argued, would have created an open vista appealing to high-end hotel companies. Some implied that the entire Alamo compound could be done away with. "We do not want to appear sacrilegious," remarked one prominent businessman, "but we realize that the time has come to stop mentioning the Alamo in the same breath with San Antonio. . . . By doing it we are advertising San Antonio not as a modern and enterprising city . . . but are associating her with a name that carries with it the idea that San Antonio is still a Mexican village."

After leaving the Menger Hotel, I stroll over to explore the place myself. William Travis's famous letter is transcribed on a bronze plaque in front of the church. I've read it numerous times now, and it never loses its kick. Personally, I find Albert Martin's bravery even more impressive; after smuggling Travis's message out of the Alamo, he slipped back in, knowing full well he probably wouldn't survive the forthcoming attack. And he didn't.

Next to the church is the restored long barracks, which has been expanded into a museum—just as Adina De Zavala had envisioned. Her fight with Clara Driscoll and the DRT continued for years after the February 1908 standoff, and there's no indication that the two women had reconciled when Driscoll died in July 1945. De Zavala passed away almost ten years later on March 1, 1955, the eve of Texas Independence Day. She was ninety-three.

In stark contrast to the apathy De Zavala and Driscoll faced, Texans are now fanatical about historical preservation (which, being a fellow fanatic, I say respectfully) and have instituted the most prolific state-marker program in America. This, too, is thanks partly to De Zavala; in 1912 she established the Texas Historical and Landmarks Association, and she pushed to name local public schools after Texas revolutionaries.

Before checking out of the Menger Hotel, I ask Ernesto Malacara his theory as to why the Alamo had been neglected for so long.

"I've never thought about that," he says. "I guess for all those years people just took it for granted. When you pass by something every day, you stop noticing it."

Ernesto also points out that the Alamo hadn't sat idle after Santa Anna's victory. Five different armies had used (and sometimes abused) the fort between 1836 and 1865 alone. Santa Anna's men occupied it until his surrender at San Jacinto, and during their withdrawal they set the entire compound on fire. Texas militia took it over and then lost it briefly in 1842 when Mexican troops invaded San Antonio. The federal government assumed control at the outset of the Mexican-American War and held on to it until 1861, when David Twiggs, the Georgia-born general who commanded all U.S. Army soldiers in Texas, switched his allegiances to the South and handed the Alamo over to the Confederacy. The United States regained it after the Civil War and garrisoned soldiers there until Fort Sam Houston was built in 1876.

Any reluctance to commemorate the Alamo during the late 1800s and early 1900s might also have had something to do with the fact that the site did represent a defeat, and military victories, not unreasonably, tend to be celebrated before losses. Texans placed their first historical marker at San Jacinto in 1856, followed by a towering memorial modeled after the Washington Monument. (Texans, God bless them, made theirs fifteen feet higher and crowned it with a 220-ton concrete star. It's the tallest stone-column memorial in the world.) Both San Jacinto and the Alamo firmly established themselves as emblems of Texas sovereignty in 1936, the state's centennial, and eventually the Alamo's fame eclipsed San Jacinto's as the old fortress increasingly became a national symbol and rallying spot for embattled causes.

Skirmishes over how the Alamo itself should be remembered are still being waged. Some Mexican American organizations have lobbied for the Tejano martyrs to receive better recognition, while others insist that the whole site is a tribute to Anglo aggression and should be bulldozed. Critics also contend that Texians were fighting not for "freedom" but for the right to enslave others after Santa Anna had attempted to end slavery throughout Texas. *Their* critics counterargue that many Texians didn't own slaves, and abolition was only one grievance among many; Santa Anna had deprived Texians of numerous civil liberties, including religious freedom and trial by jury.

If she were alive today, Adina De Zavala would be squarely aligned with the "they died for independence" crowd, and regardless of the feuds and controversies that persist around her beloved site, overall she'd have to be pleased by the Alamo's popularity. It is the most visited historic landmark in Texas and one of the top tourist destinations in America. Two and a half million people stream through here each year, which is more than twice the number of visitors who see the Charters of Freedom at the National Archives in Washington, D.C.

Six blocks away, at the corner of Fourth and Taylor Streets, is where Adina De Zavala's primary residence in San Antonio once stood. A parking lot—the bane of history, I'm coming to realize—is there now. The land is next to the Toltec Apartments, and I duck into the building to say hello to the owner, Paul Carter. Fifty years old, Paul is a fifth-generation San Antonian and also living proof that many developers are devout history buffs; he is working to make the entire street a historic site with a marker that specifically mentions De Zavala.

"My father grew up right beside her," Paul tells me. "He used to deliver chocolate pudding to her house when he was a boy."

"In most of what I've read, Clara Driscoll is called 'the savior of the Alamo,' and De Zavala receives less attention, if she's mentioned at all. Why does Driscoll get so much of the credit?" I ask Paul.

"Because she cut a check," he replies without hesitation.

Paul makes clear that he isn't diminishing Driscoll's role, and we both feel that their falling-out was especially sad because, despite holding different views of how the Alamo should be remembered, the two women were its most stalwart advocates and jointly responsible for its survival.

Paul invites me to lunch, but I have to rush to Dallas. We agree to keep in touch and work on getting De Zavala a plaque where her home used to be. Between that and some sort of recognition at the Menger Hotel, she'll be well represented.

I've tried to cut down on these detours, but I'm flying out of Dallas anyway, and there's a rare document on display at the main public library that I'd be remiss not to see while I'm in Texas. When I reach the city, I find the library, park my car, and take the elevator up to the seventh floor. I enter the Rare Books and Manuscripts Room and walk into a semicircular alcove that features just one item: an original Declaration of Independence printed by John Dunlap. This was the broadside discovered at Leary's Book Store in Philadelphia forty years ago. Displayed in an oak case, the document is dimly lit and, from the way it's mounted, appears almost to hover behind its protective glass cover, creating an effect that's both solemn and arresting.

Within seconds I hear footsteps off to the side. A guard comes around the corner, looks at me, and nods. I say hello and ask him if the Declaration gets many visitors.

He shakes his head. "I don't think a lot of people in Dallas even know it's here," he says, and walks away, having confirmed that I'm not wielding a baseball bat and don't seem like a raving lunatic intent on doing harm. Several closed-circuit security cameras maintain vigilant watch as well.

It's unfortunate that this Declaration—which, again, predates the engrossed copy at the National Archives and is the only Dunlap broadside freely exhibited on a permanent, year-round basis—doesn't draw much of an audience. And yet there's something wonderfully intimate about experiencing it this way, without hordes of other tourists angling for a glimpse. One can actually read the words and reflect on their import and the context in which they were written. Had we lost the Revolution, a likely prospect in July 1776, when our ragtag militia was challenging the world's most powerful army, members of the Continental Congress could have been hanged for treason. They were not, like William Travis and his men at the Alamo, surrounded by enemies in Independence Hall when they drafted their declaration, but they had placed themselves in real and imminent danger. And like Travis's climactic "Victory or death" sign-off, Jefferson's last line alludes to what was at stake. "And for the support of this declaration," he concluded, "with a firm reliance on the protection of Divine Providence, we mutually pledge to each other our lives, our fortunes and our sacred honor." The currency of patriotism is easy to counterfeit, but these were genuine sentiments.

I head downstairs and am almost out the main entrance when I remember having read that a copy of Texas's own Declaration of Independence used to hang next to the Dunlap broadside. (This same source, I believe, also noted that Texans literally battled one another over where to house their historic documents, including the state's original declaration. In what became known as the Texas Archive War, President Sam Houston ordered that the manuscripts be moved from Austin to Houston, the city already named for him, but the men he sent to grab the papers were hunted down and shot at by an Austin posse. Eventually, they surrendered and forked over everything at gunpoint.) I approach the general information desk on the first floor and ask a librarian about the two declarations once being side by side and why Texas's is no longer there.

"You should really check with the staff on the seventh floor," she tells me. "They'll know for sure. But I think we put it back in storage for its own protection, to keep it safe."

"What about the actual Declaration of Independence that's still up there?" I ask. "I mean, isn't there concern about its safety, too?"

"Oh, absolutely," she says, "but goodness gracious, if anything happened to the Texas declaration, folks around here would never forgive us."

MOUNT BAKER

Statistically, the probability of any one of us being here is so small that you'd think the mere fact of existing would keep us all in a contented dazzlement of surprise.

—From The Lives of a Cell: Notes of a Biology Watcher (1974) by the scientist and etymologist Dr. Lewis Thomas

IN A PARKING lot near the base of Mount Baker in northern Washington State, Ed Hrivnak opens the hatch to his Subaru Outback, pulls out a giant rucksack bulging at the seams, and hoists it over his shoulders. Feeling somewhat self-conscious, I glance at my own back-pack, which is so small and flimsy compared with Ed's that it might as well have "Hello Kitty!" written in pink puffy letters on the side.

"Aren't we only going on a day hike?" I ask rhetorically. "You look like you're about to scale Everest."

Ed, an old friend and skilled mountaineer who lives in Washington, is guiding me to an area on Mount Baker close to where a PV-1 Ventura plane crashed in 1943 and was accidentally discovered fifty-one years later.

Not without reason, Ed is ignoring me, and I ask more directly: "What do you have loaded in that thing?"

"A bivy tent, sleeping bags, extra clothes, food," he says. "I like to be prepared. The weather could change."

The sky is an endless sheet of clear-blue cellophane.

"Ed, it's at least seventy degrees out, and there isn't a cloud in sight."

"You never know. And considering your age and how overweight you've gotten, I assumed you couldn't handle all of this, and I figured I should carry it myself."

"I'm younger than you are and in better shape," I shoot back. Ed is indeed older, but only by six months, and having served twenty years in the Air Force, he's built like a triathlete. I, to put it mildly, am not.

Variations of this ridiculous banter have been going on between us for the past five years now, and, truth be told, Ed is one of my favorite people on the planet and someone I admire enormously. I don't quite understand why we mock each other constantly, but I suspect it's because we're both desperately clinging to our youth, and trading adolescent taunts sustains our delusional mind-set. (Just for the record, though, Ed started it.)

We first met while I was involved with a government initiative called Operation Homecoming, which encouraged U.S. military personnel to write about their experiences in Iraq and Afghanistan. The troops sent in thousands of short stories, poems, diary entries, letters, and e-mails related to their wartime service, and my job was to pore over and help organize the bins of submissions. Ed contributed eight months of journals chronicling his medevac missions with the Air Force's 491st Expeditionary Aeromedical Evacuation Squadron. He never recorded names or betrayed confidential information, but he described the horrors of war in gut-wrenching detail and captured both its physical and emotional toll on service members and their families.

In one entry, Ed wrote about a fellow medical officer who'd been delivering humanitarian supplies to local Iraqi hospitals when a rocket-propelled grenade exploded in his Humvee. His head was burned so badly that the tops of his ears were seared off and his face had melted into a red, expressionless mask. Covered in ointment and bandages, the officer confided in Ed that his greatest concern was how his wife and children would react when they saw him. Before deploying, he had assured them he'd be safe because he wouldn't be anywhere near the front lines, and he felt he had broken that promise.

Another patient told Ed how traumatized he'd been by the sight of Iraqi kids being forced at gunpoint onto a highway by insurgents trying to make a U.S. military convoy brake to a halt. Knowing it was an ambush and under strict orders not to stop, the drivers barreled forward, and their multi-ton vehicles struck and killed the helpless, screaming children.

Ed's entire life has centered on military and public service. He joined the Air Force while in high school and was only seventeen at the time; his father—a Korean War–era veteran—had to cosign the enlistment papers. Ed served in Desert Storm, then flew peacekeeping operations in Rwanda, Somalia, South America, and Vietnam, earning almost two dozen medals. While on reserve duty he volunteered for the Tacoma Mountain Rescue Unit, and he's now a fireman.

Ribbing aside, I'm hassling Ed about his cumbersome backpack for his own good. Less than two weeks ago, he burst a blood vessel in his left calf while fighting a wildfire, and he's supposed to be taking it easy. Carrying excess weight will only exacerbate his condition, and he probably shouldn't be hiking at all. I had told him we could postpone the trip, but Ed, being Ed—obstinate, reckless, proud, and incredibly loyal—was adamant about not canceling. "Any later in the year," he said, "and the weather becomes too unpredictable."

When Ed first mentioned his injury to me, he downplayed its severity. I asked a doctor friend of mine to tell me honestly how serious these ruptures were, and he explained that they usually healed within a month but hurt like hell. "Every time you take a step," he said, "it feels like someone's firing a blowtorch inside your leg."

Ed has brought along a buddy and fellow veteran, Mike Vrosh, who retired from the Air Force in 2003 as a colonel after thirty years in uniform. He, too, served in Desert Storm and has led multiple special operations and peacekeeping missions. I'm guessing Mike is in his early fifties, but he looks like he could run circles around us both. And he's as selfless and tough-minded as Ed; Mike recently came down with pneumonia but also refused to back out of the trip.

While Mike finishes stuffing his own behemoth backpack to the brim, Ed unfolds a topographical map of Mount Baker and shows me where we're headed.

"We'll start up that way," he says, referring to a narrow, zigzagging trail, "and then cross along this ridge."

I ask Ed how his leg feels, and before he answers we hear Mike in the throes of a coughing fit.

Making light of their ailments, Ed jokes, "One of us should get you up and down the mountain alive." While I'm concerned about their health, I know I couldn't be in more capable hands. As it so happens, Mike and Ed are among only a few people in the world who know precisely where the PV-1 crash site is.

The first was Chuck Eaton, a welder from Ferndale, Washington. On October 6, 1994, Eaton was hiking with his dog, Candy, through a ravine on Mount Baker's western face when he spotted a curved black object jutting out of a rock pile. As he got closer, he realized it was a tire still attached to its landing struts. And then he saw two large engines. Eaton quickly contacted Whatcom County authorities, who, ironically, had just finished combing Mount Baker for a lost exchange student (sadly, they found him dead in a creek) but hadn't noticed the PV-1 wreckage.

After Eaton's call, a recovery team from McChord Air Force Base in Tacoma was quickly assembled and dropped in to search for ordnance and human remains. From the plane's identification number and dog tags retrieved at the site, investigators were able to determine that the aircraft was an antisubmarine PV-1 Ventura that had gone missing more than half a century earlier.

Records indicated that the plane was conducting navigational drills between Bellingham and Everett, northeast of Seattle, on August 29, 1943. Radioman Pete LaValle had communicated with Whidbey Island's Naval Air Station at approximately 3:20 P.M. to report an engine malfunction. This was his last transmission, and the PV-1 never returned. For several days Navy planes scoured hundreds of miles over land and sea to locate the aircraft but found no evidence of a crash. Squadron commanders assumed the plane had plunged into Puget Sound, killing all six crewmen: radioman LaValle; the pilot, Lieutenant Commander Ralph Beacham; copilot Charles Nestor; and machinist's mates Carl Brown Jr., Robert Gray, and Livio de Marco. Beacham, at thirty-one, was the oldest. Nestor was twenty-four, and the rest were all just twenty-one.

Having made our way up a short but steep ascent, Ed, Mike, and I come to a wide and less precipitous ridge. I stop for a second to take pictures of Mount Baker's 10,781-foot summit, which mercifully we do not have to climb, since the crash took place well below its peak. Named after Joseph Baker, the young lieutenant who spotted it in April 1792, the mountain is technically a glaciated volcano and capped with snow throughout the year. Local Lummi Indians referred to it as Koma Kulshan, which translates roughly to "white sentinel." Even at this elevation and in direct sunlight, there are patches of snow everywhere.

"Ed, why is that snow over there pink?"

"Algae," he says. "Don't eat it."

"I wasn't planning on it," I say. But now that I think of it: "Is it okay to drink from the little streams up here?"

"No, they might have parasites."

Ed is maintaining a brisk pace ahead of us and turns around every so often to check that I haven't wandered off to gorge myself on discolored snow or contaminated water. He doesn't say a word about his leg, but from the way he's limping, the pain must be increasing.

"We don't have to go so fast," I call up.

"Getting tired?" Ed goads me.

"No." (Actually, I am winded.) "I just don't want you to push yourself too hard."

"Don't worry about me," he says.

Mike, a few paces back, is holding up the rear to make sure I don't lag behind.

We hike on, and at the top of another trail I peer down to marvel at the fir trees clinging defiantly to the mountain wall. Several appear as if they're growing sideways. I snap some pictures.

"You couldn't ask for better conditions," Ed says over his shoulder. "You're really lucky."

It's true. I've been fortunate throughout my entire journey, and never more so than with this trip. I knew early on I wanted to conclude my travels by focusing on "found" history, and this story jumped out because it represented such a rare and serendipitous discovery. There was one glitch: Nobody could tell me where exactly the PV-1 had gone down. I sought out Chuck Eaton, but he wasn't listed in the phone book. I called the regional forest service office, but they didn't want to disclose the spot because there could still be unexploded rounds in the immediate vicinity. I contacted outdoor-adventure stores in the area, the local historical society, and anyone else I thought could be helpful. All dead ends.

I had already started my travels when Ed, who knew I was bouncing around the country, asked me when I planned to visit Washington.

"Not sure," I said, "and I'm getting anxious about it. My original story was about this plane that vanished during World War II and then was randomly found fifty years later on a mountain outside of Bellingham."

"You're talking about Mount Baker?"

"Yeah," I said, surprised he'd heard of it. "But I can't track down anyone who knows where it crashed."

"I know where," Ed said.

"Like, generally speaking or specifically?"

"I worked on the recovery."

Ed was clearly putting me on, and I wasn't falling for it.

"You're joking," I said.

"I'm not."

"Ed, this is a serious story."

"I'm being serious."

"You *personally* were part of the team that went to Mount Baker and helped identify the PV-1 lost in 1943?"

"I was actually one of the first people on the scene after it was called in."

Floored, I could barely respond. "Ed, I'm . . . I mean the odds of this, that you were there is, it's a million to one."

I felt especially guilty for doubting him in light of what I had to say next. "So, I know you're *really* busy, and Bellingham is pretty far north of you, but I kind of have a huge favor to ask you—"

"Let me look at my calendar, and we'll lock in a date."

We both arranged our schedules to meet this weekend, and when Ed got injured, he called Mike Vrosh to come along for good measure. Ed couldn't have enlisted a more ideal wingman; aside from being an expert mountain climber, Mike had served as the team leader on the PV-1 salvage mission.

We hike for another hour, and Mike's coughing has gotten worse. He's now ahead of me, next to Ed, and I see them stop, exchange a few words, and wait for me to catch up.

"See that slope over there?" Ed says, and I follow his finger to where it's pointing.

"I got it."

"That's the site. It's snowed over again, but it's underneath there."

Ed tells me we can get closer, and we continue walking.

"You guys came in by helicopter, right?" I ask.

They nod. "We landed below the glacier, where the ground levels off," Ed says, and goes on to recall how quiet everything was. No wind. No birds. And very little talking among the team. Just the crunching of their feet on the ground as they surveyed the site.

From the wreckage, Ed could make educated guesses about the plane's final instant before it slammed into the wall of ice.

"One propeller wasn't bent," Ed says, "which means the blade wasn't spinning at the moment of impact." This corroborates with Radioman LaValle's report that an engine had conked out. "I also remember coming across an altimeter and holding it in my hands, and I knew the copilot must have had his own fingers on it while he was adjusting the barometric pressure before they crashed. That little detail has always stayed with me."

"I wasn't thinking about the crew when we first got there, to be honest," Mike says. "We had a thousand logistics to deal with. But I uncovered a dog tag, and that's when it all started becoming real for me."

Other personal items they collected included LaValle's sailor's cap and quarters that had fallen out of the airmen's pockets.

Mike made the day's most horrifying find. "I picked up what I thought was a long, thin strip of foam padding from one of the seat cushions," he says, "and I realized it was a spine."

Ultimately they gathered together more than 350 bone fragments. Blood-testing kits were later sent to relatives of the six crewmen, and at the Armed Forces DNA Identification Laboratory in Maryland, experts positively identified the remains.

Unlike Pete Ray's disappearance in Cuba, there was no conspiracy by higher-ups to keep the PV-1's fate cloaked in secrecy. Government officials truly didn't know what had happened. Nor was there anything particularly unusual about the mission or its crew. They were six ordinary young men, five of them practically kids, on a routine exercise that went awry.

And it's the very "ordinariness" of this story that makes it so remarkable to me. More than twenty-five thousand Navy and Army Air Corps troops were killed *within* the United States during World War II, mostly while testing new aircraft, training other airmen, or flying coastal patrols. These stateside losses represent one out of every sixteen U.S. fatalities in the war, and yet they're hardly ever acknowledged. One story is cited with some frequency, but only because it involved the world's tallest building (at the time) and fourteen deaths, the majority of them civilians. On July 28, 1945, a B-25 bomber lost in low-hanging clouds over New York City collided with the Empire State Building, killing the three-person crew on impact. Eleven office workers on the seventy-ninth floor died instantly or in the ensuing fireball, and one of the bomber's engines crashed into the elevator shaft and onto an elevator roof, causing the car to plunge almost eighty stories. Emergency brakes installed by the Otis Elevator Company prevented it from slamming into the basement at full speed, and the two passengers inside survived, albeit banged up and badly shaken. The Empire State Building crash made headlines, but for the most part these home-front accidents were quickly forgotten.

"Would you guys mind if we rested for a bit and ate something?" I ask. "I'm starving."

"Sure," Ed says.

"I'm ready for that," Mike agrees.

We park ourselves on three small boulders conveniently clustered together and drop our gear. From his backpack, Ed pulls out several plastic containers and starts handing them to me. I peel off the lid to the first one and find freshly sliced tomatoes and cucumbers inside. The aroma alone makes my mouth water. In the next little bin are feta-stuffed olives drizzled with oil. Ed unwraps a block of sharp cheddar and hard, herb-crusted salami, cuts off several chunks with his pocket-knife, and passes them around.

"That's *really* good," I say to Ed, savoring the tangy cheese and spicy meat pressed together.

Hunger makes the best sauce, the saying goes, but even if I weren't famished, the small feast Ed has prepared is the best meal I've had in months. He's thought of everything.

"Chocolate-covered almonds?" he asks.

"If you insist." I grab a handful.

We all sit there contentedly, eating and soaking up the sunshine.

"I can't thank you all enough for doing this."

"We've been wanting to come back for years," Ed says.

"How old were you again when you were first here?"

Ed does the math in his head. "Twenty-four."

"Looking back on it, how do you think it affected you?"

"You know, when we first arrived," Ed says, "we had a job to do, inspecting the site and setting up ropes for the ordnance and mortuary teams behind us. As Mike said, once we started finding personal items, that's when it got real. I became much more aware of what these guys had lost, and I think the whole experience made me more grateful, as a person."

Mike agrees. "When you realize what other people have gone through or, like these guys, sacrificed, it gives you a different perspective on life," he says, "and you become more appreciative of things in general." To the best of my recollection, no one else on the trip has explicitly made this connection, but it does seem that all of the people who've guided me around various sites and shared their love for history have exuded a similar sense of passion and gratitude.

Within a year of the 1994 recovery mission, details about the airmen and their loved ones began to emerge. Upon first receiving the news that her husband's plane had gone missing, Charles Nestor's wife got into a car with her parents and circled the twisting roads around the flight path in hopes of finding something the Navy search planes had overlooked.

Carl Brown's mother and stepfather didn't own a telephone and drove up from their ranch in Northern California to Whidbey Island. They stayed near the base for a week, waiting for news.

Ralph Beacham, the oldest member of the crew, left behind a child, and his wife gave birth to their second son two months after he died. For more than fifty years Mrs. Beacham clung to the belief that somehow, somewhere, her husband was still alive, and she never remarried.

Pete LaValle's brother Angelo was shot down over Papua New Guinea in a B-24 bomber six weeks after the Mount Baker crash. The Western Union man wouldn't show Mrs. LaValle the telegram from the War Department until her husband came home from work. He didn't want her to be alone when she learned that another one of her boys had been killed.

Once the men were positively identified in 1996, relatives were finally able to arrange proper funerals. Ralph Beacham and Carl Brown were laid to rest at Arlington National Cemetery, and the others were returned home. For many of their loved ones, the recovery mission brought a measure of comfort. "It's put closure on this," Helen Gray McConnell said after burying her brother Robert in a cemetery close to the South Dakota farm where they were raised. "We knew he was gone, but it's a relief to know what happened."

Ed, Mike, and I finish resting, pack up our gear, and check to make sure no food or trash has been left behind. Ed winces as he stands, and Mike begins coughing again after taking a slug of water.

"We really need to do this more often," Ed says to Mike.

At first I assume he's being sarcastic, considering their condition.

"I was just thinking that," Mike says. "It's been too long." His tone is serious.

We all stand there for a minute, admiring the glorious scene around us, before venturing on.

"God, it's good to be alive," Mike says.

Ed shifts his weight to his right leg and smiles.

"Amen, brother," he says. "Life is good."

And they mean it.

HOME

I haven't been everywhere, but it's on my list.

—*Susan Sontag*

RETURNING TO WASHINGTON, D.C., feels more like a layover than a homecoming. Wonderful as it is to be sleeping in a familiar bed, I soon find myself thumbing through my tattered road atlas, plotting the next getaway. The stories keep accumulating. The manila files keep getting fatter.

"Out of all the places you went, what was your favorite?" a dear friend and professional genealogist named Megan Smolenyak Smolenyak (that's really her name) asks me days after I get back.

"I'm going to have to think about that," I say.

Megan and I have known each other for so long I don't remember how we met, but we bonded over a shared interest in military history. A self-described "Army brat," Megan has spent the last ten years helping the U.S. government locate family members of American troops killed overseas whose remains, some dating back to World War I, are still missing. She's also become a rock star in the genealogy community for several high-profile finds. On September 14, 2006, the *New York Times* ran a front-page feature about Megan's efforts to identify the first immigrant through Ellis Island, an Irish teenager named Annie Moore. Megan was responsible for linking President Barack Obama's maternal family to Moneygall, Ireland, and she scored another front-page *New York Times* article for tracing Michelle Obama's roots to a young slave girl from South Carolina. Megan tracked down an 1850 will that mentioned the First Lady's great-great-great grandmother Melvinia Shields, among other "property." Six years old, little Melvinia was valued at $475.

During our phone conversation, Megan tells me that when she comes to Washington she wants to show me a little-known site relating to the man responsible for creating the Statue of Freedom atop the U.S. Capitol Building.

"It's not a huge story," she says, "but I thought it was interesting."

"I like the smaller stories," I say. "I just need some time to unpack and get settled."

Travel is a glorious form of procrastination, allowing us to put off the daily deluge of e-mails, phone messages, and countless burdens with a simple, socially acceptable excuse: "Sorry, I'm on the road . . ." Now that I'm back, those obligations beckon, along with some new and unexpected demands. The most unusual involves an appointment with the FBI; a close buddy of mine named Jay Michael is applying to the agency and has listed me as a reference.

Within forty-eight hours of coming home I find a business card stuck in my apartment door from an FBI special agent who stopped by while I was out running errands.

I phone him that afternoon and say, "I can come down to your office or talk here, whatever's easiest for you."

"Let's meet at your place if that's okay, and does now work?"

"Now is fine, I guess."

"Be there in half an hour."

Twenty-nine minutes later, he buzzes on the intercom. I go to the lobby and encounter not one but two men, both in their early thirties and dressed in khaki slacks and white button-down shirts, no tie or jacket. (I was sort of hoping for the whole sunglasses/black-suit G-man getup.) The lead agent, my initial contact, is leaner and shorter than his partner, who's built like a rugby player.

In the elevator, the three of us stand there silently.

"I probably shouldn't tell you this," I blurt out and then pause, realizing that any sentence beginning with those words is best left uncompleted, especially in the presence of FBI agents. Too late now, I figure, and continue: "But I was slightly paranoid about your visit. I thought you might have done a little digging on me in preparation for this, and I've been researching some controversial topics lately as part of a cross-country trip I took to find unmarked historic sites. Sooooo, if by chance you noticed that I bought a handful of books online about domestic terrorism, al-Qaeda, secret government medical tests on Americans, CIA cover-ups, that sort of thing, those were all work-related."

Neither agent responds.

We step into my apartment, and I quickly change the subject. "Can I offer you all something to drink? Coffee, water, anything?"

"We're fine," says the lead agent.

They sit on the sofa and pull out legal-sized notebooks.

"I'm not sure what you need to know about Jay," I begin, "but I can honestly say that he's one of the most hardworking and trustworthy people I've ever met."

The lead agent gives me a quizzical look. "You mentioned him before. Who's Jay?"

"I'm sorry?" I say, laughing, amused by the idea that they've possibly mixed up their application files.

"Who is Jay?" the agent asks again, not laughing.

Who is Jay? That doesn't make sense.

"Aren't you doing a background check on him?"

They glance at each other.

"No," the lead agent says. "We have nothing to do with that."

Trying not to sound impolite, I ask, "Then . . . why are you here?"

"We're investigating what you were doing at the Deseret Chemical Depot in Utah, where military police caught you taking pictures of the base."

Those words, *investigating* and *caught,* hang in the air. My heart starts racing and multiple images flash through my mind. I recall the sign, the valley, the white cars pulling up out of nowhere, and the circle of MPs around me.

I want to answer right away so I don't come across as evasive, but I feel self-conscious about not seeming nervous, which only makes me more nervous.

"The reason, well, actually, I wasn't photographing the base, only the sign at the entrance, as part of a photo journal of my trip, to remind me where I'd been," I say. "And you really can't see the facility from the road anyway because it's miles away. Have you all been there?"

"No," the lead agent says.

"It's far down in this valley, and you can barely make out anything. Also, I honestly thought it was closed. I can show you . . ."

I spin around to the mammoth filing cabinet behind me and pull out the folder marked UTAH/HUMAN EXPERIMENTS. I shuffle through the papers and hand the lead agent the article that, erroneously, reported that the base had been shuttered years ago. He reads it and jots down notes.

"I actually came across Deseret by chance. My main story was about the Dugway Proving Ground farther east."

"That's also a restricted area," the agent says, giving the paper back to me.

"Right, I know, and I ended up pursuing an entirely different story in Utah related to Richard McCoy."

They look at me blankly.

"The guy who might have been D. B. Cooper," I say.

Agent #2 perks up. "The hijacker?"

"The hijacker."

I relate McCoy's story, and they seem genuinely interested. To prove I'm not obsessed with domestic terrorism or classified government projects, I briefly tell them about David "Carbine" Williams and then Ralph Teetor, who created cruise control.

"He was *blind*?" Agent #2 asks.

"Since childhood."

One story leads into another, and after I ramble on for twenty minutes straight the agents have closed their notebooks and are cracking smiles. My initial heart-pounding fear has subsided, and they begin discussing some of their own favorite sites. Agent #2 tells me his father is "a history nut" and frequently loaded up the car and drove the family to battlefields and other landmarks all over the country.

"I dreaded those trips as a kid," he remarks, "but I miss them now."

"I hear that from a lot of people," I say.

They get up, we shake hands, and the mood is certainly more jovial. I'm tempted to ask what they're going to write in their report, but I don't want to push my luck. I doubt they consider me a national-security threat, although I suspect the phrase "prone to chattiness" is now part of my permanent FBI file.

Joe Rogers, my eighty-eight-year-old neighbor, notices the agents leaving and approaches me in the hallway. "What sort of trouble have you gotten yourself into now, Andrew?" he asks with a grin.

I sheepishly describe what I did in Utah and how the FBI felt my actions warranted further inquiry. This prompts Joe to mention that he's friends with a number of retired agents who've told him about various stakeouts that have taken place right in this building and on our block. I've heard inklings of these stories before, but not the full details.

As we're standing there, it hits me that I've lived across the hall from Joe for more than a decade and never really talked with him about his own military background. Like most veterans, he's humble about his service, and I pry gently. Joe tells me that he volunteered for the U.S. Army Air Corps as soon as he turned eighteen and ended up piloting B-17 bombers over Europe. After the war, he was stationed in China and became an aviation advisor to Chiang Kai-shek, leader of the country's anti-Communist party.

"In 1946, I had the pleasure of dancing with Chiang Kai-shek's wife, Soong Mei-ling," Joe says, recalling what was clearly a high point of his time in China. He was introduced to her at a dinner banquet, and she commented on his Georgia accent—something they shared. Although born in Shanghai, she was educated in the United States, primarily Georgia (Joe's home state), and spoke English with a southern inflection.

Joe seems prouder of having danced with Soong Mei-ling, one of the world's most powerful women, than of his historic flight into Beijing at the height of China's revolution. I ask if he'd experienced any harrowing moments during the upheaval, and he describes flying from Shanghai to pick up two U.S. State Department workers before Mao's Communist forces invaded Beijing. Joe had to land on the old polo grounds in front of the Imperial City, becoming the first—and, presumably, last—American to use the spot as an improvised runway. The grounds, today, are better known as Tiananmen Square.

After our one-hour conversation, the longest we've had in ten years, I tell him I hope we can do this more frequently.

"Anytime," he says.

Desk cleared, bills paid, phone calls answered, and FBI agents placated, I contact Megan and we schedule our D.C. get-together.

"Is it all right if my sister Stacy joins us?" Megan asks.

"Of course. Is she also a genealogist?"

"No, she's a defense contractor and mother of four, but she's helped me with my research and wants to tag along."

"Great. The more the merrier."

On the morning of our rendezvous, I walk up from my apartment to meet Megan and her sister in front of the Marriott Wardman Park Hotel, on the corner of Connecticut Avenue and Woodley Road.

We exchange hugs and hellos and get into Megan's car.

"I know you're both familiar with Washington, and I'm not going to lead us on a wild-goose chase through the city," I say, "but I thought I'd show you some lesser-known sites on our way to the Capitol."

Starting with the Wardman. "One of America's greatest writers was discovered here by happenstance," I say as we pull out of the hotel's driveway. "In December 1925 the poet Vachel Lindsay was eating in the hotel's dining room, and a young busboy timidly placed three poems he'd written on Lindsay's table. Lindsay was initially annoyed by the interruption, but when he looked over the poems, he thought they were quite good. Later that night he was giving a speech and declared that he'd encountered a brilliant new poet and then read the works aloud. Newspapers profiled the 'busboy poet,' and that's how Langston Hughes launched his career."

We head south on Connecticut Avenue and approach my building. I tell Megan and Stacy about my conversation with Joe Rogers after the FBI paid me a visit.

"That's my apartment, above the entrance," I say, "and Joe told me that during the Cold War one of the previous tenants was this 'big redheaded gal'—his words—who used to spend her days in front of the window knitting or quietly reading to herself. Turns out, she was actually an FBI agent taking down license plate numbers and physical descriptions of everyone who went in and out of the building across the street, which back then was the Soviet consulate."

From the car, our view of the apartment is partly blocked by a twenty-foot oak.

"See this row of trees here," I say, "and how this one is shorter than the others?"

Megan and Stacy peer out the window and nod.

"Joe said that the FBI kept pruning the tree that used to be here so the agent had a clearer view, and they ended up 'killing the damn thing.' The FBI eventually replaced it, and the new one's not as tall as the others."

We hit a red light on the corner of Connecticut and California, and I point out one last espionage site.

"I don't know if you all remember Felix Bloch, the State Department official accused of being a spy in the late eighties—"

"Oh, sure," Megan and Stacy say in unison.

"Well, halfway down this street is a blue mailbox that, according to Joe's FBI sources, Bloch and his Soviet counterparts would mark in chalk to signal when they were going to meet. Bloch was never convicted, but the State Department fired him, and he ended up moving to North Carolina, where he got a job bagging groceries and driving a city bus in Chapel Hill. He was later arrested for shoplifting."

The light turns green, and we continue down Connecticut.

Family lore is obviously Megan's area of expertise, and I confess to her that until I went on my trip, I had never asked my parents about their own brushes with history.

"After visiting Peoria," I say, "I was talking on the phone with my mom and telling her how penicillin was mass-produced there, and she made this offhand comment that when she was about twelve, Howard Florey had briefly stayed at their home on Long Island during World War II. I'd never heard this before. I knew my grandfather was a doctor, but I had no idea he was friends with both Florey and Alexander Fleming. She vividly remembered how giddy Florey became, almost like a child, when they served him fresh strawberries, which were a rarity back in England because of rationing. Ten years later, when my mom was sightseeing in Europe, she visited Fleming at his home in London. I asked what she thought of him, and her recollection was that he was a very sweet, soft-spoken man. She also said he had a stunning wife, also very nice. Greek. And '*much* younger than he was.'"

"As a genealogist, I'm always telling people to talk to their parents and elders before it's too late, and my biggest regret in life was not recording my mom's stories," Megan says. "My husband has been good about getting my dad to open up about his Vietnam experiences, and the women in our family usually live into their nineties, so I figured I had plenty of time with my mom. And then she was abruptly diagnosed with stage-four lung cancer at the age of sixty-five. We had a few months before she passed away, but it seemed inappropriate to interview her because she was very resistant to the possibility of dying. Now I encourage others to do as I say, not as I did. I was, however, able to interview my grandmother just three months before she died at ninety, and when I listened to the tape a few years later, I couldn't believe how many details I had either forgotten or misremembered."

"This was your grandmother on the Smolenyak side?"

"No, my mom's mother."

Megan's maiden name is Smolenyak, and in 2001 she married a man named Brian Smolenyak—thus her "double" name.

"How many times removed are you from Brian?" I ask.

"He's my tenth cousin. There are only four Smolenyak families in the world, all tracing back to this rural village in Slovakia, but the funny thing is, none of them share the same direct bloodline. When Brian and I went there in 2006 on vacation, I asked some of the villagers if I could test their DNA and discovered that they have different genetic identifiers. Smolenyak must have been an occupational name."

Farther down Connecticut Avenue, we make a left on I Street and pass behind Blair House, where foreign leaders often stay during official state visits. "Did you all read what happened when Boris Yeltsin got drunk here in September 1994 while visiting with President Bill Clinton?"

Megan and Stacy shake their heads.

"Clinton is on the record talking about it in Taylor Branch's book *The Clinton Tapes,* and if I could put up a historical marker anywhere in D.C., it would focus on this incident," I say somewhat facetiously.

"In the dead of night," I continue, "Yeltsin, who was president of Russia at the time and theoretically in control of all their nuclear weapons, got hammered, slipped past his security detail, and wandered out of Blair House *in his underwear.* He was found by our Secret Service agents stumbling around Pennsylvania Avenue half naked trying to hail a cab. When the agents started escorting him back inside to, among other things, avert an international scandal, Yeltsin apparently threw a small tantrum, claiming he just wanted to find some pizza. Taylor Branch asked Clinton how the situation resolved itself, and the president shrugged and said, 'We got him a pizza.'"

We reach the Capitol, and I tell Megan and Stacy I've been quizzing friends who are longtime Washingtonians about their knowledge of the Statue of Freedom, the highest, most visible statue in our nation's capital and an iconic image of American independence. "Overall the consensus is that it's either some Roman goddess or a Native American princess—possibly Sacagawea. I didn't know myself until I read the Architect of the Capitol's website, which said the model was just an anonymous 'classical female figure.'"

"Well, it's got a Roman soldier's helmet crowned with Native American feathers, so the confusion is understandable," Megan says. "The original design actually called for a 'liberty cap,' but Jefferson Davis, who was secretary of war at the time, vehemently opposed the idea because it was associated with the antislavery movement."

Sculpted in Rome by an American artist named Thomas Crawford, the plaster model for the statue arrived in 1859 and then sat around for several years because construction on the Capitol Building itself was delayed during the Civil War. Washington was under constant threat of invasion, and many able-bodied laborers were off fighting.

Clark Mills, the foundry owner in charge of casting the nearly twenty-foot-tall, fifteen-thousand-pound bronze statue, was facing his own personnel crisis; in 1861 the Italian craftsman Mills depended on to supervise the job realized that no one else had his experience and refused to begin unless he received an exorbitant pay raise. Infuriated, Mills fired him.

"Philip Reed was another skilled plasterer in the foundry," Megan says, "and although he had never done anything as large and intricately designed as this, Mills entrusted him with the project. Using stress tests and pulleys, Reed painstakingly figured out how to disassemble the plaster model so it could be cast properly. If mishandled, the whole thing could have been ruined." Thanks to Reed, the statue was assembled seamlessly and placed atop the Capitol's dome in December 1863.

Megan shares with me a file containing Reed's biographical information, including an 1870 census report that proves his D.C. residency and Clark Mills's own handwritten records detailing how much he initially paid for him. Reed—one of the individuals most responsible for crowning the U.S. Capitol with the Statue of Freedom—was a slave. In 1862, Mills wrote that he had purchased Reed for $1,200 "many years ago when he was quite a youth" and described him as "mulatto color, short in stature, in good health, not prepossessing in appearance, but smart in mind, [and] a good workman."

"Mills spelled Reed's name R-e-i-d," Megan says, "and before Reed gained his freedom, official documents recorded it that way, too. But I prefer the spelling Reed—like *freed*—used, and I think he earned the right to name himself."

Megan also tracked down Reed's death certificate and hands me a copy. He died on February 6, 1892, at the age of seventy-five, from "erysipelas of face," a painful skin infection that can now easily be cured by penicillin.

Washington's Graceland Cemetery is listed as Reed's original place of burial, but that was later crossed out, and the words "To Harmony June 21, 1895," were written above. Megan explains that Reed's body was disinterred—twice. The third and final cemetery isn't recorded on the certificate.

"We'll show you where he ended up," Megan says. "And Stacy, I should emphasize, gets the credit for doing most of the sleuthing on this. She helps me with a lot of my searches."

Stacy demurs, brushing off the compliment. "I love doing it."

Within a few short minutes we're pulling up at the intersection of Neal Street and Maryland Avenue NE, in front of a massive construction site for a new apartment complex.

"That's where Graceland used to be," Stacy says, "and you can see that it's still in sight of the Capitol, which is fitting."

We then drive to the Rhode Island Avenue-Brentwood Metro station, which is where the old Harmony Cemetery used to be.

"There *is* a marker here for Harmony," Stacy tells me, "but nothing about Reed."

"Can I take a brief look?"

"Sure," Stacy says. "It's above the newspaper stands."

I sprint over and find the plaque. "Many distinguished black citizens including civil war veterans were buried in this cemetery," it reads. "These bodies now rest in the new National Harmony Memorial Park Cemetery in Maryland."

That will be our next and last stop, directly across the D.C. border.

Meticulous attention to detail apparently runs in the family, and Stacy gives me a stack of papers she's prepared about the three cemeteries, complete with full-color photos and maps.

"I do this type of research whenever we go on family vacations," Stacy says. "I love taking my husband and kids on long hikes to find remote sites. My youngest son, who's sixteen, calls them 'the forced marches,' but these have been some of our best times together. I want to create experiences they'll remember, and hopefully the trips change how they see the world around them."

Two hands clasped in prayer are etched in marble on the entrance-way sign to Harmony National Memorial Park, which bills itself as "Washington's Most Naturally Beautiful Cemetery." I might quibble with the geographical reference, since we're technically in Maryland, but the spacious, sloping grounds certainly appear beautiful and well maintained. And according to one of Stacy's documents, it was the D.C. government that contracted the removal of some thirty-seven thousand remains—most of them Washingtonians—from the old Harmony Cemetery and transferred them here.

"Where is Reed's grave?" I ask.

Stacy did the legwork on this, too. When she first called the cemetery, they didn't know his location but suggested she speak with their off-site historian, Paul Sluby, and he was able to map out the general area for her.

Megan slows her car down in front of a polished gray marker that references the old cemetery. Stacy points to an empty acre of grass and says, "Philip is somewhere in there. Mr. Sluby told me that before the bodies were moved from old Harmony, the descendants—if they could be found—were sent letters notifying them about the change. If nobody responded, the remains were buried here without a headstone. We don't think Philip had any ancestors still alive then, and no one claimed him."

Stacy goes on to remark how sad it is that Reed has been pushed farther and farther away from his most notable achievement. First, he was in a marked plot in clear view of the Statue of Freedom, and now he's miles away, his bones lost under mounds of earth with no hope of ever being identified.

"What initially drew you to Reed?" I ask Megan.

"You know, we're raised studying kings and presidents and generals, but I'm more interested in the historical underdogs, in slaves and immigrants and anyone who's gone overlooked. Each story adds another pixel to the overall picture and gives us a better understanding of the past and a clearer image of who we really are."

I press Megan and Stacy on why this matters.

"Our ancestors faced enormous hardships in their time," Megan replies, "and their experiences remind us that we're here because of what they endured."

"And the more we recognize what they sacrificed, the more grateful we become for what we have in our own lives," Stacy adds, echoing Ed Hrivnak's sentiments to me on Mount Baker almost verbatim.

"Not to sound all 'Kumbaya' here," Megan continues, "but from a genealogical standpoint, we're all related, and we tend to treat others more respectfully when we realize that they're part of our family. History reminds us how interconnected we are, and how much we've benefited from those who've come before us."

This strikes a particular chord with me. Throughout my journey, nothing has surprised me more than discovering how personal and intimate history can be, that it's not just some distant, abstract idea we study from afar. When I was trying to find Dr. Loring Miner's house in Kansas to research the Spanish flu pandemic, by sheer coincidence the first person I called, Helen Hall, happened to own Miner's old home. In Washington state, my close friend Ed Hrivnak was part of the recovery team that found the PV-1 lost on Mount Baker in 1943. And when I mentioned in passing to my mom about visiting Peoria to see where penicillin was manufactured, I learned that—through her father—she had gotten to know its inventor, Dr. Alexander Fleming, when she was only a teenager.

"For its significance alone," I say to Megan after my mom's story came to mind, "the place that probably most affected me was the lab in Peoria, where British and American scientists worked together to figure out how penicillin could be mass-produced. Their efforts have saved tens of millions of lives, maybe more, and when you think about it, we or people we love are alive today because of what they did." The same could also be said of Maurice Hilleman, Joseph Goldberger, and countless other doctors, scientists, and innovators whose names are barely remembered.

Megan, Stacy, and I drive across the Maryland border back into Washington, and the U.S. Capitol emerges into view over the city's rooftops. I've passed that building ten thousand times before and never paid much attention to the statue above its dome. Because of Philip Reed, I'll never see it the same way again.

If learning about the past only infused our lives with a sense of passion and wonder by enriching our perception of the world around us, that alone would make it worthwhile. I realize, however, that more is demanded of history. We call upon it for guidance in times of crisis. We refer to it during national debates about when or if we should go to war, which economic policies to implement, how we conduct our foreign affairs, what restrictions we allow on individual liberties in the name of domestic security, and whom we elect to political office. Even if it fails to offer up definitive answers, a knowledge of past events and precedents helps us to engage in a more thoughtful and informed public dialogue.

But Megan and Stacy, I think, have articulated history's most overlooked value: its ability to influence the way we live our lives and how we treat one another on a day-to-day basis. At its best, history nurtures within us humility and gratitude. It encourages respect and empathy. It fosters creativity and stimulates the imagination. It inspires resilience. And it does so by illuminating the simple truth that, whether due to some cosmic fluke or divine providence, it's an absolute miracle that any one of us is alive today, walking around on this tiny sphere surrounded by an ocean of space, and that we are, above everything else, all in this together.

ACKNOWLEDGMENTS AND SOURCES

As to that night, I slept in that room in the corner away from the fireplace. One comfort was over me, one comfort and pillow between me and the dark floor. . . . There was every reason to infer that the pillow and comfort came from my [hosts' own] bed.

They slept far away, in some mysterious part of the empty house. I hoped they were not cold. I looked into the rejoicing fire. I said: "This is what I came out into the wilderness to see. This man had nothing, and gave me half of it, and we both had abundance."

—From A Handy Guide for Beggars, Especially Those of the Poetic Fraternity (1919) by Vachel Lindsay

AUTHORS, LIKE TRAVELERS, frequently depend on the kindness of friends and strangers alike, even if their endeavors seem to be mostly solitary affairs. This book, and my trip across America, would not have been possible without the generosity and assistance of a host of extraordinary individuals to whom I am forever grateful.

Beginning, first and foremost, with my editor, Rick Horgan, at Crown Archetype. Rick is a passionate history buff who understood the spirit of this book—and the larger project behind it—from the very beginning. Rick is every author's dream editor; he is brilliant and a sensational writer himself. This book became more ambitious than either of us had expected, and Rick helped me contain my somewhat peripatetic ramblings while maintaining its free-spirited style. Rick shepherded this book along with infinite patience and offered the necessary words of encouragement when they were needed. I truly cannot thank him enough. Along with Rick, there is Julian Pavia, who did much of the initial editing of the manuscript and saved me from careening too wildly from topic to topic. (I still careened more than Julian would probably have preferred, and I'm responsible for these unwieldy parts, but it's in my nature to jump from topic to topic.) I also want to thank Nate Roberson, Rick's right-hand man, who endured a barrage of e-mails and questions on a range of matters and deserves a medal for his patience and kindness throughout this whole process. Copy editors are the unsung heroes of the publishing world, and I am grateful for all of the labor Chris Tanigawa has put into fine-tuning the manuscript. On the publicity and marketing side, I've been especially fortunate to have Catherine Cullen and Christina Foxley help me spread the word about this book. They're a joy to work with and a truly dedicated and creative team. I am also deeply indebted to Crown Archetype's phenomenal publisher, Tina Constable, who has been enormously supportive. I can't imagine a more caring or thoughtful publisher.

I wouldn't have found Crown without my agent, Miriam Altshuler, who is not only the best agent but simply the greatest friend that a writer could hope to have. Miriam's wisdom, sense of humor, guidance, integrity, and encouragement were indispensable throughout this process, and I never would have made it through in one piece without her. Words cannot express the extent of my gratitude and admiration for her. I am also indebted to her assistants Emily Koyfman, Sara Mc-Ghee, Cathy Schmitz, and especially Reiko Davis, who has helped me lurch (reluctantly) into the twenty-first century and set up a Facebook page and other social media.

And speaking of newfangled technology (at least it is to me), I'm extremely grateful to my gifted Web designer, Tim Kopp, for setting up www.HereIsWhere.org.

Along with my parents, who have been incredible throughout this whole project, there are numerous family members and friends to whom I am extremely grateful for their words of support and, in many cases, their ideas for stories: Allison Agnew, Ted Alexander, Sharon Allen, Chris Aprato, Meredith and Monica Ashley, Scott Baron, Chris and Janet Beach, Kate Becker and Darell Hammond, Peter Benkendorf, Rob Berkley and Debbie Phillips, Bob Bergman, Margaret Bernal, Cliff and Anna Blaze, Ursula Bosch and Gerard Petersen, Todd Boss, Doug Bradshaw, Chad Breckinridge and Joy Drachman, Lawrence Bridges, Doug Brinkley, Chris Buckley, Jon Burrows, Allen Caruselle, Chris and Elizabeth Mechem Carroll, Lucinda and Sophia Carroll, Lisa Catapano and Bill Thomas, Ross Cohen, John Cole, Craig Colton, Alison Hall Cooley and Benjamin Simons, Frank Correa, Allan Cors, Dan Dalager, Dave Danzig, Richard Danzig, Connie and Tom Davidson Sr., Elissa and Tommy Davidson, Chris Davies and Stephanie Martz, Frank Davies, Riki Dolph, James Dourgarian, Ashley and Jono Drysdale, Chris Dunham, Tom Dunkel, Deanna Durrett, Chris Epting, Dave Felsen, Katia and Mike Fischer, Ken Fisher and Amanda Godley, Skyla M. Freeman, Dave Gabel, Joan Gillcrist and Will Strong, Larry D. Goins, Bill and Karen Graser, Dave and Debbie Grossberg, Erin Gruwell, Parker Gyokeres, Joyce A. Hallenbeck, John and Meredith Hanamiriam, Tom Hare and Liz McDermott, Mim Harrison, Mike Healy, August Hohl, Cory-Jeanne Houck-Cox, Linda Howell, Nick Irons, Kelly Johnson, Greg Jones, Steve Karras, Ryan Kelly, David Kennedy, Austin Kiplinger, Andrew Kirk, Yumi Kobayashi and Peter Sluszka, Mia Kogan, Chrissy Kolaya and Brook Miller, Jerome Kramer, Zoltan Krompecher, Gene and Joanna Kukuy, Henry Labalme, Greg and Maureen Lare, Simone Ledeen, Steve and Lori Leveen, Heather and Tom Leitzell, Jack Lewis, James Loewen, Jim and Kathy Lowy, John Madden, Peter Marks, John McCary, Pam McDonough, Mike McNulty, Jimmie Meinhardt, James and Meribeth McGinley, Sylvia Medley, Ann Medlock, Doug Meehan and Caroline Suh, Justin Merhoff, Brad and Cori Flam Meltzer, Mike Meyer, John Meyers, Jay Michael, Nathan Mick, Allen Mikaelian, De'on Miller, Marja Mills, Felicia Norton, K.K. Ottesen and Matthew Wheelock, Jon Peede, David Pelizzari, James Percoco, Elise and Tripp Piper, Alice Powers, Gary Powers Jr., Pam Putney, Cheryl Richardson, Joe Rubinfine, Cathy Saypol, Jeff Shaara, Thad and Gabby Sheeley, Katie Silberman, Denis Silva, Albert Small, Lucy Roberts Smiles, Charles Smith, Kelsey Smith, Kerner Smith Jr., Kerner Smith III, Maggie Smith, Patty Smith, Adrian Snead, Steve Stevenson, Sean Sweeney, Adrian and Sandra Talbott, Chris and Becca Tessin, Chuck Theusch, Anne Tramer, Kyriakos Tsakopoulos, Erika Tullberg, Meg Tulloch, Todd Vorenkamp, Jamie Wager, Stephen Webber, Megan Willems, Don Wilson, Rob Wilson, Ellen Wingard, Martin Vigderhouse, Thomas Young, and Lydia Zamora.

Sadly, two of my closest friends lost their moms while I was working on this book. Brook Miller's mother, Helen, and Adrian Talbott's mother, Brooke Shearer, were extremely kind in sharing with me suggestions of little-known places I should seek out. Helen was the one who told me about Charles Lindbergh's grave in Hawaii, and Brooke pointed me to several spots around our hometown of D.C. They were both extraordinary women and are deeply missed.

I want to extend a special thanks to John Elko, not only for being such an influential teacher but also for connecting me with several of his students who proved to be outstanding assistants: Antonia Hitchens, Dimitry Kislovskiy, and Massimo Young. Similarly, I want to thank my good friend Joel Swerdlow for enlisting Ben Oreskes—a terrific researcher—in this endeavor. I'm indebted as well to Elizabeth Velez, both for her support and for putting me in touch with her son, Nick, who's been a lifesaver on a variety of projects.

At Keener Management, I'm indebted to David Beasley, Okey Mbarah, Alison Sowers, and Gabrielle Weiss. And at the Weider History Group, I want to thank Aleta Burchyski, David Grogan, and Karen Jensen.

I'd also like to thank Dear Abby, who, in 1998, helped me launch the Legacy Project (a national effort to preserve American war letters), and, ultimately, further deepened my love for history. The Legacy Project's letters are being donated to Chapman University and will become the foundation of the newly created Center for American War Letters. At Chapman I am grateful to Dennis Arp, Charlene Baldwin, Richard Bausch, John Benitz (a phenomenal director and now dear friend who first introduced me to the Chapman community), Larry and Sheryl Bourgeois, William Cumiford, Erika Curiel, Doug Dechow, Jim Doti, Patrick Fuery, Ryan Gattis, Marilyn Harran, Jennifer Keene, Anna Leahy, Nina Lenoir, Jan Osborn, Ronald and Kyndra Rotunda, Bob Slayton, Daniele Struppa, Yolanda Uzzell, Char Williams, and the casts of *If All the Sky Were Paper*. (You all were sensational.) And I owe special thanks to Tom Zoellner, who read through an early draft of the book and had wise counsel to offer.

Along these lines, I cannot express enough how grateful I am to Jenny Moore, who put up with my frequent bouts of hermitic isolation throughout this process and, most important, read through the first version of the manuscript and gave invaluable feedback. Jenny is an exceptional writer herself, and she is simply one of the most remarkable persons I've ever known.

I'm also grateful to several individuals at the National Geographic Society, who were supportive of the larger Here Is Where initiative from the start, particularly Keith Bellows at *National Geographic Traveler* and Beth Lizardo, Janelle Nanos, Gio Palatucci, and Dan Westergren.

Finally, I want to thank Jim Basker, Lesley Herrmann, Sandra Trenholm, Susan Saidenberg, Richard Gilder, and Lewis Lehrman at the Gilder Lehrman Institute of American History, one of the best organizations in the United States promoting history and supporting teachers.

The people and published sources I relied on are listed below, and, in the interest of space, I've refrained from repeating book titles, newspaper articles, and other publications already cited within the chapters. Also, some sources conflict with others, and when there were discrepancies I tried to the best of my abilities to determine which were the most reliable. Mistakes sneak into even the most trusted historical records, and I will make every effort to correct information that turns out to be demonstrably wrong. Indeed, one of the points I wanted to make in this book is that far from offering us concrete rules and intellectual certainty, the study of history often fosters healthy skepticism and teaches us to think critically about what we had once believed to be absolutely true. But again, I think the search is half the fun.

The Exchange Place

Special thanks to: James Cornelius and Jennifer Ericson, who sent me a copy of Robert Todd Lincoln's February 6, 1909, letter to Richard Gilder, from the Abraham Lincoln Presidential Library; Archivist Ryan McPherson at the Baltimore & Ohio Railroad Museum's Hays T. Watkins Research Library; Jane Singer, who wrote a great article about Luke Pryor Blackburn, "The Fiend in Gray," *Washington Post* (June 1, 2003); and Mariani Tooba at the New-York Historical Society for helping me locate sites associated with the November 1864 plot to burn down Manhattan. *Publications:* John S. Goff, *Robert Todd Lincoln: A Man in His Own Right* (Norman: University of Oklahoma Press, 1969); Clint Johnson, *A Vast and Fiendish Plot: The Confederate Attack on New York City* (New York: Citadel Press, 2010); Phil Scott, "1864 Attack on New York," *American History* (January 2002); and Ronald C. White Jr., *A. Lincoln: A Biography* (New York: Random House, 2009).

Niihau

Special thanks to: Keith Robinson, whose family owns Niihau; Dana Rosendal and Shandra at Niihau Helicopters; Floyd Mori and Crystal Xu at the Japanese American Citizens League; Albert Nason at the Jimmy Carter Library; Glen Reason and Bob Timmermann at the Los Angeles Public Library; and Linda Sueyoshi at the Hawaii State Library. *Publications:* Allan Beekman, *The Niihau Incident: The True Story of the Japanese Fighter Pilot Who, After the Pearl Harbor Attack, Crash-Landed on the Hawaiian Island of Niihau and Terrorized the Residents* (Honolulu: Heritage Press of Pacific, 1982); Richard B. Frank, "Zero Hour on Niihau," *World War II* (July 2009); Anne Gearen, "US Prepares for Possible Missile Launch," Associated Press (June 18, 2009); Michelle Malkin, *In Defense of Internment: The Case for "Racial Profiling" in World War II and the War on Terror* (Washington, D.C.: Regnery Publishing Inc., 2004); "Hawaiian, with Three Bullet Wounds, Beats Japanese Airman to Death Against a Wall," *New York Times* (December 17, 1941); and Clarice B. Taylor, "Hawaiian Woman Slays Jap Pilot," *Washington Post* (December 17, 1941).

Ona Judge's Home and Grave

Special thanks to: Vicky Avery, my wonderful guide in New Hampshire; Valerie Cunningham, executive director of the Portsmouth Black Heritage Trail, who put me in touch with Vicky Avery; Evelyn Gerson, who wrote a sensational online article about Judge titled "Ona Judge Staines: A Thirst for Complete Freedom and Her Escape from President Washington," which is posted at www.seacostnh.com/blackhistory/ona.html; Carl Westmoreland at the National Underground Railroad Freedom Center; Lish Thompson and Dot Glover at the Charleston County Public Library's South Carolina History Room; and Kitt Alexander, who provided me with information about Robert Smalls. *Publications:* Battle of Bennington Committee letter to John Stark from the Papers of John Stark, New Hampshire Historical Society; David W. Blight, *Passages to Freedom: The Underground Railroad in History and Memory* (New York: Collins, 2004); Charles L. Blockson, *Hippocrene Guide to the Underground Railroad* (New York: Hippocrene Books, 1994); Betty DeRamus, *Forbidden Fruit: Love Stories from the Underground Railroad* (New York: Atria Books, 2005); Robert B. Dishman, "Ona Maria Judge Takes French Leave of Her Mistress to Live Free in New Hampshire," *Historical New Hampshire* (vol. 62, no. 1, spring 2008); Dennis Brindell Fradin, *Bound for the North Star: True Stories of Fugitive Slaves* (New York: Clarion Books, 2000); George and Willene Hendrick, *Fleeing for Freedom: Stories of the Underground Railroad as Told by Levi Coffin and William Still* (Chicago: Ivan R. Dee, 2004); Dennis J. Pogue, "George Washington: Slave Master," *American History* (February 2004); and Henry Wiencek, *An Imperfect God: George Washington, His Slaves, and the Creation of America* (New York: Farrar, Straus and Giroux, 2003).

Mound City

Special thanks to: Jerry O. Potter, who guided me around Arkansas and Tennessee and is the author of *The Sultana Tragedy: America's Greatest Maritime Disaster* (Gretna, Louisiana: Pelican, 1992). *Publications:* Mary Koik, Civil War Trust, "Deadly Duty in the Arsenals," *Hallowed Ground Magazine* (winter 2009); Denise Gess and William Lutz, *Firestorm at Peshtigo: A Town, Its People, and the Deadliest Fire in American History* (New York: Henry Holt and Company, 2002); and Leslie Miller, "Pilot Error Blamed for Flight 587 Crash," Associated Press (October 26, 2004).

Richard "Two Gun" Hart's House

Special thanks to: Enrique and Lucille Castillo for help with information on César Chávez's birthplace; Harry Hart for his hospitality; Kelly King, who owns Richard Hart's house in Homer, Nebraska; and Jane Shadle, who put me in touch with Marjorie Teetor Meyer (and I'm especially grateful to Marjorie for sharing her father's story with me). *Publications:* William H. Armstrong, *Warrior in Two Camps: Ely S. Parker, Union General and Seneca Chief* (Syracuse: Syracuse University Press, 1978); Laurence Bergreen, *Capone: The Man and Era* (New York: Touchstone, 1994); Richard Griswold Del Castillo and Richard A. Garcia, *César Chávez: A Triumph of Spirit* (Norman: University of Oklahoma Press, 1995); Harry H. Hart, Jeff G. Hart, Angela S. Beekman, and Corey R. Hart, *Capone-Hart: Two Italian Brothers: Two-Gun Hart, Lawman—Al Capone, Gangster* (Lincoln, Nebr.: The "Two-Gun Project" and JC & H Productions, 2000); John Kobler, *Capone: The Life and World of Al Capone* (New York: Da Capo Press, 1971); Jacques E. Levy, *César Chávez: Autobiography of La Causa* (New York: W. W. Norton, 1975); and Robert J. Schoenberg, *Mr. Capone: The Real—and Complete—Story of Al Capone* (New York: Quill, 1992).

Fort Meade

Special thanks to: Bob Johnson at the Fort George G. Meade Museum and Albert Nason at the Jimmy Carter Library. *Publications:* Bill Blass, *Bare Blass* (New York: Harper Perennial, 2003); CNN, "Carter: CIA Used Psychic to Help Find Missing Plane" (transcript, September 21, 1995); Jack Kneece, *Ghost Army of World War II* (Gretna, La.: Pelican, 2001); Joseph McMoneagle, *Remote Viewing Secrets: A Handbook* (Charlottesville, Va.: Hampton Roads

Publishing Company, 2000); David Morehouse, *Psychic Warrior: The True Story of America's Foremost Psychic Spy and the Cover-up of the CIA's Top-Secret Stargate Program* (New York: St. Martin's Press, 1996); Jim Schnabel, *Remote Viewers: The Secret History of America's Psychic Spies* (New York: Dell Publishing, 1997); and Douglas Waller, "The Vision Thing," *Time* (December 11, 1995).

Mary Dyer's Farm

Special thanks to: Leigh Ivey and Betsy Merritt at the National Trust for Historic Preservation; Cory D. Nelson, President of the Western Psychiatric State Hospital Association, which includes the Human Resources Center in Yankton, South Dakota; Ruth S. Taylor, Loraine Byrne, and Bert Lippincott at the Newport Historical Society; Pat Redfearn at the George Hail Free Library in Warren, Rhode Island; C. Morgan Grefe at the Rhode Island Historical Society; and Kathy MacKnight at the U.S. Naval Hospital in Newport. *Publications:* Robert S. Burgess, *To Try the Bloody Law: The Story of Mary Dyer* (Burnsville, N.C.: Celo Valley Books, 2000); Michael Farquhar, *A Treasury of Foolishly Forgotten Americans* (New York: Penguin Books, 2008); John Williams Haley, *"The Old Stone Bank" History of Rhode Island, Volume III* (Providence: Providence Institution for Savings, 1939); Ruth Talbot Plimpton, *Mary Dyer: Biography of a Rebel Quaker* (Boston: Branden Publishing Company, 1994); and Horatio Rogers, *Mary Dyer of Rhode Island: The Quaker Martyr That Was Hanged on Boston Common, June 1, 1660* (Providence: Preston and Rounds, 1896).

The Paisley Five Mile Point Caves

Special thanks to: Dennis Jenkins and his team for letting me join them on their dig; Michelle Huey, owner of the Sage Rooms motel; and K. Kris Hirst, editor of *The Archaeologist's Book of Quotations* (Walnut Creek, Calif.: Left Coast Press, 2010). *Publications:* J. M. Adovasio, J. Donahue, and R. Stuckenrath, "The Meadowcraft Rockshelter Radiocarbon Chronology 1975–1990," *American Antiquity,* published by the Society for American Archaeology (vol. 55, no. 2, April 1990); Paul Aron, *Unsolved Mysteries of American History: An Eye-Opening Journey Through 500 Years of Discoveries, Disappearances, and Baffling Events* (New York: John Wiley & Sons, 1997); Jeff Benedict, *No Bone Unturned: Inside the World of a Top Forensic Scientist and His Work on America's Most Notorious Crimes and Disasters* (New York: Perennial, 2003); Andrew Curry, "How Did People Reach the Americas? Ancient DNA Sheds Light on the Prehistoric Humans Who Colonized a Hemisphere," *U.S. News & World Report* (August 4, 2008); Franklin Folsom, *Black Cowboy: The Life and Legend of George McJunkin* (Lanham, Md.: Roberts Rinehart Publishers, 1992); Evan Hadingham, "America's First Immigrants," *Smithsonian* (November 2004); Marc Kaufman, "Human Traces Found to Be Oldest in N. America," *Washington Post* (April 4, 2008); Michael D. Lemonick and Andrea Dorfman, "Who Were the First Americans?," *Time* (March 13, 2006); Julian Smith, "Proof of a Pre-Clovis People?," *American Archaeology* (winter 2009–2010); and John Noble Whitford, "New Answers to an Old Question: Who Got Here First?," *New York Times* (November 9, 1999).

The Remains of Prometheus

Special thanks to: Betsy Duncan-Clark at Great Basin National Park; my terrific guide Bryan Petrtyl; and Terry Marasco at the Silver Jack Inn. *Publications:* Peter Browning, *John Muir in His Own Words: A Book of Quotations* (Lafayette, Calif.: Great West Books, 1988); Michael P. Cohen, *A Garden of Bristlecones: Tales of Change in the Great Basin* (Reno: University of Nevada Press, 1998); Donald R. Currey, "An Ancient Bristlecone Pine Stand in Eastern Nevada," *Ecology* (vol. 46, no. 4);   Carl T. Hall, "Staying Alive: High in California's White Mountains Grows the Oldest Living Creature Ever Found," *San Francisco Chronicle* (August 23, 1998); Ronald M. Lanner, *The Bristlecone Book: A Natural History of the World's Oldest Trees* (Missoula, Mont.: Mountain Press Publishing Company, 2007); National Park Service, "Ancient Trees: Great Basin Bristlecone Pines" (undated fact sheet); Michael L. Nicklas, *Great Basin: The Story Behind the Scenery* (Las Vegas: KC Publications, 1996); and Richard Preston, "Tall for Its Age: Climbing a Record-Breaking Redwood," *The New Yorker* (October 9, 2006).

Mound Key Island

Special thanks to: Susanne Hunt at Florida's Historic Preservation/Division of Historical Resources; Bobby Romero, who took me to Mound Key Island on his boat; and Robert Charles Brooks and Michael M. Heare at the Koreshan State Historic Site. *Publications:* Daniel B. Baker, ed., *Explorers and Discoverers of the World* (Detroit: Gale Research Inc., 1993); Marjory Stoneman Douglas with John Rothchild, *Voice of the River: An Autobiography* (Englewood, Fla.: Pineapple Press, 1987); B.F. French (editor), *Historical Collections of Louisiana and Florida, 2d ser.: Memoir of Hernando d'Escalante Fontanedo [sic] on the country and ancient Indian tribes of Florida. Translated from Ternaux Compan's French translation from the original memoir in Spanish* (New York: A. Mason, 1875); Robin Hanbury-Tenison, ed., *The Seventy Great Journeys in History* (New York: Thames & Hudson, 2006); Tony Horwitz, "The Real First Pilgrims," *American History* (August 2008);   Shelley Sperry, "A World Transformed," map supplement to *National Geographic* (May 2007); and David O. True (editor), *Memoir of Do. D'Escalante Fontaneda Respecting Florida, Written in Spain, about the year 1575, Translated from the Spanish with Notes by Buckingham Smith: 1854* (Coral Gables, Florida: Glade House, 1945).

The Grand Prairie Harmonical Association

Special thanks to: Peggy Ford at the Greeley History Museum; Kay E. Lowell at the University of Colorado's James A. Michener Library; and Terri Wargo (the library director at the West Lebanon–Pike Township Public Library, as well as the president of the Warren County Historical Society), who did an enormous amount of research on Grand Prairie for me and guided me to its former site. *Publications:* Kamal Abdel-Malek, *America in an Arab Mirror: Images of America in Arabic Travel Literature: An Anthology* (New York: Palgrave Macmillan, 2000); Daniel Brogan, "Al Qaeda's Greeley Roots," *5280 Magazine* (June/July 2003); Thomas A. Clifton, *Past and Present of Fountain and Warren Counties Indiana* (Indianapolis: B. F. Bowen & Company, 1913); Coy F. Cross II, *Go West Young Man!: Horace Greeley's Vision for America* (Albuquerque: University of New Mexico Press, 1995); Harry Evans, "Grand Prairie Harmonical Institute [sic]," *Indiana Magazine of History* (vol. XII, March 1916); Gerald and Patricia Gutek, *Visiting Utopian Communities: A Guide to the Shakers, Moravians, and Others* (Columbia: University of South Carolina Press, 1998); Mark Holloway, *Heavens on Earth: Utopian Communities in America,* 2nd ed. (New York: Dover Publications, 1966); Edward R. Horgan, *The Shaker Holy Land: A Community Portrait* (Boston: Harvard Common Press, 1987); Arthur Melville Pearson, "Utopia Derailed: How the 1894 Pullman Strike Ended One Magnate's Vision of a Working-Class Paradise," *Archaeology* (January/February 2009); Mike Peters, "Roots of Terrorism," *Greeley Tribune* (February 24, 2002); Martha Smallwood, "Warren County's Socialist Experiment on Prairie Township Farm," *Williamsport Pioneer* (March 9, 1950); Jyotsna Sreenivasan, *Utopias in American History* (Santa Barbara: ABC-CLIO, 2008); David Von Drehle, "A Lesson in Hate," *Smithson-*

ian (February 2006); Richard Frothingham, *Life and Times of Joseph Warren* (Boston: Little, Brown & Company, 1865); and Lawrence Wright, *The Looming Tower: Al-Qaeda and the Road to 9/11* (New York: Knopf, 2006).

Pikes Peak's Summit

Special thanks to: Leah Witherow at the Colorado Springs Pioneers Museum. *Publications:* Richard E. Bohlander, ed., *World Explorers and Discovers* (New York: Macmillan Publishing Company, 1992); Eugene W. Hollon, *The Lost Pathfinder: Zebulon Montgomery Pike* (Norman: University of Oklahoma Press, 1949); Milbry Polk and Mary Tiegreen, *Women of Discovery: A Celebration of Intrepid Women Who Explored the World* (New York: Clarkson Potter/Publishers, 2001); Frances Rooney, *Extraordinary Women Explorers* (Toronto: Second Story Press, 2005); Lynn Sherr, *America the Beautiful: The Stirring True Story Behind Our Nation's Favorite Song* (New York: Public Affairs, 2001); Gayle C. Shirley, *More Than Petticoats: Remarkable Colorado Women* (Guildford, Conn., and Helena, Mont.: Globe Pequot Press, 2002); Agnes Wright Spring, ed., *A Bloomer Girl on Pike's Peak—1858, Julia Archibald Holmes: First White Woman to Climb Pike's Peak* (Denver: Denver Public Library, 1949); Rebecca Stefoff, *Women of the World: Women Travelers and Explorers* (New York: Oxford University Press, 1992); and Claude Wiatrowski, *All Aboard for America's Mountain: The Manitou and Pike's Peak Railway* (Manitou Springs, Colo.: Manitou and Pike's Peak Railway Company, 2007).

Madison Grant's Residence

Special thanks to: Eric Robinson at the New-York Historical Society for finding the *New York Times* obituary about Madison Grant. *Publications:* Joel K. Bourne Jr., "Redwoods: The Super Trees," *National Geographic* (October 2009); Frederick Russell Burnham tribute from the Library of Congress, Kermit Roosevelt papers, "Boone & Crocket Club 35-38" folder, container 106; Wayne Gard, *The Great Buffalo Hunt* (Lincoln: University of Nebraska Press, 1959); Martin S. Garretson, *The American Bison: The Story of Its Extermination as a Wild Species and Its Restoration Under Federal Protection* (New York: New York Zoological Society, 1938); Andrew C. Isenberg, *The Destruction of the Bison: An Environmental History, 1750–1920* (New York: Cambridge University Press, 2000); Michael Punke, *Last Stand: George Bird Grinnell, the Battle to Save the Buffalo, and the Birth of the New West* (Washington, D.C.: Smithsonian Books, 2007); and Philip Shabecoff, *A Fierce Green Fire: The American Environmental Movement* (Washington, D.C.: Island Press, 2003).

The Sonoma Developmental Center

Special thanks to: Karen Litzenberg at the Sonoma Developmental Center, who couldn't have been more helpful, especially in light of the sensitive nature of this topic. *Publications:* Edwin Black, *War Against the Weak: Eugenics and America's Campaign to Create a Master Race* (New York: Four Walls Eight Windows, 2003); Harry Bruinius, *Better for All the World: The Secret History of Forced Sterilization and America's Quest for Racial Purity* (New York: Knopf, 2006); Peter Irons, "Forced Sterilization: A Stain on California," *Los Angeles Times* (February 16, 2003); Wendy Kline, *Building a Better Race: Gender, Sexuality, and Eugenics from the Turn of the Century to the Baby Boom* (Berkeley: University of California Press, 2001); Stefan Kuhl, *The Nazi Connection: Eugenics, American Racism, and German National Socialism* (New York: Oxford University Press, 1994); Mark A. Largent, *Breeding Contempt: The History of Coerced Sterilization in the United States* (New Brunswick, N.J.: Rutgers University

Press, 2008); Paul A. Lombardo, *Three Generations, No Imbeciles* (Baltimore: Johns Hopkins University Press, 2008); Nuremberg-related documents are from the Harvard Law School Library's "Nuremberg Trials Project—A Digital Document Collection," http://nuremberg.law .harvard.edu; Andrea Pitzer, "Terrible Legacy of U.S. Eugenics," *USA Today* (June 24, 2009); Peter Quinn, "Race Cleansing in America," *American Heritage* (February/March 2003); Jonathan Peter Spiro, *Defending the Master Race: Conservation, Eugenics, and the Legacy of Madison Grant* (Burlington: University of Vermont Press, 2009); Alexandra Minna Stern, *Eugenic Nation: Faults and Frontiers of Better Breeding in Modern America* (Berkeley: University of California Press, 2005); Aaron Zitner, "Sterilization in California," *Los Angeles Times* (March 16, 2003); and https://supreme.justia.com, for a full transcript of all the Justices' opinions in *Buck v. Bell.*

Haun's Mill

Special thanks to: Karen Sadler and Benjamin Pykles at the Church of Latter-day Saints. *Publications:* A copy of Governor Christopher "Kit" Bond's statement on June 25, 1976, rescinding Governor Lilburn Boggs's October 1838 Executive Order #44, can be accessed online from the Missouri State Archives (Missouri Mormon War collection) at http://www.sos. mo.gov; Juanita Brooks, *The Mountain Meadows Massacre* (Norman: Oklahoma University Press, 1962); Paul Hodson, *Never Forsake: The Story of Amanda Barnes Smith—Legacy of the Haun's Mill Massacre* (Salt Lake City: Keeban Productions, 1996); Jon Krakauer, *Under the Banner of Heaven: A Story of Violent Faith* (New York: Doubleday, 2003); Stephen C. LeSeuer, *The 1838 Mormon War in Missouri* (Columbia: University of Missouri Press, 1990); and Beth Shumway Moore, *Bones in the Well: The Haun's Mill Massacre, 1838* (Norman, Okla.: Arthur Clark Company, 2006); and Joseph Smith III and Heman C. Smith, *The History of the Reorganized Church of Jesus Christ of Latter Day Saints 1836–1844, Volume 2* (Independence, Missouri: Herald House, 1897).

Union Pacific Mine #6

Special thanks to: Bob Nelson, my trusty guide in Rock Springs. *Publications:* Henry Chadey, *The Chinese Story and Rock Springs, Wyoming* (Green River, Wyo.: Sweetwater County Museum, 1984); Cathy Newman, "Together Forever: Chang and Eng Gave the World 'Siamese Twins'—and Brought a Small Town an Enduring Legacy," *National Geographic* (June 2006); Jean Pfaelzer, *Driven Out: The Forgotten War Against Chinese Americans* (New York: Random House, 2007); Craig Storti, *Incident at Bitter Creek: The Story of the Rock Springs Massacre* (Ames: Iowa State University Press, 1991); Russel L. Tanner and Margie Fletcher Shanks, *Images of America: Rock Springs* (Mount Pleasant, S.C.: Arcadia Publishing, 2008); Amy and Irving Wallace, *The Two: The Story of the Original Siamese Twins* (New York: Simon & Schuster, 1978); and Ralph Zwicky testimony, U.S. House of Representatives, report no. 2044, "Providing Indemnity to Certain Chinese Subjects" (May 1, 1886).

Dowagiac Train Station

Special thanks to: Kay Gray and Mike Shamalla at the Dowagiac District Library; Muriel Anderson and Amanda Wahlmeier at the National Orphan Train Complex; and Vickie Phillipson, who works for the Greater Dowagiac Chamber of Commerce. *Publications:* Mary Bigger, "Alice Bullis Ayler Story," http://www.orphantraindepot.org/AliceAylerStory.html; John Eby, "Orphan Train Mystery Solved?," *Dowagiac Daily News* (March 9, 2007); Marilyn Irvin Holt, *The Orphan Trains: Placing Out in America* (Lincoln: University of Nebraska Press, 1992);

and Stephen O'Connor, *Orphan Trains: The Story of Charles Loring Brace and the Children He Saved and Failed* (Boston: Houghton Mifflin, 2001).

Paris-Cope Service Station

Special thanks to: Tom Eberle, deputy clerk at the Oklahoma Supreme Court; Andy Hollinger and Geoff Megargee at the United States Holocaust Memorial; Debra Spindle at the Oklahoma Historical Society; Patricia Presley and Kathy Stanley at the Oklahoma County Court; and Janice Thompson at the Oklahoma Department of Corrections. *Publications:* Gary Hartman, Roy M. Mersky, and Cindy L. Tate, *Landmark Supreme Court Cases: The Most Influential Decisions of the Supreme Court of the United States* (New York: Checkmark Books, 2007); David Cay Johnston, "William Pierce, 69, Neo-Nazi Leader, Dies," *New York Times* (July 24, 2002); Lou Michel and Dan Herbeck, *American Terrorist: Timothy McVeigh and the Tragedy at Oklahoma City* (New York: HarperCollins, 2001); Victoria F. Nourse, *In Reckless Hands: Skinner v. Oklahoma and the Near Triumph of American Eugenics* (New York: W. W. Norton, 2008); and https://supreme.justia.com, for a full transcript of all the Justices' opinions in *Skinner v. Oklahoma.*

Slip Hill Grade School

All of the U.S. Supreme Court decisions cited in the following chapters can also be found at: https://supreme.justia.com. Special thanks to: Marie Barnett for sharing her story with me; Debra Basham at the West Virginia State Archive; and Midge Justice at the Kanawha County Records Office in West Virginia. *Publications:* American Civil Liberties Union, *The Persecution of Jehovah's Witnesses* (New York, 1941); Richard J. Ellis, *To the Flag: The Unlikely History of the Pledge of Allegiance* (Lawrence: University Press of Kansas, 2005); Kermit L. Hall and John J. Patrick, *The Pursuit of Justice: Supreme Court Decisions That Shaped America* (New York: Oxford University Press, 2006); Peter Irons, *A People's History of the Supreme Court: The Men and Women Whose Cases and Decisions Have Shaped Our Constitution* (New York: Viking Penguin, 1999); Shawn Francis Peters, *Judging Jehovah's Witnesses: Religious Persecution and the Dawn of the Rights Revolution* (Lawrence: University Press of Kansas, 2000); and Robert H. Jackson Center and the Supreme Court Historical Society, "Recollections of West Virginia State Board of Education v. Barnette," *St. John's Law Review* (September 24, 2007).

Saluda County Jail

Special thanks to: Paige Hogge and Karlee Steffey at the Virginia Cooperative Extension for Middlesex County; and Dannielle Traylor, the visitor relations specialist and tour guide at the Rosa Parks Library and Museum. *Publications:* Raymond Arsenault, *Freedom Riders: 1961 and the Struggle for Racial Justice* (New York: Oxford University Press, 2006); Catherine A. Barnes, *Journey from Jim Crow: The Desegregation of Southern Transit* (New York: Columbia University Press, 1983); Jim Carrier, *A Traveler's Guide to the Civil Rights Movement* (New York: Harcourt, 2004); Larry Copeland, "Parks Not Seated Alone in History," *USA Today* (November 38, 2005); Wayne Greenhaw, "Rosa Parks, 'One of Many Who Would Fight for Freedom,'" *Alabama Heritage* (summer 2007); Katharine Greider, "The Schoolteacher on the Streetcar," *New York Times* (November 13, 2005); Kermit L. Hall, ed., *The Oxford Guide to United States Supreme Court Decisions* (New York: Oxford University Press, 1999); Phillip Hoose, *Claudette Colvin: Twice Toward Justice* (New York: Farrar, Straus and Giroux, 2009); Russ Kick, *50 Things You're*

Not Supposed to Know (New York: Disinformation Company, 2003); Yvonne Shinshoster Lamb, "Obituary: Irene M[organ] Kirkaldy; Case Spurred Freedom Ride," *Washington Post* (August 13, 2007); Kimball Payne, "Woman Who Fought Bus Segregation Dies," *Daily Press* (August 12, 2007); Lea Setegn, "Irene Morgan," *Richmond Times-Dispatch* (February 13, 2002); and Jessie Carney Smith, *Black Firsts: 4,000 Ground-Breaking and Pioneering Historical Events* (Detroit: Visible Ink, Second Expedition, revised and expanded, 2003).

James Johnson's Landing Spot (via the Deseret Chemical Depot)

Special thanks to: the Utah National Guard soldiers who, mercifully, did *not* arrest me at the Deseret Chemical Depot after they saw me taking pictures of the facility, which I thought had been shut down; and Ruth Bybee at the Springville police department. *Publications:* Patty Henetz, "Dugway Suit Takes New Twist: Appeals Court Overturns Whistle-Blower Discrimination Judgment," *Salt Lake Tribune* (February 14, 2007); Bernie Rhodes, research by Russell P. Calame, *D.B. Cooper: The Real McCoy* (Salt Lake City: University of Utah Press, 1991); "CRIME: The Real McCoy," *Time* (April 24, 1972); and Robert E. Tomasson, "Jet Out of La Guardia Is Hijacked; Bomb Left in New York Goes Off," *New York Times* (September 11, 1976).

Heights Arts Theatre

Special thanks to: Peter Fletcher, the former chairman of the Michigan State Highway Commission; Ellen Seibert at the Supreme Court of Ohio; and Billy Zavesky at Johnny Malloy's Sports Pub. *Publications:* Henry Alford, "Not a Word," *The New Yorker* (August 29, 2005); Peter Krouse, "Cleveland Heights Theater Recalls 1959 Nico Jacobellis Controversy over 'The Lovers,'" *Cleveland Plain Dealer* (April 23, 2009); W. Ward Marsh, "Adventure in Filth: Full Condemnation for 'The Lovers,'" *Cleveland Plain Dealer* (November 13, 1959); Mark Monmonier, *How to Lie with Maps,* 2nd ed. (Chicago: University of Chicago Press, 1996); Richard Parker, ed., *Free Speech on Trial: Communication Perspectives on Landmark Supreme Court Decisions* (Tuscaloosa: University of Alabama Press, 2003); Jeffrey Rosen, *The Supreme Court: The Personalities and Rivalries That Defined America* (New York: Times Books, 2006); George R. Stewart, *Names on the Land: A Historical Account of Place-Naming in the United States* (New York: New York Review of Books, 1945); Jeffrey Toobin, *The Nine: Inside the Secret World of the Supreme Court* (New York: Doubleday, 2007); Michael G. Trachtman, *The Supremes Greatest Hits: The 34 Supreme Court Cases That Most Directly Affect Your Life* (New York: Sterling Publishing, 2006); and Bob Woodward and Scott Armstrong, *The Brethren: Inside the Supreme Court* (New York: Simon & Schuster, 1979).

Neal Dow's Birthplace, H. H. Hay Drugstore, and Monument Square

Special thanks to: Herb Adams for taking me on a tour of Portland; Bill Barry at the Maine Historical Society; Wesley M. Oliver; and Rob Quatrano at the Neal Dow House. *Publications:* Donald W. Beattie, Rodney M. Cole, and Charles G. Waugh, eds., *A Distant War Comes Home: Maine in the Civil War Era* (Camden, Me.: Down East Books, 1996); Frank L. Byrne, *Prophet of Prohibition: Neal Dow and His Crusade* (Gloucester, Mass.: Peter Smith, 1969); Peter Carlson, "Uneasy About Alcohol," *American History* (December 2008); Henry S. Clubb, *The Maine Liquor: Its Origin, History, and Results, Including a Life of Hon. Neal Dow* (New York: Maine Law Statistical Society, 1856); Betsy Hart, "Those Misunderstood

Puritans," *San Francisco Chronicle* (November 22, 2001); Richard Higgins, "Puritans and Sex: Myths Debunked," *Boston Globe* (April 21, 1987); Maine Writers' Project, *Portland City Guide (American Guide Series) Compiled by Workers of the Writer's Program of the Works Projects Administration in the State of Maine* (Portland, Me.: The Forest City Printing Company, 1940); Wesley M. Oliver, "Portland, Prohibition, and Probable Cause: Maine's Role in Shaping Modern Criminal Procedure," *Maine Bar Journal, The Quarterly Publication of the Maine State Bar Association*; (vol. 23, no.4, fall 2008); Thomas R. Pegram, *Battling Demon Rum: The Struggle for a Dry America, 1800–1933* (Chicago: Ivan R. Dee, 1998); Charles Phillips, "A Day to Remember," *American History* (February 2005); Neal Rolde, *Maine: A Narrative History* (Gardiner, Me.: Harpswell Press, 1990); W. J. Rorabaugh, *The Alcoholic Republic: An American Tradition* (New York: Oxford University Press, 1979); Richard Shenkman and Kurt Reiger, *One-Night Stands with American History: Odd, Amusing, and Little-Known Incidents* (New York: Morrow, 1980); and Roger Thompson, *Sex in Middlesex: Popular Mores in a Massachusetts County 1649–1699* (Boston: University of Massachusetts Press, 1986).

Caledonia Correctional Institution

Special thanks to: Joseph B. Cutchins Jr., who provided me with the location of where Jack Johnson died; Superintendent Grady Massey at Caledonia, who graciously approved my visit to the prison, and Daryl Williams for giving me a tour; James Zobel at the MacArthur Memorial. *Publications:* Ross E. Beard Jr., *Carbine: The Story of David Marshall Williams* (Lexington, S.C.: Sandlapper Store, 1977); Alfred W. Cooke, *Caledonia: From Antebellum Plantation 1713–1892 to State Prison and Farm 1892–1988* (Raleigh, N.C.: Sparks Press, 1988); Jack Johnson, *The Autobiography of Jack Johnson—In the Ring and Out* (New York: Carol Publishing Group, 1992); Tracy Thompson, "Prison Inventor Wins Recognition; Court Rules Process in Helmet-Making Is His," *Washington Post* (November 24, 1991); and Geoffrey C. Ward, *Unforgivable Blackness: The Rise and Fall of Jack Johnson* (New York: Knopf, 2004).

Elisha Otis's Birthplace

Special thanks to: Jackie Calder and Paul Carnahan at the Vermont Historical Society; Ruth Ann Nyblod in the office of public affairs at the United States Patent and Trademark Office, who provided me with specific history about the office (there's also a wealth of information on the department's website: www.uspto.gov); Stephen Showers at the Otis Elevator Company, who provided me with dozens of press releases and two informative booklets published by the corporation; and, most of all, my wonderful "team" in Halifax: Connie Lancaster, Douglas Parkhurst, Bernice Barnett for Sally Pratt, Stephen Sanders, and Laura Sumner. *Publications: The First One Hundred Years* (New York: Otis Elevator Company, 1953); Arrol Gellner, "Laying the Foundation for Today's Skyscrapers," *San Francisco Chronicle* (August 23, 2008); Jason Goodwin, *Otis: Giving Rise to the Modern City* (Chicago: Ivan R. Dee, 2001); Charles Otis, *E. G. Otis: Inventor, Originator of Otis Safety Elevator Business 1811–1861* (New York: Otis Elevator Company, 1911); and Nick Paumgarten, "Up and Then Down: The Lives of Elevators," *The New Yorker* (April 28, 2008).

William Morrison's Laboratory

Special thanks to: my incredible guide Bill Jepsen; and Michael Smith and Bill Johnson at the State Historical Society of Iowa. *Publications:* Thomas Ayers, *That's Not in My American History Book: A Compilation of Little-Known Events and Forgotten Heroes* (Dallas: Taylor Publishing Company, 2000); Neil Baldwin, *Edison: Inventing the Century* (New York: Hyperion,

1995); Ruth S. Beitz, "Whirlwind on Wheels," *Iowan* (summer 1963); Margaret Cheney, *Tesla: Man Out of Time* (New York: Simon & Schuster, 2001); Jonathan Glancey, *The Car: A History of the Automobile* (London: Carlton Books, 2008); Sungook Hong, *Wireless: From Marconi's Black-Box to the Audio* (Cambridge, Mass.: MIT Press, 2001); Tom Longden, "Famous Iowans: William Morrison," *Des Moines Register* (February 7, 2009); Keith McClellan, "The Morrison Electric: Iowa's First Automobile," Annals of Iowa (vol. XXXVI, no. 8, spring 1963); Clifford Pickover, *Strange Brains and Genius: The Secret Lives of Eccentric Scientists and Madmen* (New York: Harper Perennial, 1999); Ronald A. Stringer, "The Morrison Electric: America's First Automobile!?!," *Antique Automobile* (January/February 1984?); and Steven Watts, *The People's Tycoon: Henry Ford and the American Century* (New York: Random House, 2006).

The Farnsworth Farm

Special thanks to: Mike Miller, who went out of his way to find the old Farnsworth property. *Publications:* R. W. Burns, *Television: An International Story of the Formative Years* (London: Institution of Electrical Engineers in association with the Science Museum, 1998); George Everson, *The Story of Television, The Life of Philo T. Farnsworth* (New York: W. W. Norton & Co, 1949); Elma G. Farnsworth, *Distant Vision: Romance and Discovery on an Invisible Frontier* (Salt Lake City: Pemberly Kent Publishers, 1989); Donald G. Godfrey, *Philo T. Farnsworth: The Father of Television* (Salt Lake City: University of Utah Press, 2001); Andrew F. Inglis, *Behind the Tube: A History of Broadcasting Technology and Business* (London: Focal Press, 1990); Evan I. Schwartz, *The Last Lone Inventor: A Tale of Genius, Deceit, and the Birth of Television* (New York: Harper Perennial, 2002); and Daniel Stashower, *The Boy Genius and the Mogul: The Untold Story of Television* (New York: Broadway Books, 2002).

Robert Goddard's Backyard

Special thanks to: Barbara Berka, who showed me Goddard's boyhood home in Massachusetts and generously gave me the bulk of information about Goddard; and Guy Webster at NASA, who provided me with details about the *Voyager* records. *Publications:* Robert H. Goddard, *The Autobiography of Robert Hutchings Goddard* (Worcester, Mass.: Achille J. St. Onge, 1966); Milton Lehman, *This High Man: The Life of Robert H. Goddard* (New York: Farrar, Straus and Company, 1963); Jim Mann, "The Story of a Tragedy That Was Not to Be," *Los Angeles Times* (July 7, 1999); Michael J. Neufeld, *Von Braun: Dreamer of Space, Engineer of War* (New York: Knopf/Smithsonian National Air and Space Museum, 2007); Jeanne Nuss, "Goddard Foresaw Apollo 11: Father of American Rocketry Made Space Program Possible," Associated Press (July 19, 2009); Carl Sagan, *Murmurs of Earth: The Voyager Interstellar Record* (New York: Random House, 1997); A. Bowdoin Van Riper, *Rockets and Missiles: The Life Story of a Technology* (Baltimore: Johns Hopkins University Press, 2007); and Andrew Walker, "Project Paperclip: Dark Side of the Moon," BBC News (November 21, 2005).

Hartford Union Hall

Special thanks to: Jack Eckert at Harvard University's Center for the History of Medicine; and Cynthia Harbeson and Diana McCain at the Connecticut State Historical Society. *Publications:* W. Harry Archer, B.S., D.D.S., "Life and Letters of Horace Wells, Discoverer of Anesthesia," *Journal of the American College of Dentists* (vol. 11, no. 2, June 1944); Henry K. Beecher and Charlotte Ford, "Some New Letters of Horace Wells Concerning an Historic Partnership," *Journal of the History of Medicine and Allied Sciences* (vol. IX, no. 1, 1954); John Carey, *Eyewitness to History* (New York: Avon Books, 1987); Julie M. Fenster,

Ether Day: The Strange Tale of America's Greatest Medical Discovery and the Haunted Men Who Made It (New York: HarperCollins, 2001); "Dr. Horace Wells Discovered Anesthesia, Not Morton," *Hartford Daily Courant* (November 28, 1920); "Dispelling the Curse of Cain: Hartford Dentist Frees Mankind from Age-Old Torture by Discovery of Anaesthesia," *Hartford Courant* (December 7, 1924); M. A. DeWolfe Howe, *Memories of a Hostess: A Chronicle of Eminent Friendships Drawn Chiefly from the Diaries of Mrs. James T. Fields* (Boston: Atlantic Monthly Press, 1922); Peter H. Jacobson, "Horace Wells: Discoverer of Anesthesia," *Anesth Prog,* published by the American Dental Society of Anesthesiology (issue 42, 1995); Craig Lambert, "An Aristocrat's Killing," *Harvard Magazine* (July/August 2003); James McManus, *Notes on the History of Anaesthesia* (Hartford: Clark & Smith, 1896); Max E. Soifer, "Discoverers (?) of Anesthesia: The Claimants," *Journal of the American Dental Association* (September 1942); Max E. Soifer, "Dr. Horace Wells the Discoverer of Anesthesia,'" *Dental Items of Interest* (December 1939); Max E. Soifer, "Horace Wells 'Rediscovered,'" *Dental Items of Interest* (November 1941); and Helen Thomson, *Murder at Harvard* (Boston: Houghton Mifflin, 1971).

Minnesota Riverbank

Special thanks to: Bill Lass in Mankato, who took me to the site; and Anne Stenzel at the Minnesota State University, Mankato Memorial Library. *Publications:* Gary Clayton Anderson and Alan R. Woolworth, eds., *Narrative Accounts of the Minnesota Indian War of 1862* (St. Paul: Minnesota Historical Society Press, 1988); Randy Dotinga, "Med Schools Cut Out Cadavers," *Wired* (March 19, 2003); Linden F. Edwards, "Body Snatching in Ohio During the Nineteenth Century," *Ohio History: The Scholarly Journal of the Ohio Historical Society* (vol. 59); Robert Elder, "Execution of Dakota Indian Nearly 150 Years Ago Spurs Calls for Pardon," *New York Times* (December 14, 2010); Judith Hartzell, *I Started All This: The Life of Dr. William Worrall Mayo* (Greenville, S.C.: Arvi Books, 2004); Jerry Keenan, *The Great Sioux Uprising: Rebellion on the Plains, August-September 1862* (Cambridge, Mass.: Da Capo Press, 2003); Norman M. Keith and Thomas E. Keys, "The Anatomy Acts of 1831 and 1832: A Solution of a Medical Social Problem," *AMA Archives of Internal Medicine* (vol. 99, May 1957); C. Brian Kelly, *Best Little Ironies, Oddities and Mysteries of the Civil War* (Nashville: Cumberland House Publishing, 2000); Jules Calvin Ladenheim, "The Doctors' Mob of 1788," *Journal of the History of Medicine* (winter 1950); Charles Donald O'Malley, *Andreas Vesalius of Brussels, 1514–1564* (Berkeley: University of California Press, 1964); Lisa Rosner, *The Anatomy Murders: Being the True and Spectacular History of Edinburgh's Notorious Burke and Hare and of the Man of Science Who Abetted Them in the Commission of Their Most Heinous Crimes* (Philadelphia: University of Pennsylvania Press, 2009); Duane Schultz, *Over the Earth I Come: The Great Sioux Uprising of 1862* (New York: Thomas Dunne Books, 1992); Suzanne M. Shultz, *Body Snatching: The Robbing of Graves for the Education of Physicians in Early Nineteenth Century America* (Jefferson, N.C.: McFarland, 1992); Aaron D. Tward and Hugh A. Patterson, "From Grave Robbing to Gifting: Cadaver Supply in the United States," *Journal of the American Medical Association* (March 6, 2002); John C. Warren, *Boston Medical and Surgical Journal,* published by the Massachusetts Medical Society (vol. 103); and D. T. Wheeler, "Creating a Body of Knowledge," *Chronicle of Higher Education* (February 2, 1996).

Rankin Farm

Special thanks to: Russell Archer and William L. Thompson, who work in the Historic Preservation Division of the Mississippi Department of Archives and History. *Publications:* Ethan Blue, "The Strange Career of Leo Stanley: Remaking Manhood and Medicine at San Quentin State Penitentiary, 1913–1951," *Pacific Historical Review* (vol. 78, no. 2, 2009); Alfred Jay Bollet, "Politics and Pellgra: The Epidemic of Pellagra in the U.S. in the Early Twentieth Century," *Yale Journal of Biology and Medicine* (issue 65, 1992); Joann G. Elmore and Alvan R. Feinstein, "Joseph Goldberger: An Unsung Hero of American Clinical Epidemiology," *History of Medicine,* published by the American College of Physicians (vol. 121, no. 5, September 1994); Allen M. Hornblum, *Acres of Skin: Human Experiments at Holmesburg Prison* (New York: Routledge, 1998); Allen M. Hornblum, "They Were Cheap and Available: Prisoners as Research Subjects in Twentieth Century America," *BMJ,* published by the British Medical Association (November 29, 1997); Zereena Hussain, "MIT to Pay Victims $1.85 Million in Fernald Radiation Settlement," *The Tech,* published by the Massachusetts Institute of Technology (January 7, 1998); Gina Kolata, "Vanderbilt Sued on Radiation," *New York Times* (February 2, 1994); Alan M. Kraut, *Goldberger's War: The Life and Work of a Public Health Crusader* (New York: Hill and Wang, 2003); Susan E. Lederer, *Subjected to Science: Human Experimentation in America Before the Second World War* (Baltimore: Johns Hopkins University Press, 1995); Barron H. Lerner, "Subjects or Objects? Prisoners and Human Experimentation," *New England Journal of Medicine* (May 3, 2007); Jonathan D. Moreno, *Undue Risk: Secret State Experiments on Humans* (New York: Routledge, 2001); Leo L. Stanley with the collaboration of Evelyn Wells, *Men at Their Worst* (New York: D. Appleton-Century Company, 1940); Eileen Welsome, *The Plutonium Files: America's Secret Medical Experiments in the Cold War* (New York: Delta, 1999); and Tom Zoellner, *Uranium: War, Energy, and the Rock That Shaped the World* (New York: Viking Penguin, 2009).

USDA National Center for Agricultural Utilization Research

Special thanks to: Patrick Dowd, Cletus Kurtzman, Katherine O'Hara, and Jackie Shepherd at the USDA National Center; Bob Killion at the Peoria Historical Society; and Sherri Schneider and Karen Deller in the Special Collections Center of Bradley University's Cullom-Davis Library. *Publications:* Alexander Fleming Laboratory Museum, "The Discovery and Development of Penicillin 1928–1945" (November 19, 1999); C. Verne Bloch, "'Moldy Mary' Gave Penicillin a Boost," *Peoria Journal Star* (May 8, 1962); Kevin Brown, *Penicillin Man: Alexander Fleming and the Antibiotic Revolution* (Stroud, U.K.: Sutton Publishing, 2004); Robert D. Coghill, "Penicillin: Science's Cinderella," *Chemical and Engineering News,* published by the American Chemical Society (vol. 22, no. 8, April 25, 1944); Gail Compton, "Spoiled Melon Fruitful Field for Penicillin: Good Mold Producer for Wonder Drug," *Chicago Daily Tribune* (May 7, 1944); Eric Lax, *The Mold in Dr. Florey's Coat: The Story of the Penicillin Miracle* (New York: Henry Holt and Company, 2004); Frank H. Stodola, "Penicillin: Breakthrough to the Era of Antibiotics," *USDA Yearbook of Agriculture* (1968); Stevenson Swanson, "How Peoria-Produced Penicillin Helped Win WWII," *Peoria Journal Star* (April 23, 1995); U.S. Department of Agriculture, Agricultural Research Service, "Always Something New: A Cavalcade of Scientific Discovery" (Miscellaneous Publication Number 1507, November 1993); U.S. Department of Agriculture, Science and Education Administration, "Chronology Contrasts Penicillin Research with War Needs," *Research News* (August 11, 1980); and Robert Weidrich, "Beer Size Vats Put Penicillin in Reach of All: It's American Story of Free Science," *Chicago Daily Tribune* (September 25, 1952).

Dr. Maurice Hilleman's Birthplace

Special thanks to: Art and Nancy Larson for kindly showing me around Miles City; Jeryl and Lorraine Hilleman, for sharing Dr. Hilleman's story and autobiography with me; and

Mayor Joe Whalen. *Publications:* Lawrence K. Altman, "Obituary: Maurice Hilleman, Vaccine Creator," *New York Times* (April 13, 2005); John E. Calfee, "Medicine's Miracle Man: Maurice Hilleman's Remarkable Period of Industrial Scientific Research Yielded the Most Cost-Effective Medicines Ever Made," *The American, the Journal of the American Enterprise Institute* (January 23, 2009); Huntly Collins, "The Man Who Saved Your Life—Maurice R. Hilleman," *Philadelphia Enquirer* (August 30, 1999); "Maurice Hilleman, Pioneer of Preventive Medicine, Died on April 11th, Aged 85," *The Economist* (April 21, 2005); Thomas H. Maugh II, "Maurice R. Hilleman, 85; Scientist Developed Many Vaccines That Saved Millions of Lives," *Los Angeles Times* (April 13, 2005); Paul A. Offit, MD, *Vaccinated: One Man's Quest to Defeat the World's Deadliest Diseases* (New York: HarperCollins, 2007); Christopher Reed, "Maurice Hilleman: Medical Scientist Whose Vaccines Saved Millions of Lives," *The Guardian* (April 15, 2005); Caroline Richmond, "Maurice Hilleman: Inventor of More Than 40 Vaccines," *The Independent* (April 20, 2005); Patricia Sullivan, "Maurice R. Hilleman Dies; Created Vaccines," *Washington Post* (April 13, 2005); and "Maurice Hilleman: Trail-Blazing Biologist Whose Vaccines Saved Millions from Death—and Tens of Millions from Disease" *The Times* (April 19, 2005).

Dr. Loring Miner's House

Special thanks to: Helen Hall and Jamie Wright at the Haskell Township Library for all their assistance; William McKale, director of the 1st Infantry Division Museum at Fort Riley; and Paul and Bill Miner, who kindly shared stories about their father with me. *Publications:* John M. Barry, *The Great Influenza: The Story of the Deadliest Pandemic in History* (New York: Viking Penguin, 2004); William E. Connelley, *A Standard History of Kansas and Kansans* (Chicago: Lewis Publishing Co., 1919); Ceci Connolly, "A Grisly but Essential Issue: Pandemic Plan Skims Over How to Deal with Many Corpses," *Washington Post* (June 9, 2006); Alfred W. Crosby, *America's Forgotten Pandemic: The Influenza of 1918, New Edition,* 2nd ed. (New York: Cambridge University Press, 2003); Jack Fincher, "America's Deadly Rendezvous with the 'Spanish Lady,'" *Smithsonian* (January 1989); John F. Kelly, "1918, Washington's Season of Death," *Washington Post* (January 22, 2004); Christine M. Kreiser, "Influenza 1918: The Enemy Within," *American History* (December 2006); Naval Historical Center, "A Winding Sheet and a Wooden Box," *Navy Medicine* (vol. 77, no. 3, May/June 1986); Alice Park, "A Flu Strain Goes Kerflooey," *Time* (March 23, 2009); PBS, "Influenza 1918," *American Experience* (transcript); Gustav Person, "The Flu Strikes Belvoir: Camp A.A. Humphreys and the Spanish Influenza Pandemic of 1918," *On Point,* published by the Army Historical Foundation (fall 2008); Steve Sternberg, "What a Pandemic Taught Us," *USA Today* (April 22, 2010); and U.S. Department of Health and Human Services, "The Great Pandemic: The United States in 1918–1919," http://1918.pandemicflu.gov/your_state/kansas.htm.

Brevig Mission

Special thanks to: Pastor Brian Crockett; Lisa Fallgren, my fellow passenger between Brevig Mission and Nome; Laura Samuelson, director of the Carrie M. McClain Memorial Museum, which is where I found the Levi Ashton letter; and Dr. Jeffery Taubenberger. *Publications:* T. A. Badger, "Nome-Area Residents Recall Deadly 1918 Flu Epidemic," *Northland News* (May 1993); David Brown, "On the Trail of the 1918 Influenza Epidemic," *Washington Post* (February 27, 2001); R. S. Henry, *The Armed Forces Institute of Pathology—Its First Century 1862–1962* (Washington, D.C.: Office of the Surgeon General, Department of the Army, 1964); Christopher C. Kelly, "Breaking the Genetic Code; AFIP's Taubenberger Unlocks Mystery to 1918 Spanish Flu: Findings Play Major Role in H5N1 Pandemic Preparations," *AFIP Newslet-*

ter (vol. 163, no. 3, fall 2005); Gina Kolata, *Flu: The Story of the Great Influenza Pandemic of 1918 and the Search for the Virus That Caused It* (New York: Touchstone, 1999; reissued, 2005); Elizabeth Pennisi, "First Genes Isolated from the Deadly 1918 Flu Virus," *Science* (vol. 275, March 21, 1997); and Ned Rozell, "Permafrost Preserves Clues to Deadly 1918 Flu," *Alaska Science Forum* (article #1386, April 29, 1998).

Henry Laurens's Grave

Special thanks to: Thomas Ashe Lockhart for taking me to Mepkin Abbey to see Henry Laurens's grave; and Clay Kilgore and Janet Wareham at the Washington County PA Historical Society. *Publications:* Brown University, "Slavery and Justice: Report of the Brown University Steering Committee on Slavery and Justice" (February 2007); John Duffy, *The Sanitarians: A History of American Public Health* (Urbana: University of Chicago Press, 1992); Margaret C. McCullough, *Fearless Advocate of the Right: The Life of Francis Julius LeMoyne, M.D., 1798–1879* (Boston: Christopher Publishing House, 1941); "Baron De Palm's Request. His Remains to Be Cremated on Wednesday," *New York Times* (December 4, 1876); "Another Body to Be Cremated: The Remains of Samuel D. Gross to Be Reduced to Ashes," *New York Times* (May 8, 1884); Stephen Prothero, *Purified by Fire: A History of Cremation in America* (Berkeley: University of California Press, 2001); David Ramsay, ed., *Memoirs of Martha Laurens Ramsay, Who Died in Charleston, S.C., on the 10th of June, 1811, in the 52d Year of Her Age with Extracts from Her Diary, Letters, and Other Private Papers* (Philadelphia: American Sunday-School Union, 1923); Fred Rosen, *Cremation in America* (Amherst, N.Y.: Prometheus Books, 2004); Lori Stiles, "Eugene Shoemaker Ashes Carried on Lunar Prospector," *University of Arizona News Services* (January 6, 1998); Ethan Trex, "10 Bizarre Places for Cremation Ashes," *Mental Floss* (August 2, 2010); and David Duncan Wallace, *The Life of Henry Laurens* (New York: G. P. Putnam's Sons, 1915).

Daniel Boone's Grave

Special thanks to: Steven Caudill, who took me to Boone's gravesite in Frankfort, Kentucky, and shared with me a wealth of information about Boone's life. *Publications:* Nancy Disher Baird, *Luke Pryor Blackburn: Physician, Governor, Reformer* (Lexington: University Press of Kentucky, 1979); Dan Barry, "Restoring Dignity to Sitting Bull, Wherever He Is," *New York Times* (January 28, 2007); Leo A. Bressler, "Peter Porcupine and the Bones of Thomas Paine," *Pennsylvania Magazine of History and Biography* (vol. 82, no. 2, April 1858); Meredith Mason Brown, *Frontiersman: Daniel Boone and the Making of America* (Baton Rouge: Louisiana State University Press, 2008); CBS News, "Jesse James Grave Mix-up: Misplaced Headstone Shifted over the Years" (transcript, June 30, 2000); David W. Chen, "Rehabilitating Thomas Paine, Bit by Bony Bit," *New York Times* (March 30, 2001); Paul Collins, *The Trouble with Tom: The Strange Afterlife and Times of Thomas Paine* (London: Bloomsbury, 2006); Lyman C. Draper, Ted Franklin Belue, ed., *The Life of Daniel Boone* (Mechanigsburg, Pa.: Stackpole Books, 1998); John Mack Faragher, *Daniel Boone: The Life and Legend of an American Hero* (New York: Henry Holt and Company, 1992); Harvey J. Kaye, *Thomas Paine and the Promise of America* (New York: Hill and Wang, 2005); Robert Morgan, *Boone: A Biography* (Chapel Hill: Algonquin Books, 2007); Edwin W. Murphy, *After the Funeral: The Posthumous Adventures of Famous Corpses* (New York: Citadel Press, 1995); "The Paine Monument at Last Finds a Home," *New York Times* (October 15, 1905); Paul W. Prindle, "The 1752 Calendar Change," *American Genealogist* (October 1964); George B. Wilson, "Genealogy and the Calendar," *Maryland Magazine of Genealogy* (fall 1978); and Henry C. Young, "The Gregorian Calendar and Its Effect on Genealogical Research," *Niagra Frontier Genealogical Society Magazine* (June 1944).

Thomas "Pete" Ray's Grave

Special thanks to: Erin Duck and Cass Shirley at the Forest Hill Cemetery and, most of all, to Janet Ray, who shared with me her memories of her father and his military service. *Publications:* John Arnold, "Young Bay of Pigs Pilot Returns to Long-Delayed Funeral," *Miami Herald* (December 6, 1979); Andrew Carroll, editor, Dwight D. Eisenhower letter excerpt from *War Letters: Extraordinary Correspondence from American Wars* (New York: Scribner, 2001); Edward B. Ferrer, *Operation Puma: The Air Battle of the Bay of Pigs* (Miami: International Aviation Consultations, Inc., Spanish ed., 1975; English ed., 1982); Howard Jones, *The Bay of Pigs* (New York: Oxford University Press, 2008); Peter Kornblush, ed., *Bay of Pigs Declassified: The Secret CIA Report on the Invasion of Cuba* (New York: New Press, 1998); Alejandro de Quesada, *The Bay of Pigs: Cuba 1961* (New York: Osprey Publishing, 2009); Warren Trest and Donald Dodd, *Wings of Denial: The Alabama Air National Guard's Role at the Bay of Pigs* (Montgomery, Ala.: NewSouth Books, 2001); and David Wise and Thomas B. Ross, "The Strange Case of the CIA Widows," *Look* (June 30, 1964).

Hart Island

Special thanks to: Beverly Fields in the Washington, D.C., Office of the Chief Medical Examiner; Michael J. Desmond, a family service counselor at Cypress Hills Cemetery in Brooklyn, New York, who took me on a tour of the cemetery, which I had originally visited to find the forgotten grave of Thomas Holmes (in 1861, Holmes popularized embalming in America); and Melinda Hunt, who is the author, with Joel Sternfeld, of the book *Hart Island* (Zurich, Berlin, New York: Scalo, 1998) and could not have been more generous with her time in taking me out to the island and educating me about its history. *Publications:* Percy H. Epler, *The Life of Clara Barton* (New York: Macmillan, 1915); Stephen B. Oates, *A Woman of Valor: Clara Barton and the Civil War* (New York: Free Press, 1994); and John F. Walter, *The Confederate Dead in Brooklyn* (Bowie, Md.: Heritage Books, 2003).

Leary's Book Store

Special thanks to: Lee Arnold at the Historical Society of Pennsylvania, who located where Leary's had once been and provided me with an abundance of information about other Philadelphia landmarks; Carole Herrick, who helped me find where Stephen Pleasonton hid the Declaration of Independence and other valuable documents near the Chain Bridge in Washington, D.C; Miriam Kleiman, the public affairs specialist at the U.S. National Archives; and Courtenay Singer, manager of the Global Health Initiative at the USC Annenberg Norman Lear Center. *Publications:* Eleanor Blau, "Declaration of Independence Sells for $2.4 Million," *New York Times* (June 14, 1991); Julian P. Boyd, "The Declaration of Independence: The Mystery of the Lost Original," *Pennsylvania Magazine of History and Biography* (October 1976); Julian P. Boyd and Gerard W. Gawalt, eds., *The Declaration of Independence: The Evolution of the Text,* rev. ed. (Lebanon, N.H.: University Press of New England, 1999); Marc Eepson, *Saving Monticello: The Levy Family's Epic Quest to Rescue the House That Jefferson Built* (New York: Free Press, 2001); Dorothy S. Gelatt, "$8.14 Million Dunlap Declaration Has Checkered Past," *Maine Antique Digest* (August 2000); George W. Givens, *500 Little-Known Facts in U.S. History: The More We Know About the Past, the Better We Understand the Present* (Springville, Ut.: Bonneville Books, 2006); Frederick R. Goff, *The John Dunlap Broadside: The First Printing of the Declaration of Independence* (Washington, D.C.: Library of Congress, 1976); Milton Gustafson, "Travels of the Charters of Freedom," *Prologue Magazine* (vol. 34, no. 4, winter 2002); Richard Luscombe and Daniel Nasaw, "Houston, We Have a Problem: Original Moon Walk Footage Erased," *The Guardian* (July 16, 2009); Pauline Maier, *American Scripture Making the Declaration of Independence* (New York: Knopf, 1997); John McPhee, "Travels of the Rock," *The New Yorker* (February 26, 1990); Milestone Documents in the National Archives, *The Declaration of Independence* (Washington, D.C.: National Archives and Records Administration, 1776); National Archives and Records Administration, "The Declaration of Independence: A History," http://www.archives.gov/exhibits/charters/declaration_history.html (December 4, 2010); Wilfred J. Ritz, "From the *Here* of Jefferson's Handwritten Rough Draft of the Declaration of Independence to the *There* of the Printed Dunlap Broadside," *Pennsylvania Magazine of History and Biography* (October 1992); Russell Frank Weigley et. al., *Philadelphia: A 300-Year History* (New York: W. W. Norton & Company, 1982); Linda Wheeler, "Founding Documents Will Get New Cases," *Washington Post* (March 18, 1999); and Ted Widmer, "Looking for Liberty," *New York Times* (July 4, 2008).

The Menger Hotel and
Adina De Zavala's Residence

Special thanks to: Paul Carter, who helped me find where De Zavala once lived; Ernesto Malacara for guiding me around the Menger Hotel; Carol Roark in the special collections department of the Dallas Public Library; Margaret Schlankey at the Dolph Briscoe Center for American History (University of Texas at Austin); Ryan Schumacher at the Texas State Historical Association; and Richard Bruce Winders at the Alamo. *Publications:* Elaine Ayala, "Preservationist Adina De Zavala Getting Her Due as Historical Figure," *San Antonio Express-News* (November 28, 2006); Paul Bourgeois, "Dallas Library Displays Rare National Document," *Dallas Star-Telegram* (July 6, 2001); Van Craddock, "Texans Didn't Like Santa Anna, by Gum," *Longview News-Journal* (June 20, 2010); Ann Fears Crawford and Crystal Sasse Ragsdale, *Women in Texas: Their Lives, Their Experiences, Their Accomplishments* (Austin: State House Press, 1992); James E. Crisp, *Sleuthing the Alamo* (New York: Oxford University Press, 2005); Ruth Eyre, "City to Get Declaration of Independence Copy," *Dallas Times Herald* (July 2, 1978); Lewis F. Fisher, *Saving San Antonio: The Precarious Preservation of a Heritage* (Lubbock: Texas Tech University Press, 1996); Will Fowler, *Santa Anna of Mexico* (Lincoln: University of Nebraska Press, 2007); Kim Horner, "The Pursuit of History: Dallas Boasts Display of Rare Declaration Copy," *Dallas Morning News* (July 4, 2000); Frank W. Jennings with Rosemary Williams, "Adina De Zavala: Alamo Crusader," *Texas Highways Magazine* (March 1995); Randy Roberts and James S. Olson, *A Line in the Sand: The Alamo in Blood and Memory* (New York: Free Press, 2001); "San Jacinto Battleground State Historic Site," Texas Parks & Wildlife (www.tpwd.state.tx.us); Timothy J. Todish, Terry Todish, and Ted Spring, *Alamo Sourcebook, 1836: A Comprehensive Guide to the Battle of the Alamo and the Texas Revolution* (Austin: Eakin Press, 1998); Docia Schultz Williams, *The History and Mystery of the Menger Hotel with Special Recollections of Ernesto Malacara* (Dallas: Republic of Texas Press, 2000); and Dorman H. Winfrey, Texas Historical Association, "The Texan Archive War of 1842," *Southwestern Historical Quarterly* (October 1960).

Mount Baker

Special thanks to: Ed Hrivnak and Mike Vrosh for spending an entire weekend with me in order to hike up Mount Baker and show me the PV-1 crash site; and Tom Philo, a military historian who helped me determine the number of service members who died in the States during World War II. *Publications:* James Barron, "Flaming Horror on the 79th Floor; 50 Years Ago Today, in the Fog, a Plane Hit the World's Tallest Building," *New York Times* (July 28, 1995); Bureau of Naval Personnel and US Marine Corps Headquarters, "US Navy

Personnel in World War II: Service and Casualty Statistics," *Annual Report, Navy and Marine Corps Military Personnel Statistics* (June 30, 1964); Jonathan Goldman, *The Empire State Book* (New York: St. Martin's Press, 1980); Anthony J. Mireles, *Fatal Army Air Forces Aviation Accidents in the United States 1941–1945* (Jefferson, N.C.: McFarland & Company, 2010); TSgt. Linda L. Mitchell, "McChord Personnel Recover Navy Anti-Submarine Aircraft Wreckage," *Northwest Airlifter* (October 14, 1994); Leo Mullen, "World War II Tragedy on Mount Baker: Lost Crew Returns from Clouds," *Bellingham Herald* (September 3, 1995); and United States Forest Service, "A Brief History of Mt. Baker," http://www.fs.usda.gov/main/mbs/home.

Home

Special thanks to: Megan Smolenyak Smolenyak and her sister Stacy Neuberger, my two wonderful guides in Washington, D.C. (and much of the information I acquired about Philip Reed—also spelled Reid—came from an early draft of Megan's sensational book, *Hey, America, Your Roots Are Showing: Adventures in Discovering News—Making Connections—Unexpected Ancestors—Long-Hidden Secrets—and Solving Historical Puzzles*); Gene and Patricia Godley, who first told me the story behind the Statue of Freedom; my neighbor Joe Rogers; Mark Indre and Kathleen Matthews at Marriott; Kenneth Despertt, a librarian in the "Washingtoniana" department of the Martin Luther King Jr. Memorial Library; and Cecelia Logan and Ayeta Heatley at National Harmony National Park. *Publications:* Taylor Branch, *The Clinton Tapes: Wrestling History with the President* (New York: Simon & Schuster, 2009); Jon Elliston, "Spy Like Us?: Felix Bloch, One of the Great Unsolved Mysteries of Cold War Espionage, Is Back in the Headlines—and Still Driving a Bus in Chapel Hill," *Indy Week* (March 7, 2001); Sam Roberts, "First Through Gates of Ellis I., She Was Lost. Now She's Found," *New York Times* (September 14, 2006); Rachel L. Swarns and Jodi Kantor, "First Lady's Roots Reveal Slavery's Tangled Legacy," *New York Times* (October 8, 2009); Dr. Eugene Walton, "Philip Reid: Slave Caster of Freedom," *The Examiner* (March 1, 2005); and David Wise, "The Felix Bloch Affair," *New York Times Magazine* (May 13, 1990).

Along with the stories profiled in this book, there are several others that, for one reason or another, could not be included. But I'm extremely grateful to the people who shared them with me either during or after my main cross-country journey, and they deserve recognition:

Sandra Cano, who was the "Mary Doe" in the influential—but overlooked—January 1973 U.S. Supreme Court case *Doe v. Bolton*. This decision was announced the same day as *Roe v. Wade* and was, in fact, pivotal in changing abortion laws throughout the country. Sandra has mostly stayed out of the media spotlight and was incredibly generous with her time in telling me the behind-the-scenes account of her case, which I think could be a book in itself.

Martin Cooper, "the father of the mobile phone." Somewhere

around Sixth Avenue and Fifty-fourth Street in Manhattan on April 4, 1973, Marty (he said it was okay for me to call him that) made the first public cell phone call in history. Marty was general manager of Motorola at the time and just about to go into a press conference at the Hilton to herald this new invention. Mischievously, he phoned his competitor, Joel Engel, who was head of research at Bell Labs. I asked Marty if he made a play on Alexander Graham Bell's "Watson, come here, I want to see you" line, but he said no; he just called Engel and casually said something like, " 'Hey, it's Marty, and I'm calling you from a cell phone.' He knew what that meant and got real quiet." Marty also sent me a map of Sixth and Fifty-fourth and pinpointed with an *x* exactly where he was standing when he made his famous call. He added a second *x* and a note right in the middle of Sixth Avenue to indicate where, distracted while simultaneously walking and talking on the phone, he almost stepped in front of a car and had history's "first cell phone accident." Marty also told me, "If you look at when the telephone was invented, it was around the time Nikola Tesla was experimenting with radio waves, so there's no reason mobile phones couldn't have come first. We could have skipped landlines entirely." At the end of our conversation, Marty mentioned one more thing: "I recently saw a performance of *The Farnsworth Invention* about Philo Farnsworth. I don't know where you could see it, but maybe you could get a copy of the script somewhere." This offhand comment is what led me to Philo Farnsworth's farm in Rigby, Idaho. (Along with Marty, I'd also like to thank his executive assistant Jaye Riggio for all of his help, as well as Adrian Acosta and Donald Trump Jr., who I accidentally bumped into at the Trump Tower in New York, and who pointed me in the direction of Sixth and Fifty-fourth.)

Diane Cremeens at the Alcor Life Extension Foundation in Tucson, Arizona, who gave me a tour of the building and patiently answered all of my questions about cryonic preservation (or, "freezing" people after death so they can be revived in the future, when scientific advances might enable such a process to be possible). What makes the Alcor facility historic is that the first person to be cryonically preserved—

James Bedford—is in one of Alcor's "dewars," as the containers are called.

Kenneth Emery in Columbus, New Mexico, who helped me locate Hermanas, New Mexico. The town no longer exists, but it's where, in July 1917, approximately 1,300 striking mine workers were dumped without food or water after being forced on a train at gunpoint in Bisbee, Arizona. The "Bisbee Deportation," as it became known, was the largest mass kidnapping in U.S. history.

Rob Florence, who's one of the best tour guides in New Orleans, Louisiana, and took me to the old Karnofsky building at 427 South Rampart, where Louis Armstrong had his first job. Armstrong credited the Karnofskys, a family of second-generation Jewish immigrants from Lithuania, for nurturing his love of music and caring for him when he was virtually homeless. Throughout his life, Armstrong—considered one of the greatest jazz musicians in the world—wore a Star of David as a tribute to, in his words, "the Jewish family who instilled in me Singing from the heart." (I'm also grateful to Suzanne N. Blaum at the Preservation Resource Center of New Orleans for helping me find other little-known jazz-related sites.)

Ed Furman, in Palestine, Texas, who assisted me in locating the field near his home where a part of Ilan Ramon's diary was found; Ramon was an astronaut aboard the *Columbia* space shuttle, which exploded over Texas on February 1, 2003, and, incredibly, pages of Ramon's diary survived the blast and almost forty-mile descent to earth.

John Imes, who let me use the John Muir Room in his Arbor House Inn as my temporary base of operations during my visit to Madison, Wisconsin. I was there to visit the dormitory on Bascom Hill where Muir had lived while a student at the University of Wisconsin. Most important, it was outside this dorm that a fellow student gave Muir an impromptu tutorial about locust trees that, in Muir's words, "sent me flying to the woods and meadows in wild enthusiasm" and caused him to be one of America's greatest advocates for nature and the great outdoors. (Special thanks also to Michael Hoel and Eve Robillard for the impromptu tour of Bascom Hill.)

Susan Johnston, who let me visit her home in Dover, Delaware, which is where the famed astronomer Annie Jump Cannon was raised. (The house is actually owned by Wesley College and is the school's president's home; Susan's husband is Dr. William Johnston, president of Wesley.) Cannon used to go on the roof when she was a little girl and gaze at the stars. Later, while working at the Harvard Observatory, Cannon discovered 300 variable stars and, in the early 1900s, came up with the stellar classification system that is used to this day to categorize all stars. She became the first woman to receive an honorary degree from Oxford University and the first woman to earn the Henry Draper Medal, the highest award given in the field of astronomy.

Lisa Kobrin, reference librarian at the May Memorial Library in Burlington, North Carolina, who helped me track down the former site of the Alamance General Hospital, where Dr. Charles Drew died on April 1, 1950, after being in a car accident. Drew was the prominent African American surgeon who helped revolutionize how blood was stored and used in transfusions.

James Lewis, at the Newark Public Library's Charles F. Cummings New Jersey Information Center, who helped me find the general location of where Clara Maass's home in Newark would have been. Maass was the heroic American nurse who volunteered to be bitten by mosquitoes thought to be carrying yellow fever to see if the virus was spread by the bugs or some other factor. Maass was aware of the health risks of these experiments, and they indeed proved fatal; she died on August 24, 1901.

Christine McKeever, at the 6th Cavalry Museum in Georgia, who showed me where the internment camp at Fort Oglethorpe had been constructed to detain Americans suspected of being spies or simply unpatriotic during World War I. Bridget Carr, the archivist at the Boston Symphony Orchestra, also provided me with information about one of the camp's most famous inmates—Karl Muck, the fifty-seven-year-old German-born conductor of the BSO. Muck had been (unfairly) accused of not playing the national anthem during a concert, and he was imprisoned for more than a year. In Georgia, I'm extremely grateful as well to Jonathan Lewis for taking me on a tour of Atlanta and pointing out various little-known historic sites.

Dennis Northcott at the Missouri History Museum, who helped me find the office building at 1222 Spruce Street in downtown St. Louis, Missouri, where a man named Henry Grant sold Underwood typewriters in the 1940s. What makes Grant an intriguing character is that his real name was Hugo Gutmann, and he was the Jewish lieutenant in the German army who, during World War I, nominated a young corporal named Adolf Hitler for the Iron Cross. (Hitler received the prestigious award and, although furious that a Jewish officer had recommended him, cherished the medal more than almost any other possession.) Obviously Gutmann didn't know that Hitler would turn into the monster he became, and Gutmann himself fled Germany in 1940 for the United States, where he changed his name and tried to live a life of obscurity.

Deb Novotny, a battlefield guide at Gettysburg National Military Park, who introduced me to the story of Elizabeth Thorn. Thorn became the caretaker of the Evergreen Cemetery near Gettysburg after her husband, who would otherwise have been responsible for managing the property, joined the Union Army. Despite being six months pregnant, Thorn took on the responsibility of burying more than one hundred soldiers killed during the historic battle. She became known as the "Angel of Gettysburg," and while there is a statue at Evergreen in her honor, her name is not on it, nor is there a marker explaining her significance.

Jimmy Ogle, a Memphis historian who gave me a whirlwind tour of the city, including through its storm drains—which are historic in themselves and influenced how numerous other municipalities constructed their sewage and draining systems. I'm also indebted to Toni Holmon-Turner in the Memphis mayor's office for telling me about Jimmy Ogle; sewer historian Jon C. Schladweiler for background information on Memphis's system; and Ronald Kirby, who was at the Memphis Department of Public Works at the time and took me to one of their waste treatment facilities. (This was all much more exciting than it might sound.)

Antonio M. Perez, the chairman and chief executive officer of Kodak. Mr. Perez brought my attention to an extraordinary American patriot and publisher named Mary Katherine Goddard, who printed in January 1777 the first edition of the Declaration of Independence with the names of the signers. (Since the War for Independence was still raging, the very act of printing and distributing the Declaration was considered treasonous by the British and could have resulted in harsh reprisals against Goddard.) I'm grateful to M. J. Kraus and Maria Day at the Maryland State Archives and Bruce Kirby at the Library of Congress for providing me with additional information about Goddard. And I'm also indebted to Francis O'Neill and Damon Talbot at the Maryland Historical Society for helping me locate the former site of Goddard's print shop at what is now 125 East Baltimore Street in downtown Baltimore.

Inée Slaughter, executive director of the Indigenous Language Institute, who was instrumental in helping me find Edwin Benson, the only living Mandan Indian still fluent in the Mandan language. Edwin very kindly met with me in Twin Buttes, North Dakota, and he's been working with the linguist Sara Trechter to record as much of the language before it's lost forever. They usually meet at the Twin Buttes Elementary School, which is also where I met Edwin. I'm grateful to him for sharing his story, and he reminded me that some of the most important things we need to save aren't always tangible.

Finally, to everyone I met in passing throughout my trip who told me about their own favorite little-known spots, thank you for your recommendations—and please keep them coming; the journey continues. . . .

INDEX

ABOUT THE AUTHOR

ANDREW CARROLL is the editor of several *New York Times* best-sellers, including *Letters of a Nation, Behind the Lines,* and *War Letters,* which inspired an acclaimed PBS documentary. Carroll's book *Operation Homecoming* was the inspiration for an Oscar-nominated and Emmy-winning film.